NO FORGOTTEN
FRONTS

NO FORGOTTEN
FRONTS

FROM CLASSROOMS TO COMBAT

LISA K. SHAPIRO

NAVAL INSTITUTE PRESS
ANNAPOLIS, MARYLAND

Naval Institute Press
291 Wood Road
Annapolis, MD 21402

Library of Congress cataloging-in-publication data is available.
978-1-68247-272-9 (hardcover)
978-1-68247-273-6 (eBook)

♾ Print editions meet the requirements of ANSI/NISO z39.48-1992
(Permanence of Paper).
Printed in the United States of America.

26 25 24 23 22 21 20 19 18   9 8 7 6 5 4 3 2 1
First printing

All *News Letters* and letters can be found in the World War II San Diego
State College Servicemen's Correspondence Collection, 1941–1946, Special
Collections and University Archives, San Diego State University.

Unless otherwise credited, all photographs are from the University Archives
Photograph Collection, Special Collections and University Archives, San Diego
State University.

[For Deborah K. Reed, fellow author and best friend]

Like other games it is a great game or a small game, according to the intellectual and moral caliber of the players. . . . Within the Great Game which Fate plays with Destiny are the little games which the puppet-pieces play with each other—the games of politics, war, ambition, avarice, and the joy or sorrow of living.

E. H. (Yorick) Clough
Epigraph in *Del Sudoeste*
San Diego State College Yearbook
June 1943

This war-time record of a college year is dedicated to those who carry a memory of our campus in their hearts, wherever the Great Game calls them.

Editors of *Del Sudoeste*
San Diego State College Yearbook
June 1943

Contents

Illustrations

INTRODUCTION

A t the beginning of World War II, a professor from San Diego State College asked students entering military service to write to him. For the next five years, he received thousands of letters from places like Pearl Harbor, North Africa, and Normandy that began with the salutation "Dear Doc" and gave vivid accounts of training, combat, and camaraderie. War took the students from State to places all over the world, but they never lost their connection to their campus. Their mascot was Montezuma, ruler of the Aztec Empire, and they called themselves the Fighting Aztecs.

Lauren Chester Post was part father figure, part mentor to those who wrote to him. Through their shared correspondence, he followed these servicemen and servicewomen as they completed training and took up the tasks of war. Every month, with help from campus fraternities and clubs, he excerpted their letters for publication and mailed the *Aztec News Letter* around the world. His efforts helped his students endure hardship, homesickness, and the death of friends.

April 28, 1944
Dear Dr. Post,

. . .

Sometimes, doc, the going gets pretty tough—even on a battlewagon—and you feel discouraged and disgusted. And somehow the word *News Letter* flashes in your brain, and you pick out an old issue at random and start thinking of the other

1

fellow—fellow Aztec. You think of the guy who used to drop by for you every morning and drive you out to State. It wasn't much of a car, and we invariably had engine trouble, and I don't recall ever making an 8 o'clock class on time. But you can't help thinking of what a swell guy he was and how badly you felt when you learned that—that he had been killed in a bombing raid over Germany.

You read about others who have been killed or wounded. And you read about others who have been away from the States a hell of a lot longer than you have. It's then that you realize that things aren't tough at all—that you've just been kidding yourself!

. . .

Respectfully,
Lt. (jg) R. J. (Bob) Noel, USNR
USS *Mississippi*
c/o FPO
San Francisco, California

Born in Louisiana on Labor Day in 1899, Post attended the University of California, Berkeley, where he studied geography. He researched cultural landscapes and the interplay between people, their heritage, and their surroundings and published *Cajun Sketches from the Prairies of Southwest Louisiana*. In one of his classes, he was seated alphabetically next to Valeria Postnikova, a young chemistry major who later became his wife. Post went on to earn his PhD, but at that time women were denied admission to doctoral programs, so Valeria became a high school science and chemistry teacher.

The couple moved to San Diego, where Dr. Post took up a teaching position and Valeria Post served as president of the light opera company. They never had children but pursued interests that kept them involved in the lives of their students. She taught aspiring singers in their home, and he coached the freshman football squad. He loved to show off his skills at trick roping and always complied with requests to say a few words in Cajun French.

During World War II, students and their families wrote more than 4,500 letters to Dr. Post. He read every letter, responded personally to many of them, and abridged others for inclusion in the monthly *Aztec News Letter*. When the latest edition arrived, servicemen and servicewomen halted the war to read about their friends. Places that their professor had shown them on a map came into new focus during the war, and the students sent all kinds of gifts—Japanese occupation money from the Philippines, sand from Iwo Jima, Nazi flags from Germany.

On November 3, 1944, in a letter to the San Diego Junior Chamber of Commerce, Dr. Post provided some statistics on the costs of publishing and distributing the *News Letter*: "At present we mail 800 *News Letters* to men overseas, about 2,000 more go to service men and their families inside the United States and the students on the campus buy about 500 copies each month at 10c. each. The printing bill is about $112.00 per month, while the postage is about $88.00 per month." One hundred dollars in 1944 was the equivalent of about $1,400 in 2018.

Those at home also relied on the *News Letter* for firsthand information about their loved ones. Pilots wrote about seeing planes shot down, and mothers, hoping for word about sons missing in action, anxiously read each issue for details. Men in POW camps alerted Dr. Post to the whereabouts of other prisoners, and he passed on their reassurances to frantic families.

One of Post's students, James "Jim" Hurley Jr., was pinned under enemy fire on the beach at Anzio during the invasion of Italy. He wrote, "I blew my stack & lost my marbles. No permanent after effects except a little deafness and visual trouble. If this letter seems incoherent please forgive me, I'm still a bit rusty in spots." Dr. Post, himself a veteran of World War I, recognized the signs of shell shock, and he dashed off a letter to another fellow Aztec, an army chaplain. On April 15, 1944, the serviceman's father, J. R. Hurley, wrote to Dr. Post:

Thank you so much for your interest in James, Jr., and for asking the Chaplain of the 7th Infantry to look him up, and for letting us know about it. It was kind of you indeed, especially when you have so many Aztecs to remember, who are now serving their country. I do hope that the 7th is billeted near the 15th so that the Chaplain Dyreson can easily find James. The latter is having a rather difficult time of it, and to think that *somebody* was interested in him, and one who was capable of giving him spiritual consolation besides, will, I'm sure, give his morale a big uplift.

Another group of Aztecs trained together as a unit with the United States Naval Reserve. On July 31, 1943, Robert F. Smith wrote, "Close to 60 anxious AZTECS received their August *News Letters* at today's mail call and one and all were happy to feel remembered. I believe that at least 50% of the value of the *Letter* comes from this assurance that one is not forgotten, which runs through a fellow as he huskily yells 'Here!' at mail call."

Initially, training camps were full of young men boasting of an early victory, but by 1943 that naive assurance had been replaced with grim determination. In 1944 a note of cautious optimism returned, but those seasoned in combat warned that the fighting would be bitter to the end.

The words of these articulate, college-educated writers were set on paper while their hearts were homesick and the heat of battle seared their blood. Letters were often scribbled in a hurried moment after chow and before lights-out. In pencil or pen, on whatever stationery was at hand, the students revealed their deep-seated love for home and family. They had no way of knowing the outcome of the war, and yet they knew in their hearts that good would triumph over evil. Preserved in the timeless amber of letters is these students' respect for their country and its values and their willingness to fight for what they held most dear.

WORKING WITH LETTERS

Letters capture thoughts and emotions as events are unfolding. They offer a narrower view of history than a textbook, and they are written in the moment, instead of in reminiscence, as in memoirs. Most letters are sent to friends and family, and so their tone is intimate and honest. This honesty extends to bias. Letters are powerful because they convey the original voice of the writer, a voice that hasn't been filtered by time and shouldn't be filtered after the fact by an editor.

The World War II San Diego State College Servicemen's Correspondence Collection, 1941–1946, contains many letters in which enemy forces are discussed in derogatory terms. For example, writers refer to "Japs" and "Nips," and servicemen unabashedly express their preference for "white" as opposed to "native" women. The letters that have been included here portray the time, place, and events from the viewpoint of a specific group of students and their families at a unique moment in history.

San Diego State College had been home to a Japanese club, but Japanese and Japanese Americans were expelled from the West Coast during World War II. Some Japanese American students enlisted in the United States military, while others were transported to internment camps, as documented in chapter 12, "Aztecs of Fine Caliber." A Chinese student,

Some Ching, provided one of the most pointed verbal attacks against the Japanese in his letter in chapter 5. To better place that letter in context, I provide details about Japanese aggression in China during the decade leading up to World War II.

Each chapter includes information about battles, key leadership decisions, and significant social events. Many of the letter writers only hinted at these current affairs, partly because of censorship restrictions, but also because they frequently assumed that the reader had seen news accounts. They preferred to use their brief time and limited space to share personal thoughts. The intent in this volume is to add enough historical background to make the letters accessible without drowning them in details.

Spelling such as the shorthand *altho*, *thru*, and *nite* remain as they were penned. Dr. Post always wrote *News Letter* as two words, and this spelling is used throughout for consistency. I have followed the example of Bernard Edelman, Vietnam veteran and editor of the collection *Dear America: Letters Home from Vietnam*, who corrected minor spelling errors. I have not altered punctuation, with the exception of apostrophes for possessives and contractions, commas, and other minor corrections for the sake of consistency and clarity. Ellipses indicate that a line or a section has been omitted. My omission of certain portions of the letters reflects a balancing act between honoring the essence of the letters and managing the length of the book. Acronyms and abbreviations in the letters are defined in the list of abbreviations at the end of this book.

The World War II San Diego State College Servicemen's Correspondence Collection, 1941–1946, fills ten boxes in the Special Collections and University Archives at San Diego State University. Some letters are signed with just a first name. Many times, a portion of the envelope bearing the full name and address of the writer has been saved with the letter. In a few instances, the letter writer has been identified by the archivists, who have studied and cross-checked the letters against other correspondence and excerpts from the *News Letters*. I have included as much information with the letters as possible about the full name and address of each writer.

Dr. Post liked to include positive excerpts in the *News Letter*, but he also gave updates in every issue of those who had been wounded or were missing or killed in action. In order to spare their families from harsh realities, writers sometimes noted that a passage was intended for Dr. Post alone, but most letters were meant to be shared. They contain the poignant thoughts and feelings of men and women at war.

Edited by Dr. Lauren C. Póst
San Diego State College
San Diego, California
May 6, 1942

To and from the Aztecs who are in the service and their friends:

This NEWS LETTER is a news service experiment intended to serve you.
Send us news and ask us questions. We will try to oblige in every way that we
can in keeping you in touch with State College and your friends. We want your
names and addresses and would like to get news of promotions and activities.
(We don't want any infractions of the censorship rules, so tell us only that
which you don't mind having published.) This first issue will be given over
largely to letters received so far. We intend to run lists of addresses also,
and perhaps later we will run news items and comments, but for the present we
have room only for letters received and addresses. We will try to get the
NEWS LETTER to you as often as possible.

To all Aztecs and Faculty Members:

Have you done your share of writing to the service men? You should be
writing more than they do, not less as has been reported. When you receive
letters from the men, we would appreciate it if you would let us have addresses
and paragraphs from them that are of general interest and which they would not
mind having made public.

We are compiling for the college a list of names of San Diego State College
Aztecs (both graduate and undergraduate) who are in the armed forces of the
country. Since there is no possible way of getting an absolutely complete and
accurate list, we do appreciate any help that you can give us. If you want any
addresses from the file, we shall be glad to let you have them.

This letter serves as an expression of appreciation we have for the services
of our men in the armed forces. With the NEWS LETTER go our wishes for a certain
and early victory.   Lauren C. Post, Editor

* * * * *

From: Wallace McAnulty, Btry D, 251st C.A.,A.P.O. 954, c/o Postmaster, S.F.

Dear Doc: April 26, 1942

I received your letter yesterday -- good to hear from you.
Yes, some of the fellows have started to write to me already. I received a
letter from Norm Wier a couple of days ago. It sure does bring a guy back home
to get all the news of the fellows that he used to know back home. I didn't
realize that so many of the old gang were in the service. I guess that I am about
the only old timer among the bunch. Heck, in only a couple of months I can consider myself a native of this place. I catch myself speaking pidgeon English
every now and then.
I sure do feel sorry for poor old Kita. What the heck, this wasn't any
fault of his...Oh, well maybe one of these days this old world of ours will settle
down a bit and get wise to itself.
Maybe I can help fill up that file of yours of men in the service by giving
you the names of the Aztecs in our outfit. Some attended a number of years back,

1

LITTLE BOX OF CARDS

In 1943 Lt. Lionel Chase, a World War II pilot with an Air Medal, four oak leaf clusters awarded for meritorious achievement in flight, and a Silver Star for gallantry in action against an enemy, wrote to a professor at his alma mater: "Will never forget the day you started wandering around the campus with a little box of cards in your hand collecting Servicemen's Addresses." The campus was San Diego State College, the professor was Dr. Lauren Chester Post, and the "little box of cards" turned into a mailing list with hundreds of names.

Dr. Post had served in the Navy on board a destroyer during World War I, went to France and Germany, and worked as an electrician's mate building ships at the Mare Island Naval Shipyard, northeast of San

Francisco. After earning his doctoral degree, he accepted a position as a geography professor, and he made sure his students understood topography and map reading. Infantrymen and navigators later wrote to him to say how glad they were to have acquired those essential skills. Dr. Post had a knack for helping his students find their way in the world, and he forged a link that would keep them connected—to their campus and to one another—throughout the biggest armed conflict in human history.

October 15, 1943

Dear Dr. Post,

The last time I saw you, you were out spinning the lariat in your backyard as I drove by one day. I'd come and be your audience every day, if I could get back in San Diego to do it.

. . .

Jim Kinsella

March 24, 1944

Dear Dr. Post,

I received number 24 a couple of days ago and was very glad to get it. I always read each *News Letter* from beginning to end the same day it arrives even though I have to stay up half the night to do so. . . .

I don't know if you remember me or not as I never had the good fortune of taking a Geography course from you. I did go on one Geography field trip with you in the fall of 1939. (A trip which I enjoyed very much.) You also took me home from college in your 1932 Model B on my first day at San Diego State. I appreciated that ride very much as I was a bewildered freshman in a strange city and I didn't know a single student at San Diego State. . . .

Thanks again for sending me the *News Letter*.

Respectfully yours,

George L. Stillings

Ensign, SCV-G, USNR

USS *Delta*

Fleet Post Office

New York, New York

After a brief visit with Dr. Post, Lieutenant Chase had taken up residence in his bachelor officer quarters, where he tried without much luck to master a few rope tricks.

December 2nd, 1943

Dear Doc,

Well, here I am, settled down in a B.O.Q. and quite happy and contented. Flying schedules here are a little rough, but at least there's no one shooting at us. Doc, that afternoon we spent over at your house spinning ropes was more fun than a red wagon. I've been anxious to get going on the roping, so I could learn that "Texas Skip," but the rope and book of instructions are somewhere on the railroads in my parachute bag. "C'est la guerre."

. . . We only have one kind of weather here, and that's instrument weather, but there's no Tunisian sand in the food or the engines so I can't complain. Will let you know about the rope spinning after the old A-3 bag gets here.

Happy Landings

1st Lt. Lionel E. Chase

Student Pilot Group

Lockbourne A.A.B.

Columbus 17, Ohio

Dr. Post's experience as a war veteran combined with his academic understanding of the world and its conflicts compelled him to offer support to the young students who were trading the comforts of campus for the rigors of military service.

In the very first edition of the *News Letter*, dated May 6, 1942, Dr. Post wrote,

Dr. Lauren C. Post performing rope tricks.

To and from the Aztecs who are in the service and their friends: this *News Letter* is a news service experiment intended to serve you. Send us news and ask us questions.

As Dr. Post worked in a small office on the sun-splashed San Diego campus, enlisting the aid of typing classes, collecting dollars from mothers to help pay for postage, and placing ads in the local paper to obtain even more addresses, his "experiment" became an organized campaign that amassed more than 4,500 pieces of handwritten correspondence. Some of the letters still bear the notes he penciled as he prepared excerpts for publication.

Dr. Post knew a global war would likely take years to reach a conclusion, yet even a prescient geography professor could not have foreseen that his students would set up camps on islands in the Pacific, fight desperate battles under horrific conditions in New Guinea and the Solomon Islands, trek into the heart of the North African campaign, and wing across Europe in bombers they had only just learned to fly. They were also learning war's unique language. In the following letters, "ack-ack" is shorthand for antiaircraft fire, and "williwaws" is a local term for severe squalls in the Aleutian Islands.

April 14, 1943
Middle East Forces
Dear Doc:
The present dust storm reminds Alex of Indio, both of us, of the fact that also in Southern California is Montezuma and his prophet, Doc Post. We have never thanked you for your persistence. It has made us feel pretty swell to know that the *News Letters* will follow us no matter where we go.

Alex (G. C. Alexander) known by many Aztecs as "Benny," and myself are learning a bit of geography from up above as well as how to take on fighters or classify ack-ack by sight, sound, and accuracy. Approaching the enemy land we think it very beautiful, a fact the cartographers leave out. Over the target we damn his ack-ack, his fighter's and himself and peer down to see our hits.

. . .

Alex and I as Kappa Phi and Omega Xi still have our minor differences of opinion, but we are united in our thanks for every *News Letter* and your well wishes.
Very sincerely,

2nd Lt. Maxton (Max) Brown 0-729411
515th Squadron 376th Bomb Group
APO 681 c/o Postmaster
New York City, N.Y.

September 13, 1943

[Dr. Post made a note on this letter: "Wrote from a Sub in Pacific."]

. . .

In six war patrols we have had some varied experience in dodging torpedoes, aerial bombs, depth charges, williwaws, typhoons, and we have had considerable fun in raising hell with Japanese shipping. However, don't underestimate the Japs; they are far from licked, and it will take continuous pounding by all branches of the service before they will throw in the towel.

. . . Come hell or high water we make our cokes and ice cream. During depth charging or during an approach on an enemy ship the men make cokes and turn the ice cream freezer. The ice cream freezer is kept in the pump room, and once during a storm we took lots of water aboard and the pump room was flooded about two feet above the deck plates, but the man turning the ice cream freezer turned away with the air jack with water up to his knees. We're not completely crazy—just a little "pressure happy."

. . .

It seems rather strange writing to a person whom you have only seen while traveling across campus, however, the prime motive of all this chatter is to thank you for sending me the *News Letter*, and to congratulate you and your organization in reminding us that all this hell (a great understatement) is not in vain. I think the people at home have a tougher job in making adjustments to the trying times than adjusting yourself to depth charging, after all you people hear a lot of different tunes that must be very confusing; hell, all tunes from depth charges are the same except some are close and others are too damn close.

Please accept the enclosed money order to use as you see fit.

Sincerely,

Emmett W. Fowler Jr.
Lt. (jg) DE-V-(g) USNR
USS *Whale*
Fleet Post Office
San Francisco, California

As a professor with a keen sense of folk culture, Dr. Post was ideally suited to collect the stories of students turned soldiers. He had studied the Louisiana Cajuns, whose ancestors had journeyed south from Nova Scotia and Quebec following wars in their native regions. Dr. Post understood the ways in which war could force populations to shift, causing new cultures to take root. He was trained to trace the migrations of people, exploring how they lived, learned, and changed. When his students began migrating to battlefields the world over, he tracked them and collected their stories. Their words were always on his mind.

September 5, 1943

. . .

Doc., I often think of you in your Geography 1 class. I wonder if you still look up at that class and say: "I have a letter from John Jones from somewhere in the South Pacific (or etc.). Just a year ago, he sat in this class. He sat in that corner seat where Miss Brown is now sitting." I guess those memories will continue to

Dr. Lauren C. Post, professor of geography, San Diego State College

be with you for as long as the war lasts. I know now that we too remember those not so long ago sessions. I think we all wish they were back.

Pfc Warren C. Golson, 19111022

43rd Base Hq. and Air Base Sq.

McChord Field

Tacoma, Washington

The servicemen and servicewomen left for boot camps, ports of embarkation, and overseas posts. Paul Arriola, a young private at Camp Wolters, Texas, wrote on April 18, 1943, "I remember, just before I left, your saying that you were apprehensive about the day when we would all be out here and there would be no one left to do the sending." Another former student, Herman J. Branin, at Camp Roberts, California, also recalled Dr. Post's warnings. On January 4, 1943, Branin wrote, "I can remember last year when you stated in class that many of us would be overseas within a year. It certainly was hard to believe then, but it looks like it sure was the truth."

The war took the students far away from Dr. Post's class, but they never stopped yearning for their campus and friends:

July 18, 1942

Pearl Harbor

Hello Doc:

Sorry I haven't written sooner to thank you for the copies of the *Aztec* and the *News Letter*. Believe me, I certainly have a great deal of enjoyment out of them. My former classmates and fraternity brothers are often on my mind and any news of them is most welcome.

How I would like to be lying out in the quad waiting for football practice or drowsing through one of your classes (the warm weather of course). Speaking of Geography, this island would really be an ideal place to have field trips. . . .

It is too bad that so many of the old guard have left school to do more important things, but I know that they can sense the importance of everyone doing his share, and I know many of them will return to enjoy college life once more.

Thanks again "Doc," and I hope all is well with you.

Sincerely,

Armond Ault

Advance Destroyer Base One

December 19, 1942

Somewhere in the Pacific

Dear Dr. Post:

Sometimes I believe a more appropriate caption would be "Everywhere in the Pacific." Naval censorship is normal, so don't expect much "dope" herein.

Thanks muchly for the *News Letters* (8 & 9). . . . The greatest regret of a college man is losing touch with the lads he knew, worked and played with at college. Your *News Letter* therefore was not only a brilliant stroke, but timely in that, in this time of stress and strain and broken homes and lives, it has brought the old campus to every part of the world under all conditions, and lets you know that the boys you played football with are *still* by your side (although in a slightly spread formation).

The recent *News Letters* have me with mixed emotions. Happy to learn of the State boys in service everywhere, and sad that some fine men gave their lives for us.

. . .

Get 'em Aztecs,

Dexter Rumsey

Lieutenant, U.S.N.

Incredibly, nearly every *News Letter* reached its destination, thanks in part to Dr. Post's diligent work in updating his hand-typed mailing list and help from the military postal service. Students and parents weren't the only ones writing to Dr. Post. His publication soon caught the attention of the censors, who sent him detailed instructions on what he could put into print. The censors got their hands on the December 22, 1942, *News Letter* and sent Dr. Post a long list of items to be corrected. Their press release contained these words of caution:

DO NOT TELL the names of ships upon which sailors serve.

DO NOT TELL the troop units in which soldiers serve overseas.

The Nazis and the Japs want to know these things about our forces. Their agents assemble the information like this: from one paper, an item reveals the 600th Infantry is in Australia; another, that the U.S.S. *Wisconsin* is in the Mediterranean; another, that the 206th Tank Battalion is in North Africa.

Add hundreds of these bits of information together, and our enemies have a too-accurate estimate of American military strength.

These are *our* soldiers—Americans all—whom we endanger by these "little slips."

In the January 31, 1943, issue of the *News Letter*, Dr. Post wrote this comment:

> **Censorship has made a difference. Remember, now your letters go through two rigid censorings. The first is the official one and then mine. I have received definite instructions as to what to leave out of the *News Letter* and I have made every effort to cut out every item that could possibly help the enemy or prolong the war.**

He also sent a copy of that edition to his contact at the Office of Censorship and received praise:

February 9, 1943

Dear Dr. Post:

It is putting it mildly to say that we are immensely appreciative of your conscientious efforts to comply with censorship requests in editing your *News Letter* for Aztecs in the services. We are also grateful for your sympathetic understanding of our problems.

The issue of January 31 which you sent for our examination is beyond criticism so far as censorship is concerned. Indeed, in your efforts to comply with the Voluntary Press Code you have gone further than we requested in the matter of addresses.

. . .

Your cheerful cooperation is deeply appreciated. Please do not hesitate to call upon us whenever we can be of service.

Sincerely Yours,

N. R. Howard

Assistant Director (Press)

THE OFFICE OF CENSORSHIP

WASHINGTON

The *News Letter* kept the servicemen and servicewomen updated on the general location of other Aztecs. When Lieutenant Chase wasn't flying, he made it his mission to track down his former classmates in person. On

March 15, 1943, he complained, "I have looked all over North Africa for another Aztec without meeting one. I've looked in every bar, hospital and guardhouse without results." On May 29, he wrote, "I drew a short leave and started a long, slow hitch hike to see Bob Wade and Griff Williams. After crossing 'about half' of North Africa, I discovered they had just recently moved to the half of North Africa I didn't cover! What a war!"

The letters tell a war story that began in the classroom:

✉ May 24, 1942

. . .

Remember the contour maps you taught me to read? Well, that is something that the army uses a lot of, and my "small" knowledge of them came in very handy. As for the terrain of Texas, I have made a very close study of it. By crawling all over it on my stomach.

. . .

Respectfully yours,
Pvt. Warren W. Brown
Co. B, 60th Infantry Training Battalion
Camp Wolters, Texas

✉ Undated
Somewhere at Sea

. . .

When I left State to don the Navy Blue I never realized that one day the fellows in my chem lab or math class would be fighting by my side like this. No, I would not have believed it if someone had told me that the Staters who endangered my life in the parking lot by swooshing by in "go-jobs" would one day be just as dangerous to the Japanese. . . .

No one doubts what will be the final outcome—that when the smoke from the last gun has cleared the enemy will have been taught the meaning of war and will be glad to settle down along more peaceful lines.

It seems most surprising how important things like football, liberties, and seeing certain people again appear when compared with this business of war. Most all of us now have smelled the smoke of battle and have come to look upon things like raids and attacks and torpedoes as merely daily incidents. Many volumes could be written about the deeds of our many heroes, but they won't be for now to be a hero is commonplace and not worthy of special note.

. . .

William M. (Bill) Goode
Ensign USN
U.S.S. *St. Louis*

For some students, the story began at Pearl Harbor:

March 4, 1942
Somewhere on Oahu
Dear Doc Post,

. . .

You really missed something over here Doc. It was really something the seventh of December. I'll tell you it was just the same as waiting for a kick off. Your old stomach was just as tight as it could be but when the first gun was fired, boom, it was gone and you were figuring ("figgering") how to run one through tackle. I must admit it was something like our game in '39 against Compton, but there will come a day and soon I hope.

I have been acting as an officer since a week before the war and have high hope of making it in the not too far future. No kidding Doc I'm a changed man. I have been studying pretty hard since I've been in the Army and I have my math, as applied to Anti Air Craft Gunnery, down fairly well. . . .

Well Doc I hope you can see it to forgive me as I did "goof" off something awful. . . .

Aloha
Wally (Mac) McAnulty

The letters testify to the sacrifices made by students and their families:

October 8, 1942
. . . Most of us have been thrust from petty, individual, personalized living, into a spearhead of vast proportions. All our efforts are now directed toward the creation of something beyond ourselves, though well we know that many will perish in the attempt. We must impersonally charge forward through this long and fiery ordeal. . . .

Herman G. Goldbeck
Hq. Co., 2 Bn., 11 Infantry
APO #5 c/o Postmaster
New York, New York

For Lieutenant Chase, the war meant doing his duty and adapting to difficult conditions, which he did gladly as he waited for one of Dr. Post's *News Letters* to arrive.

November 3, 1942
Walla Walla, Washington
Dear Doc,
Where in hell is my *News Letter*? The new address is B.O.Q. 712 Army Air Base, Walla Walla, Wash. It won't be the address over a month, so hurry my *News Letter* so I can get in touch with the boys. . . . We're really waiting for our chance to get over, get even, get back, get drunk. Doc I've gotta run, so I'll sign off "Roger" and wish you happy landings.
     Sincerely,
     Lt. Lionel E. Chase

April 7th, 1943
Dear "Doc" Post,
Has the *News Letter* gone out of print, have you lost my address, or what? I'd sure love to see one right now. . . .

     We're fairly comfortable over here. We've had to improvise stoves, beds, tables, chairs, lockers, showers, etc. But you'd be surprised at what the boys get together with a little ingenuity, and old airplane parts and empty Bomb Cases. We've even got a window in our tent, and the fuel control on our home-made stove can be adjusted without getting out of bed. We shave in our helmets, and all that, but we're having a great time, and we're really giving 'em the works! . . .

     That's thirty for tonight
     Happy Landings
     Lt. Lionel E. Chase

That same winter, Lieutenant Chase was still pleading for the "Doc" to send a *News Letter* and still trying to master the Texas Skip.

December 17, 1943
Dear "Doc"
S.O.S. S.O.S. where is my *News Letter*? Please get one on the road right away.

     Doc, this rope-spinning is a rough, rough, racket! In the first place, the size of a B.O.Q. room is somewhat restricting, and it's too damn cold to go outside and practice. I've been practicing faithfully since the rope and instruction book got here, but don't seem to get very far. But you wait, someday I'll come barreling into your office, take you down to the quad, and do a Texas Skip for you!

Doc, after Tunisia, this Ohio weather is horrible. How I long for those dusty days of hitching from Cairo to Casablanca looking for Wade. Seems as I left the old outfit just before the real fun of plastering Germany began. The States has a lot of advantages, but I'm "eager as a beaver" to get back over.

. . .

Doc, I've got to tear over to ground school, so I'll sign off—
Happy Landings
1st Lt. Lionel E. Chase

Dr. Post concluded his personal column in the *News Letter* with his own distinctive wish. Month after month, to all of the Fighting Aztecs, he wrote, "Best of luck!"

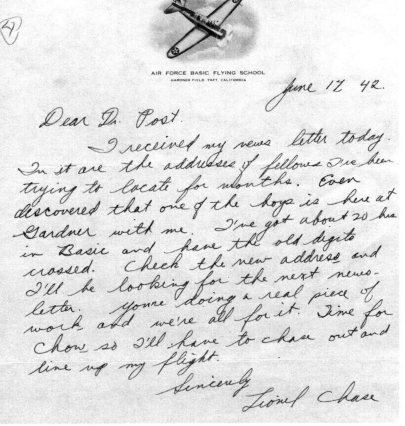

AIR FORCE BASIC FLYING SCHOOL
GARDNER FIELD, TAFT, CALIFORNIA

June 17 42.

Dear Dr. Post.

I received my news letter today. In it are the addresses of fellows I've been trying to locate for months. Even discovered that one of the boys is here at Gardner with me. I've got about 20 his in Basic and have the old digits crossed. Check the new address and I'll be looking for the next news-letter. You're doing a real piece of work and we're all for it. Time for chow so I'll have to chase out and line up my flight.

Sincerely
Lionel Chase

Letter from
Lionel Chase,
June 17, 1942

THE AZTEC NEWS LETTER

Edited by
DR. LAUREN C. POST
San Diego State College
San Diego, California

January 31, 1943
No. 11
HATS OFF to the HODS and PHI SIGMA NU'S for sponsoring this issue of the NEWS LETTER.

To All of the Aztecs in the Service and Their Friends:

The News Letter looks different but that is not all. It **is** different.

CENSORSHIP

Censorship has made a difference. Remember, now your letters go through **two** rigid censorings. The first is the official one and then mine. I have received definite instructions as to what to leave out of the News Letter and I have made every effort to cut out every item that could possibly help the enemy or prolong the war.

The effort was conscientious—there is not a ship name in the whole News Letter; no combat unit is named; no important military or official personnel names reveal any plans or movements or troop movements and embarkations; and every other precaution was taken to prevent the enemy from getting or keeping tab on our war plans or the strength or distribution of our forces.

EDITING and RE-WORDING

Personally, I would rather see 10 words from you in the News Letter than 100 from myself. Unfortunately, I have had to cut more than ever and the opposite is sometimes the case. In many letters the cutting and re-wording have come down to the stock sentence which the girl received after the Censor got through with the letter.

"Your boyfriend still loves you, but he talks too much." Signed: The Censor.

FORWARDING LETTERS

Since we no longer publish addresses, we may be able to help out some. We will forward a letter to anyone for whom we have the address. We will do the best we can.

DATES

Dates were left out of all letters purposely. Since many of the letters were written in the latter part of last year, any bit of information that could possibly have slipped through would now have much less value than then.

THE WEATHER

Mention of the weather was omitted in practically all cases. If it is mentioned, its value has long since been outdated.

STREAMLINING

We hope the streamlined version meets with your approval, and that you will still send in the news and new addresses which makes it possible. Your friends on the Home Front have approved the News Letter idea and they have indicated that they want to see it continued.

AN OPTIMISTIC NOTE

This war isn't going to last forever. The day will come when the things you write won't help either the Japs or the Germans, and in the meantime, it's my duty, and yours, to see that they don't get the information—but still to help all of the Aztecs, wherever they are, to keep in touch with each other. And again, Best of luck to every one of you.

Lauren C. Post, Editor of the News Letter

2

WAITING FOR
SOMETHING TO POP

SAN DIEGO STATE COLLEGE SERVICE MEN'S NEWS LETTER
No. 4, June 18, 1942
The campus has not been as crowded as some of you remember it. The Quad was rather sparsely populated during the past semester. The Cafe likewise has been less crowded. No longer is one certain that it will be an athlete that will wait upon you. Jobs have been more plentiful than men, and girls are filling them more and more.

July 27, 1942

Dear Doc,

. . .

I can see just how you must feel about some of the fellows meeting death at the hand of this devilish enemy we are fighting against. . . .

The fellows are always gathering at night to have a great "bull session" and it seems funny to hear men talking of killing and meaning it. Sometimes I wonder just how it will affect them in late life. You know something like that will linger in a guy's mind and really leave some sort of an impression. Probably the greatest cause for it all is the (sweating) waiting for something to pop. I know that I would enjoy another little encounter with our little friends especially knowing that the next time I'll be fully armed. It gives a lot of confidence when one has his rifle in hand.

. . .

Aloha,
Wally (Mac) McAnulty

Lt. Wallace McAnulty trained in San Diego and was stationed at Pearl Harbor as part of the 251st Coast Artillery (Antiaircraft) Regiment (CA [AA]). Wally survived the Pearl Harbor attack and was transferred to the South Pacific. He wrote faithfully to Dr. Post, sending in the names of the men in his battery. One of his letters appeared in the very first edition of the *News Letter*, and it inspired others to write.

Wally's mother also wrote to Dr. Post, describing her son's "shellback" initiation as his ship crossed the equator.

July 21, 1942

. . . Wally says, being top sergeant he really took a beating during the initiation. When reading this I thought how typical of American youth, even in the midst of great danger they could let themselves go and have a little fun, in upholding an old tradition of the Sea.

Audrey E. M. McAnulty

Throughout the first half of the twentieth century, the U.S. Army Coast Artillery Corps' heavy guns defended the coastline and harbors.[1] Many young men from San Diego were part of the 251st CA (AA), and their mothers were enthusiastic supporters of Dr. Post's *News Letter*, though not everyone was careful about following the censor's guidelines. Servicemen, servicewomen, and their families typically sent from one to ten dollars with their letters to Dr. Post. (Ten dollars in 1943 was the equivalent of about $144 in 2018.) The accompanying notes usually stated that the writer wished he or she could send more.

May 19, 1942

Dear Sir,

. . .

Lieut. Chas. H. Cardwell is a Reserve officer serving with the 251 C.A. (A.A.) Btry. G. There are many other lads from State College at the same outfit.

. . .

That they are in Hawaii is supposed to be a "military *secret*." Several of the lads from the 251st were wounded in the attack on Pearl Harbor but luckily most of them escaped harm.

I understand numbers of the regiment are serving in small groups over all the Islands in the Hawaiian group. The band has just got together again after five and a half months of other duties.

Btry. G. is a 50 cal. and 37 m.m. outfit.

. . .

I think you are doing a real service for the former students of S.C.
Thanking you
Mrs. H. E. Cardwell
4138 Swift Ave.
San Diego, California

May 5, 1943
Mothers of the 251st
Coast Artillery, A.A.
Dear Dr. Post;
The Mothers of the 251 C.A. (A.A.) wish me to send you ten dollars to help with your Aztec *News Letters* to our boys in service. Many of the boys write home that they look forward to these *News Letters* even more than the newspapers for news about their friends so you see they are appreciated.

Sincerely yours
Alice E. Chedsey
(correspondence secretary)
4249 47th Street
San Diego, California

Dr. Post's students were careful not to reveal the name of a country or island, but they described enough details of culture, topography, and vegetation to keep their geography professor well informed. The following letter refers to "two Aztecs" and "the Aztec service letter." The college's student newspaper was called the *Aztec*. Dr. Post's *Service Men's News Letter* was later renamed the *Aztec News Letter*.

July 1, 1942
Dear "Doc,"

. . .

They have us now, on a little island in the South Pacific. We had a swell trip over and naturally crossed the equator. We're all a bunch of hard shell shell backs now.

This isn't such a bad place but they sure did have us snowed under when we first arrived. The English money system and all their driving on the wrong side of the road. . . . I know darn well the natives over here gave us a skinny when we first arrived. Their prices were always three times what they wanted, now that we are on to them we argue them down and get a good price.

They are a friendly bunch of people and like the Americans very much. They are still somewhat primitive and live in swell grass huts. The outside isn't much to look at but the inside is clean and comfortable. I made friends with one of the local chiefs and had dinner at his shack one night. During the course of the evening he gave me three of his villages and made me chief of another. He has his wife and daughters do all of my laundry free, but I'm beginning to feel I'd be better off if I did it on my own. The women all go down the river and beat the devil out of the clothes.

I have received two Aztecs and a copy of the Aztec service letter. Thanks. I really enjoyed them. . . .

Aloha

Wally (Mac) McAnulty

The Pacific theater of war encompassed a swath of the globe that stretched from the Aleutian Islands in the north to the Solomon Islands and New Guinea in the southern Pacific. For the purpose of command and operations, conducted jointly by both the Army and Navy, the theater was further divided into ocean and mainland areas, and it included what was at the time the Dutch East Indies and Southeast Asia.[2] The servicemen didn't count on staying in one place for long. The military's strategy of island hopping brought them ever closer to Japan.

With thousands of islands spread over millions of square miles, the terrain and climates were as varied as the insects and illnesses that plagued those stationed at each island. In their letters to Dr. Post, the men described monsoons and tropical jungles, offered reports on the local food and liquor, and complained about the women.

June 17, 1943

Dear Dr. Post,

The question here isn't when are we going to get home, but when will we see an American Beauty. The native girls are all rather dark and plump, with muscle enough to K.O. any fair U.S. heavyweight. They use their shoe leather to supplement the beef ration. . . .

When we shoot a wild boar we give the bones and tusks to the natives—they use them to make fish hooks, and the hide they use to flavor their version of American stew.

The most wonderful invention for which they are noted is called Hullo-eu-whew. It's the only known drink that can kill a man and still have enough potency to make him jump around. At least that was my impression after the first teaspoonful. They sometimes call it sunshine because it's the only thing that can approach the heat of the sun. Wally McAnulty and I used to like to bathe in the stuff.

So much for that Doc, because the place is really as endurable as a bee hive.

Lt. T. N. Chavis 0-104359

Hqs. 64th CA (aa)

APO #958

c/o P.M. San Francisco, California

September 8, 1943

Hello, Dr. and all,

. . .

I'm still stuck here on this "South Pacific Island" (there are millions of them) and I'm still "beating my gums" in true Leatherneck style. They say that as long as a Marine is beefing about something, he is happy. When he stops beefing, watch out!

. . .

A lot of new mosquito stories have come out lately. Yesterday, for example, we heard of a large one that landed on the airfield. He was gassed up and loaded with bombs before the ground crew discovered that it wasn't a B-17.

PFC J. A. (Jack) Chandler

HQ Co. 2nd Bn 9th Mar

c/o fleet P.O.

San Francisco, California

December 22, 1943
Dear Dr. Post:—

. . .

The jungle here is really something to talk about. It's so dense we usually cut through rather than trying to cut the whole business down.

There is always some humor with each situation. Not being much of a horticulturist I selected rubber trees to make my 1840 model bed from. The first night I used it found me once again on the ground with the thousands of varmints there are here. I knew better the next day.

. . .

Sincerely,
Wm. O. Mobley
CUO Bandleader

August 25, 1944
Dear Dr. Post:

. . .

In the months I've been out here I've learned several things about the South Pacific. Firstly, I've discovered it rains. Not just plain rain that falls and gets everything wet. It comes down in great gobs that threaten to tear one limb from limb. I've also found out that the sun shines. It's a big beautiful sun than can fry the hide off an ox. And then there are coconuts, billions and billions of the things. They fall from tremendous heights to create a hazard to persons traveling on foot, in jeeps, or just standing about. And I learned there are lots of crawling things out here that have no inhibitions about where they go. They would just as soon nestle in a man's coffee as sleep in the same bunk with him. I've found out there were Japs around here. I asked a native [about the Japanese] who said, "No two bucks" when I tried to buy a souvenir from him for one. . . . "Marine kill!" he said as he slid a finger across his neck and made a nerve-racking cutting sound. Lastly, I've learned that there has never been any greater truth said than "There's no place like home." I'm sure all the men out here will agree to that.

. . .

Sincerely yours,
H. Wagner White, Jr.

San Diego was home to the Navy's U.S. Destroyer Base, which grew to become Naval Base San Diego. Since the arrival of the Spanish Conquistadors and Franciscan Friars, religious conversion and military presence shaped the settlement of San Diego. In California, missions and forts were built side by side, and San Diego emerged steeped in a history of conquest.[3]

The city's Spanish colonial heritage influenced the architecture on the San Diego State College campus. Situated over a river valley that was tinder-dry in summer and filled with floods in the winter rains, the white-washed adobe buildings with fired red tile roofs and tile floors were styled in the Spanish tradition. The campus bell tower overlooked a central quad-rangle, or quad, as the students called it, and was reminiscent of a Southern California mission courtyard.

An atmosphere of enlightened learning, the sunny quad, and the Spanish Colonial architecture were the vision of Dr. Edward L. Hardy, the president who oversaw the construction of the original buildings.[4] Like Dr. Post, Hardy was a veteran of World War I, and he envisioned a campus modeled after historic civilizations. Students needed a symbol worthy of such ambitions, and the university adopted as its mascot Montezuma, ruler of the Aztecs. For the Fighting Aztecs, the spirit of athletic competition translated easily into the spirit of combat.

October 5, 1942
Dear Dr. Post

. . .

I see from our letterhead that Montezuma is with us on the warpath. One look at that grim face ought to put the fear of God into those Axis mugs. And apparently anywhere an Axisman sticks his head out he apparently will meet a fighting Aztec, cause we are spreading fast.

. . .

Yours for a quick Victory & a snappy discharge
Sgt. Owen F. Asberry

The war as a whole was spreading fast, and Wally McAnulty was still sweating it out. He offered updates on island life, then signed off with the Hawaiian words that meant his letter was finished.

Undated
Dear Doc
Back again and with not too much lapse of time since my last letter.

I dropped around to see my friend the chief the other day. What a guy, always trying to give me something. Sometimes I'm afraid he is trying to get me in his family. I had my camera with me and asked him and his daughters if they would like to have their pictures taken. One of his daughters said no, when all the time she was walking towards the door of the grass hut combing her hair and asking where to stand.

They really are great people, although the Americans have ruined them. Their main vocabulary now is "one buck, two buck," and on up the line. Everything a fellow buys now is three times the price it was one year ago.

. . .

I sure did enjoy reading Ernie's letter in the last *News Letter*. It was kind of like getting a letter from him.

. . .

Well Doc, I'll call it all pau for now. I'll try and write again soon. I'll be looking for your mail.

Wally (Mac) McAnulty

While Wally was in the South Pacific with a defensive regiment, his brother, Ernie, was flying in North Africa and keeping an eye out for German fighter planes. Dr. Post had coached Wally on the football field and followed Ernie's gridiron record at Herbert Hoover High. Now he kept the lines of communication open and even visited Mrs. McAnulty. Both boys thanked him for looking in on their mom.

January 25, 1943
North Africa
Dear Doc Post;
You probably don't remember me but I'm Ernie McAnulty, Wally's brother. I received a copy of the *News Letter* No. 8 so thought I would drop you a line and let you know how the boys in North Africa are doing.

. . . I am flying Fighters over here which is a bit nerve racking at times, one develops what we call the Messerschmitt twitch, from looking around. Jerry is pretty good and flys a very good air craft. We have been knocking them down though. Our Fighter Sweeps are quite a lot of fun, blowing up trucks, tanks, and a number of other things. When the Boche see the P38s sticking that deadly nose towards them, they take cover damn quick.

You know, I was very glad to read my brother's letter. I haven't heard from him for a long time, but he can take care of himself with those Japs.

At the present time I'm in an English hospital recovering from a pair of burned legs, I hope to rejoin my squad very soon though. The writing must be excused as I'm lying in bed and getting very tired of it also.

Thanks for stopping in to see my mom. Tell her not to worry.

Well Doc this is all for now—

Sincerely,

E. McAnulty

P.S. I would appreciate it if you would see what can be done about sending some good old American girls over here to keep us company. Blonds preferred.

In the March 26, 1943, edition of the *News Letter* (No. 13), Dr. Post wrote,

Ernie is Wally's younger brother whom all Hooverites will remember as the great punter of about 1937. He didn't go to State but we'll make him an honorary Aztec being that he's Wally's brother. We are awfully glad to hear from him and hope that he can be up and at 'em again soon and also that we'll be seeing him soon.

Unfortunately for Ernie, his dating days would have to wait. As soon as he recovered, he was back in action, and news about him filtered in from other writers. Jim McColl earned a letter in varsity football, and he took notice of the "great punter" in North Africa.

March 29, 1943

Dear Dr. Post—

Just a page to say hello and [word cut by censor] that I haven't forgotten the "Halls of Montezuma" even tho I haven't written to you & "Monty" for several months.

I know you must be bored stiff by this time with letters dealing with the mud and blood and horror of it all, so I'll lay off the war angle this trip—you've probably a better idea of what's going on in regard to the war than most of us over here anyway.

. . . Also bumped into Ernie McAnulty up in Algiers awhile back—he'll have some hair-raising stories to tell when he comes home.

. . .

As Ever,

Jim

James Q. McColl

Less than two weeks after Jim's letter, Wally wrote again:

April 10, 1943

Dear Doc,

Your letter of March 15, the one with the pictures, was received today with a hearty welcome. Shades of Will Rogers, you really spin a mean loop.

I can imagine it would [be] great exercise but I'm kind of handicapped for want of rope. Guess I could get one of my chief's boys to fix me up a bark rope. You know they are quite handy people. They can make practically anything out of nothing.

. . .

I guess Ernie has had some time since he arrived in Africa. It seems as though the only news I get of him is what you and my mother write. I haven't heard from him for quite some time now. From everything I've heard he did pretty good for himself before he got hurt.

. . .

Guess I'll call it all pau for now Doc. Thanks for writing as I always look forward to your letters. Well nothing else so—

Aloha

Wally (Mac) McAnulty

A month and a half later, Wally got news of his brother, and his next letter is full of uncharacteristic mistakes, as though he can't settle his thoughts or his pen.

Monday, May 24, 1943

Dear Doc,

What a week end this last one has been. Bad news one day and good news the next.

I received a letter Saturday telling me Ernie was missing in action. She (Mom) seem[ed] terrible [*sic*] broken up about [it], naturally. If only something would turn up and he could be found, even as a prisoner of war. The kid deserved a lot of credit. One of the first to volunteer, then over to Africa to plenty of action. Always travelling in bad luck. Well I have my fingers crossed for him. Well that is the bad news.

Good news, oh yes, they called me in yesterday and pinned a silver bar on the old collar. Yes it really happened. The order was dated May 14, which made it exactly 6 months and 15 days since I was commissioned. . . .

Sincerely,

Wally (Mac) McAnulty

Two weeks later, Ernie's news reached Dr. Post:

June 7, 1943
Lt. McAnulty E. U.S.A.F.
Gefangenennummer: 1123
Lager-Bezeichnung:
M.—Stammlager Luft 3 [penciled in: Block 100 Prn. 6]
Deutschland
Dear Doc;
This card is being written under a bit different circumstances than my last letter to you. I'm a Prisoner in Germany. I would appreciate it if you would let my friends know I'm O.K. and any letters will be gratefully received. Hoping to hear from you soon.
    Sincerely,
    E.M.

Stammlager (Stalag, for short) Luft III, was near the border, and the grounds are now part of Poland. Ernie was in a prison camp designed for captured pilots. "Luft" was short for Luftwaffe, the German term for air force. A preprinted lined postcard had just enough room for him to pencil in his *Gefangenennummer* (prisoner number) and Dr. Post's address on one side, and a few lines on the opposite side of the card.

Following World War I, the *Convention relative to the Treatment of Prisoners of War* had been adopted but wasn't universally enforced. After World War II, the convention was updated, but it didn't become part of the Third Geneva Convention until 1949.[5] Before that, the terms for treatment drawn up in 1929 required countries to notify one another about captured prisoners and also specified that prison camps be similar to military camps. According to these terms, a prisoner could expect the same kind of food and housing that he would get as a soldier in his own country.

The convention also laid out expectations for the delivery of letters and packages. Families were supposed to be able to send food, clothes, and even books. The American Red Cross prepared relief packages of medicine and food, including chocolate and cigarettes, but also dried milk, peanut butter, tuna, and even cheese and meat.[6] Some packages were confiscated, while others, containing rations intended for one, were shared by several servicemen.

Ernie's name caught the attention of a former high school classmate, Ethyle Bradshaw Smith.

March 31, 1943

Dear Dr. Post,

As I do the larger part of my husband's writing so he may have more time for studying, I decided that I should write to thank you for those much welcome *News Letters*. Kit has been intending to write to you but just doesn't get around to it.

The *News Letters* are very interesting to me as well as Kit. While I am not an ex-Aztec, I did graduate from Hoover in the '38 class and I know a great deal of the many in the service who write to you.

Last Sunday on the radio in an Oakland news broadcast I heard that Ernie McAnulty's life had been saved, by two brothers, from a Messerschmitt after his motor had failed. I didn't hear all of it, so I don't have details. You probably know all about it anyway.

Kit and Wally McAnulty are good friends and if you could send us Wally's address I know that Kit would appreciate it.

. . .

Kit has recently received his instrument rating and had his first flight to Honolulu two weeks ago. He had a good trip and said he learned a great deal. (He brought me back a large pineapple, aren't I lucky?)

. . .

Thank you again, Dr. Post.

Sincerely,

Ethyle Bradshaw Smith

(Mrs. Clinton E. Smith)

1055 Aileen Street

Oakland, California

When news came of Ernie's capture, the letters between Wally and Dr. Post flew as fast as the postal service could deliver them. Dr. Post heard from all theaters of the war, with everyone writing to tell him details about who had been seen alive and who had been captured, which meant he sometimes had news before the official reports were released.

June 19, 1943

Dear Doc,

My letter writing has really hit a new low this past couple of weeks. I received your really swell letter telling me about Ernie being a prisoner. It was bad news but at the same time very welcome news. I know it made my mom feel swell to hear it. I do know Ernie will appreciate your writing to him Doc, thanks. I guess I'll have a pretty hard time trying to write him with all the regulations covering a serviceman writing a prisoner of war.

. . .

Well guess I'd better sign off for now and try and catch a few winks before supper.

Aloha

Wally (Mac) McAnulty

July 21, 1943

Dear "Doc"

. . . You probably know I'm on the Bn. staff now. Hq 1st Bn 251st CA (AA) same address as before.

. . .

Guess Ernie is getting along ok, as he is able to write home fairly often. Mom is able to send him a package every three months. If he receives it, he will have some good American chow now and then anyhow.

. . .

Aloha

Wally (Mac) McAnulty

July 21, 1943

Lt. McAnulty E.E. U.S.A.A.F.

Gefangenennummer: 1123

[Penciled in: "Mit Luft Post Noch Nord Amerika . . . Air Mail"]
[Stamped: U.S. Censorship Examined by 845]

Hi Doc. I hope you have received the other card I wrote you. This P.O.W. life sure gets monotonous after a while. How are things at home? Have you heard from my bud lately? If you see anybody not doing anything tell them to drop me a line. Say hello to everyone for me. Sincerely. E.E.M.

The summer passed, and toward the end of 1943, Wally took a moment to reflect on the war.

November 7, 1943

Dear Doc.

What a war. Here I sit in the Paradise of the Pacific while so many of the fellows have had places and battles like Africa, Sicily, and Italy. Not forgetting the Solomons, New Guinea and all the air raids in the Pacific. It doesn't seem quite right does it?

. . .

These wars are funny things. The way it started out I figured that I'd get to see lots of it and end up as a sightseer. I can't say I haven't enjoyed the sights however it's just that they get old after watching them for a year and a half. I know darn well it's not fun further up the line but would still like a crack at it.

. . . Lionel Chase and the rest of the guys jockeying those ships around have certainly raised a lot of rumpas from a grandstand seat. They all have my wishes for the best of luck as they have really done a swell job.

Hated to hear about Williams and Frost being prisoners but such is war, I guess.

We all enjoyed the picture on the front of this last *News Letter*. Everything you are doing back there is appreciated . . . and we're all looking forward to the day we can drop in out at school and see the picture panel.

Well Doc guess I'll call it pau for now as my sails are really blown out. Guess I must be slipping because I used to be able to think of lots to say. Will be looking for the next *News Letter*.

Aloha

Wally (Mac) McAnulty

For Wally McAnulty in the South Pacific and for his brother Ernie in a German prison camp, the war had become a terrible test of endurance.

THE AZTEC NEWS LETTER

No. 24, March 1, 1944

REMEMBER "SAN DIEGO'S OWN"

THE 251ST CA AA

Millions of American families should be interested in what happens to the San Diego regiment of CA AA. By the time this

Wally McAnulty at San Diego
State College

Wally McAnulty, 251st Coast
Artillery (Antiaircraft) Regiment

note comes off the press they will have been overseas for three
and a half years. Many of those men had their educations suddenly disrupted when they were called out, and their being
away from their families, wives, and children has been an
unusually great hardship. Some of the men have children now
in nursery school whom they have never even seen.

Let any family asking for the return of their loved ones after
two or even one year's service in the tropics think first of the
original "forgotten regiment." Because of their far-sightedness
they were among the first to prepare for this war. They led the
way over; now let's have them lead the way back.

SAN DIEGO STATE COLLEGE SERVICE MEN'S
NEWS LETTER No. 6

Edited by Dr. Lauren C. Post
San Diego State College
San Diego, California
August 28, 1942

(The addresses of this Letter supplement
those in No. 4 and No. 5. Only the additions,
changes, and promotions appear in this
letter. See those two numbers for about
500 addresses that have not changed in the
past few weeks.

We now have available re-runs of all of
the News Letters from its beginning.
Write us if you want to complete your
file. Specify which numbers you deisre.

Be sure to send in your own full address and
rank as well as any that have been omitted.

A complete new directory is to be issued after
the beginning of the new semester.)

MONTEZUMA says:

"The sun never sets on
the FIGHTING AZTECS of
San Diego State College"

To all of the Aztecs:

Thanks for all of those nice letters. They are appreciated both here and
"over there". We want you to feel that you are still one of us no matter how
far away you are as measured in miles. And we want you to feel that you are not
alone in this war. Really, the Quad is empty.

The number of Aztec mothers and wives on our mailing list has been growing
fast. If you have friends who enjoy reading the News Letter, just send their
addresses in. Perhaps they can keep your file complete for when you return just
in case your own copies are lost or worn out.

At this moment the mimeograph is running off the other pages--1000 copies of
each--and soon we will be assembling and mailing them. No small job but we always
have more offers for help than we can use.

We get back very few of the News Letters, and we hear of some being forwarded
as many as four times. Are you getting yours?

Write to us and we will keep them rolling.

Sincerely, L.C.P.

P.S. Send us some new slogans!!! I wonder what Phil Thacher meant when he said
"Remember the Houston!"

3

DEAD AHEAD

The military was under pressure to get more men prepared for air, sea, and land assaults, and San Diego State College was ideally suited to assist in war preparations. In 1935, the same year that Consolidated Aircraft dedicated a new factory in San Diego, the college added engineering to the curriculum. Consolidated Aircraft quickly began production of the patrol boats and B-24 bombers that were used early in World War II.[1] Blair Burkhardt, a young Aztec alumnus, worked with another aircraft company, North American Aviation, based in Inglewood, California. North American Aviation made the B-25 bomber that was used throughout the war, notably in the April 19, 1942, Tokyo raid led by Lt. Col. James "Jimmy" Doolittle.[2]

Burkhardt was attached to a bomb group, close enough to the service-men to see how they fared in combat, and he took a natural interest in pilots because he worked on their planes.

November 1, 1943

. . .

Really Doc, when I do hear about another of our close friends having a little bad luck, I wish that I had taken a job where I could really get at their throats and give it a twist. Sometimes my job seems dull watching the planes go and come, day in and day out, and me staying behind really not doing much about it. About all I can do is give the fellows the best possible break that I can by continually improving their planes, but sometimes I wonder if I shouldn't have learned to fly and be right with them and let my job fall to some guy who is really 4F. After all, Doc, we just build them, but the credit is to the fellows that fly them.

. . .

As ever,

Mr. H. B. (Blair) Burkhardt

Representative

North American Aviation, Inc.

XII A.F.S.C. Hd.

APO 528 New York, New York

Burkhardt's efforts to improve the planes went hand in hand with the Tokyo bombing raid. Sixteen B-25 bombers were used in the first attack on Japan, which was planned as a direct retaliation for Pearl Harbor. A number of logistical problems had to be overcome in order to execute a long-range assault with medium-range bombers. Although they could be launched from an aircraft carrier in the Pacific, bombers of that size weren't designed to land on the carrier, so after striking targets in Japan the bombers were to continue on to China.

The United States was rushing to build planes and train pilots, and it risked significant losses in carrying out the raid on Tokyo and other Japanese cities. The damage inflicted wasn't meant to turn the tide of war but to show the Japanese that they were vulnerable to invasion. The need to strike back at Japan outweighed all other factors, including the possibility that the planes wouldn't return.

Those who volunteered didn't know the details until they were on board the aircraft carrier and heading out to sea. En route, a Japanese patrol was spotted near the American position, and Doolittle called for takeoff earlier than anticipated. Even after the launch time was moved up, forcing the planes to use more fuel to reach China, the mission was a "go." Everything pointed toward a one-way trip for the pilots and their crews.[3]

For a young, idealistic college student, this type of attack was the perfect mission—a daredevil raid designed to show the enemy who was boss. Everything about the Doolittle Raid signaled a desire to teach a lesson to a country that Americans viewed as underhanded and cowardly. Many pilots volunteered, but only a handful were chosen for the job. Each of the sixteen planes on the mission had a crew of five men, and the copilot on plane 15 was a young lieutenant named Griffith Williams, known to fellow Aztecs as "Griff" or "Grif."

Williams survived a harrowing escape from China, and when he returned to San Diego, he was invited to speak on campus on July 8, 1942. Dr. Post published an excerpt of his talk in the next issue of the *News Letter*:

SAN DIEGO STATE COLLEGE SERVICE MEN'S NEWS LETTER
No. 5, August 5, 1942
We have all been given orders not to talk about anything that took place before or after the raid—only what took place during the actual raid. What took place before and after is a "military secret."

The whole flight was made at low elevation in order to escape detection. They had no idea we were coming. Our particular target was Kobe—not Tokyo. We arrived at Kobe at about 1:30 P.M. their time and about an hour and a half after Tokyo had been bombed, but it seemed that the population was carrying on as usual. We dropped all our bombs before they did any firing at all.

On our way to Kobe we had to cross about 50 miles of land. This was planted mostly in rice and the workers and a lot of people waved at us. After they discovered we were enemy planes the boys threw rocks at us and shook their fists at us— that was the only opposition we had.

Every ship was assigned a definite target. The kind of ammunition we had depended on the kind of target we were after. We carried incendiary bombs in our ship. We had reports that the fires we started were burning three days later. We bombed two aircraft factories and some warehouses. Probably six or eight aircraft factories were bombed in all. We were given instructions not to bomb the emperor's palace.

Some warships fired on some of the planes after they left the land and were over the water. Some fighter planes took after us but we just pulled away from them without opening the throttle all the way.

The planes were all manned on a volunteer basis. More men volunteered than could go. Sixteen planes started and sixteen planes came back. A lot of pictures were taken—both stills and movies. I have never seen them. They are in the hands of the Intelligence Office.

Toward the end of his life, Williams wrote a personal account of the Doolittle Raid titled "WW II Revisited: The First Air Attack against Japan." In it he remembers the moment he volunteered for the mission, just weeks after the Pearl Harbor attack. "If you had asked me at that time why I volunteered, I could probably have given you a good answer. But looking at it from a distance of fifty years, I'm not certain I could explain why. Perhaps it was just the enthusiasm of youth, the search for excitement, perhaps even patriotism."[4]

All those years later, Williams was finally free to disclose the rest of the "military secret," including his training leading up to the attack. Initially, twenty-four crews were trained at Eglin Field, Florida. Williams wrote, "We would train in short field takeoff techniques, long range cruise control at low altitudes, and low level bombing. . . . To lift a B-25 off the deck of a Navy aircraft carrier we had to use techniques that were contrary to everything we had been taught."[5]

The pilots were given leeway in choosing their targets. Williams' pilot was 1st Lt. Donald Smith, and Williams recalled that their strategy was to attack warehouses near the waterfront using incendiary bombs that would set fire to shipping facilities where war materials were manufactured and stored.

The day of the mission arrived, with Colonel Doolittle in the first position for takeoff. On an aircraft carrier, the planes didn't have the luxury of a long runway to gain speed for lift-off. Normally, a hydraulic catapult would propel the planes off the short deck.[6] The modified planes lifting off from the *Hornet* were at such low airspeeds that they were in danger of stalling.

Williams wrote,

As you would guess, we were more than a little interested in that first takeoff with Jimmy Doolittle at the controls. As we stood to one side and watched, he ran the engines up to full power and waited for the "go" signal from the Navy controller kneeling beside the airplane. At that moment I will guarantee that all of us were doing one or more of the following: holding our breath, crossing our fingers, or praying. As the carrier approached the bottom of a trough, the controller gave the go signal and the colonel released his brakes. The airplane accelerated slowly into the brisk wind and, as the flight deck rose, became airborne with at least 100 feet of deck space remaining. The cheer that went up should have been heard in Tokyo.[7]

Williams was on the fifteenth of the sixteen planes to launch. Describing the tense moments in the cockpit during takeoff, he wrote,

Because of the extremely low airspeed, Don was fighting to keep the airplane from falling off to one side or the other by the quick use of ailerons and rudder. As the gear came up, he was able to lower the nose a bit and gain some airspeed. As airspeed increased, I retracted the wing flaps a few degrees, further reducing the drag and allowing an additional increase in airspeed. This process of 'milking' up the flaps was continued until we were in a normal takeoff configuration and we could start to breathe again. During the entire takeoff process, I had been calling out airspeeds and flap positions to Don so that he was constantly aware of how close he was to a complete stall and could react accordingly.[8]

Williams and his crew flew over Japan at midday, looking down on a peaceful landscape with no sign of resistance. His focus sharpened as his target came into view. He wrote, "There it was, dead ahead. All the planning and practice and apprehension of the previous two and a half months was about to come together in a 20 second bomb run over storage and warehouse facilities."[9]

Williams, in the cockpit, heard the navigator and bombardier, Lt. Howard Sessler, as he called out the bombing sequence. "From the nose, we heard Sessler over the intercom, 'Ten degrees left, steady, three degrees right, good, doors open, 1 and 2 away, five degrees left, 3 and 4 away, doors closed.' That was it. I was heard to say (although I don't remember it), 'Let's get the hell out of here.' Don dove for the water of Kobe harbor and headed for the open sea at ten feet altitude."[10]

The planes were under orders for radio silence. To make matters worse, they were forced to increase speed in order to out-distance enemy fighters, which meant consuming more precious fuel. As they flew over the China Sea, the crew debated whether to use all the fuel in an effort to get closer to land, or to ditch the plane in a controlled manner in the choppy water. Darkness descended as the crew made their preparations for a rough landing on the water. The pilot turned on the landing lights to illuminate the dark sea.

Williams described the impact: "As the nose dropped into the water, the plexiglas [*sic*] nose section collapsed and we were immediately sitting in water up to our waists. I opened the upper hatches and after picking up our emergency gear, Don, Sessler and I climbed out onto the upper wing surface."[11]

The other crew members—the engineer, Sgt. Edward Saylor, and a doctor, Lt. Thomas White—released the life raft from the rear of the plane, then also climbed onto the wing. White, the designated medic for the mission, dove back into the water to retrieve his medical case from the partially submerged plane. For risking his life in this way, he was later awarded the Silver Star. The crew had just enough time to load their emergency gear, rations, and weapons into the life raft and push off.

Williams recalled, "My last view of the airplane is still fresh in my mind because of one simple detail; *the landing lights were still on!* The lights, wiring, and battery system were somehow insulated from the sea water and the result was an eerie, underwater glow."[12]

SAN DIEGO STATE COLLEGE SERVICE MEN'S
NEWS LETTER NO. 5

Edited by Dr. Lauren C. Post
San Diego State College
San Diego, California
August 5, 1942

(The addresses of this Letter supplement
those in No. 4. Only the promotions,
changes, and additions appear in this
Letter. See No. 4 for the 345 old
addresses. Write for it if you didn't
get it. Be sure to send in your own
change or promotion.)

Dear Fellow Aztecs:

Doc Post asked me to write this letter for his fast growing
publication, not because he thought I could write an inspiring
message, but because I was fortunate enough to get to go on a
trip in April which I am sure any of you would have given your
next three months' pay to have been in on.

I've just had my first chance to take a look at the
Aztec News Letter and it's really swell to get some of the
news from the bunch. From the looks of the addresses, you
are spread all over the globe and I suppose some of you have
had some good licks in already. I just hope that all of you
have the satisfaction of seeing the Axis' buildings topple
and their ships and planes go down, because there is going
to be a lot more of that going on pretty soon.
Am I right?

Give 'em hell, fellas, and we'll all have Christmas
dinner in Tokio.

Best of luck,

Griffith Williams
1ST. LT. AAF

4

THE MISSING
AMERICAN AIRMEN

In preparing for the Doolittle Raid on Japan, every effort was made to supply the planes with as much fuel as possible, including adding extra storage tanks. The weight of the extra fuel combined with the aircraft carrier's short runway made it even more difficult for the planes to get into the air.

In his account of the raid, "WW II Revisited," Griffith Williams wrote, "In addition to wing tanks (the normal fuel load), there was a specially made 225 gallon tank in the upper third of the bomb bay and a 65 gallon tank in the rear of the airplane replacing a lower gun turret that had been removed. A collapsible rubber tank occupied the tunnel space that separated the cockpit from the rear of the airplane, and finally, 10 five gallon cans of gasoline were stored in the rear fuselage to be manually emptied into the turret tank as fuel was used."[1]

When the *Hornet* and its accompanying ships were alerted to the presence of enemy vessels, Colonel Doolittle decided to launch the bombers early,[2] so the extra fuel that had been meant to get the planes to an airfield in China was instead consumed en route to the target cities. After the bombing run, 1st Lt. Donald Smith was forced to land on the water. His plane had settled underwater but was still partially afloat because of the extra fuel tanks that were now full of air. As the crew pushed the life raft away from the plane, the raft suddenly collapsed, probably punctured by the wreckage.

Now, with only the pilot's sidearm for protection, the crew was in the water, hanging on to what was left of the raft. Darkness had fallen, and the carefully stowed supplies were lost. The bombardier, Sessler, left the deflated raft and tried to swim to shore on his own. The rest of the group pushed and pulled their damaged raft toward shore and, nearing total exhaustion, dragged one another out of the water. Their sodden clothes were no match for the cold wind. Fearing hypothermia, the men carefully headed in the direction of a light, and came upon a cottage with a straw-filled lean-to alongside it. Quickly, they took shelter inside the lean-to.

Williams continued, "We were no sooner settled comfortably, when the light reappeared, this time from around the corner of the cottage and right behind it, a face peered cautiously at us. The first exchange of words were obviously not understood, but the emotion on both sides of the light was definitely tentative. These were probably Chinese farmers or fishermen, but were they friendly? And from their viewpoint; this group of Occidentals who appeared suddenly on their doorstep—who were they?"[3]

The men were invited inside and given food. To communicate, they used a school book that belonged to a young girl who lived in the cottage.

It wasn't until they pointed to a picture of the flag of the United States that the Chinese family understood who they had invited to supper.

In the morning, the crew was reunited with their bombardier, who had made it ashore farther up the coast. They also discovered that instead of landing near the mainland, as they had hoped, they were on Tantou Shan, an island just across a channel from Shipu, a port occupied by the Japanese. They stayed hidden until nightfall when locals took them to a small fishing boat.

Williams described their nighttime escape from the island: "Two of the Chinese followed us aboard and we were instructed to lie down in the bottom of the craft so as not to be visible from the side. There was a partial moon in the sky and without the cloud cover, close objects were easily recognized. I was quite apprehensive at this point as I'm sure the rest of crew was, because our fate was now completely in the hands of alien strangers. We had no choice but to trust these people, since it would be virtually impossible for us, by ourselves, to leave the island or avoid almost certain capture by the enemy."[4]

The Chinese were no strangers to Japanese hostility. Their country had been locked in battle with Japan for decades. As World War II spread across continents, the Second Sino-Japanese War became one more complexity in the greater global warfare. While Europe succumbed to Hitler's smashing blitzkriegs, China was trapped in civil turmoil, teetering between nationalist and communist factions whose leaders were unified only in their desire to escape Japanese domination. At first, Chinese military forces fared badly against brutal Japanese assaults, but they gradually honed their guerrilla tactics.[5]

When the Doolittle raiders crashed, swam, and limped ashore in occupied China, the local resistance fighters wasted no time in helping them escape. Plane 15, the one that Williams copiloted, had managed to touch down intact before sinking. The crewmen of another plane weren't as lucky. When the pilot tried to land on the beach, the engines cut out, and the plane plummeted into the surf, flipped, and forcefully ejected the crew.

Williams learned this from an English-speaking guide. He wrote, "The guerrilla forces on the island took immediate action to remove the injured crew from the island and start them on their way toward a missionary hospital at Lin Hai in unoccupied China."[6]

When a second group of raiders showed up, the local guerrillas responded again, taking precautions to hide Williams and his fellow crewmen from the Japanese who were scouring the coast.

Williams described his precarious journey as it unfolded: "We started walking, dutifully following our guides. That walk was an almost mystical experience that I can still visualize clearly. In the faint moonlight, we hustled along narrow paths between rice paddies; made our way through groves of exotic trees; oriental, pagoda-like buildings resolved magically out of the darkness as we approached; and we eventually found ourselves high on the side of a mountain inside a Taoist temple."[7]

The priest allowed the Americans to use his cottage to keep watch through the next morning, when word reached them that a Japanese search party was on the way.

Williams continued, "We were quickly led into a back bedroom of the cottage where the priest removed a curtain-like covering from the wall behind the bed to reveal an opening, or cave, dug into the side of the hill. The opening was about three feet wide by five feet high and extended straight back into the mountain for 12 to 15 feet."[8]

The five American crewmen and their two Chinese guides crawled into the tunnel and sat on the dirt floor. After the priest put the covering in place, the crewmen and their guides were in absolute darkness.

In this cramped hiding place, Williams and his companions waited. He wrote, "The silence in that tiny cavern was almost complete. A few low whispers, but there was really nothing to discuss. Within 20 minutes or so after moving into our 'tomb,' we heard a great deal of activity and a lot of loud, angry conversation. The enemy patrol had entered the house looking for the missing American airmen. I'm sure we all wondered what would happen if the opening were discovered. Would we suddenly find a grenade rolling at our feet? Or would they simply order us out. We still had the 45-automatic—with one clip of ammunition—big deal!"[9]

Later that night, the men were put on another boat and again hidden from view as they sailed along the coast to a point where they could escape from the occupied territory. They journeyed by bus and train to Chongqing, where Chiang Kai-shek awarded the Doolittle raiders the Military Order of China. Ten weeks later, in Washington, they received the Distinguished Flying Cross. The pilot of plane 15, Don Smith, who had made such a heroic landing in the China Sea, was killed in action in Great Britain seven months after the Doolittle Raid.[10]

Toward the end of his life, when Williams wrote about the raid, the plane he had copiloted still lay submerged in deep water near Tantou Shan. The landing lights, once visible beneath the China Sea, had long since been extinguished. Griffith Williams passed away in 1998 and is buried at Fort Rosecrans National Cemetery in San Diego.

Of the sixteen planes that launched from the USS *Hornet*, all reached their targets, and all but one of them made it to China, where they either crashed or were ditched. (One plane reached an airfield in the Soviet Union.) The Japanese were relentless in their search for the Doolittle raiders, and yet they succeeded in capturing only eight men. Any Chinese people who were discovered to have helped the Americans escape suffered brutal retaliation. To further deter civilians from assisting the Allies, the Japanese carried out an extended campaign against the local population. Some estimates place the death toll of Chinese civilians from Japanese reprisal at 250,000.[11]

Another pilot from San Diego State College, Lt. Earl Allison, also described the role of the Chinese in helping Americans. In editing Allison's letter, Dr. Post, who was always thinking of the censors, crossed out the mention of B-25s and substituted the generic word "planes."

✉ June 30, 1943

Doc, we have B-25s up here now & what a honey of a ship. Lots of power, speed, bomb load & fire power. Turning a lot of pilots out too so Tojo, Adolf & his hench-men had better get plenty well prepared when Uncle Sam turns his Aztecs loose.

. . .

This post is rather unique Doc. We just finished training about 60 or 70 Chinese pilots in B-25s & they'll go back to China to fly American built B-25s. One of them gave a bunch of us a lot of good information & also the attitude of the Chinese. His very words were, "We'll fight the Japs another 100 years if need be." This was in answer to the question "Aren't you losing a lot of Chinese people in this war?" He says the Chinese will never give up. They would rather be killed than live under the Japs. He says they figure they're better off fighting with a weak army than giving up like the French. At least part of China is free & parts will always be free.

When the Japs found the wreckage of the planes of Doolittle's Tokyo raid— every Chinese man, woman & child in a radius of 70 miles were killed because they wouldn't tell where the party had gone. With allies like that on our side & the guerillas of occupied Europe plus our own power plus Great Britain—well— the Axis can never defeat the Allied cause. Tell the fellows in the front lines, Doc, that there are plenty of men coming across very shortly to help keep things going that they have started with such hardships.

Lt. Earl L. Allison

THE AZTEC NEWS LETTER

Edited by
DR. LAUREN C. POST
San Diego State College
San Diego, California

June 1, 1943
NO. 15

This Issue Sponsored, in part, by the Class of 1945

To All of the Aztecs in the Service and Their Friends:

This letter to you can be short because the News Letter now speaks for itself. Some of the features in it will tell you that we are really in a war.

Editing is more of a problem than ever, but I try to include as much as possible of the foreign mail. That means that the domestic letters often get cut nearly to the vanishing point. But to those of you who have gone to the trouble of sending in long, well-written letters, let me say that I enjoy them immensely and I feel that they are a fine personal reward for my efforts in trying to keep up old ties.

I'll repeat my request for news names, addresses, and promotions of any men who ever went to State College. We are still short of pictures for the AZTECS IN SERVICE panel. Tell your families to send us snapshots—head size, not over 2x2 inches. Also let us know who has been decorated. All who have been decorated get blue stars. About 300 of the 1,500 Cetza address cards have been returned.

Civilians may still get on our mailing list. Are your families keeping your News Letters on file for you? We still have some older issues but we are about out of No. 14. This time we will get 2,600 copies printed.

The war picture looks much brighter from here. Hope it does to all of you from your vantage points.

And again, best of luck,

Lauren C. Post,
Editor of the News Letter.

"I'll meet you in front of the archway."

Lt. George J. R. Ewing

Lt. George J. R. Ewing was killed in a plane crash near Orlando, Florida. He had received his wings at Willliams Field, Arizona, in April.

Lt. Joseph Norman Gates

Lt. Joseph Norman Gates was reported missing in action over France last October. Less than a month ago his mother, Mrs. Nanette D. Bailey, received word from the war department that Lt. Gates had been "killed in action over Europe."

Lt. Jerry Thomas

Lt. Jerry Thomas was reported "missing in action." He had been stationed in England and from there he had participated in the "daylight bombing raid over Lille, France." Charles Byrne who is in Portland wrote of him: "I read several interesting V-Mail letters he had sent from England after he had started dropping 'eggs' on the continent. He had five Fortresses shot up under him and he had brought them all back safely. Apparently he couldn't bring No. 6 back."

Jerry had received several decorations, one of which was the Oak Leaf Cluster. (Again, I'm sorry I don't have more information. His home town was listed as South Gate and the local papers sometimes miss such stories. L.C.P.)

Lt. Augustine Apra'

It has been reported that Lt. Augustine Apra' is a prisoner of the Japanese.

Lt. Richard Kenney

Lt. Richard Kenney who has been flying P-38's in North Africa, was mentioned in the press for "shooting down a Messerschmidt and dropping a bomb squarely on an enemy ship off North Africa." Previously Richard had been shot down, wounded, and badly burned, but he fell in friendly territory. He had an opportunity to return to the States, but being a real **Fighting** Aztec, he chose to stay and fight. The next thing

5

HAPPY LANDINGS

A Chinese student at San Diego State named Some Ching became an infantry lieutenant. He'd been on the college fencing team, and he was used to close combat. While he was at war, he went after the Japanese with a vengeance. Ching's vicious and exuberant writing should be balanced against the consideration that he had family in China and therefore a personal vendetta against the Japanese. The Second Sino-Japanese War had begun escalating in 1937, and as the fighting increased, so did the cruelty, culminating that year in the infamous Rape of Nanking. Witnesses reported mass executions and the brutalization of troops and civilians.[1]

In the following letter, Ching described the way dead bodies polluted the streams. Accounts of the Nanking Massacre testified to a similar scene: "Every pond, stream and river was polluted with decomposing bodies."[2] The language used by Ching in the aftermath of battle was the same as that used to describe the death of his countrymen at the hands of the Japanese. Ching's blithe tone veiled his anger, and his wrath wasn't confined to the battlefield. Dr. Post noted that while he was still on campus, Ching had unapologetically heckled a Japanese speaker.

Like many who wrote to Dr. Post, Ching began his letter with a jab at the highly decorated pilot Lieutenant Chase.

August 14, 1943

Dear Sir;

Enjoyed your July issue immensely. I see Lt. Lionel E. Chase is covering himself with glory. These Air Corps glamour boys live a charmed life, besides living in luxurious quarters and being decorated with medals. I suppose when the war is over, he will have enough medals to open a hardware store.

Nothing exciting ever happens to us "Dough Boys". After sweating out [material cut by censor].

Our leading units have annihilated the Japs here, killing several thousands and capturing only a few. Dorothy Thompson, who calls us brutes and wants to take away our American citizenships, doesn't understand that those Sons of Yamamoto's don't surrender en mass like the "Supermen" of Hitler's in Africa, but fought to the last man. It was a tedious job for the boys to carry a Tommy-gun and a sackful of grenades, ferreting them out from foxhole to foxhole, because they are extremely well camouflaged. Many Japs, however, have done us a favor, committing Hara Kiri by holding a grenade against their chests or heads. For a long time the cadavers sprawled all over the hills and streams, stinking and polluting our water. Every time I take a drink, I can't help thinking it is Jap juice. No more live ones left. Ho hum, back to the picks and shovels again. And dig and dig and dig! Our morale is excellent.

The Germans die for the Fuhrer; the Japs for Hirohito, but the Yanks don't die for Franklin because we have many staunch Republicans here. To this day I have not yet figured out what my men's incentive is. I guess it is a mixture of: love of the country, personal pride, adventure and last but not the least, the desire for souvenirs. Nothing of monetary value of course, but little things like Japanese battle flags, insignias, coins, blankets and swords carried by the Jap officers entreat them. As the story goes, one Yank was about to hand-grenade a Jap but was stopped by his buddy who hollered, "Don't do that, shoot him. He's got a watch on." We traded souvenirs for Coleman Lanterns and electric generators from the Navy and sold the flags for as high as fifty dollars a piece.

And speaking of swords, I am glad I have learned a few fundamentals of parry and thrust from Mr. Manzeck's fencing class, because when the Japs attack, their officers lead their men with a sword, according to the spirit and tradition of the Samurais. So you see I still have a chance to win an Athletic Letter from Monsieur Manzeck when I come back.

. . .

One more gripe while I am at it. I thought victory is sweet and glamorous like Marching into Tunisia with women and children cheering and throwing flowers and kisses at you. Well, the only reception we got was from weird cries of the well fed black ravens. . . .

War will be over soon, I hope. I have a cousin at Hawaii, one in the Chinese Air Corps and me at the third corner of the triangle. We have the Japs surrounded now.

1st Lt. Some Ching
Infantry

The Japanese had initially seemed invincible, but as the war continued, flaws began to appear in their strategy. Lieutenant Ching got a good look at their weaknesses and strengths. The samurai code to which he referred filtered into every Japanese attack, from the pointed swords that led the charge to the deeply ingrained cultural values of the fighting men.[3] Their tradition called for warriors to remain in combat until victory or death.

THE AZTEC NEWS LETTER
No. 24, March 1, 1944
1st Lt. Some Ching sent a captured Japanese propaganda Christmas card from the Aleutians. "Not much doing here now so I play chess to keep from getting Aleutianations." (Some of you will remember Lt. Ching as the little Chinese student who heckled the Jap lecturer in the Little Theater at State College back in about 1939. The lecturer told of cooperation between Japanese and Chinese after the "incident" and Ching told the Jap what the Chinese would really do to them. The third man in the ring was Dr. Lewis B. Lesley. LCP.)
Dr. Lauren C. Post, Editor

The "glamour boy," Lieutenant Chase, could look forward to rotating home, but he was more concerned with locating his friends and his next drink. One of his beverages was named for a German dive bomber, the Stuka.

Doc, I saw 17,000 cases of Coca-Cola the other day. I tried everything from bribery to theft but to no avail. The stuff is guarded a lot closer than Bombsights. To make it worse, we've run out of "Stuka Juice." We nailed some Spanish Banana Brandy, but it hits harder than the first Typhoid-Tetanus Group—Wheels down, Pressure up!
    Lt. Lionel E. Chase

January 8, 1943
Peterson Field
Dear Doc'
. . .

News from here is scarce. Hell, a navigator is always too busy working to see anything. I joined the Air Corp to see action and I wind up a blasted flying bookkeeper. Phooey. Next time I'll go in the Paratroops. I see about as much as a company clerk.

    Thanks again for the *News Letter* & tell Chase to quit making me jealous with tales of his exploits or next time we go hunting I'll really shoot at him.
    So Long
    Lt. Le Roy A. Morgan
    0-695688
    383 Heavy Bombard. Grp.
    Colorado Springs, Colorado

More letters from Lieutenant Morgan are in chapter 15.

March 28, 1944
Italy
Dear Dr. Post;
    . . . Only one year in North Africa and Italy has brought home to me some of the immense import of these basic international problems. Truly, college credit should be allowed for lessons learned over here.

    This is certainly not intended as a dissertation of affaires politiques; I wish only to express my gratitude for the *News Letter* which is a symbol of those happy days of academic life at "State"; bull sessions in the Quad; campus politics, Fraternity doings; lemon-cokes in the Coop; the beautiful sanctity of the library; football and proms; mid-term exams. . . . . can this be the same planet?
    . . .

As I read these constant references to Lionel Chase, I am wondering if this swashbuckling daredevil of the Air Corps is the same person as the blushing, timid Lionel Chase whom I knew in the 8th grade in Woodrow Wilson Jr. High School; had you seen this bashful lad in the school play, "Billy," you would not wonder at my incredulity.

. . .

Tennyson was right. . . . "The old order changeth, yielding place to new and God fulfills Himself in many ways lest one good custom should corrupt the World."

Respectfully,
1st Lt. Bernard B. Siner
Class of '39
Med. Adm. C.
Headquarters, Peninsular Base Sections
Office of the Surgeon, APO 782
c/o Postmaster, New York, New York

In addition to vexing his friends and searching for Coca-Cola, Lieutenant Chase sought Aztec stickers, which Dr. Post promptly sent. They were one of the servicemen's most requested items and were especially prized by pilots.

For the most part, Lieutenant Chase's letters to Dr. Post had an upbeat tone. Because everyone was reading excerpts in the *News Letter*, Chase was aware of the need to boost morale. Occasionally, though, his good cheer faltered.

July 26, 1943

Dear Doc,

Your card and the Aztec stickers came this afternoon. There'll be one on the old "fuel-consumer" in the morning. The other day I set down at a Medium Bomb field for gas. It just happened to be the—bomb group and I immediately inquired after Griff Williams. It sure hurt to learn he was "M.I.A."

. . .

We had a real treat tonight. From materials obtained by "Midnight Requisition" methods we made 25 gallons of *Chocolate Ice Cream* (note capitals). Oh, brother! Get that old *News Letter* on the way and Happy Landings.

Lt. Lionel E. Chase

Lt. Griffith Williams, who copiloted a plane on the Doolittle Raid (discussed in chapters 3 and 4), continued to fly until his plane went down over Italy. Pilots who were lost or captured, like Williams, were soon replaced by others with good training. Lieutenant Chase had perhaps one of the most important advantages of pilots anywhere in the world—he had been trained by combat-tested instructors.[4] American and Japanese strategies differed in their approaches to pilot training and combat.

The decision to move experienced pilots from the combat theater to the classroom, where they became the teachers, proved motivational to men like Lieutenant Chase. For these athletes-turned-pilots, exerting themselves toward one more lap of the field, one more quarter of the game, or one more combat mission before they earned a rest was as familiar as the uniforms they wore. They trained, excelled, got the job done, and then taught others how to do the same.

The Japanese, who had taken such a commanding lead in the early battles in the Pacific, adopted a different strategy, a natural outgrowth of their reverence for the warrior class and the honor that warriors sought through combat. Their pilots continued to gain experience, making those who survived more menacing. The strategy to pit battle-tested experts against relative novices made sense, and it worked well until major conflicts inflicted heavy losses all around. Ultimately, the American training practice paid off. No matter how many planes went down in battle, the Americans still had experienced personnel behind the lines.

The tide of war in the Pacific theater began to turn with the Battle of the Coral Sea and culminated decisively the following month at the Battle of Midway, in June 1942. Military historians have noted that the Coral Sea was the first battle in which planes from both sides were launched before the carriers had even sighted the enemy. This type of fighting emphasized the important role of pilots. Naval battles were now fought from the air as well as the sea.[5]

The fighting in the Coral Sea lasted for days. Aircraft carriers, light carriers, destroyers, and oilers were damaged or disabled, and both fleets suffered significant losses. Based on just the numbers—the Allies are estimated to have lost more ships in terms of tonnage—the Japanese appeared to have come out on top. American industrial operations were at full power, however. Damaged vessels were repaired or replaced, and in the Battle of Midway a short time later, the Americans had a slight edge.[6]

The Japanese, believing they had the advantage, hoped to decimate the American fleet. What the Japanese didn't know was that the Americans had deciphered enough of their communications codes to successfully track Japanese military movements. At Midway, the Americans delivered a pounding to an already weakened Japanese force, and Japanese dominance in the Pacific came to an end.[7] One after another, Japanese pilots plunged from the sky, their combat experience and their aircraft disappearing into graves rimmed with fire and filled with seawater. The massive battles of the Coral Sea and Midway took a severe toll on ships on both sides, and Japan lacked the industrial strength to regroup and rebuild. Equally devastating for Japan was the loss of experienced combat pilots. Seemingly overnight, Japan's warrior class, a tradition perfected for hundreds of years, was swallowed by the Pacific.

In Lieutenant Chase's part of the war, the fighting was also taking a toll on him:

September 6, 1943

Dear Doc,

Another Aztec has been added to the missing in action list. Because of regulations, I can't yet send his name or his story. The story is not a long one, but it is one that makes me proud to be an Aztec. It's getting so that I hate to ask the question, "Is there a fellow named 'Jonnie Jones' in your outfit" for the answer is too often, "there *was* a fellow named 'Jonnie Jones'"—

Don't print any of this one "Doc," it's too discouraging for the ole *News Letter*.

Well, I'm still counting on doing my Christmas shopping in San Diego. I'm gonna loaf on the Quad, visit all my old faculty friends, and drink Clarence and Andy clear out of coffee and eat *all* their toasted Tuna sandwiches. . . . The Malaria ward just let me out today, so I have to take it easy for a while.

Happy Landings

Lt. Lionel E. Chase

Three things helped Lieutenant Chase make it through the war. First was looking forward to seeing family, friends, and even Clarence and Andy Randeques, who ran the college café and soda fountain. His campus was waiting to embrace him when he got home. The second was that he could confess his darker thoughts to Dr. Post. When Chase needed to get his doubts off his chest, he had the sympathetic and understanding ear of his old professor. Third, Chase knew that he was nearing the end of his combat tour and would soon be rotating home.

Shortly before Christmas in 1943, Blair Burkhardt, who worked on planes and kept track of pilots, reported with a sense of relief, "I was glad to hear that Lionel Chase had completed his 50 combat missions and that he had returned to San Diego."

THE AZTEC NEWS LETTER

"FAITHFUL FOREVER"

August 1, 1943

NO. 17

This Issue Sponsored, in part, by the Faculty Dames

Edited by
DR. LAUREN C. POST
San Diego State College
San Diego, California

To All of the Aztecs in the Service and Their Friends:

If your News Letter had to be forwarded to you, we don't have your latest address. Some News Letters are returned, and if yours is returned you probably won't receive another until the correct address is sent in. We still have a list of about 300 'addresses wanted.'

Editing was more difficult than ever, partly because of the great number of letters received and partly because they were so fine. Many a good long letter was cut to a mere line. The overseas letters still get priority space. Some letters had to be omitted, but they will appear next time. Hope **yours** was not among them.

The war news still continues to improve so our Victory editions must not

be forgotten.

And again, best of luck!

Lauren C. Post,
Editor of the News Letter.

FIRST LT. RAYMOND L. ADAIR
was listed in **Life Magazine**, July 5, 1943, as killed in action. Previously he had been reported "missing in action since August 29, 1942."

"Lt. Adair had been on duty in the Alaskan area about four months. He piloted a B-17 Flying Fortress, presumably in the Aleutian fighting, and was decorated prior to the action in which he was reported missing."

CAPT. JOHN W. BASSETT
was reported killed in action in the Aleutians, May 29. Capt. Bassett was in the army medical corps.

CAPT. WESLEY P. EBY
was killed in the crash of an army plane near Fresno. He was stationed at the Merced Army Flying School at the time of his death. Eby's plane was one of two that crashed a mile apart when caught in a downdraft while flying low in search of a 15-year-old Fresno boy.

LT. RICHARD F. KENNEY
was reported "missing" in the North African area. See News Letter No. 15 for

a story on how he had chosen to stay and fight even after he had been shot down, wounded, and badly burned. One of several newscasts told of him shooting down three Axis planes in one day with his P-38. On June 5th Richard had been awarded the Air Medal, the Distinguished Flying Cross, and the Cluster. He has been missing since June 15th.

S/SGT. EDWARD WEISENBERG
was reported missing in action in the European area. Sgt. Weisenberg left for the European area April 1.

MAJ. ROBERT I. BACHRACH
of the Army Air Corps received the Distinguished Flying Cross in North Africa. His brother, **1st Lt. Herbert R. Bachrach,** is in an anti-aircraft outfit and is also in North Africa.

CAPT. MACARTHUR GORTON
received the Distinguished Flying Cross from Gen. Douglas MacArthur after nearly a year spent in New Guinea. Following is part of the story:

"While piloting a B-17 on a reconnaisance mission in the Southwest Pacific the latter part of 1942, Lt. Gorton and his crew sighted a Jap convoy. They shadowed the convoy for six hours during which time they were attacked five times by Zeros. The citation was

6

SUCH SWELL KIDS

THE AZTEC NEWS LETTER
No. 12, February 26, 1943
MISSING IN ACTION
Bill Goodchild had been missing in action just one month when the news reached home—and campus.

The telegram which his mother received from the Adjutant General read: "The Secretary of War desires to express his deep regret that your son, Second Lieutenant William S. Goodchild, Air Corps, has been reported missing in action in the Southwest Pacific area since Jan. 7. Additional information will be sent . . ."

Charles Byrne, Y2c, U.S.M.S.

For two years in a row, in 1939 and 1940, the San Diego Aztecs basketball team took the runner-up trophy at the national tournament. The team was led by star forward Milton "Milky" Phelps and coached by Morris "Morrie" Gross with help from his student manager, Paul "Punchy" Fern. Finally, in Kansas City in 1941, the Aztecs claimed the championship, but their trophies hadn't even had time to collect dust before the teammates went to war.

Paul Fern was drawn to good causes, and nicknames seemed to stick to him. Known as "Stump," "Stumpy," and "Punchy," he worked tirelessly, and his energy was infectious. In addition to managing ballplayers, he served as the college's Associated Men's president, building esprit de corps on campus. He sweetened events with doughnuts and ice cream, and his quest for campus entertainment included Wild West movies, a minstrel show, and men's ballet. Fern kept a lucky nickel, but he lost it during the 1940 basketball season when his team was runner-up.

May 22, 1943

Dear Dr. Post,

I just received a letter from my husband, Ensign Paul Fern, who has been on active duty in the South Pacific for two months now. In the letter he asked me to give you his latest address, because he enjoys receiving the *News Letter*.

. . .

I, too, would like to have my name on the mailing list for the *News Letter* if it is possible. When we were living in San Francisco and were receiving the *News Letter* regularly, I certainly did look forward to hearing about our old college friends.

Thank you kindly.

Sincerely,

Mrs. Paul A. Fern

5502 Madison

San Diego 5

California

September 9, 1943

Dear Sir:

. . .

Speaking of friends, I was terribly sorry to hear about Lt. Paul Fern's death. He and I grew up together and were very dear friends throughout the past years. It is a shame that fine young men like him have to go. But I guess to maintain a country blessed with Democratic Ideas, a lot of young men have to be sacrificed.

Last year while I was stationed at the San Diego Naval Training Station, I was able to make a couple of cruises with his father who was Captain of a Navy tanker running between San Diego Harbor and the San Clemente Islands. Lt. Fern was surely proud of his son, and that he was in the Navy with him.

Thomas W. Downey

C.Sp. (A) USNR
c/o Cary Halls
Purdue University
West Lafayette, Indiana

September 12, 1943
It has been a long time since I have written, Doc . . .

. . .

The word on Paul Fern was sad indeed to us. Naturally I had a lot of contact with him during the period he managed Morrie Gross' great basketball team, but my acquaintance with him far antedated that. I knew him first when he played football and baseball at San Diego High. It's strange how details sometimes become so firmly fixed in your memory. One of my strongest recollections concerning Paul goes back to an afternoon in 1937 when I covered an Escondido-Grossmont football game at Grossmont. Paul rode back into town with me, and I could repeat to you right now a good part of our conversation. The little guy, who was one of the most courageous athletes I ever knew, (did you know of his neck injury in football?) will be missed by many.

    Charles T. Byrne, Y 1/c

September 18, 1943
At Sea In A Saloon
(or Visa Versa)
Dear Dr. Post,
At present I am writing this letter in the officers mess while the ocean outside is madly pitching and rolling this ship around like nobody's business.

    . . . I am deeply sorry to hear of Paul Fern's death, and I understand that he left a young baby. I've known Paul for quite some time and played with him on teams; it just doesn't seem possible that such swell kids like him must pay with their lives.

    Sincerely
    Eddie Preisler

THE AZTEC NEWS LETTER
No. 18, September 1, 1943
LT. (JG) PAUL A. FERN
was killed in action in the South Pacific where he had been on duty on a ship for seven months.

(Paul was married last fall to the former Miss Dorothea Salyers. His daughter, Linda Ellen, whom he never saw, is five weeks old.)

THE AZTEC NEWS LETTER
No. 24, March 1, 1944
Lt. (jg) Wilbur S. Kelley wrote from his YP on patrol duty:
. . .

"Would you send the *News Letter* to Paul Fern's father, Lt. Al Fern. He is skipper of a yard YF and I see him quite often. So far he has been able to get one from someone else, but he would appreciate getting one of his own since he knew so many of Paul's friends." (Sure. You know, Paul's father and I were on the same destroyer in 1918. Lt. Fern probably doesn't remember me as I was just a radio operator, and he didn't see me very often. Those were the days. Just think—Destroyer No. 15—and a coal burner at that. And Tony Ghio thinks his tin can is old! Would you like to see a picture of a *real* destroyer on the front of the *News Letter* some time? LCP)

Dr. Lauren C. Post, Editor

THE AZTEC NEWS LETTER
Christmas Edition
No. 45, December 1, 1945
AMERICAN LEGION POST 364
made a substantial contribution toward the support of the *Aztec News Letter. . . .*

One of the members of Post 364 is Lt. Fern, father of Lt. (jg) Paul Fern who was killed in action in the South Pacific about three years ago. A very great many of you will remember Paul as a basketball manager and football player back in the good old days. His cheerfulness as a basketball manager brought the team through many a tight game, and we always associate Paul with our finest teams. That is where he belonged.

It was your editor's idea that this note be "In Memoriam" but Mr. Fern preferred it otherwise. So, our thanks go to Mr. Fern and American Legion Post 364, LCP.

Dr. Lauren C. Post, Editor

✉ Undated
Dear Mr. Post,

. . .

After reading of Bill Shropshire and Paul Fern, you can't imagine how I felt. I was in Corpus Christi when Milky was there & it was the same feeling I had as when I heard of his terrible accident.

The thing that makes you feel so bad is knowing that you won't have the pleasure of speaking to those boys again. "Milky," "Punchy," & "Shropy" were real, 100% American men and if for no other reason we should work harder to achieve victory.

. . .

Sincerely,
Lt. S. J. (Samuel) Patella

✉ December 20, 1943

. . .

And now it's Sammy Patella. Seems like there is at least one whom I claim as a good friend in every issue. . . .

Charles T. Byrne, Y 1/c

✉ August 20, 1944
Dear Dr. Post,

. . .

The only sad part about the letter is the names of those who have left us and whom we can never hope to see again. It seems almost unbelievable that fellows like Sammy Patella won't be around again to throw that million-dollar smile at everyone and everything. Not only him, but all those others whom we were so used to seeing on the gridiron and on the basketball courts. They seem so damned alive in a fellow's mind that you can't quite conceive their being gone. They all put on a great show, Dr. Post, both on the athletic field and on the battle field, and now—they are sitting in the grand stands. I only hope and pray that the post-war show that is put on for them is worth the price of admission they paid.

. . .

As always your friend—
Ricardo de la Cruz
c/o Fleet Post Office
New York, New York

THE AZTEC NEWS LETTER
No. 47, February 1, 1946
LT. SAM PATELLA, USNR
who was reported missing from a bombing mission in the
Pacific in October, 1943, has since been declared legally
deceased. There has been no additional news about him.

During World War II, notifications to families of the loss of a loved one often arrived by telegram. Sometimes personal letters were written and signed, and even the president might write a letter as a way of noting appreciation for special service or significant loss. In many cases, however, the notification began, "We regret to inform you . . ." After World War II, the military began the practice of informing families in person. Today, special teams are trained for that purpose.[1]

✉ November 7, 1943

. . .

Casualty lists are somewhat impersonal until a friend's name or that of a fellow alumnus shows up. . . .

Bill Shropshire was forced down before I came into the Army. I was ninety percent reconciled to his loss and the official notification by the Navy Dept. reluctantly made up my mind the remaining ten percent.

Bill and I were next door neighbors for eleven years and I knew him for sixteen years in all. . . .

Received recent word of the loss of another friend, Parker Smith, who was feared to have been on the tanker which collided with an ammunition ship with such tragic results. Parker, Shrop and I lived within four doors of each other during those aforementioned eleven years.

Sgt. MF Morton 39529212
387th Base Headquarters & Air Base Squadron
Hobbs Army Air Field
Hobbs, New Mexico

Bill Shropshire's mother passed notification regarding Bill's death to Dr. Post and also enclosed five dollars (the equivalent of about seventy-two dollars in 2018) with her letter. Dr. Post printed the personalized letter to the Shropshire family in the September 1, 1943, *News Letter*.

August 6, 1943

Dear Dr. Post:

I want to thank you for the *News Letters* I received yesterday.

The extra copies I shall send to friends of Billy's, who did not attend "State" but had met many of the boys. I am sure they will be interested.

I am having some black and white pictures printed from the color picture of Billy in uniform—if they are a success I shall send you one. I am enclosing copy of letter we received from "Secretary of the Navy"—use any part you think advisable.

Mr. Shropshire joins me in wishing you continued success with the *News Letter* and hope our small contribution will help.

Very Sincerely,

Mary P. Shropshire

Point Loma

The Secretary of the Navy

Washington

7 July, 1943

Mr. William B. Shropshire, Sr.

820 Golden Park Avenue

San Diego, California

Dear Mr. Shropshire:

After a full review of all available information, I am reluctantly forced to the conclusion that your son, Ensign William Bryan Shropshire, Jr., United States Naval Reserve, is deceased, having been reported missing, when the plane of which he was pilot was lost on patrol in the Pacific area.

In accordance with Section 5 of Public Law 490, 77th Congress, as amended, your son's death is presumed to have occurred on the 28th day of June 1943, the day following an absence of twelve months.

I extend to you my sincere sympathy in your great loss and hope you may find comfort in the knowledge that your son gave his life for his country, upholding the highest tradition of the Navy. The Navy shares in your sense of bereavement and feels the loss of his services.

Sincerely yours,

JAMES FORRESTAL (Signed)

Acting Secretary of the Navy

THE AZTEC NEWS LETTER
No. 39, June 1, 1945
Mr. and Mrs. William B. Shropshire visited our picture panel recently. Mr. Shropshire told of his son's first combat experience. He had just been assigned to duty aboard his cruiser and on the morning of Dec. 7, 1941, he took over his first Officer of the Deck watch. Just as his watch began the Japs struck.

As previously reported, Ens. Shropshire was first reported missing from the battle of Midway, and later reported killed in action.

Milton "Milky" Phelps was the physical opposite of little "Punchy" Fern. Phelps, a lanky forward for the varsity team, was considered by many on campus to be one of the best basketball stars in the history of the college. Everyone who watched him talked about his grace on the court. He was one of the first players to introduce a one-handed shooting style to his team, and he captained the All-American National Association of Intercollegiate Basketball small college team. His leadership and talent were a crucial part of the college's championship season.

On October 27, 1942, Herbert Tompkins, a member of Class 10A, Cadet Regiment, at U.S. Naval Air Station, Corpus Christi, Texas, wrote, "Although San Diego is at a distance to me in miles it is very close to me in friends. . . . I see Milky Phelps, Jack Adams and others when we get a chance at a liberty weekend. These are few for we fly seven days a week."

November 15, 1942
Dear Dr. Post—

. . .

No doubt you have received notification of "Milky" Phelps loss in a crash in Texas. I read of it in the Denver papers and was at a loss to express my feelings— I've spent many hours watching him play on the basketball court even before I went to State and I know that all Staters regret the loss of such a man.

. . .

Pvt. Alexandros (Alex) D. Regas
768 Tech School Sq. (Sp)
Barracks E 540
Army Air Force
Buckley Field, Colorado

Wally McAnulty, the young man who was "sweating it out" in the South Pacific, waiting for his chance to fight, was one of the first to send his condolences:

December 22, 1942
Dear Doc,

. . .

All the fellows in the battery that are from San Diego really felt the death of Milky Phelps. . . .

I sure do envy some of those fellows writing from England, India, New Guinea, and the Solomons. Who knows, maybe one of these days. . . .

Wally (Mac) McAnulty

April 18, 1943
South Pacific
Dear Doc Post;—

. . .

Was very glad to hear about the trophy put up in honor of "Milky." Enough can never be said about him, both as an athlete and a fellow Aztec—Glad to hear the Basketball team made out so well—too bad such good boys had to end their careers under these conditions but that's life I guess—

. . .

An Aztec for always
Lt. Chester S. (Chet) DeVore
Second Marine Raider Battalion
c/o F.P.O.
San Francisco, California

August 14, 1943

. . .

Certainly sorry to hear about the fellows who haven't made out so well, but I suppose it's to be expected. I was happy to hear about the faculty presenting "Milky" with his diploma. I'm sure he'll never be forgotten.

. . .

Lt. Chester S. (Chet) DeVore
Second Marine Raider Battalion
c/o F.P.O.
San Francisco, California

✉ July 5, 1943

. . .

Many names I have read have hurt very deeply. I can only say that they gave the full measure of devotion to God and country the same as all of us are willing to do. I know wherever they may be, their spirits will be an inspiration and a guidance to a better and fuller life for those they and perhaps we will leave behind. You at State can be proud of your sons and daughters, you taught us courage and truth, we will fight to keep you there to teach the ones that will come after us to be better equipped to run this world after this mess is over. You, Dr. Post, and men like you hold our future, and our children's future in what you give them now. Make them men, strong men as you have made us, give them visions and thoughts of good government and how to run it, make them conscious of God and his divine Guidance. Make them *HARD* for theirs will be a hard row to hoe. Turn out men like Milky Phelps, you can do no better.

Lt. Ray W. Fellows
Anti-Tank Co., 134th Inf.
A.P.O. 35
Camp Rucker, Alabama

THE AZTEC NEWS LETTER
No. 16, July 1, 1943
ENS. ATWELL MILTON PHELPS
The faculty voted to award a degree posthumously to Ens. Milton Phelps so his name appeared on the commencement program with those of the other graduates. Following the reading of his name all stood for a minute in silence. By coincidence the exercises were held indoors this year—on the very floor on which Milky had endeared himself to all Aztecs through his sportsmanship.

After Milky Phelps lost his life in a training crash, San Diego State retired his jersey number, 22. Unfortunately for pilots, training accidents, sometimes caused by wind and rain, were a fact of the job.

✉ June 7, 1943

. . .

Went on a little cross country hop yesterday afternoon & had my first experience with rain squalls. It's really a helpless feeling to be cruising along with ten other

San Diego State College championship basketball
team, *News Letter* No. 21, December 1, 1943

planes & not able to see a foot in front of you. It made it a little worse thinking about our two classmates who turned into each other about two weeks ago.

Turned out to be an uneventful trip, but my instructor knocked a bit of wind out of my sails. He dashed out on the runway as soon as the wheels touched. I taxied up to him & he said, "Sure glad to see you back, Boy. Awful glad to see you back." Sometimes I wonder whether he has any confidence in me at all.

. . .

Sincerely,

Lt. J. A. (John) Muelchi

Class L-21 Box H-5

25th A.A.F.L.T.D.

Denton, Texas

More letters from Lieutenant Muelchi are in chapter 14.

July 12, 1944

Dear Dr. Post,

. . .

For the past few months I've been in the "Baffin Bay theatre of operations" as a fighter pilot instructor. We fly "sorties" out over the Gulf of Mexico, strafe lonely sea-gulls and terns with machine-gun fire as they sit on our targets among the sand dunes of Padre Island. We load our planes with bombs and make relentless attacks against "enemy positions." We climb two miles up and fight it out among ourselves in fierce "dog fights." Night operations are very hazardous with many fledglings getting their owl eyes. There are frequently a number of accidents on the darkened runways, planes taxiing into one another and chewing up wings and tails. The other night, one of our aircraft failed to return, crashed into the brush and cactus of the south-west. Yesterday while doing an inverted spin, my engine caught fire and it began to get a little warm in the front cockpit. Flames were licking back under the floorboards and around the front seat. My cadet was halfway out of the cockpit when I extinguished the fire.

This instructing business, Doc, is actually pretty monotonous, but there's nothing that can be done about it. There are no medals, no ribbons, no glory. But there is some satisfaction in knowing that students that leave here are equipped with the best training we can give them, are able to meet the enemy in the acid test and show good account of themselves. We give 'em our best because we know we'll be out there someday with them—maybe in the same squadrons. And that's the day we look forward to.

. . .

"Semper fidelis"
1st Lt. D. E. (Ed) Totten USMCR
TS-14C N.A.S.
Kingsville, Texas
Harding Field, Louisiana

World War II strategy hinged on planes and the training of pilots to fly them into combat. The world had learned a lesson during World War I that it wasn't eager to repeat. Trench warfare was a bloody slugfest with artillery attacks that lasted for days and miles upon miles of supply lines to support the troops stalled on the front lines. In World War II, ground troops still endured protracted campaigns, but battle strategies called for faster assaults combined with air support.[2]

In the summer before Pearl Harbor, the U.S. Army's small Air Corps became the Army Air Forces and rapidly began training pilots.[3] Accelerated training programs were also taking shape in Great Britain, Canada, and Australia. Germany was already a leader in aerodynamic design, and the

Germans and the Japanese used aggressive air attacks from the very beginning of World War II. The Germans were known for their fast, overpowering force—blitzkrieg, or "lightning war"—which combined troops and fast-moving tanks with air attacks. Their strategy prevailed until they met their match in the British skies during the Battle of Britain. The Germans had the Messerschmitt Bf 109, and the British countered with the Supermarine Spitfire. The United States developed long-range fighter-bombers, like North American Aviation's P-51 Mustang and long-range bombers such as the B-17, made by Boeing and dubbed the Flying Fortress.[4]

For pilots, this meant learning to fly rapidly developing technology. The AT-6 Texas trainer, mentioned in the following letter, was designed by North American Aviation, and the P-36 Hawk and P-40 Warhawk were made by the Curtiss-Wright Corporation.

May 27, 1942

Dear "Doc,"

. . .

I'm in pursuit A.T. #6s, none of that straight and level flying like Gene Erdman, Fred Smith and Don Peck are going into. I've been kidding them about being "Jap-bait" and "clay-pigeons"! I'm in 42-F while they are in 42-G and they enlisted before I did, ha, ha.

These A.T.s are sure sweet ships; bow wing; retractable landing gear; all metal job that really handles like a "kitten." We get one hour transition in P36s before we leave. That's what's going to be fun. The P36 is just like the P40, only it has an air-cooled engine, instead of an inline engine.

. . .

Took a cross-country hop, the other day, altitude 24,000 feet. I had to wear an oxygen mask, but man was it fun. At that altitude, you only have to take 5 deep breaths of the outside air and it will knock you cold. By the way it does get sort of chilly up there, enough to freeze your control cables, sometimes. . . .

As ever,

H. G. Harold (Hal) Hevener, Jr.

Lieutenant Hevener, who boasted that he didn't want any "straight and level flying," got his wish and lived to laugh about it. His awards included the Silver Star for gallantry in action against an enemy, the

Distinguished Flying Cross for heroism, and the Air Medal for meritorious achievement while participating in aerial flight. Oak leaf clusters signified that he had received an additional medal.[5]

✉ September 10, 1943

Hi "Doc",

. . . You know I just missed Bill Goodchild by a few days when I got over here. And I was certainly hit hard to learn he had gone down over by India. Bill and I came from the same town and had gone through school all the way together. Even in the army, he and Eddie were in my lower class, in primary. You never can tell though, they both may come hiking back someday, cause it often has happened over here. . . .

A lot of things have happened since the last time I wrote, like I now am pushing 300 combat hours damn close, so maybe one of these days, not so far distant, I'll be dropping around out at "State" to shoot the bull! Say here's a picture that was taken the day the boys in the 90 Bomb Grp. got decorated by General Ramey. I got the "Silver Star," "D.F.C." and Airman's Medal that day, but I'm still sweating out the D.F.C. Oak Leaf Cluster. . . . By the way, Doc, did you know I'm the proud father of a son? No kidding! Hope I get to see him before his number comes up in the draft, Ha! Ha! My claim to fame over here is—I'm the only guy to hit a mountain and live and at the same time hitch hike back from a combat mission, Ha! Ha! I'll tell you the sordid details when I see you, it's quite a story, one of those truth is stranger than fiction deals. Say Doc, you ought to see the victory garden my navigator has outside our tent. The only trouble is, that our tent is becoming the headquarters of "House & Garden" over here and it often gets a bit crowded inside. I have to run 'em out every once in a while just so I can get some quiet.

I want to get out of [censored] and back home pretty soon, so I can see some of the "State" football games this season. By the way Doc, can they still scrape enough men together for a team or are them days gone forever?

1st Lt. H. G. Harold (Hal) Hevener, Jr.

The "swell kids" who came from San Diego State College belonged to a larger team captained by Dr. Post. The ballplayers and fraternity brothers held fast to their camaraderie. When battles wore them down and the loss of friends weighed on their hearts, the *News Letter* bolstered everyone's spirits. In its pages, the servicemen and servicewomen and their families found words of common cause and comfort. That sense of unity and purpose stayed with them even as the war threatened to tear them apart.

Pat Allard, who wrote the following letter, could often be seen helping out around campus. Photos of her appear in the *News Letters* in chapters 13 and 22.

August 30, 1943

Dear Dr. Post,

Your mail box is full of letters that are much more important than this, I know. In fact, this isn't important at all. It's just something I felt after reading the last *News Letter* and as it's along congratulatory lines, I decided to tell you. . . .

It's about feeling close to people I don't even know which sounds a little strange but this is what I mean. Last night before I went to sleep I read the latest *News Letter* and it left me with a very warm feeling and I felt a little bit wise. . . . or maybe I mean enlightened. War has seemed to me to be a conglomeration of P 38s and commandos and riveters and Casa Blancas and Remember Pearl Harbor-ish ideals—all pulling in the same ultimate direction, but using different routes. I saw a unity of cause, of purpose, of aim, but none of action. When I began to think about, after reading letters of the boys from State who are now in North Africa and Kiska and New Zealand and a million places that two years ago were foreign to our ears, I saw that there really is a unity of action—something that started in the green of the quad and swing of the caf' and mortuary-air of the lib'—a something that has been carried thru starless nights on "Monty" bombers, and batteries of red gunfire . . . even the deathlike stillness of a steaming desert. And it is this unity which ties me to the people I read about—most of whom I don't know because I just started State last February. But to someone who sat in the same classrooms and gazed at the same tower and crowded in the same booths, I cannot be a complete stranger. And I'm sure that many of the *News Letter's* most avid readers cherish, as I do, these one-sided friendships which make the realization of this unity a more stable, a more certain to succeed reality.

. . .

Sincerely,

Pat Allard

THE AZTEC NEWS LETTER

September 1, 1943

NO. 18

This Issue Sponsored in full by "San Diego's Own"

Edited by
DR. LAUREN C. POST
San Diego State College
San Diego, California

To All of the Aztecs in the Service and Their Friends:

Nothing much to say in this spot today. I have been busier than ever with the editing and the new addresses. Keep sending in new names, changes, promotions, and also, pictures for the Panel.

In case a News Letter is sent to a former address, please forward it, and send me the new address. Unless our turn for a telephone comes up real soon, the Post's new home will be without a telephone after September 1st. The address is 4538 Norma Drive. Since I have no phone in my office either, about the easiest way to get a new address to me is to mail it.

Thanks for all of the nice letters. Sorry I couldn't use all of them.

And again, best of luck,
Lauren C. Post,
Editor of the News Letter.

PS. See longer letter to 1st Lt. Wallace McAnulty on last page.

2ND LT. MAXTON BROWN

was reported killed in action in the North African area. (See News Letter No. 16 for a letter by Max which he wrote from the Middle East and in which he mentioned **Lt. George C. Alexander**, the enemy fighters, and the ack-ack. LCP)

LT. (JG) PAUL A. FERN

was killed in action in the South Pacific where he had been on duty on a ship for seven months.

(Paul was married last fall to the former Miss Dorothea Salyers. His daughter, Linda Ellen, whom he never saw, is five weeks old.)

ENS. WILLIAM B. SHROPSHIRE

The Secretary of the Navy
Washington
7 July 1943
Dear Mr. Shropshire:

After a full review of all available information, I am reluctantly forced to the conclusion that your son, Ensign William Bryan Shropshire, Jr., United States Naval Reserve, is deceased, having been reported missing, when the plane of which he was pilot was lost on patrol in the Pacific area.

In accordance with Section 5 of Public Law 490, 77th Congress, as amended, your son's death is presumed to have occurred on the 28th day of June 1943, the day following an absence of twelve months.

I extend to you my sincere sympathy in your great loss and hope you may find comfort in the knowledge that your son gave his life for his country, upholding the highest traditions of the Navy. The Navy shares in your sense of bereavement and feels the loss of his services.

Sincerely yours,
JAMES FORRESTAL (Signed)
Acting Secretary of the Navy
Mr. William B. Shropshire, Sr.
820 Golden Park Avenue
San Diego, California

1ST LT. WILLIAM EARLE SAGE, U.S.M.C.

was reported missing by the Navy Department. He was a pilot of a navy fighter plane and saw service in New Caledonia, New Hebrides, and the Solomon Islands.

CAPT. GRIFFITH P. WILLIAMS

was reported missing in action in the North African area. Capt. Williams was mentioned a few months ago on the anniversary of the bombing of Japan which he, General Doolittle and 13 others celebrated in Africa. Last summer Griff paid State College a visit during which he spoke in assembly.

(About 15 minutes before assembly time that day I walked over that way and saw a tall, distinguished looking pilot sitting all by himself on a bench in the Quad, in fact he was all alone in the whole Quad. I introduced myself to him, and we sat there in the stillness of the morning and talked for a few minutes. At that time I didn't even know that the planes had taken off from a carrier, or anything about the trip. One could tell that Griff had a lot on his mind, but I didn't know how much. I certainly hope that I can meet him a second time and in the very same Quad. LCP)

LT. JOHN MEGREW

Mrs. Edith MeGrew whose address is Box 107, Rancho Santa Fe, and who is the mother of 1st Lt. John MeGrew wrote as follows: (John is a prisoner of

**Capt. Griffith P. Williams
Missing in Action**

the Japanese)

"Thank you very much for your letter. It has been so helpful during the past months to hear from John's friends. We have had no further news of him. However, each month we receive a Prisoner of War Bulletin published by the Red Cross. The last issue says that in one of the camps the men are permitted to write five letters a year. We are hoping that this may be so in other camps and that we shall hear from John.

"We have written him a few letters but understand that the boys are allowed to receive but one from the folks at home. The censorship regulations are very rigid indeed, so we could scarcely tell him a thing. As soon as ever we hear that restrictions are lifted I shall tell you so that friends may write him. It would make him very happy to hear from them.

"We are pleased to have your News Letter. San Diego State surely has a great many boys of whom to be proud in the service. Of the several colleges that John attended before going to State he always said he liked that one best of all."

LT. RICHARD F. KENNEY

Mrs. Doris Kenney of Coronado phoned in this very welcome telegram:

"Report received through the International Red Cross stating that your son, **2nd Lt. Richard F. Kenney**, is a prisoner of war of the German government."

7

AFRICAN BRANCH OF SAN DIEGO STATE COLLEGE

THE AZTEC NEWS LETTER
No. 12, February 26, 1943
To All of the Aztecs in the Service and Their Friends:
Keep writing even if your letters are cut down. If yours was cut, so were many others. Oftimes I don't have the courage to cut a nice letter so I lay it aside for later editing—then pressure of time and work force me to crowd them in close.

And don't get discouraged if your wedding and furlough were omitted. They are being left out. This is a shooting war.
Lauren C. Post, Editor

In 1942 it was hard for Americans to ignore the British request for assistance in North Africa, where they were fighting the Germans and Italians, as well as troops loyal to France's Vichy government. (The Germans had allowed the French puppet regime to keep its colonies in Africa, but Vichy forces were forced to fight the British.) Initially, American military leaders weren't interested in diverting resources to North Africa. They focused their attention on the war in the Pacific, and they had their sights set on Europe. They were persuaded to rethink a North African strategy after Erwin Rommel, the cunning commander in charge of German Panzer divisions, began to gain ground. Strategically, whoever dominated the region controlled the Mediterranean. When it was clear that Rommel was heading for the Suez Canal, the United States finally committed to sending troops.[1]

The U.S. assault began at Oran in November 1942, and attacks peppered the Algerian and French Moroccan coastline. Gen. George S. Patton's troops landed ten miles north of Casablanca and fought their way south for days. Patton planned a smashing bombardment, but the Vichy commander surrendered in time to preserve the city.[2] The British and Americans quickly took up residence. Prime Minister Winston Churchill and President Franklin D. Roosevelt met there to plan the invasion of Europe, specifically by way of Sicily. Afterward, Roosevelt announced that the only terms he would accept from the Axis were unconditional surrender.[3]

Lt. Al Slayen reached his post in time to see history being made, and he sent Dr. Post a stream of cards, letters, photographs, and even local papers as a way of documenting the war as it unfolded at his feet. The photo that Slayen refers to in the following letter was probably returned, as requested, to Slayen's family. It is no longer with the original letter.

✉ Undated

Dear Dr. Post—

I really haven't the time to write you a long letter. I wanted to get this photograph to you.

To me this is the one picture that covers a great event in history. This is the first American Flag to parade the streets of French Morocco (Casablanca). The date this picture was taken was the 11th of November 1942. The civilian walking with the officer was an interpreter and guide for the 1st American commander in the area.

. . .

I regret that I cannot say more about this picture. I do hope that it may prove of interest to the students if you see fit to display it.

As this is a very rare and valuable photograph I would like to have my wife receive it after you have finished showing it at "state."

. . .

Always an Aztec

A. E. (Al) Slayen

Note—This photo cannot be reproduced or published in any newspaper—Slayen.

April 23, 1943

Dear Dr. Post—

Just a word of greetings from the "Dark Continent." I'm supposed to be in a war and here I am further away from the war than when I was in the states.

Am quartered in a beautiful city in Africa. I am living with a very nice French Family at the present time. I have seen many strange and interesting sights. Enough to last me a life time. However nothing can compare to good old San Diego—

The weather here is grand—It is a little better than you will find in San Diego—many of the buildings are really beautiful. Here in town we have French and people from the continent. On the outskirts of town live the Arabs. . . . They do add color to the scenery with their flowing robes and assorted modes of transportation. There is a continual clashing of the old & new worlds. The Arabs seem to come out of the past into an ultra-modern city—most of them barefooted riding on donkeys loaded down with tremendous loads. . . .

I have seen donkeys hitched up with camels pulling wooden plows. The filth and poverty of the Arab population is indescribable, however they seem happy and without a worry. Many of the women are veiled. Most of the men are named Mohammed (Arab). There is a lot of trash written about the customs here. I have seen many women remove their veils. It has some religious significance. But they are not as strict in the belief of their religion as one reads. Some may be, but the majority are not. I can go on for hours. . . .

Always an Aztec,

Lt. A. E. (Al) Slayen

B.C.D. BASE H.Q.

APO #759 c/o P.M. N.Y.C.

December 25, 1944

Dear Dr. Post,

. . .

At the present time I am overseas two years. Have seen all of Africa and most of Italy—By truck, Jeep & plane. Have been north of Rome—south of Naples and both coasts . . . I have had my share of fun and tough breaks—I think that I'm about ready to go home. Anyway, I do hope that I can at least spend my next Xmas at home—

. . . In all my travels I found one city that I like especially well. Casablanca—I was fortunate to meet some very fine people there and I am seriously planning a return trip. The most interesting city in Italy is Bari. . . . The partisans are really rugged looking—Tall, dark, lean, & ugly—This describes both the men & women.

. . .

As Ever

1st Lt. A. E. (Al) Slayen

225 QMSR Co. APO 388

c/o P.M. New York, New York

In North Africa, British and American forces pushed for Tunisia, and the Germans and Italians pushed back. Across the desert, ground troops and tanks battled for the upper hand, and at every encounter the Germans seemed to outfight, outflank, and outwit the Allies. Again and again they tried to push through treacherous passes to reach the coast, and the Germans repulsed them in one bloody and dispiriting battle after another. The weather, bitterly cold just a few months earlier, began to steam. In April, American troops under the command of Gen. Omar Bradley began a dogged advance that finally broke the German line. At the beginning of May, artillery bombardment and concentrated bombings left no doubt that the Allies were taking control. The coastal towns of Bizerte and Tunis collapsed under the pounding, and ships blocked any chance of a German retreat by sea.[4]

Jim McColl (the writer who had been keeping tabs on Ernie McAnulty in Algiers) saw the momentum shift. He sent a picture of a German Messerschmitt fighter plane and wrote that the battle seemed like Dunkirk. At that 1940 battle, British and French forces, divided and boxed in, staged a desperate evacuation across the English Channel. Now in 1943 the situation was reversed, and the Germans were trapped with little hope of escape.

May 9, 1943

Dear Doctor Post—

Nothing new to report that you haven't already seen in the papers but, at this writing, it looks as tho the African campaign is all but over. Way before yesterday Tunis and Bizerte fell and we now have Jerry and friends confined to a forty mile section of the coast—receiving a terrific pounding from our Air Force and artillery units—Tunisia has turned into another Dunkirk, but this time for the Germans.

Slowly but surely, the war on all fronts, seems to be swinging our way—here's hoping the rest of it doesn't take too long.

Have received the *News Letter* only once in the past several months but then, all of our mail has been slow coming thru of late.

Here's a picture of a Jerry M.E. 109, a little the worse for wear—be seeing you, doctor.

As Ever,

James Q. (Jim) McColl

Bob Wade was well known at San Diego State for his good writing and mischievous antics. In 1940 his original one-act play, "Finis," earned him first place in the college drama tournament. Wade then learned that a movie set designed to look like a French fort had been abandoned in the desert east of San Diego. The set had been left behind by a production company after filming the epic story *Beau Geste*, starring Gary Cooper. The classic-looking fort was irresistible to Wade. He enlisted a friend's grandmother to sew French foreign legionnaire costumes, rounded up his fraternity brothers, and embarked on making a parody of *Beau Geste*. Fearing copyright infringement, the campus initially refused to let the fraternity show their remake of the movie. Undaunted, Wade and company went to Hollywood and wrangled their way into a meeting with a studio lawyer who gave them "unofficial" permission. According to campus lore, Wade was supposed to burn the film after three showings, but he never did.[5]

Soon Wade's battles were more than fiction. His letters from North Africa span more than a year between late 1942 and the end of 1943. As his bomb group put pressure on General Rommel, Wade understood that his mission in Africa was setting the stage for more combat in Europe. One of Wade's buddies was Griffith Williams, who took part in the Doolittle Raid and was now back in action in North Africa.

November 24, 1942

Dear Doc—

Just a line or two to let you know that I am now "somewhere in North Africa." No fooling. I have been "somewhere in something" for so long that when I get home I think I'll use "somewhere in San Diego" as my permanent address.

. . . The outfit I was with was among the first to land in the invasion and I got in on a little excitement before everything calmed down. Of course, it wasn't much compared to what some of the boys saw, and it was plenty for me. I was shelled, strafed and swiped at, and generally wore out the knees of my GI pants diving into ditches. But that is, for the moment anyway, a thing of the past.

At present, we are living in pup tents and trying hard not to freeze to death. Whoever spread this rumor of Africa being hot didn't have all his buttons, because, brother, it's cold! . . .

We eat from a field kitchen and wash and shave from our helmets and generally suffer the other discomforts of living outdoors. But there is really little to complain about—our food is surprisingly good and we're not worked to death, either. And then there's the satisfaction that comes with the feeling that you are helping to end this war in the right way—and that makes up for a lot of discomforts.

. . .

The geography around here is very familiar, Doc. It reminds me a lot of central California—up in the San Jose valley section. The soil seems to be a sort of clay, which forms a sticky mud when it rains, which is often. If I remember correctly, this part of Africa has a Mediterranean type climate, doesn't it? Principle crop over here seems to be grapes, with tangerines second.

. . .

Haven't gotten one of the *News Letters* for a long time now, and I'm anxious to see the back issues. It's hard for me to picture State buzzing along as usual. Let's see: football season must be just about over now. Thursday night is the Turkey Trot, and soon the Christmas formals will be starting. It seems a long, long way from here.

Cpl. R. A. (Robert) Wade, 39022529
437 Bomb Sq. 319 Bomb Gp.
APO 520, c/o PM, NY NY

March 19, 1943
Dear Doc:

. . .

In a spurt of ambition when we first got here, my tentmate and I took a day off and fixed ourselves a home of which I am very proud—and which is very luxurious, according to local standards. We dug down about two feet, lined the sides with tin, built a framework to hold the tent and eliminate the center poles, and thus just about doubled our lebensraum. And when two of you are living in the small space a pup tent provides, that is mighty important. Then we added such homelike touches as shelves, gun racks, wash stand and gasoline lamp. For this country it's a veritable palace—and most of our spare time is spent wallowing in our new luxury and telling each other what clever fellows we are, after all.

. . .

Take care of the home front—we'll do our best with the others.

Bob Wade

April 3, 1943

Dear Doc:

. . .

There is little doubt that this war is going to be won in Europe—but that can't be accomplished until we've gotten Rommel out of Tunisia. The drive seems to be on now, so maybe that day isn't far off.

I had a real surprise, and a pleasant one, the other day. I was sitting in the orderly room, doing some routine work, when a captain walked in, and said:

"Do you have a man named Wade in this outfit?"

Naturally, I looked up—and there was Grif Williams, now Captain Williams! He's been a member of the 319th since last September some time, but this was the first time I've seen him. . . . Believe me, Doc, it was quite a reunion—two Aztecs meeting in the middle of this forsaken continent. We talked and talked, about the war and our adventures in foreign service and so on—but mostly of the college and the friends we'd left there. . . .

While I was damn glad to see him, it made me a little homesick, too—especially when I recalled that the last time Grif and I talked was in the middle of the quad. It made everything seem very far away—even farther than usual. Those were happy days.

. . .

Give my regards to the whole Aztec gang,

Bob Wade

July 7, 1943

Dear Doc:

It's 1900 hours and the breeze has cooled off the tent enough to make it livable again, so I'll spend a little spare time in writing to you. We've moved twice since I wrote you the last time, so there's a little time to catch up on.

Africa is finally living up to her reputation. Hot weather has arrived, but definitely. Yesterday our first real sirocco (or *khamsin*) hit us: a scorching hot wind, carrying plenty of dust, which makes everyone miserable. I've never seen anything like it; it's like a blast from a smelting furnace. Everything heats up—the metal chairs in the orderly room become so hot that you can hardly sit on them. Water in the lister bags is practically boiling. Temperature yesterday hit 122 degrees here, and I'm told it was even hotter out on the line. And when it gets that warm, it's time for me to head for Old Mission.

. . .

Liquor, particularly beer, is very hard to get. Wine, of course, is always available anywhere in Africa at any time, but I've had enough of that Purple Death to last me a long time. In this hot weather I'd sooner take poison. Nearly everyone feels the same way, and the demand is for beer. Since it's scarce, anyway, you really have a tough time finding it. The other day I stepped into a bar at 1200 (which is the time beer sales begin), gulped down two fast glasses of beer—and the place was sold out. That's the way it is everywhere. The big sale here is lemonade and a sweetish orange drink—every shop, every house, every street peddler has a pitcher from which he will supply you at 2 francs a glass. It's ice cold and, after five or six glasses, doesn't taste too badly.

Aside from going to town, our only other recreation is to go swimming in a river that passes within a mile of our base. There's a dam, with a miniature waterfall, and after these scorching days it's wonderful to wander down to the river and lie under the falls. Nearly every outfit in the vicinity comes there, and about 1800 it resembles Old Mission on a Sunday in July. Of course, the girls are missing, which spoils the whole illusion.

. . .

I intended to write sooner, but I haven't had the heart, since I've been feeling low, due to reasons that I can't mention. But such is war. See you soon.

Love,

Bob Wade

When Wade was overheated and homesick, he longed to escape to the Old Mission Dam in San Diego. In the following letters, he described his chance meeting with an old friend. He was so surprised, he claimed he was "struck with cafard," an expression loosely translated as having a fit. He wasted no time setting up a reunion.

July 29, 1943

Dear Doc:

. . .

It all began with a sudden decision of mine to take a day off and ramble around the country. There are too many soldiers in town to suit me, so I thought I'd strike off in the opposite direction and see a few other places of interest. So off I went, stopping by one town after another, and finding very little of note anywhere. After four or five hours of this I was pretty well disgusted, and had about decided to come back home. Now the action begins.

I was standing by the side of the road, trying to thumb a ride without much luck, when along comes a weapons carrier, with an officer riding in the front seat. I waved my arm in the approved fashion, but the truck rolled right on past me. This burned me up, so I took another look at the officer—and started shouting and waving my arms as if I had suddenly been struck with cafard. The officer, startled, looked back and then stopped the truck. Then Larry Devlin and I fell into each other's arms. Yep, it was Larry, same old guy that I used to lie on the quad with.

. . .

Well, you can imagine the rest of the day. It was spent largely in talking; I don't believe there was a moment of silence till we finally parted about 2400. It was "Do you know that—" and "Do you remember when—" for hour after hour.

. . .

What I can't get over is the amount of luck involved. I almost took the other road out of town, I almost didn't go there in the first place—and it was only on the spur of the moment that I even left camp. Furthermore, it was the one day that Larry was in that area: his camp lies in the opposite direction. . . . Furthermore, we're sweating out Lionel Chase. He's due to arrive in this area sometime around the first of August. If this keeps up, we can open an African branch of SDSC.

. . . I hope it won't be too long before I can be listening to your wife sing again—preferably Lindy Law. Let's make it a date, shall we?

Love,

Sgt. R. A. (Bob) Wade, 39022529

437 Bomb Sq. 319 Bomb Gp (M)

APO 520, c/o Postmaster NY

August 23, 1943

North Africa

. . .

A few weeks ago, I was driving through a little town about seventy-five miles from my headquarters when I noticed a soldier trying to thumb a ride. Since I was only going as far as the next block, I did not stop, but just as I drove past someone yelled my name. The old car stood on end and I was out before it had come to a complete stop, because I recognized the voice of Bob Wade, an old Sigma Lambda fraternity brother. It was really quite a coincidence, because Bob was just seeing the sights on his day off. . . .

A few days later, I learned that Lionel Chase had moved in near my place. I called him up right away, and I think that he was surprised (understatement) when he was greeted with the suggestion that he run over to the cafe for a coca and then go out to Mission Beach for a swim. I will not quote his answer, but it certainly would make Clarence and Andy realize how much the old Aztec gang miss the cafe and everything that went with it.

. . .

Well, Doc, that is about thirty for tonight, but I do want to thank you again for the *News Letter*. I just can't tell you what it means to me; all that I can say is that it is TOPS.

2nd Lt. Lawrence R. Devlin 0-1050632

Hq. 31st C.A. Brigade (A.A.)

APO 512, c/o Postmaster

New York, NY

August 18, 1943

Dear "Doc"—

The other day I was called to the telephone. A voice said "Say old man, let's go over to the caf' for a coke, grab a couple gals and go out to Mission Beach for a swim!" The "funny man" was Lt. Larry Devlin. We got together that afternoon. . . . Next day Larry and I visited a guy I've chased all over Africa, Bob Wade. What a big reunion we had, with an even bigger one in the offing. Larry and I sat up 'til about 1 A.M. for the best time I've had in Africa.

Lt. Lionel E. Chase

416 Sqdn 99 Bomb Grp (H)

APO # 520 New York

Wade and his friends carved out a few moments of pleasure amid the bitterness of war. The battles in Africa had been won, but the cost in lives continued to rise. In the September 1, 1943, issue of the *News Letter*, Dr. Post published a notice that Griffith Williams had been listed as missing in action. When Wade wrote the following letter, dated August 30, he hadn't yet received the news that Griff might still be alive.

August 30, 1943

Dear Doc:

. . .

I'd like to say something about Grif Williams. Since the news is known back at home, I can say something I wanted to say before but wasn't able to, due to censorship. He was a grand guy and a good friend, and his death hit me very hard. We came up from grammar school together, always sitting next to each other, due to our last names beginning with "W." In those years, we grew to be good friends. Meeting him again over here and having him in the same outfit brought us even closer together. He was one of the best fliers in the Group, a flight commander. The last time I saw him, he was cheerful and full of plans for the future—Grif had planned to go back to school for engineering work after the war. There is a bare chance that he may have gotten out alive, but those who saw him go down don't think so. The irony of the whole business is that Grif was scheduled to go back to the States as an instructor. So passes a grand guy.

A week ago, Larry Devlin, Lionel Chase and I got our schedules to agree, and we held our long-awaited reunion. And what a reunion it was, too! . . . three Aztecs together in this god forsaken corner of the world. We adjourned to a luxurious (by African standards) hotel in a little town near Larry's outfit and spent the evening in reminiscence and recollection. We also had a quart of Seagrams. It was a wonderful evening—by far the best I've had in a year of foreign service. . . . Doc—I think I'd go crazy if I was someplace where nothing happens. Not much danger as long as I stick with the 319th, though: we were the first medium bomb group in England, the first in North Africa, and we'll probably keep on like that. Last to come home though. Well, say hello to the whole Aztec gang for me, and I'll see you about 1945 sometime.

Bob Wade

October 22, 1943

Dear Doc:

. . .

Of course, the best news of this or any other month is about Grif. A few days after I wrote Barbara the details of his last flight, Intelligence was notified that he was a prisoner of war. This made me happier than anything I can remember in a long long time. Grif is a swell guy, one of the best, and it would have been one of the real tragedies of the war if he had gone down. We'll be getting him out before long, too.

The North African branch of SDSC is really getting along in fine shape. Rare indeed is the weekend that doesn't see Larry and me together in some bistro or the other, drinking moderately and talking immoderately. Many are the memories and friends that are recalled in those sessions. . . .

Bob Wade

In the preceding letter, Wade referred to Barbara Williams, Capt. Griffith Williams' wife. It was common for the Aztec community to share details between themselves, even before official notification was made. Pilots had access to eyewitness accounts and could offer family members more information than was customary through the usual military channels. Williams' plane went down over Sicily, and a lot of Aztecs expressed relief that their friend had been captured instead of killed in action.

In the following letter, the reference to escaping prisoners was accurate. Several well-known escapes were staged from Stalag Luft III, the prisoner-of-war camp where Williams was held. One escape attempt was made from block 104, not far from where Williams stayed for a time, in block 105.[6]

October 22, 1943

Dear Doc,

. . .

Am plenty glad to know that Grif Williams is safe. According to one of our boys who flew for the RAF until recently, the Luftwaffe treats English & American flyers very well—and some escape, too.

. . .

Respectfully,

Lieut. Charles M. Witt

U.S. Naval Air Station

Jacksonville, Florida

November 2, 1943

Dear Dr. Post:

. . .

Lately, I've been receiving the *Aztec News Letter*, which I've appreciated very much, as most of the fellows who are in the *Letter* are old friends of mine such as, Ernie and Wally McAnulty. . . .

I was particularly interested in this issue, Nov. 1, 1943, as I learned from it that my brother-in-law, Capt. Griff Williams, and Lt. Ernie McAnulty were in the same prison camp together, which certainly ought to be a morale lifter for both of them. I had written Griff, a few months back, and asked him, that if, by chance, he should run into Ernie, would he tell Ernie I said "hello." I've always remembered Ernie from high school days, as one of the best Triple Threat men I've ever seen on a high school football team. A punt of sixty yards was just in the day's work for him.

. . .

I remain

As always

Ralph (Butch) Sunderhauf, MOMM 2/c

U.S.S. YP37 Section Base

San Diego 49 California

The Aztec News Letter

No. 26, May 1, 1944

Lt. Ernest McAnulty who is Wally's young brother writes from a prisoner of war camp in Germany to his mother:

"You asked several times how my capture came about. Well all I can say is that when you blow up out in the middle of the Mediterranean and come to floating around some hours later and a torpedo boat picks you up, there isn't much you can do about it. Or is there? All I can do is chalk it up to experience.

"Griff (Williams) and I have a time re-living our high school days (at Hoover) and tell Dr. Post to say hello to all the fellows for me in the *News Letter*. And tell people to write to me. There is no limit on the number of letters coming in."

(Ernie's address is: Lt. Ernest McAnulty, American Prisoner of War No. 1123, Block 105, Stammlager Luft 3, Germany, Via New York City, N.Y. LCP)

Dr. Lauren C. Post, Editor

Letters from the McAnulty brothers and from their mother are in chapter 2.

Ernie McAnulty was shot down in April of 1943. A few months later, in July, Griff Williams' plane went down, and he joined Ernie in Stalag Luft III.

McANULTY

267. McANULLY, EARNEST E 2LT. 0729351 USAAF 125/18 PILOT
SAN DIEGO, CALIF.   1123   P-38   4-5-43
FERRYVILLE, TUNISIA HOSP. 4-7 TO 4-14-43 TUNIS(CONF) 4-
14 TO 4-17-43 DULAG LUFT 4-20 TO 4-23-43   STALAG LUFT
III 4-25-43.
SHOT DOWN BY FLAK.   CRASH LANDED IN SEA ON FIRE 14M OFF
BIESERTA, TUNISIA.   7 HRS. IN DINGHY.   PICKED UP BY
ITALIANS TORPEDO BOAT.   DISLOCATED SHOULDER AND KNEE IN
CRASH.
FIGHTER SEA SWEEP, MEDITERRANEAN
SINGLE- P-   28-9-20   37   O

POW record of Ernest McAnulty,
Stalag Luft III, block 125, room 18
Courtesy of the Stalag Luft III Museum,
Zagan, Poland

GRIFFITH

631. WILLIAMS, GRIGGITH P CAPT 0421366 USAAF 125/18 PILOT
4164 30 ST.   B-26
SAN DIEGO, CALIF.   1764   7-4-43
DULAG LUFT 7-9 TO 7-16   STALAG LUFT III   7-18-43
SHOT BY FLAK. STRAGGLED. ATTACKED BY FW190-MACCHI 202.
BAILED OUT- LANDED AT GEPBINI AIR FIELD, SICILY.   CAPT
IMM. BY LUFTWAFFE.
AIRFIELD, CATANIA, SICILY.
D.F.C.-MILITARY ORDER OF CHINA
MARRIED-P- 7-10-20   11   A

POW record of Griffith Williams,
Stalag Luft III, block 125, room 18
Courtesy of the Stalag Luft III Museum,
Zagan, Poland

In September, along with other American prisoners, Ernie and Griff were transferred to the south compound of the camp, where they became roommates in Block 125, Room 18.

June 5, 1944
Dear Dr. Post:
. . .
I received a letter from my sister, Barbara Williams, a few days ago and she had received three letters and a picture of Griff and she said that he was still doing okay. Thank God he and Ernie are together. They will get through it all alright.

. . .

Yours Truly
Ralph A. (Butch) Sunderhauf MOMM 2/c
Division 49 Hut 441
Motor Torpedo Boat Squadrons Training Center
Melville, Rhode Island

Williams and McAnulty were lucky to survive plane crashes, but not all Fighting Aztecs fared as well.

THE AZTEC NEWS LETTER

Edited by
DR. LAUREN C. POST
San Diego State College
San Diego, California

February 26, 1943
NO. 12

This issue sponsored by
TAU DELTA CHI
and
EPSILON PI THETA

Salute to the Aztecs in Service

To All of the Aztecs in the Service and Their Friends:

There isn't much to say in this column now. It looks a lot better, it's easier to mail, it makes less work, but some people miss the addresses.

The Office of Censorship in Washington wrote a nice letter approving the last issue. We will keep it so that it will be approved by all but our enemies.

Your friends and families can still get on the mailing list if you only send in their addresses. And we want them to send us bits of information about you but especially your changes in address and promotions.

Our list of "unknowns" is still very long. We pay postage on all News Letters that come back and still the fellows don't get them. But the percentage of returns is very low.

About 600 Aztecs now have commissions in the various branches of the armed forces. That many more are enlisted personnel or are cadets or in O. C. S. If we had all of the names there probably would be several hundred more in each group.

Keep writing even if your letters are cut down. If yours was cut, so were many others. Oftimes I don't have the courage to cut a nice letter so I lay it aside for later editing—then pressure of

time and work force me to crowd them in close.

And don't get discouraged if your wedding and furlough were omitted. They are being left out. This is a shooting war.

Don't forget all of your war experiences. When the war is over we will want some Victory Letters for a Victory Edition of the News Letter. Keep that in mind. More later.

The city library is compiling a record of the part played by San Diegans in the war. Needless to say, we have the same ideas in mind and will do some pooling.

And again, best of luck!

Lauren C. Post, Editor of the News Letter.

The Service Men's Panel

Did you know that many of your pictures are in what amounts to our Service Flag? About 700 pictures are already up and the names of the other 500 Aztecs in service are there on white cards awaiting the pictures which we hope you or your friends will send us.

This panel is really quite unique. It consists of four sections each six feet long so that the overall length is 24 feet. It is 3½ feet high and has 12 rows of mounts for cards 3 inches high. The

1,200 mounts look very impressive arranged in alphabetical order so that names can be immediately located.

To get the pictures we cut up two sets of Del Sudoestes for about 10 years back. In general we used the best picture we could get but we favored graduation pictures.

Some of you ex-freshmen look pretty young to be piloting B 17's so we will replace the older pictures with new ones as they come in but try to keep them down to about 2x2 inches for the head dimensions.

Tell your friends to visit the panel sometime on a week day or on Saturday morning (the building is not open on Sundays) or better yet, come and see it yourself. It is in the hall of the Administration Building near Dean C. E. Peterson's office.

Miss Haman drew the architectural blue prints for it, Ruth Kimball made the block letters for the title and "motto," the class of 1945 sponsored it, Robley Baskerville and her friends did most of the picture mounting, and the editor of the News Letter did the rest.

The title is simple: AZTECS IN SERVICE, and below in block letters also is the "motto," ONCE AN AZTEC, ALWAYS AN AZTEC.

The 29 gold stars certainly tell us that San Diego State College is in a war. For

8

IN OUR GREAT SORROW

THE AZTEC NEWS LETTER

No. 13, March 26, 1943

The Service Men's Panel has visitors practically throughout the day. It now has over 1,400 names and probably 800 pictures. More and more "uniform" pictures are coming in. By the way, do you think that your public relations offices would send us your pictures? Tell them it's really important. At least, it's an idea.

Your families are invited to come out to the campus (on school days) to see the Panel. Ask them to send us pictures in case you didn't have one in a rather late *Del Sudoeste*, and don't forget to tell them that they also can get on our mailing list.

And again, best of luck!

Lauren C. Post, Editor

A long with their letters, Dr. Post asked servicemen and servicewomen to send photographs—the preferred size was two and a half by three and a half inches—which he arranged in a display case called the Service Men's Panel. He got his hands on pictures any way he could, even if he had to cut up the campus yearbook, *Del Sudoeste* ("From the Southwest"). A gold star next to a picture denoted killed in action.

On February 26, 1943, Dr. Post wrote, "The 29 gold stars certainly tell us that San Diego State College is in war." *News Letter* no. 12 described the Service Men's Panel:

> This panel is really quite unique. It consists of four sections, each six feet long, so that the overall length is 24 feet. It is 3½ feet high and has twelve rows of mounts for cards 3 inches high. The 1,200 mounts look very impressive arranged in alphabetical order so that names can be immediately located. To get the pictures we cut up two sets of *Del Sudoestes* for about 10 years back. . . . Some of you ex-freshmen look pretty young to be piloting B-17s . . .

On May 11, 1943, Bob Schneider, who signed his letter, "A Former Aztec," wrote, "I don't know if I am eligible to have my picture in your collection; please let me know in your *News Letter*." Dr. Post wrote his answer in red pencil directly on the letter, and his message was later typed into the *News Letter*: "Yes, tell someone to send us your picture. Your name is there waiting for it. LCP." The panel of names and photos was constructed to remind those on campus that their friends were fighting, and some were dying. The *News Letter* reminded the servicemen that their campus would never forget them.

Before the gold stars were placed beside pictures in the display case, telegrams arrived in mailboxes in San Diego homes. Basketball players, fraternity brothers, a club president—their talent may have been extinguished when they died, but Dr. Post made sure that memories survived.

✉ April 3, 1943
Dear Doc:

. . .

I note with growing anxiety the growing gold stars list of Aztecs. I guess it is something we have all grown to take in stride to expect it if comes to us personally, but it is hard to realize the empty places that must be if and when an Aztec reunion takes place. I guess we can only offer that fervent prayer that they didn't die in vain. Certainly we can all be proud to have known them.

. . .

Capt. Jos. (Joe) A. Rodney
Btry C 251st CA (AA)
APO #913

Grief was a rising tide in the Aztec community, and the *News Letter* served as an anchor. Its pages had always been a source of information, and they became a way to share eulogies and memories. Dr. Post did his best to find out about all who were killed in action or captured, as well as those who lost their lives in other ways while in the service.

The New Hebrides (today Vanuatu) is a group of islands in the Pacific, but unlike many of the other islands that had been captured by the Japanese during World War II, this chain was under Allied control. The New Hebrides provided a base from which the Allies could defend Australia from Japanese aggression, and it supported the Marines as they prepared to invade Guadalcanal.

Like other volcanic archipelagos, the New Hebrides are surrounded by treacherous reefs. These relatively young volcanoes rise steeply and drop away below the waterline just as suddenly. One of the factors adding to the danger is that there is little landmass underwater. By contrast, the beaches of San Diego, like any continental coastline, continue underwater in a gradually sloping shelf, which means the water also deepens gradually. Without a continental shelf, the shore around the New Hebrides plunges unexpectedly into deep ocean waters.

The Pacific islands were also host to a different threat—illnesses transmitted by mosquito. Even today there is no vaccine for dengue fever.

November 18, 1944

Dear Doctor Post,

Thank you very much for sending me those two copies of the *News Letter*. . . .

Yes, the Lt. (j.g.) T.J. Davies your article mentioned is my brother. Joe went to State for two years, 37-39, finished at Cal, 39-41, got his M.A. in Agricultural Economics at the U. of Maryland, June 42, received a commission in the Navy, trained at Harvard and then went down to the New Hebrides. He was there for six months, till Aug. 29, 1943. . . .

He had had Dengi fever (spelling only a guess), in June, and was left very weak. The surf was a favorite sport, for relaxation, until that Sunday when a heavy ripping current was too much for him to fight.

His body was recovered Monday morning, and the "San Diego Union" carried a description of his funeral.

A crash boat and an airplane searched for him to come up, and another man risked his life to save Joe, so we know he had every help—had God not found him ready.

. . .

Milky Phelps & Paul Fern, I noticed, have gone "Home" too. Joe's among friends.

Thank you again Dr. Post.

Sincerely,

Mary Davies

Dr. Post kept in touch with families, and they updated him as they learned the news about their loved ones. One mother was uncertain about her son's fate following the Japanese assault on the Philippines. The U.S. Navy's Asiatic Fleet was based in Manila Bay and defended by several Coast Artillery (Antiaircraft) Regiments similar to the one Wally McAnulty served in at Pearl Harbor. The air and naval bases were irresistible targets to the Empire of Japan. During the prolonged attack, the Americans and the less-experienced Filipino forces fell back, regrouped, and fought for longer than expected, but they couldn't halt the enemy's advance.[1]

When Japanese capture of the position was imminent, Gen. Douglas MacArthur was forced to withdraw, vowing famously to return. The following letter was written just months later.

May 22, 1942

I saw in the Union you are editing the *State College Servicemen's News Letter*, and you would like addresses and information of former college students now in the service, among the names mentioned I find my son's name Bob Newsom. At present I have no address, but I can give you a little information.

I had a telegram from Washington D.C. from the commandant of the U.S. Marine Corps that according to the records of the headquarters, Corp. R.S. Newsom U.S. Marine Corps was performing his duty in the service of his country in the Manila Bay area, when the station capitulated, and he will be carried on the records as missing pending further information. No report of his death has been received, and he may be a prisoner of war.

I hope and pray he is alive and well, but it may be months before I hear anything. If I get an address, I will send it to you. I know he would be so glad to get the *Servicemen's News Letter*. I think you are doing a fine thing for our boys.

Mrs. R. P. (Bertine L.) Newsom

1404 Golden Gate Dr.

San Diego 3, California

Ten months later, Mrs. Newsom finally received news, which she immediately shared with Dr. Post.

March 22, 1943

Dear Dr. L.C. Post,

I have just received a message from Headquarters U.S. Marine Corps Washington, concerning Bob. He is alive. I had just about given up hopes, so you can just imagine how I felt. Never in my life been so glad. The following is the message I received.

A partial list of American prisoners of war in the Manila Bay area has just been received from the International Red Cross, containing the name of your son Pfc. Robert S. Newsom U.S. Marine Corps confirming the fact that he is alive and a prisoner of war.

The report fails to state the place of internment but you may communicate with him by mail at the following address,

Private First Class Robert S. Newsom U.S.M.C.

Serial Number 271846

Prisoner of War

Philippine Islands

c/o Japanese Red Cross

Tokyo, Japan

Via: New York, N.Y.

The Red Cross failed in giving the place of internment. I would like to know where he is, but I am so happy he is alive.

I wish to thank you so much for sending me the *Aztec News*, I enjoy them, and I am saving them in hopes that some day not before long, Bob will be home, and I know he will be very much pleased to have them. I think it is a wonderful thing for the boys to see where their friends are. I don't think I can send them to him.

I see you would like to have a picture of all the Aztec boys in the service. I have no good picture of Bob, but I have a Kodak picture of him taken in Shanghai which I enclose, in hopes you can use it.

Mrs. R. P. (Bertine L.) Newsom

1404 Golden Gate Dr.

San Diego 3, California

P.S. This message has him as P.f.c. I received a letter from him written in the Philippines, Feb, 1942. He was then Corporal. Washington may not have received the Marine records from there, so guess his address has to be written like Washington has it.

The International Red Cross worked diligently on behalf of prisoners and refugees. It was flooded with thousands of requests for information, and its success depended on the cooperation of the countries at war. In addition to finding out the names of those captured, the organization did its best to ensure that prisoners had adequate food and medical care. In this regard, it was more successful in Europe than in Asia. It generally fared better in countries that had signed the Geneva Convention.

THE AZTEC NEWS LETTER
No. 34, January 1, 1945
Lt. Jason M. Axsom is a prisoner of war in Germany. A message that he sent his parents read: "I am OK, not hurt or maimed in any way. I never was so glad to get anything in my life as I was to get the Red Cross kit they gave me. It had practically every-thing in it. I hope the notice didn't upset you too much. That's the result of the game we play."

He was a pilot on a B-17 that was shot down over Northern Germany in August. His address is:
Lt. Jason M. Axsom
American Prisoner of War No. 6974
Stalag Luft 3
Germany, Via New York.

Prison camps often limited the amount of correspondence and care packages that prisoners and their families could send and receive. For those held prisoner by Japan, the situation was more extreme. Like many nations fighting a war, Japan was low on supplies, and not much food was spared for prisoners, who often existed in a state close to starvation. Although Japan had signed the Geneva Convention before World War II, it neither ratified nor abided by its conditions. In fact, the International Red Cross found that Japan actively tried to interfere with its efforts. Names of those captured were withheld, care packages were not delivered, and medical staff were permitted only limited access to check on the well-being of prisoners.[2]

More evidence of the brutal treatment the Japanese inflicted on prisoners emerged after World War II. In the Philippines, where Corporal Newsom was captured, prisoners were forced to endure death marches and were confined under inhumane conditions.[3] Many of the servicemen wrote to Dr. Post that they didn't want their families to know about the worst aspects of war. Japanese camps required messages to be typed, and prisoners were given a limit of just twenty-five words. Newsom used what little space he had to reassure his mother.

September 11, 1943

Dear Dr. L. Post,

I just received a card from my son Robert, Corporal in U.S. 4th Marines now interned by Japanese at Philippines Military Prison Camp No. 2. He states his health is good. He is uninjured and well, and please take care of yourself and don't worry.

Thought you would like to know I heard from Bob. The card is type written but he has written his name. His writing looks as usual, shows he is well.

I wish to thank you so much for the *Aztec New Letters* you send me.

Sincerely,

Mrs. R. P. (Bertine L.) Newsom

1404 Golden Gate Dr.

San Diego 3, California

Undated

[A partial postmark is visible on an envelope fragment: Dec]

Dear Dr. L.C. Post.

I have just been informed by the Provost Marshall General Washington D.C. that my son Robert Sherley Newsom has been transferred from the Philippines to Osaka Camp, Japan.

I have not heard from Bob since March so I was happy to get news of him, but I am very much grieved about him being taken to Japan. I was in hopes the Philippines would soon fall, and he would soon be coming home, but all we can do is to hope and pray that this war will soon be over.

I thank you so much for the *Aztec News Letters* you send me, and I hope before long Bob will be home to read them. He sure will be happy to have them, and I thank you again.

Mrs. R. P. (Bertine L.) Newsom

1404 Golden Gate Dr.

San Diego 3, California

Bertine Newsom wasn't alone in her concern and grief. Other parents in San Diego were also trying to make sense of unthinkable news, and to learn everything possible about the details of personal tragedy.

Lt. John Burdette Binkley, called Burdette by his parents and "Bink" by his friends, played tennis and acted in dramatic productions on campus. Like his fellow Aztec, Bob Wade, he had an eye for detail, and he didn't forget what he had learned from his former professor. In an early letter to Dr. Post, written on April 7, 1942, from Randolph Field, Texas, he wrote, "I am sure glad I had your Geography courses. They have helped me considerably in my ground school, and I am not saying that just to flatter you, I really mean it." Binkley was soon overseas, posted first in Great Britain.

October 15, 1942

Somewhere in England

I will repeat a few of the impressions I have, which may prove of interest. The small farms with every inch of ground in use; the stone houses with their many chimneys . . . ; the narrow streets and roads; the very few autos and the many bicycles. The accent which I'm beginning to understand. The universal food of potatoes and cabbage; tea at 4 o'clock; and many other things which make this seem like a giant movie with me in the center.

. . .

The blackouts here are really blackouts. There are absolutely no lights at night except from small torches and small shielded lights on bicycles and autos.

. . .

Clothing, soap, much of the foodstuffs, etc. all need coupons. There are practically no eggs, very little milk, little meat, sugar is scarce, candy is rationed, etc.

Lt. John B. Binkley

By the beginning of 1943 Binkley was part of the North African campaign.

Tunisia has ports on the Mediterranean and terrain that stretches from the Atlas Mountains to the Sahara Desert sands. In the sixteenth century, it became part of the Ottoman Empire, and it remained as such until the French took control in the late 1800s. Tempted by oil and the Suez Canal, the Axis Powers seized it early in World War II. The Allies, who planned to invade Sicily and reach Europe, made capturing Tunisia a priority.

Before the war, the mythical lore of North Africa, full of intrigue, with tales of daring raids and enticing harems, was already popular in Hollywood and on Broadway. In San Diego State's 1940 production of *The Desert Song*, a Broadway musical, Burdette Binkley played the role of Sid El Kar, an Arab who assists the French leader of a rebel group. Everyone on campus helped with the production, including the a cappella choir and two other singing groups, the Men's Glee Club and Treble Clef, an all-women's ensemble.

Like *Beau Geste* (the movie parodied by Bob Wade), *The Desert Song* was set in North Africa and loosely based on fabled stories drawn from World War I, including the exploits of Lawrence of Arabia. Those adventures may have fueled the imaginations of students like Bob Wade, who donned a French legionnaire's uniform, and Binkley, who sang the tenor role while ensconced in Arab garb. But when these students-turned-pilots went to North Africa, they were wearing American military uniforms. In many ways, the battles they fought were a continuation of the colonial conflicts that had taken root before World War I. Suddenly the young State College students weren't acting but fighting in earnest. Binkley was looking at Tunisia from the cockpit of his plane, and Africa was no longer the setting of a musical but a battleground.

On January 30, 1943, Burdette's father, John P. Binkley, sent two dollars with a brief note to Dr. Post. Just a few weeks after sending his contribution to the *News Letter*, he wrote again, this time enclosing a letter he had received from his son.

February 16, 1943

Africa

Dear Mother & Dad:

Got a couple more letters today, Jan 13. #2 and Valentine and picture and a V mail from Bob.

Glad to hear you got my money OK although, (as I have asked before) I wish you would tell me the special amount you have received. Also I have mailed you a check for $100.00. You can do most anything you wish with this money. I have about four hundred more I am going to send as soon as the P.O. gets some money order blanks. You can't cable from here, not much need for money here.

Bob says he is now engaged, lucky boy, of course, that is probably old news to you.

Thanx for the Valentine and pictures. The pictures were very nice. Hope to get some more.

There isn't much news I can tell you. Don't worry about me and how the war will affect me, that is, without regard to actual physical injury. I mean emotionally and mentally. I believe I am more stable now than ever before. What I mean is that I have probably reached a greater peace of mind. I am, shall we say, exposed to death fairly constantly, yet I can truthfully say that there is really no fear present. An occasional moment of nervous terror, yes; however if my number should come up, I am ready. As you know, I am not a particularly religious person, yet I do have a very strong faith. It is not a faith to be put in words but rather to be kept in the heart. The 23rd Psalm and the "Lords Prayer" are about the only passages of scripture that I know, yet they give me a peace of mind that is real. Sometimes when I am flying I look out [at] the tremendous blue sky, the fleecy clouds, the earth below, I realize what a small, yet somehow integral part of things I am. It constantly amazes me, this flying. I know the theory of flight, the mechanics of flight, the airplane, can all be explained with figures, graphs, charts etc., yet there is something more that is there. I believe I have written other letters regarding my feelings along this line.

I don't know why I am writing on this way except that I have nothing much else to do. I probably wouldn't talk like this but it is easier to write. Also, it gives you a little insight as to my thoughts and feelings.

I don't know how you all feel about this war and how long it will last, but I am afraid it is going to be a long one. It is going to be hard on you people at home, and it will get harder. Hitler has a great deal of fight left in him. I know that we in the army are going to see this really through: I sincerely pray for peace, but I also pray that peace will not come until the great cancer that is Germany & Japan, and all their present manifestations, are totally obliterated from the earth. I hope that people at home do not tire of war until this [is] accomplished. When I look ahead I see a rather morbid picture, however, I also look back in history and see many which are equally frightful. Along with this morbid picture I also see a very bright one. Air transportation, medicine, and machinery are some of the countless industries and science which are receiving tremendous impetus from the war. A few years after the war our standards of living will be changed to a new undreamed of level. Possibly this war will wipe out racial and political boundaries, uniting the world in an intelligent peace with plenty for all. Theoretically this should be possible however, in actual practice it will probably not happen.

Jealousies, retribution, reprisals, etc. will probably mar any attempt at a sane, sensible peace.

Say, I am getting tired so I will say good night. I am going to seal this up without reading it, otherwise I probably would never mail it.

Love.

Burdette.

Lt. John B. Binkley

[USS] *Mizpah*

April 19, 1943

Dear Sir:

I am enclosing a copy of [the] letter we recently received from our dear son Burdette, who was fighting for his country in North Africa. The letter has been copied in its entirety and if you see fit to use it or any part of it, I want you to know it is perfectly all right with his mother and myself.

Perhaps it is only parental pride, but we feel his letter should help many others to see how our boys feel and think in their line of duty on the battlefront.

In our great sorrow we have nothing but the kindest feeling toward the whole world and sincerely hope you will be able to continue your good work with the *News Letter* to our boys and girls in the service of their country, I remain

Sincerely Yours

John P. Binkley

3168 Grape St

San Diego, California

May 19, 1943

Portland, Oregon

Dear Doc—

. . .

I think Burdette Binkley's letter in No. 14 was one of the finest and most inspiring letters I ever read. It rather choked me up with emotion, and made me proud to think that my college produces *fighting* men of such caliber. I imagine that many fighting men experience his same feelings, but not many are capable of expressing themselves so lucidly.

. . .

Charles T. Byrne, Y 1/c

U.S.M.S. Graduate Station

11733 NE Sandy Blvd.

Blair Burkhardt, the man who worked on planes and looked out for the pilots from San Diego State College, got some inside information on John Burdette Binkley. Burkhardt sent the following information to Dr. Post, who passed it along to Burdette's father, John Binkley.

August 12, 1943

. . .

I ran into the Captain of Burdette Binkley's outfit and found out that Bink was flying Douglas attack airplanes when he was shot down. Bink was flying on this captain's right wing when he was hit from behind by an explosive shell. The ship crashed and Bink apparently didn't have a chance. He was one of the best liked boys in his outfit and their best pilot, but he had a little bad luck. . . . He was a classmate of mine for years and I consider myself very fortunate to have known a fellow like him.

. . .

HB Burkhardt, NAA Representative
XII Air Service Command, Hdq.
APO 528 New York, New York

HONORING FIVE FORMER MEMBERS OF THE MEN'S GLEE CLUB

Lt. John Burdette Binkley — Killed in action
Lt. Joseph Norman Gates — Killed in action
Lt. Victor R. Talbot — Missing in action
Lt. Ross A. Tenney — Missing in action
Lt. Frank R. Verdusco — Missing in action

Lt. John Burdette Binkley and other members of the San Diego State College Men's Glee Club, *News Letter* No. 23, February 1, 1944

From March 28 through April 1, fierce clashes took place around El Guettar, in Tunisia. In less than a week, thousands perished in what was one of the worst periods of fighting in North Africa.[4] Air attacks hammered targets across northern Tunisia, including the port cities of Bizerte and Tunis.

Binkley's plane went down on April 2, 1943. By May, the North African campaign, which had spanned the desert and reached the coast, was drawing to a close. British troops suffered 38,000 casualties. Estimates place Axis casualties at 40,000 to 50,000. The Americans suffered more than 18,000 killed, wounded, and missing, and overall Allied casualties were approximately 70,000.[5] These losses set the stage for the fight in Italy.

Lt. John Burdette Binkley, who sang in *The Desert Song* on his college campus and found peace in the Lord's Prayer as his plane crossed "the tremendous blue sky," is interred in Carthage, Tunisia, along with more than 2,800 other American servicemen at the North Africa American Cemetery and Memorial.

THE AZTEC NEWS LETTER

FIRST ANNIVERSARY EDITION

Edited by
DR. LAUREN C. POST
San Diego State College
San Diego, California

April 29, 1943
NO. 14

This issue sponsored by
PHI LAMBDA XI
and SHEN YO

To All of the Aztecs in the Service
and Their Friends:

A year ago this month a little mimeographed publication made its debut on the campus. It immediately gained popularity with the FIGHTING AZTECS as well as with those on the Home Front. This issue is the 14th and also the ANNIVERSARY EDITION of what has become the Aztec News Letter. An attempt was made to make each issue better than its predecessor even though the many chores connected with the project have grown in all dimensions.

It has grown rapidly during every month of its existence, and it has more than met all of the services that were originally expected of it. The address file has proved useful to faculty and students as well as to the men themselves. The AZTECS IN SERVICE panel has been an outgrowth of the News Letter and the address file.

And to our new members, we hope that you will always keep us informed of changes in address and promotions. Be sure to ask other Aztecs if they are getting their News Letters. In case they are not, please send in their addresses. Also, we still want your pictures showing the uniforms if possible.

And to the parents whom we sometimes place on the mailing list—please forward the News Letters unless they are addressed to you. In that case, your son is getting his own copy.

Cetza, a women's service organization on the campus, sponsored the enclosed cards. We read that some mail ships had been lost, but we sincerely hope that the News Letter always gets through. Please fill out the cards. DO IT NOW!

Thanks again for the nice letters. There were more than ever this time and consequently, more of them had to be cut down. Many a fine letter was reduced to a single sentence in this issue. The letters that you have written compensate many times over for all the work done on the News Letter. It makes one

Montezuma says: "The sun never sets on the FIGHTING AZTECS of San Diego State College." (Why shouldn't some of the **Sons of Montezuma** name their planes for old Monty?)

proud to be associated with such men. When you read Burdette Binkley's letter you will see what this means.

And again, best of luck,
Lauren C. Post
Editor of the News Letter

Lt. John Burdette Binkley

Lt. John Burdette Binkley was reported by the war department to have been "killed in action in Africa."

Recently he had written to his Mother and Dad in part:

"Dear Mother and Dad:

"Don't worry about me and how the war will affect me—that is without regard to actual physical injury. I mean emotionally and mentally. I believe that I am more stable now than ever before. What I mean is that I have probably reached a greater peace of mind. I am exposed to death fairly constantly, yet I can truthfully say that there is really no fear present. An occasional moment of nervous terror, yes—but if my number should come up, I am ready. . . . Yet I do have a very strong faith. It is not a faith to be put into words but rather

to be kept in heart. The 23rd Psalm and the Lord's Prayer give me a peace of mind that is real. Sometimes when I am flying I look out at the tremendous blue sky, the fleecy clouds, the earth below. I realize what a small yet somehow integral part of things I am. It constantly amazes me, this flying. . . . I don't know how you all feel about this war and how long it will last but I am afraid it is going to be a long one. It is going to be hard on you people at home and it will get harder. I know that we in the army are going to really see this thing through. I hope that the people at home do not tire of war until this is accomplished. When I look ahead I see a rather morbid picture but when I look back into history I see many which were equally frightful. Along with this morbid picture, I also see a very bright one. . . . A few years after the war is over our standards of living will be changed to a new undreamed of level. Possibly this war will wipe out racial and political boundaries uniting this world in an intelligent peace with plenty for all.

"I am getting tired so I will say good night. I am going to seal this up with-

9

AN AMERICAN KID

THE AZTEC NEWS LETTER
No. 14, April 29, 1943
To All of the Aztecs in the Service and Their Friends:
A year ago this month a little mimeographed publication made its debut on the campus. It immediately gained popularity with the FIGHTING AZTECS as well as with those on the Home Front. This issue is the 14th and also the ANNIVERSARY EDITION of what has become the *Aztec News Letter*. An attempt was made to make each issue better than its predecessor even though the many chores connected with the project have grown in all dimensions.

. . .

Lauren C. Post
Editor of the *News Letter*

During World War II, so many students and faculty from San Diego State enlisted that the college was forced to scale back on classes. At the time war broke out, about two thousand students could be found on campus.[1] By 1943, the editors of the campus yearbook noted a "constant stream of students and personnel leaving to join the Armed Forces," estimating that "at least two hundred and fifty left school after February."[2]

Some athletic events were cancelled, and band membership was "rationed," the editors' way of saying there weren't enough students to play all the parts. Students held fund-raisers and war assemblies, and the homecoming dance was reimagined as a victory ball. In 1943, pots, pans, and a few old cars were collected for a scrap drive. The university replaced glass panes in the doors with cardboard and added an air raid siren on campus.

San Diego was home to the Pacific Fleet, and the campus was designated a War Information Center. Students participated in air raid drills, and a new fitness program for men was dubbed "pre-commando training." The course included cross-country runs through local canyons and hills. Underclassmen who were physically able were required to take four and a half hours of general fitness training each week. When the instructors departed for military service, students took over running their own physical training program.

Fraternities and typing classes stayed busy helping Dr. Post assemble and mail the *News Letter*. Each edition included a note from Dr. Post, updates on promotions, and excerpts from some of the letters sent in by servicemen, servicewomen, and their families. Students also wrote personally to the servicemen and servicewomen, sending separate letters, especially during the holidays. By 1944 the holiday letter-writing campaign was sponsored by the Associated Student Council, and the yearbook staff noted that they had nearly achieved their goal of "A Christmas letter for every Aztec in the service!"[3]

On Christmas Day in 1943, when it was natural to think of family, Alfred Scott Jr. took the time to express his gratitude for a letter he had received from a student and for Dr. Post's *News Letter*.

✉ December 25, 1943

Dear Dr. Post.

I don't believe you know me, except as a listed Aztec. Let me introduce myself—I am Alfred G. Scott, Jr. . . .

Doc—this is rather a hard letter to write—since it is my first. And being my first, I feel very much ashamed for just *now* getting it off. For after all the *News Letters* I have received and the knowledge of the wonderful encouragement you have given us, there's no excuse I would offer that would be justified. Perhaps the greatest reminder of my lack of gratitude was the epistle I received from Adrienne Wueste sending me her and the School's wishes. You see I hadn't ever met her and receiving such a fine letter sponsored by you—well it kinda made me feel good. It's swell to know that there are folks at home pulling and praying for our safe return. It's what we all are fighting for, whether we realize it or not. To me— it's worth all the sacrifice. So Dr. Post—I sincerely thank you for what you have done and are doing! It helps us out here immeasurably. And to your co-workers, Adrienne & all the rest, my wholehearted thanks.

. . .

So wishing you the best New Year's I remain
Sincerely yours,
Alfred Scott, Jr.

The *News Letter* made it possible for a whole community to stay con- nected, but many private letters were also penned, their sentiments intended for Dr. Post alone. He was a father figure and confessor to those who faced battle. As they prepared to fight, they assured Dr. Post that they would emerge victorious, that their victory would be won for freedom and democ- racy, and that their efforts would lend meaning to the sacrifices made by so many. When they had no other way to express their feelings, the students turned to poetry.

June 7, 1943
Dear Dr. Post,
I want to thank you from the lowest depths of my heart for #15 issue of the *News Letter*. It's a wonderful source of news we soldiers of freedom could get from no other source. Of all the boys in the service, you, who are not actually in uniform, are doing the biggest and best job of all. We truly thank you.

Here's a poem I wrote while coming to Little Rock from California which expresses a thought that is so helpful to a soldier.

"On a Troop Train"
There's something verile about the American youth
Waving salutes to a passing troop train—
Hands full of dish rags, bats or balls
Or combing the air with their hands a-spread
What makes this commonplace thing an event?
What makes it a memory, a reflection?
What makes a kid wave and shout
To an unknown hero or a common gob?

If it's due to the signs the government prints—
"Smile—and say Hello!"—or "Give the boys a break!"—
Then may God demolish that hope-full habit!
No, tis not for some credo or order
Published from the hand that rules;
It's from the heart, the soul, and the mind
Of Americans old and new.
It's a gesture to wish Godspeed and cheer;
To remind us to think of home;
To wish each one more love and luck
Than the ones they wished before;
To remind us of faith, and hope, and care;
To remember the ones we have loved;
That and a million other "little" things.
I feel, that is a wave. Yes,
There's something verile about an American kid
Waving salutes to my passing troop train.
Pvt. James C. Cook
Co. D., 62 "Bn, 13" Reg.
1st Platoon
Camp Jos. T. Robinson
Arkansas

Dr. Post shouldered the concerns of parents too. The McAnulty family had two boys in the service—Wally, who was with the 251st Coast Artillery regiment stationed in Pearl Harbor during the attack and later in the South Pacific, and Ernie, a pilot who was captured and interned in a German prisoner-of-war camp. Mrs. Alta Grant and Mrs. Caroline Rock were two San Diego mothers who each sent several boys to war.

After World War II, the United States amended its draft laws so that families who had lost sons in combat were exempt from sending more children into service. The Special Separation Policies for Survivorship, commonly known as the Sole Survivor Policy, was updated in 1964 and again in 1971 so that any son or daughter from a family that has suffered a combat-related death may request an exemption, though the exemption may not apply if Congress declares a state of war.[4]

April 18, 1943

Dr. Post:

. . .

I had a letter from Harold last week and here is what he said. "I've met several San Diego State boys as Cadets. We all get a kick out of talking about San Diego and experiences. They sure enjoy the *News Letter* and so do I."

. . .

Russell who is a Lieut. (jg) is in Savannah, Georgia and it is warm there. I am enclosing his picture which I hope will cut down to the right size.

I hear each week from Floyd and of course you know there is little they can say except they keep busy and are well—

I forgot to say Russell said he receives the *News Letter* and enjoys it but is so busy he can't write.

Thanks again for the *News Letter* not only for myself but for each one of my boys.

Mrs. Alta S. Grant

1907 Robinson

San Diego, California

November 7, 1943

Dear Dr. Post—

You are doing such a splendid job with *Aztec News Letter* I want to show our appreciation. My sons, Rupert and Lincoln, write me they receive it regularly and I know what home news means to them when they're far away; as for myself, knowing so many Aztecs I read it from cover to cover.

Perhaps you don't remember my older sons, Gidi and Robert—they attended State. Gidi is at Consolidated—Robert went on to University of California, received his degree last June and was sent to Midshipmen's School at Columbia N.Y. He expects to graduate Nov. 24th when I hope he'll return to San Diego.

With three sons in the Navy I think I qualify as a Navy Mother, don't you?

Thanking you

I am sincerely yours

Mrs. Caroline Rock

1971 Ebers Street

San Diego, 7 California

✉ August 4, 1943
Dr. Post:

The *Aztec News Letter* has been following me to my new address, and although I do not know many of these boys that write letters to the *News Letter*, I would love to take every one of them in my arms and tell them what wonderful boys they are, and may every one of them come home better boys for their experience, horrible though it must be for a great many of them.

    Mrs. A. C. Flor
    Lakeside Farms

✉ January 21, 1944
Dr. Post:

The *News Letter* arrived yesterday, telling about the concert being given this evening by the College orchestra, for the benefit of the *News Letter*. It will be impossible to come to the concert, but find enclosed the price of two tickets. I started to say give the tickets to someone else, but don't do it, let them help in a small way also.

    Very truly yours,
    Mrs. A. C. Flor
    Lakeside Farms

Dorothy Searl had one son at Pearl Harbor and another flying the dangerous route from India to keep China supplied against the Japanese, and she was waiting to hear whether her third boy was alive. Through all of that she managed the accounts for the United States Army Mothers of San Diego.

✉ Undated
My Dear Dr. Post.

The United States Army Mothers of San Diego requested me to mail the enclosed check to you and to express our thanks for the work you are doing for our boys in service.

From time to time as our organization "enlarges" its bank account we will continue [to] send you more money to aid in this work.

I should like to add my personal check at this time also, and to request a change in the mailing address of my son. . . .

    Thanks.
    S. Dorothy Searl (Mrs. E. L.)
    4283 43rd St.
    San Diego, California

My Dear Dr. Post.

Thanks for adding my name to your mailing list, with the 14th copy. I have no back numbers but from now on will file these away for Eddy. . . .

Regarding my other sons. Herbert is not on the "Prisoner of War mailing list at Santa Tomas, Manila," we still hope he is alive, his wife, a former University of Washington girl, Janet F. Miles, is on the provost "mail list" but if the letters get in they do not let any answers out.

The second son [James Searl] attended State in 34-35 [and] played Frosh football . . . he would I'm sure appreciate any *News Letter* you could spare. The news of San Diego is scarce at Pearl Harbor; I try to send clippings.

. . .

Eddy's latest address is A.P.O. 882, 25th Fighter Squad. 10th U.S. Air Force; if you had word from him you probably know he has been in India since Nov. 16. . . . His base is Karachi and he ferries P38s from that part of Karachi to New Delhi then over into China & Burma. They return to base in a transport, then repeat.

. . .

Thanks for your work. It's grand.

Dorothy Searl

THE AZTEC NEWS LETTER
No. 16, July 1, 1943
LT. EDWARD L. SEARL, III
Lt. Edward L. Searl, III, was reported killed in action in the Asiatic area June 5th. He had been ferrying planes from Karachi into China and had more than 800 hours to his credit when he applied for and received a transfer to a combat area.

Eddy's older brother, Herbert H. Searl, is a prisoner of the Japanese in Manila. Another brother and Aztec, James Junior Searl, AMMIc, is stationed at the N.A.S. in Honolulu.

THE AZTEC NEWS LETTER
No. 38, May 1, 1945
LT. (JG) JAMES J. SEARL
is at NAS, Alameda, Calif. During his 35 months in the South Pacific he was awarded the Purple Heart for a wound received while trying to "reach his older brother, Herbert," who was just released from a Jap internment camp.

News trickled slowly from the different war theaters, and those at home had to gather up the bits and details and fit them together into a coherent global picture. In their letters, the servicemen said as much as they could, but their commentary was often limited to the perspective of their own units. Censorship didn't help; even when the men did try to give the details of their experiences, their letters were cut. Sometimes a word was omitted, and sometimes whole pages were sliced apart. And those who had been tested in battle were often reluctant to put all that they had witnessed into words.

✉ May 6, 1944
Dear Dr. Post:
I just received a letter from my son, Lt. A.H. Johnson, this morning and thought it might be of interest. He writes his letters as he used to write his college papers and they exasperate me beyond endurance. He leaves so much unsaid.

"I used the Major's brand new airplane to lead the squadron the other day, and when I got back it needed a new engine and a little patching up. He was a little browned up, so to speak, but he couldn't say much. They took a picture of the ship with a couple of hundred flak bursts in it, and sent it back to the newspapers in the States. They also sent back a shot of my bombardier and me to the papers."

The Major, I presume is Edwin Brewer of Chula Vista. And a ship holds seven men. I can only guess why they took a picture of two of them.

I do not know just who enjoys the *News Letter* most, the boys or the mothers. As many of the boys passed through my hands when they were little fellows in the Primary Dept. of the Mission Hills Sunday School, I am very much interested in the paper when I can waylay one of the college students going by and take their copy away from them.

Sincerely,
Isabel U. (Mrs. Elmer G.) Johnson
1626 Madison Ave.
San Diego, 3, California

Isabel Johnson had to wait until her son returned to learn the details of his missions, which she then proudly shared with Dr. Post. Her family was still in harm's way, however, as she had another son in the service. Some parents were fortunate to have sons return, while others endured the anguish of having a child wounded, missing, or killed in action.

December 30, 1944
Dear Dr. Post:

. . .

Arthur reached here the end of October and we did go out to State one afternoon, too late to find anyone around anywhere. So we took moving pictures of year old Arthur David on all sides of Montezuma, a favorite subject of his Dad's. . . .

Anyhow Arthur returned without a scratch after sixty five missions over Italy and France, leading the squadron or wing over thirty of them. He has the air medal with ten oak leaf clusters, the Distinguished Flying Cross, the Presidential Unit Citation, and his B-26 group were awarded the De Gaulle Croix de Guerre.

. . .

I am still interested in the *News Letter* because my younger son, who was just ready to enter State when he had to enter the army, is still planning to go when he comes back. . . . My son's last letter was from Germany. So I guess he is in the thick of it now. He is a radio man with the Field Artillery. But I'm still hoping he will get to State. . . .

Thanking you.
Isabel U. (Mrs. Elmer G.) Johnson
1626 Madison Ave.
San Diego, 3, California

January 20, 1944
Dear Sir:
I am enclosing herewith a clipping, which may be of interest to readers of your *Aztec News Letter*, if you have not already had it from some other source. I would appreciate its return in the enclosed self addressed envelope.

Jim has been in the SW. Pacific for more than six months—I turned in his address for mailing to your office. He has never mentioned receiving the *Letter*, but I know if he did, he enjoyed it, as must hundreds of your old "boys." I am enclosing a check to help a bit in continuing this service to them. You are doing a marvelous piece of war work. Jim or "Penny," as his brother Hods used to call him, is now reported "missing," having failed to return from a flight mission Dec. 5th. I am living just a day at a time, hoping and praying—trying to be a worthy mother of a marine flyer.

Yours truly,
Rose Miller (Mrs. J. A.) Parks
4805 Lee Avenue
La Mesa, California

✉ April 3, 1944
Dear Doc—

. . .

I want to thank you for Jim Park's information. I received a letter from his mother—he was last seen heading down to sea for a crash landing with 3 empty fuel tanks during a tropical storm. His wing men made it back—one landed with only 1 gal. of gas remaining—with hope that Jim (Penny) was adrift in the vicinity of the New Hebrides. This happened Dec. 5th—strangely enough, the day I was commissioned and given my wings.

His wing men claim Jimmy was the hottest pilot in operation off the "flattop." He was to have received a Lt. senior grade appointment in January. I still feel that he's O.K. He's too good a man to keep on the ground.

We have been flying P-63s—a new fast little fighter—really tops in my estimation. (But there are a few bugs in it yet to be shaken out. Last line not to be printed.)

. . .

Be good "Doctor Aztec" & best of luck Pardner—
Your Friend
Lt. Robert F. (Bob) Russell
0-762413
434th R.T.U. "Red Group"
c/o S.R.A.A.F.
Santa Rosa, California

Dr. Post tried to dig deeper into what his students had seen and done. He was driven by a desire to give them credit for their actions and to share their accomplishments with the college community. He knew that a personal narrative could convey more than a news account, and he encouraged servicemen and servicewomen to tell their stories immediately. He invited them to let ink flow onto the paper while the heat of battle still flowed through their veins. Too often, however, the servicemen found themselves unable to describe all that they'd been through, and when they couldn't tell their stories, sometimes their families tried to help.

In 1935 Dolores Bacon Gorton was a pledge to a social sorority, Sigma Pi Theta. Her photograph in the college yearbook shows a dark-haired young woman, eyes wide and serious under arched brows. Dr. Post relied on her natural inquisitiveness. When he requested information, Gorton put her research skills to work, gleaning facts from her reticent husband.

June 25, 1943

Dear Dr. Post:

This morning in the mail was a nice note from you and the *News Letter* which Mac is reading avidly at the moment. You have no idea, or maybe you do have, how much we enjoy catching up on all the dope about our old friends. It really gets better and better with each issue doesn't it?

About the decoration Mac received—it's like pulling teeth to get anything out of him but here is what I have managed to find out about it in the past three months:

While piloting a B-17 on a reconnaissance mission in the South West Pacific the latter part of 1942, Lt. Gorton and his crew sighted a Jap convoy. They shadowed the convoy for 6 hours during which time they were attacked 5 times by the Zeros. The citation was given for sticking to their job, bringing the ship home safely, and discovering the convoy in extremely bad weather. (P.S. from me: The casualties on the convoy were *terrific!*)

You see, Dr. Post—that's as much as I or my husband can tell you about it. There is still much hush, hush about so many things and we aren't sure what to let out for publication and what not to, but I hope that this will give you enough information for what you want.

Keep the *News Letters* coming and more power to you and your fine staff.

Sincerely,

Dolores Bacon Gorton (SD State 34 & 5)

(Mrs. MacArthur Gorton, Jr.)

632 North Nevada, Apartment 5

Colorado Springs, Colorado

When husbands were transferred within the states, wives were often able to go along. When the men went overseas, the women sometimes found themselves on their own in new cities. Dr. Post made every effort to send the *News Letter* to all members of each family. He also started a club for men who had never seen their infant children.

On May 20, 1943, Captain James E. Stacey, wrote, "After reading about the other Aztecs that have made their double bars and still twenty-three,

I sort of set my goal on the same principal and made it. I was promoted on May 15, 1943 to Captain and still have to reach my twenty fourth birthday. All this and heaven too."

July 7, 1943
Dear Dr. Post,

In looking at the last *News Letter*, I was interested in a letter from an Aztec who recently became a captain. He wrote that he had made his double bars before his twenty-fourth birthday, a goal he had set after reading of some other Aztecs who had received theirs while still twenty-three.

When I received a letter from my husband the very next day, telling me that he is now Captain Kenneth Scidmore, and he is still *twenty-two*, I just had to write you about it.

Naturally, I'm pretty proud of him. I think our boys are really proving themselves all over the world.

Did Kenny write you about his Airman's medal and Oak Leaf clusters? I believe he had three clusters the last time he mentioned it, which was some time ago. He's really seeing some of the geography we used to study.

Do you remember when Fern Menzel and I were always together? Since she's in Florida now with her husband, we have to be satisfied with long, "gossipy" letters.

If I ever manage to get near the college I hope I'll get a chance to see you again, but since I'm working at Rohr Aircraft (I have to help the Air Corps, of course) I seldom even see San Diego.

The *Aztec News Letter* is really splendid, and I know it means a lot to the boys. Keep up the good work, Dr. Post.

Sincerely,

Evelyn Durnbaugh Scidmore

August 10, 1943
Camp Shelby, Mississippi
Dear Dr. Post:

. . .

I would like to sort of apologize for a letter in which I sort of gloated over a promotion but it wasn't exactly that. I guess I was so happy that I didn't realize just how conceited it sounded until after I read it in the *News Letter*. I did not mean it to sound as it did for there are many men in the army, possibly Aztecs, who have made the Supreme sacrifice for their country without ever knowing the joy of a promotion. It is because of these men that others of us are having the opportunity to train for eventual combat and we appreciate it.

. . .

Sincerely,
James E. Stacey
Capt. 271st Infantry

More letters from Captain Stacey are in chapters 16 and 20.

The following short note was written on special stationery called V-Mail, or Victory Mail. After these letters were reviewed by censors, they were photographed and transported on microfilm to save space and weight. Before delivery, they were printed but only partially enlarged, and what arrived in the mailbox was a smaller version of the original.[5] Dr. Post called V-Mail letters "dehydrated mail." In *News Letter* No. 26, May 1, 1944, he wrote, "Wish someone would send me a reading glass."

March 7, 1944
V-Mail
Dear Doctor Post,

. . .

I should be eligible for your "infants' never seen" society. I have a son who will be a year old May 17th that I haven't seen.

. . .

Yours Truly,
Capt. R.W. Sullivan USNR
H & S Btry. 10th Marines
c/o Fleet Post Office
San Francisco, California

May 16, 1944
Dear Doc Post,
I was on the campus May 3 and tried to find you but without luck. I saw many of the other members of the faculty and some of the fellows I knew. I was going to make another visit to the college but couldn't find the time for it in my brief stay in San Diego.

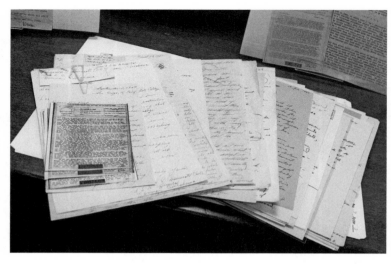

Letters in the World War II San Diego State College Servicemen's Correspondence Collection, 1941–1946, with V-Mail letters on top

. . . I spent most of my time in Coronado with my wife and daughter who was born April the eleventh. I was sure glad that my membership in your "I've Never Seen My Baby Club" was very brief.

. . .

Ens. H. B. (Horace) Walton
VP—92 F.P.O.
New York, N.Y.

Families had to endure the pain of separation, but fortunately for the wives of servicemen, the military was ready with helpful advice.

October 2, 1944
Dear Doctor Post:

. . .

The copy of the enclosed letter was sent to me by the Commandant of the Transportation Corps O.C.S., and I thought you might find it of interest.

Sincerely yours,
Jean C. Self

ARMY SERVICE FORCES
Transportation Corps School
New Orleans Army Air Base
New Orleans 12, Louisiana

27 September 1944
Mrs. Jean C. Self
4859 Monroe Street
San Diego, California
Dear Mrs. Self:
Your husband has just been enrolled as an officer candidate in the Transportation Corps School. Upon successful completion of his course he will be commissioned a Second Lieutenant in the Transportation Corps. He will then be subject, depending upon his special qualifications, to assignment to any one of hundreds of stations throughout the world. The purpose of this letter is to inform you of some of the policies which govern the operation of this school.

I think the most important rule or guide affecting your husband at this school may be summed up as follows: in dealing with officers or men, there is no arbitrary rule. Each case will be considered on its individual merits. Every officer on duty at the school prides himself in the knowledge that all of our candidates are applying themselves wholeheartedly toward gaining the maximum amount of information from their course of instruction, learning how to apply this information to problems which will confront them in their next assignments. Candidates are exerting themselves to the utmost in learning how to know, influence, and lead others.

. . .

During the time your husband is attending Officer Candidate School he will have less time for letter writing. You may not receive as many letters from him as you have in the past. This will not be because he does not want to write. It will be because his hours are crowded with hard work. On the other hand, it is important that he receive frequent letters from you. There will be times when he will be discouraged and exasperated by the exacting and arduous routine of Officer Candidate School. Therefore, it is most important that you write to him, always expressing a note on encouragement together with affirmation of your continued confidences in his success.

. . .

I want you to feel not only free, but dutybound, to communicate with me on any matter relating to the welfare and progress of the candidate in whom you are interested. I assure you that wholehearted and genuine cooperation will be your return.

Very truly yours,
Stephen W. Ackerman
Colonel, TC
Commandant

Dr. Post's nephew Bill Post was in the service, though his letters don't appear in the college's collection. He wrote privately to his family, and occasionally Dr. Post gave a report of him and his stories in the *News Letter*.

> ### THE AZTEC NEWS LETTER
> No. 26, May 1, 1944
> Cpl. W.L. Post, USMC, formerly of the Aviation Engineers, returned from the South Pacific to the San Diego Naval Hospital via the hospital in New Caledonia. When reduced to numbers or statistics his trip was simple: 18 months overseas; 13 months on Guadalcanal building air strips, digging ditches and foxholes, and loading gravel with a steam shovel; moving the steam shovel on a trailer 35 times on Guadalcanal; going out to Liberty ship to operate steam crane once; hours of liberty during 18 months, exactly zero; times in foxholes during bombings, 107.
>
> Bill's private Snow Jobs to your editor have been by far the most detailed to date, but surprisingly enough, without complaint even though the fellows often worked 12 hours per day and at times loaded 60 trucks per hour with gravel. He did admit that the rations "got awfully monotonous after the second meal." LCP.
> Dr. Lauren C. Post, Editor

Ens. George W. Peck served with an aircraft carrier task force and flew in several Pacific battles under the leadership of Vice Adm. Marc A. Mitscher. Peck put an Aztec sticker on the nose of his plane and during the Battle of Leyte Gulf was credited with sinking an enemy ship. Ensign Peck was promoted to lieutenant junior grade, and he made his father proud. The elder Peck was in New Guinea, and he tried to make light of the horrid conditions there. The Anopheles mosquito he mentions is the type that transmits malaria.

February 6, 1944
Dear Doc,

   . . .

Thanks for putting my pop on the list—I know he as well as I appreciated it. . . . He's in New Guinea now and by the way has been promoted from Warrant

Bosn' to Chief Warrant. Besides that he is now in line for (j.g.). Pretty damned good for an old Mustang with some 30 years service—how 'bout that. Doc, make some notation of that in the next issue will you? I know he wants the boys to know of it.

. . .

Best o'luck, Doc
Ens. G. W. (George) Peck
United States Pacific Fleet

February 14, 1944
In the Jungles of New Guinea
My Dear Mr. Post:
My son George W. Peck Ens. U.S.N.R. informs me he has asked that I be admitted as an honorary member to, I believe, the Student Body. I consider even the submission of my name an honor and even tho no action be taken, thank you for considering it.

I have been appointed a Chief Boatswain and as you know have been in the service 28 years and it is a great pleasure to me when George got his wings and appointment. I am Captain of the Yard now and that means Transportation here. We have principally (on the bad side) mosquitos, Anopheles, scorpions, boas (a few), and dysentery. The latter the most prevalent—on the good side beautiful butterflies, white Orchids but best of all Dead Japs.

Best of luck to you and yours,
George M. Peck
ex Bosn US Navy
Air Force
Bombing Squadron Nineteen
c/o Fleet Post Office
San Francisco, California

Vice Admiral Mitscher signed the citations decorating Lieutenant Peck. In addition to receiving the Air Medal, Lieutenant Peck was also awarded the Navy Cross, the second-highest military decoration for valor.

THE AZTEC NEWS LETTER
No. 33, December 1, 1944
Lt. (jg) George W. Peck was awarded the Air Medal for his part as a pilot in carrier based aircraft assigned to strikes against

enemy installation and shipping at islands of the Mariana, Palau, Kazan, Bonin and Philippine groups between July 18 and September 24. In spite of intense AA fire and air opposition, he performed his assignments in "an outstanding manner and materially assisted in inflicting damage upon the enemy." (The award was signed by Admiral Mitscher.)

Lt. (jg) George W. Peck received a second award during this month:

"In the name of the President of the United States, the Commander, First Carrier Task Force, United States Pacific Fleet, presents the Navy Cross to Lt. (jg) George W. Peck, USNR, for services set forth in the following citation:

'For distinguishing himself by extraordinary heroism in operations against the enemy while acting as a pilot in a carrier based bomber aircraft assigned to strike major Japanese Fleet Units on 25 October 1944, in the vicinity of the Philippine Islands. He pressed a dive bombing attack on an enemy aircraft carrier and obtained a direct hit in the face of enemy air opposition and extremely intense and continuous antiaircraft fire that appreciably contributed to the sinking of same. His courage and skill were at all times in keeping with the highest traditions of the naval service.'

M. A. Mitscher, Vice Admiral,

U.S. Navy"

Nearly half of the students from San Diego State College who lost their lives in the war were pilots.[6] Pilots got a jump start in training in the Aztec Aero Club, and State was one of the first campuses to take part in the Civilian Pilot Training Program. Beginning in 1938, young men and women at colleges around the country received flight instruction. The training was considered essential for defense, even before the United States entered World War II.[7]

The 1939 *Del Sudoeste*, the San Diego State College yearbook, shows a picture of Tom Cozens crouched in a defensive lineman position. The following year, Tom was voted the favorite Aztec player at the homecoming game. His brother Robert (Bob) Cozens also played varsity football. They along with their younger brother, Richard, all trained as pilots.

Tom Cozens' plane went down in a storm during a training exercise, and his brother Richard was killed in an accident right after he received his wings.

October 19, 1942

Geiger Field, Washington

The shock of Tom's sudden death has gradually worn away and now it is hard for me to realize that he really has left us. I feel now that I have a little personal grudge to satisfy in this war and I am becoming more and more anxious to get over there where I can do something about it.

I am flying B-17 "flying fortresses" here and really do like them. Also flew some of Consolidated's B-24 "Liberators" the first month I was here—they are a "sweet" ship also.

Lt. Robert C. Cozens

391st Bomb Squad

Undated

Can't tell you how shocked I was to read about the Cozens boys. There must have been a mistake somewhere as both couldn't have been killed. One tragedy such as that in such a fine family is certainly enuf'. I was with them both last year at this time and the memories are very poignant. I guess the war has reached a stage that a few of our fellas must go but a guy hates to hear about it.

C. Thomas McGraw

PhM 3/c USNR

Robert Cozens, who lost his brothers, became a founding member of the committee that erected a war memorial at San Diego State University, and he lived to see its dedication in 1996. Names are engraved on a smooth face, but the top edge is ragged, like metal torn from a plane. The monument stands so that students coming from the trolley station on their way to the library or heading into the student union building will pass by the names of Aztecs who died in military service.

THE AZTEC NEWS LETTER

Montezuma welcomes home Lt. Col. and Mrs. Robert C. Cozens. Mrs. Cozens is the former Patricia Ann Hamrick, Aztec cheer leader when Bob was a football hero. Bob piloted the Patsy Ann, a B-17, on 25 bombing missions over Europe without even getting his nose skinned. The Patsy Ann went down after Bob's last mission.

July 1, 1944
No. 28

**This Issue Sponsored
in part by
Theta Chi
Omega Xi**

Edited by
DR. LAUREN C. POST
San Diego State College
San Diego 5, California

**To All Aztecs in Service and
Their Friends:**

At the time of this writing the invasion is four days old. News is still meager, but it seems that the Atlantic wall has been cracked on a broad front. The part that seemed to be most terrifying in the pre-invasion thinking has been accomplished, and we are on the beach to stay and to expand. Losses have not yet been reported.

State College is represented in every phase of the invasion, and each day and hour we name a great many of you who are in on it, and we think of many more, wondering how you are faring and wishing you the best. What individual deeds of heroism you have accomplished we can never know, but we do know that you are in on everything, and that you are represented in all organizations. You have seen every type of action, and at this time we want to pay tribute to the GIs who are really down close to it with hand grenades, machine guns and mortars. Their part is as essential to the teamwork of the cause as any, but without the rank, the pay, the decorations, or the glamor. We just want to let you know that the hundreds of you, in your essential capacities, are not forgotten even while we are publicly paying tribute to those about whose exploits we have heard. We take off our hats to those who pass unnoticed. And lest we forget, we have men on all of the other fronts enduring and overcoming the worst that appears in their various theaters of operation.

The picture panel showing the AZTECS IN SERVICE has grown. We have added an extra section and a great many new pictures. We still want pictures, especially those showing you in uniform. Keep sending them in along with the changes in address and in rank. We are always glad to hear from you even though we don't have a chance to print all of your letters. Thanks just the same.

And again, best of luck!

Lauren C. Post,
Editor of the News Letter

10

ROGER AND OUT!

THE AZTEC NEWS LETTER

No. 20, November 1, 1943

I have been in the WAC since June and am thoroughly sold on it and only wish that more of our girls would decide to join.

Pvt. Ethelmae Scholder

San Diego State College was founded as a teacher's college to prepare women to become elementary school teachers, and women were part of campus life from the very beginning. The first graduating class had twenty-six students in all, and twenty-three of them were women.[1] Education had always been a priority for the women of State, and during the war years, they again turned to teaching, this time instructing pilots in flight simulators.

The Link Trainers, named for their designer, Edwin A. Link, taught instrument flying, which helped keep planes in the air even in conditions of poor visibility.[2] The Army Air Corps (later the Army Air Forces) also relied on meteorologists to assist with flight plans. Different types of training aircraft are mentioned in the following letters.

June 27, 1943

Dear Mr. Post,

. . .

I am a link trainer instructor and I've been looking forward to meeting some San Diego cadets. The cadets actually detest the links, though—just ask some of them, but they all have to go [through] the ordeal of instrument training. It is interesting work and after all the time I've spent in a link I feel like I could easily fly one of the SNJs.

> Mary E. Daggett
> SP(T) 3/c, V-10, U.S.N.R.
> T.S. TBB
> U.S. Naval Air Station
> Corpus Christi, Texas

September 23, 1943

Dear Doc—

. . .

After my boot training I was sent to Atlanta, GA to Link Trainer Instructor School. Sorority sister Pat Layton was sent to Atlanta too—to Control Tower Operator's School. We both feel that we got the "plums" of Wave schools.

I met Lt. Ed Totten U.S.M.C.R. at the base. He was taking an Instrument Flight Instructor's School course. In other words Ed teaches pilots in the Air—the same stuff I teach 'em in the "Links."

After I received my rate I was sent to Corpus Christi and thence to Beeville, Texas, an auxiliary field. Here I ran into Ed again. I can't talk to him officially—but he suggested—and I'm hoping that he can give me some real flight instruction. I rate flight time, you know—when I can get it.

. . .

Well, take good care of my Alma Mater until I get back. I know it's in good hands.

> Sincerely,
> Dusty
> $1 (encl.)
> P.S. Uncle pays me too much—
> Sp (T) 3/c Virginia L. Miller USNR
> T. Squadron 13-C

U.S.N.A.S.
Chase Field, Naval Air Training Center
Beeville, Texas

February 14, 1944
Dear Dr. Post,

. . .

I like the Marine Corps very much. This probably is due greatly to the fact that I like my work so well. I'm a Link Trainer Instructor. Flying by instruments is an entirely new world to me. All of us in this department are determined to learn contact flight when this war is over. Our pupils are the pilots, most of whom have just arrived from overseas. We really get quite a slant on the war from them. They are all grand fellows and nice to work with. It really gives one a weird feeling to be telling a Major or a Capt. or a Lieutenant what to do—especially when one is only a Corporal.

. . .

Sincerely
Corp. Shirley Schmetzer MCWR
Synthetic Training
MCAS
Santa Barbara, California

The Women's Army Auxiliary Corps was created in 1942 as an all-volunteer organization that trained women to take over men's jobs as the men shifted to combat duty. Initially the women served as civilians, but in 1943 the auxiliary status was dropped, and the Women's Army Corps became part of the U.S. Army.[3]

August 13, 1943

. . .

Seems only a minute ago since we were all happily meandering over State's campus. What a world!

I am in the W.A.C., and at present am stationed at Newark, New Jersey. I am attending Radio School (maintenance) at present and enjoying it very much. It gets rather hard at times, but doesn't anything that's worth while? The hardest part of going to school is the waiting to be sent out into the field to really *do* something. As far as army life, it's perfect; and if any prospective lass should ask you about the WAC, give her my word for it that she'd love it—that is, if she doesn't mind *working*.

I won't mind in the least if my name isn't printed in the *News Letter*, because it is certainly more interesting to hear from our boys overseas. The space is rightfully theirs. Just send me the next edition is all I ask. I enjoy it more than anything I receive thru the mail, and it must mean just that much more to the fellows overseas.

Very sincerely,
Cpl. Celia E. (Ellen) Brown
Group 10W U.R.T.I.
1244th S.U.
96-100 Washington
Newark, New Jersey

War, with its insatiable need for supply lines to deliver machines, ordnance, fuel, and food to troops around the world, created a cyclone of industrial demand, and women were pulled into the workforce. They helped the war effort through their work in communications and military intelligence, mechanics, public relations, and war industries such as shipbuilding and aircraft manufacturing. Industrial occupations offered better wages than women had earned in more traditional work, such as clerical roles. American manufacturing began to pick up the pace even before the United States entered the conflict, and by the war's end, overall national production had doubled.[4]

Women got a boost from Eleanor Roosevelt, who was never content to perform only the traditional duties of a first lady. Known for her work to further women's and civil rights, Roosevelt made an excellent role model. She traveled, wrote for the papers, and championed women as equal partners in society.[5] Following her lead, women flexed their muscles, earned rank and respect, and paved the way for the next generation of working women.

November 3, 1942
Dear Dr. Post:
Even though the *News Letter* strikes a predominately masculine note, this skirted soldier is most grateful to you for news from the home front.

My duties are to encourage the women in the state of Virginia to enroll for the duration plus six months in the Women's Army Auxiliary Corps. I find this a twenty-four hour a day job, weekends no exceptions—planning publicity, news releases, radio broadcasts, speaking before various club groups, touring the state, and interviewing and examining applicants.

. . .

But none of us are losing sight of the fact that our main purpose is to take over the jobs and replace men so they can be released for active combat duty.

Esther E. Pease

3rd Officer, WAAC

206 Lyric Bldng

Richmond, VA

February 14, 1943

Dear Dr. Post,

I'm in the army now, a full fledged Waac. It's almost a week since I arrived here at Fort Des Moines and I have really worked since that time. Scrub that floor! Wash that window! Shine those shoes! Orders, orders. Honestly we are on the go every minute. But I love it.

. . .

If the girls only realized how badly they are needed, I know that more would come. This is something more important than staying home and being comfortable and safe. It's something bigger than individual, personal lives. I just wish they could hear a few of the speeches we heard our first days here.

. . .

This is the day Mrs. Roosevelt inspects the post, so we have everything spic and span. Word has just come that she passed by. I didn't see her but I was close.

. . .

An ex-geography student,

Aux. Barbara Woollet

12 Co. 3 Regt.

A.P.O. Fort Des Moines

Des Moines, Iowa

April 29, 1943

Dear Dr. Post,

When a person is in the army, there is so little time to write. It just doesn't seem possible that one can be so busy. Tonight I am what is known as C.Q. (Charge of

Quarters) so I must remain right in the hotel every minute. Therefore I am taking this opportunity to write letters.

Radio school is still going strong. I am slowly but surely becoming a radio operator. At times we become dit crazy, but it's part of the army so we love it. It's so thrilling to realize that we are learning something that will be so useful in this war program. Every girl works so hard to come through with flying colors so she can release a man for combat duty.

. . .

As soon as the army goes into summer uniform, I'll have some pictures taken. I want to have mine up there with the "Aztecs in Service." It will make me very proud to be beside those brave boys that are really doing the fighting. We've got to hand it to them. Our Aztecs are really made of the best.

. . .

Sincerely,
Sgt. Barbara Woollet
Normandy Hotel Room 411
Kansas City, Missouri

March 6, 1944
Dear Dr. Post—

. . .

Here at Aberdeen we test all types of Army arms and ammunition. I am working at the bombing field. We photograph and compute the speed of bombs falling from an airplane and other work we don't talk or write about. It's work which directly affects the bombings in Europe.

The Wacs are doing a good job here. They do everything! Some of them test trucks and heavy artillery. They are all happy with their jobs.

Thank you so much for sending the *News Letter* to me. . . .
Pvt. Betty J. Whitaker A917916
Wac Detachment Bks. 4009
Aberdeen Proving Ground
Maryland

May 10, 1944
Dear Dr. Post

. . .

I'm going to radio operator's school for five months. . . .

The man situation is terrible here. About 5,000 girls to 500 men. Even a uniform isn't enough to get a man here.

. . .

Sincerely,
Mary L. Omar S/c USCGR
USCG Radio School
138 So. Virginia Ave.
Atlantic City, New Jersey

Women who signed on with the WAVES—Women Accepted for Volunteer Emergency Service—became part of the Navy.

February 5, 1944
Dear Dr. Post
I have been receiving *The Aztec News Letter* and I have certainly enjoyed reading it. Thank you very much for sending me each copy.

My work here is intensely interesting and, although quite confidential, I believe it is safe to give you a general idea of the type of thing I am doing. I work at the Information Center in Norfolk, and my duties are to take flight plans of all Navy planes flying in this defense area. There are four WAVE Ensigns on this assignment and we are the first four to have held such a position in the United States. We are the ones who sit up on the glassed-in balcony and identify targets as they appear on the grid.

We had to learn all types of planes as to names, like F6F etc., and type—single, bi, multi, sea or land. Also we must know this part of the country pretty thoroughly, which was a task for me. I would have been much more useful on the West Coast. We had to learn all the call signs for each field, some 100 or more. Besides we have to be able to read a grid, which I can explain to you better after this is all over.

You have perhaps gathered by now how much I love my work and how fascinating it is.

. . .

We stand watches around the clock, usually two day watches, two swing watches and one mid-watch with forty-eight hours off, twenty-four of which are used in catching up with our sleep.

I miss you all at school and will be so glad to be back and see you again. I should like to be remembered to my friends at State.

. . .

Very sincerely,
Laura E. Chase, Ensign USNR
705 Stockley Gardens
Norfolk 7, Virginia

Nursing shortages were evident even before World War I, and Congress responded by creating the United States Army Nurse Corps. A similar branch for the Navy soon followed. At about the same time, the American Red Cross was chartered to provide relief in times of national disaster and to assist the military during times of war. The National Committee on Red Cross Nursing Service was formed, and local chapters began maintaining lists of qualified nurses. The hope was to create a reserve from which nurses could be called for service, but the shortage persisted, especially during World War I.[6]

Part of the difficulty was that women who joined the Red Cross Nursing Service were required to have attended an accredited nursing school. (Other requirements included that she be a U.S. citizen and unmarried.) The strict accreditation guidelines helped to create a class of professional women, but schools couldn't train nurses quickly enough to meet wartime demand. The solution came in the form of Red Cross Nurses' Aid courses, which provided skilled volunteers to assist in hospitals during both World Wars.[7]

During World War II, government funds were allocated to the Public Health Service to develop and improve nursing programs, and the job of recruiting student nurses fell to the U.S. Cadet Nurse Corps. At the time, women had their pick of high-paying jobs, so the corps used incentives to make the rigorous nurses' training more attractive. When a student enrolled in an accredited school, her tuition was paid, and she received a monthly stipend. After graduation, she was required to serve throughout the war.[8]

July 1, 1944
Hello Dr. Post,
Just decided it was high time I sent in my thanks for the swell copies of *News Letter* that have been coming my way in recent months. Have to admit my patients

suffer whenever I come back from the post office with one for I promptly sit down and ignore all work except the CO until I have read it from cover to cover. Am afraid not many Aztecs find themselves stuck (and I do mean stuck) in this part of Texas. . . .

I've been here at Maxey for 18 months and it begins to look as if I'll be here for the duration plus. They keep sending my girls overseas about as fast as I get them trained and commissioned, but still I stay. . . . They are all in England now. Am beginning to believe I know more people over there now than I do on this side. . . .

You are certainly doing a swell job with the *News Letter*. I know how much I appreciate it, so think of what it means to the kids across the pond. Keep it up!

More another time,

L. B. (June) Prescott, 1st Lt. PTA

Regional Hospital

Camp Maxey, Texas

August 21, 1944

Dear Dr. Post—

From somewhere in New Guinea, I am wondering where you found my name and address to send me the *News Letter*. Possibly, you obtained it through my sister who is still a loyal Aztec.

. . .

At the present time we Army nurses in the Southwest Pacific are looking with envy at our fellow members in the European theatre. Before this is finished, however, I think that we will have our share of work to do.

We are living a life of luxury compared to our first weeks here. Of course, we dream of hot water showers, of dresses and feminine shoes, and of those good Stateside steaks; and now we are accustomed to this community living and the self-sufficient attitude we are developing. Never before did I do any carpenter work, and now I swing a "mean" hammer.

Your *News Letter* is a wonderful bond between us and the States, and I hope to receive more copies so that I can learn more of the Aztecs in the Service.

Sincerely Yours,

Jeanne Quint

2nd Lt. ANC

80 Gen Hosp. APO 928

c/o P.M. San Francisco, California

THE AZTEC NEWS LETTER

No. 38, May 1, 1945

Lt. Alice F. McDaniel wrote from the 226th General Hospital in France:

"Would you please tell any Aztec who might pass through our hospital to ask for me. I would be very happy to see them.

"There isn't a lot I can tell you about my work except that I would not change places with anyone I know. Believe me, we have in our great army the finest, bravest lads in the world. I have every reason to know. It is my solemn wish that they let the Army nurses plan the next world conflict. I rather fancy it would be conspicuous by its absence."

THE AZTEC NEWS LETTER

No. 43, October 1, 1945

1st Lt. Alice F. McDaniel is back from the ETO where she served with the 226th General Hospital in France just below Rheims. She was overseas for 10 months and during that time cared for patients who had been battle casualties in the Rhineland fighting. The Rhine bridgehead fighting brought their unit most of its casualties. They were flown back to them in C-47s. Lt. McDaniel's hospital gave them their first care, gave them baths and food, and in about 24 hours they were moved over to England for more permanent treatment and care.

. . . She has the Rhineland campaign badge with one battle star.

Some of the most highly trained women were WASPs, Women Airforce Service Pilots, who worked as civilians under the Army Air Forces. Many of the women received their initial flight instruction through the Civilian Pilot Training Program, overseen by the Civilian Aeronautics Authority.[9] Combat pilots were in great demand, and because women were not allowed to fight, they took over jobs in other areas, including flying transport planes, thus freeing up qualified male pilots to take fighters and bombers into battle. Only men were trained in gunnery and had military status. The WASPs completed the same basic and advanced courses and flight training as men and earned a commercial pilot's rating and military wings. WASPs were rated to fly military planes, and they transported them between bases or to airfields around the country from the factories where the planes were being rapidly constructed. [10]

The following letter was written on stationary imprinted with the WASP mascot, a female gremlin with wings known as Fifinella.

October 27, 1943

Dear Dr. Post.

What a wonderful and complete surprise it was to me to receive the *Aztec News Letter*—which heretofore was quite unknown to me! I would sincerely like to become a steady customer and receive your monthly issues.

Although Texas isn't oceans away from San Diego, hearing about old friends, acquaintances, and former classmates does wonders for the morale!

May I say a few words about my favorite subject—flying? The training offered the Women Pilot Trainees (officially WASPs—Women's Airforce Service Pilots) equals that of any Army cadet school! Imagine getting paid for "all this and heaven too!" The five months course consists of Primary, Basic, and Advanced training. We fly the same trainers as cadets and are *told* that in most ways our flying equals theirs, and in some respects even surpasses it!

Although we are still civilians, our induction into the Army Air Corps is expected in the very near future, plus commissions as flight officers with the same rank and privileges as the men. Kinda crowding the fellows, aren't we, Dr?

But we are not here for glamour, for these Army G.I. overalls ("zoot zuits") which we wear constantly are anything but! We all feel that our love of flying and the desire to help *our* country win the war makes a valuable combination!

I am now in Advanced training, flying the smoothest most ambidubilating— as P.A. Duich so aptly puts it, (—by the way, he and I made a bet in Arizona some months ago that he would have his captaincy by February—wonder if he will make it?!) training craft in the air!

The only item the fellows have in the curriculum that we do not have are formation flying and gunnery. Dr. Post, what have the girls who took the C.A.A. course at State done with their flying?

. . .

God willing, I shall graduate, about the middle of December. I am angling for B-17 school! My first visit in San Diego will be paid to see "Monty"!

. . .

My post-war plans are to return to SAN DIEGO STATE COLLEGE and finish my schooling.

May I here extend my thanks to whomever placed my name on your mailing list. I am deeply indebted to him (or her). This letter and future ones I want to write I feel will restore the grand old feeling about State that I have somehow lost since I left S.D.

. . .

As we flyers say
ROGER AND OUT!
Jeanne E. Robbins
43-W-8
318 AAFFTD
Avenger Field
Sweetwater, Texas

Women pilots flew every type of plane during World War II, including basic and advanced trainers. The P-51 Mustang, a fighter plane made by North American Aviation, was designated as a pursuit aircraft. The Boeing B-17 and the B-24 Liberator made by Consolidated Aircraft were bombers.

Unlike their WAC sisters, the women pilots remained civilians. They did not receive veteran benefits, and when they were killed in training or while on active duty, they were not accorded military honors. Jeanne Robbins stated her desire for a military commission, but her wish did not come true during the war. Veteran status was finally granted in 1977, and the women who had served as pilots were eventually awarded the Congressional Gold Medal. The ceremony took place in 2010, with some of the surviving WASPs present to receive their medals.[11]

April 18, 1944
Hello Dr. Post,

. . .

My job here is Engineering Test Pilot. (Incidentally, I graduated from Sweetwater Training School in December!) As Test Pilots the four WASPs here fly BTs and AT-6s. We test hop these ships for any and everything. This job is very interesting, and I have learned so much more about flying in the three months I

Jeanne E. Robbins
43-W-8
318 AAFFTD
Avenger Field, Sweetwater, Texas

Jeanne E. Robbins

October 27th
Avenger Field

Dear Dr. Post,

What a wonderful and complete surprise of the news letter it was to me to receive the AZTEC NEWS LETTER – which heretofore was quite unknown to me! I would sincerely like to become a steady customer, and receive your monthly issues.

Although Texas isn't oceans away from San Diego, hearing about old friends, acquaintances, and former classmates 'does' wonders for the morale!

May I say a few words about my favorite subject – flying? The training offered the Women Pilot Trainees (officially WASPs – Women's Airforce Service Pilots) equals that of any Army cadet school! I imagine getting paid for "all this and heaven too!" The five months course consists of Primary, Basic, and Advanced training. We fly the same trainers as cadets and are told that in most ways our flying equals theirs, and in some respects even surpasses it!

Although we are still civilians, our induction into the Army Air Corps is expected in the very near future, plus commissions as flight officers with the same rank and privileges as the men. Kinda crowding the fellows, aren't we, Dr?

Letter from Jeanne E. Robbins, October 27, 1943

have been here than I ever could have learned in training. The reason, I believe, is because the pressure is off now and we relax. To be able to relax is one of the keys to becoming a "Hot Pilot."

Until the bill, now in Congress, to militarize WASPs into the Army Air Corps is passed or rejected we will continue to be tossed around—alternately as "Feather Merchants" (civilians working for the Army) or J.B.s (junior birdmen— in the Army under Civil Service pay). 'Tis truly most confusing to everyone! If the Bill is passed we will be commissioned as 2nd Lts. or Flight Officers on exactly the same status as flying officers. We do hope they (the Army) will decide to want us, because we hear many rumors from numerous sources that we are unwanted.

Marana Air Field, I have discovered through gripes written me from other WASPs stationed elsewhere, is an *ideal* base. Consequently, I am not in a hurry to leave, except that I am very anxious to get checked out in a P-40, P-47, P-51, or any pursuit. (Not ambitious am I?!) The WASPs have officially been checked out in every plane except the B-24, as far as I know.

With sprinklings of XCs (cross-countrys) on weekends, and a few Ferry Trips across the continent life couldn't be and isn't all dull for me.

. . .

Until next time—best of luck with your grand, A-1 (1-A) *News Letter*.
Very Sincerely,
Jeanne E. Robbins
WASP
Marana Army Air Field
Tucson, Arizona

One servicewoman writing to Dr. Post was stationed with a WAC unit attached to the U.S. Fifth Army in North Africa, and she had a front row seat for the initial stages of the European invasion. Her letters reflect her homesickness for training grounds in Hawaii, but she learned to make do with desert privations. The Lister bag she mentions took its name from William Lyster, who served in the Army medical corps and developed a method for purifying water in large canvas bags. The bags were suspended from tent poles, and the spigots at the bottom made it easy to dispense the treated water.

Bob Wade, whose letters are in chapter 7, was in Africa long enough to endure every harsh season. In a letter to Dr. Post, he wrote, "Water in the lister bags is practically boiling. Temperature yesterday hit 122 degrees here, and I'm told it was even hotter out on the line."

August 7, 1943

Dear Doc Post:—

Here is another Aztec somewhere in North Africa. This time my Aloha sent to you is a far cry from Aloha land.

We're really roughing it at the moment, living in tents, with good clean sand for our floor; eating out of mess kits, & drinking water from a Lister bag. It's all new to me, and very fascinating. You can be sure I'm going to make the most of it. We're allowed (it seems) one candle, per day, or nite as you will, when it goes out, we go to sleep. I've never been in so early before. Oh yes, I'm also getting to be an expert washing in a helmet, god, that sounds silly, but you know what I mean.

I still can't believe I'm here, it all looks like a picture out of the Nat'l Geographic, or a Geography book. The natives in all their filth are very picturesque on the little donkeys they ride, & the first camels I've seen outside of a zoo. Even the heat isn't too bad.

I've traveled quite a bit since I last saw you haven't I. And still have not taken a picture for the service flag. See Bea, perhaps she can scare one up, and I really mean scare.

The trip over was wonderful. Not a day of seasickness, never missed a meal. Lots of sunshine, fresh air, and wonderful meals.

I know quite a few of the boys from State are somewhere in these parts also. Would like nothing better than to run into them some time.

. . . Keep the *News Letter* coming my way, it should prove even more interesting now.

. . .

Lots of Aloha as usual,

Aux. E. V. (Eleanor) Spinola

On August 12, 1944, Jim Hurley, an infantryman who was in North Africa and later in Italy, wrote to Dr. Post from Headquarters Fifth Army: "By the way, I have come to learn that Eleanor Spinola is in this headquarters. Am I right? Anyway, when the King of England was here, she was among the WAC reviewed by His Majesty. She was later interviewed by the Stars and Stripes, and it was thru this that I found out she was here."

✉ August 24, 1943

Dear Doc Post—

. . .

We are ideally situated, our living quarters sumptuous; food is excellent & the climate wonderful. In fact the Mediterranean is practically at our back door. . . .

The fellows we work with are very nice & we get along splendidly. They gave us a royal welcome. Some had never seen a Wac before so we were quite a novelty. Naturally we love being in the limelight & still are very proud to be here as we are. When will the *News Letter* catch up with me? I'm losing touch with the "outside" & State College. Send them please!

Pau for now—Aloha,

Aux. E. V. (Eleanor) Spinola, A-9028889

182d. W.A.C. Hq. Platoon, 5th Army

A.P.O. # 464, c/o Postmaster

New York, N.Y.

✉ September 2, 1943

Dear Doc Post—

Today I am a private. Yesterday was an important day in my life, when I was sworn into the W.A.C. Now I really feel as if I am "in" things. The ceremony was brief but impressive. The platoon was sworn in en masse, but our officers took their oaths individually. After taking the oath, Gen. Clark addressed us briefly, welcoming us, etc. into the army. Other high officials were there too, to sort of add a bit of prestige to the affair. Now I have two ribbons (pins) to wear. One is for reenlistment, the second for theater of operations. Along with the 5th Army patch on my sleeve, I look somewhat like a Christmas tree. Ah yes, the other day I was fortunate in catching a glimpse of [censored] and other high officials. Truly I never thought I'd be seeing these things. Join the WAC and see the world (or part of it anyway) is proving to be true for me.

. . .

Pau for now, Aloha,

Pvt. E. V. (Eleanor) Spinola, 9028889

182 W.A.C. Hq. Pltn, 5th Army

A.P.O. # 464, c/o P.M.

New York, N.Y.

Gen. Mark Clark addressed Eleanor Spinola's platoon on September 1, 1943. His Fifth Army was already poised for the invasion of Salerno and attacked at dawn on September 9. Spinola was behind the lines but following rapidly as General Clark pushed toward Naples. It was rough going, with the retreating Germans leaving destruction in their wake.[12] Spinola kept up her spirits, and the women pulled their weight, but it must have been impossible to ignore the fact that Salerno was taken at the cost of 3,500 American casualties. Additionally, Spinola found no comfort in the local cuisine; the only thing worse than the local wine, in her opinion, was a fermented concoction downed by servicemen in Hawaii. She strongly preferred Coca-Cola.

September 21, 1943

Dear Doc;

That long awaited *News Letter* finally caught up with me here in No. Africa. . . . It's strange to read letters from the boys telling about Arabs, Vino, French, the filth, and assorted smells. I don't think I'll ever forget the smells of "Arab Gulch" as we call the gully back of our quarters. At night they seem to be most potent. Then there is the whiff of garlic and wine of a Frenchman one gets passing by them. Lord deliver me from Vino, one taste was enough. That stuff seems to be almost as bad as Okolehao.

. . .

I wonder where Lionel Chase saw that Coca Cola. We had some about three weeks ago when out to a C.P.O. dance, and it was good!!! Seems the longer I stay in this town the more I find wrong with it, still I have fun, and don't think I'll ever forget it, so much of importance has happened to me here.

. . .

The usual Aloha,

Pvt. E. V. (Eleanor) Spinola, A-9028889

182 W.A.C. Hq. Pltn, 5th Army

A.P.O. # 464, c/o P.M.

New York, N.Y.

July 22, 1944

Dear Doc Post—

. . . One of the girls told me the other day I was becoming somewhat muscle bound. But that comes from lifting barracks bags & foot lockers. Believe it or not, we've been moving so fast and so often that we're old experienced hands at loading and unloading trucks of our own equipment. The only thing we haven't done yet is put up our pyramidal tents, and I won't be surprised if one of these days I find myself driving stakes etc. At first we had G.I.'s help us move, then they couldn't be spared so we had Italian help. It seems now they can't be spared either so we've been doing our own work, almost all of it, and it's fun too.

. . .

And being with Fifth Army is proving to be an education in itself, even tho I'm seeing Italy sort of on the hit or miss fashion. For instance we've made four moves in little more than a month, trying to keep up with things. . . .

I remember the day I walked into your office with the news that I had enlisted in the WAAC, as it was then, and now I'm half way round the world from home.

. . .

Pau for now—and here's the usual

Much Aloha

Eleanor V. Spinola

THE AZTEC NEWS LETTER

No. 44, November 1, 1945

T/5 Eleanor V. Spinola has returned to San Diego and is again a civilian after 31 months in the WAAC and the WAC, 26 months of which time was spent on duty in the Mediterranean Theater of Operations. Eleanor has the MTO campaign ribbon with battle stars for the Naples-Foggia, Romano, North Apennines and the Po Valley campaign. She also has a Unit Citation for Meritorious Service and the Bronze Star Medal. Altogether she had a total of 79 discharge points.

THE AZTEC NEWS LETTER

No. 47, February 1, 1946

The marriage last December 9th of Eleanor Spinola to Richard Lange of Chicago in St. Mary's church in National City culminated a courtship that, appropriately, began on Capri. Dick was a much-decorated member of the 15th Air Force, and Eleanor was a member of the first WAC contingent to reach the MTO when they drew seven-day passes and met at a rest camp on the famed and romantic isle.

Eleanor's parents who reside in Hilo, T.H., were represented by Dr. Lauren C. Post of State College who gave the bride away and Mrs. J.R. Hollingsworth. . . .

Thelma Chamberlain

THE AZTEC NEWS LETTER

October 1, 1943

This Issue Sponsored in Part by Phi Kappa Gamma

Edited by
DR. LAUREN C. POST
San Diego State College
San Diego, California

To All of the Aztecs in the Service and Their Friends:

If I were to dedicate the work of editing this issue to anyone, I would dedicate it to our men at Salerno. That beach has been in my mind during much of this work. How much we owe to those who gave so much!

The fall semester is under way as usual, but now I have a part-time secretary. Mrs. Elizabeth King helps me with the adddresses, typing, and correspondence. I now have two offices, one for Geography and one for the News Letter. The new office is A. 108½ and will be remembered variously as the Placement Office, Dr. Ray Perry's former office, and Mrs. Torbert's former office.

And by the way, the telephone is not at all a convenient way of reaching me. I am practically never near one on the campus, and besides the war has caused the number of lines to the campus to be reduced.

Please send a card or note. It is far more convenient to get the addresses and news in writing.

The Posts finally got one of those luxuries in the new home. The number is T. 5613 and the address is 4538 Norma Drive.

And again, best of luck,
Lauren C. Post
Editor of the News Letter
P.S. See longer letter to 1st Lt. Wallace McAnulty on last page.

🕮

LEO PETER VOLZ, PhM.
has been reported killed in action.

🕮

LT. KRAMER W. RORIG
was reported missing in action in the North African area. (Lt. Lionel Chase and Kramer had seen each other for a moment once previously in the height of the North African campaign when they were checking in and out between hurried missions. LCP.)

🕮

LT. JACK FROST
was reported missing in action in the North African area on August 28th. He had been flying a B-17.

Clarence gets signatures of all returning Aztec service men; Andy serves "$5.00 cokes" that the boys write about. Bill Koller, first Aztec back from the Sicilian invasion and trip around the world, is the first to sign the book. See what others have written and don't forget to sign the book when you come to the cafe. Note string beans in Ed Herzig's victory garden.

CPL. ROBERT NEWSOM
who is a prisoner of the Japanese wrote to his mother who sent in the following note:

"I just received a card from Robert who is interned at the Philippines Military Prison Camp No. 2. He states that his health is good, he is uninjured and well. 'Please take care of yourself and don't worry.' The card was typewritten but he had written his name. His writing looks as usual. I wish to thank you so much for the News Letter which you send me. Sincerely, Mrs. R. P. Newsom."

🕮

FLIGHT OFFICER JOSEPH K. ROBBINS
who was reported missing in action from a bomber raid in the European area, has since been reported a prisoner in Germany. Lt. Robbins was formerly in the 251st.

(The earlier story had been set up in type but was replaced by this last minute news which came by phone. LCP.)

🕮

CAPT. GRIFFITH P. WILLIAMS
is a prisoner in Germany according to

cards and letters he has written home. (The news came the day News Letter No. 18 went to press so a mimeographed strip was inserted with the message that he was still alive. LCP.)

🕮

LT. GEORGE C. (BENNY) ALEXANDER
was wounded in the North African area. Lt. Alexander was the navigator and Lt. Maxton Brown was the pilot of a bomber during a raid in which the latter was killed and the former wounded in the body and arm. He is recovering and will resume duty as a navigator without any trip home.

🕮

JOHN OSBORN, Y2c
was wounded during a bombing of Guadalcanal. He had been there seven months and had been in the South Pacific 14 months. He is at Mare Island and is expected home soon.

🕮

AUBURN RYAL ROGERS, RM1c
has been wounded in action in the Atlantic area. The following is part of a note from his mother, Mrs. L. B. Rogers:
"On August 15th, I received word

11

NO RELIEF IN SIGHT

THE AZTEC NEWS LETTER
No. 21, December 1, 1943
Lt. Charles Caston wrote from the South Pacific:
"I'm still kicking and I have affixed the 'tough guy' on the nose of our plane. In fact, we call our ship the [censored]. Bloody, isn't it? Believe you me, it will be for any Jap. In fact, I expect to be flying over Tokyo eventually."

The waters of the Pacific lap against the Americas, Asia, Australia, and Antarctica. This vast expanse of ocean—the largest on the planet—is dotted with islands, many of which were formed by volcanic activity. During the war, these jagged archipelagos were strategic to forces on both sides.

The Japanese wanted to create a ring of bases to provide their empire with protection and resources. They already had a military presence in China, and they began looking farther abroad. Indonesia (the Dutch East Indies) was desirable for rubber and oil. The Japanese, in addition to gathering raw materials, sought to form a defensive buffer far out into the Pacific. Diplomatic measures, such as a U.S. oil embargo designed to punish this aggressive overreaching, seemed to spur the fuel-starved country to seize even more resource-rich territory.[1]

The bombing at Pearl Harbor was closely followed by Japanese attacks on U.S. military positions in the Philippines, Guam, Wake Island, and the

Midway Islands.[2] The string of assaults was meant to put the U.S. Navy out of action and to neutralize the United States so that it couldn't interfere with Japanese positions in the Pacific. Stunned by Japan's ferocity and ambition, the United States quickly geared its vast industrial strength to build ships and planes. Unlike Japan, which became crippled as it ran low on supplies, the United States had the capacity to continually repair damaged battleships and get them back on the water. This ability to stay ahead in operations turned into a military advantage for U.S. forces.[3]

The United States developed a plan that would take U.S. troops across the Pacific: to Japan along a northerly route and to the Philippines on a southerly course. These large sweeps gradually recaptured islands and collapsed Japan's buffer zone until Japan no longer sat comfortably inside a defended perimeter. The Allies brought the war to Japan by ship and by long-range bomber. Japan was starving, and Americans were hungry too—for vengeance.[4]

In 1942 the letters of the San Diego State servicemen and servicewomen reflected a unified belief in the need for justice, along with hope for swift victory. By 1943 that early optimism had evaporated like sweat, staining seasoned combatants with the grim and bitter residue of a prolonged war. By 1944 the writers had begun to describe an enemy that fought to succeed or die rather than to surrender.

The battles to retake Pacific territories involved painstakingly brutal campaigns, one archipelago at a time. The Japanese dug into caves and reinforced bunkers from which they smothered beaches with machine-gun fire. The first phase of an island invasion brought heavy naval bombardment, intended to shake out some of the entrenched defenders, followed by a beach landing. Marines poured forth from shallow-bottomed landing craft and tried to gain ground as quickly as possible. In some cases, these landings were hampered by jagged reefs that tore open the boats. Wading to shore, the Marines tried to hold the beach and push inland, a task that might take weeks or months.[5]

As each island was secured, construction battalions moved in to build airstrips and bases from which to launch the next invasion. The war in the Pacific progressed from bloody beaches through vine-choked jungles to cave-pocked hillsides. The names of these island chains may have been known to a geography professor like Dr. Post: the Solomon Islands, including Guadalcanal and Bougainville, the Marshall Islands, and the Marianas. His students, who admitted to dozing sometimes in class, were suddenly forced to learn the topography of this terrible combat theater firsthand, mile by mile.

As the war unfolded around the world, commanders argued strategy. One thing that both sides agreed on was the usefulness of isolating an enemy from a supply line. The Allies did their best to shut down Japanese access to fuel and other resources. The Pacific strategy known as island-hopping carried Allied troops to key positions that could be captured and held, often leaving pockets of the Japanese military cut off from their main force.[6]

The Japanese intended to use a similar strategy against the whole of Australia. The continent was too difficult to capture, but it could be isolated. Toward this end, the Japanese wanted to build an airstrip on Guadalcanal in the Solomon Islands as a base from which to launch raids and sever Australia from Allied naval support. The fight to win control of Guadalcanal began in 1942 and lasted for half a year. Like the Midway Islands, where the Allies' victory against the Japanese was a turning point in the naval war, Guadalcanal was viewed as a decisive, albeit bloody victory for the U.S. Marine Corps.[7] Slowly, the Japanese were forced to give ground. After Guadalcanal, the Allies pushed on toward Bougainville.

At the beginning of World War II, the Japanese easily wrested Bougainville away from an inadequate Australian defense force. Then, as the Allies made determined progress in the Pacific, the Japanese reinforced their hold on their existing bases. On Bougainville, one bay was left relatively undefended, and the Marines landed there early in November 1943. Once again, a beach landing was followed by jungle battles that whittled down the Japanese defenses. The fighting at Empress Augusta Bay went on for months before the Allies eventually captured the high ground.[8]

Often the censor's knife neatly sliced out words or phrases from servicemen's letters, leaving rectangular holes that interrupted the writing on the opposite side of the page. The following letter by Pfc. Jack Chandler had so much material removed that the pages were cut to ribbons. One of Chandler's buddies, Sgt. Charles Ables, also wrote regularly, and the two friends reminisced about their days at State. Ables described how he had stayed calm during the landing stage of an invasion only to experience the terror of falling bombs, including one that killed men in his unit. He had a chance to return home for the V-12 Navy College Training Program. The program would have allowed him to work toward a bachelor's degree and a commission as an officer, but he passed up the opportunity because he didn't want to leave the battlefield.

December 31, 1943

Dear Dr. Post, and all,

Here it is New Year's Eve, and the day after Christmas. At least, to us it's the day after Christmas. You see, we received our packages yesterday, and I really made out.

At last the censorship regulations have been lifted so now we can tell about what's been going on down here recently. You probably remember reading about the Marines at Bougainville, about the first of November. Well, that was my outfit which hit the Empress Augusta Bay area at that time. We were the first ones in, as the Marines always are. We hit the beach early on the morning of Nov. 1st. [censored]

The whole campaign was a wonderful example of perfect coordination between units. The Navy, the Air Force, and other units carried out their jobs well. Special credit, though, must be given to the "Seabees" who were "on the ball" at all times. They are a very fine outfit, and too much credit cannot be given them. They are "tops" with the Marines who saw what they did there. [censored]

I didn't pick up any souvenirs at all, though I had every chance in the world to do so. It's odd, but one has very little interest in such things when he is surrounded by them.

All in all, I came out O.K. My only wounds were a few bad scares and the loss of a few pounds. [censored]

That's all this time,

Best Regards,

Pfc. J. A. (Jack) Chandler

HQ. Co., 2nd Bn. 9th Marines

c/o Fleet Post Office

San Francisco, California

January 4, 1944

V-Mail

Dear Dr. Post:

Now they tell us—that was no sightseeing trip we were on, and we weren't there for fun. You see it was Bougainville and we went there for the same purpose every other Marine has come to the Solomons for. Undoubtedly there were several other Aztecs there too, but the only one I managed to see was Jack Chandler. We spent a lot of time in my fox-hole talking about the old days in the shade of the trees in the Quad. We also decided that the nicest way to study Geography is out of a good old text-book, because all you have to do to change the climate is turn the page. Here it's the same month in & month out.

Sgt. C. N. (Charles) Ables
3rd Marine Div, HQ Co.
c/o Fleet P.O.
San Francisco, California

THE AZTEC NEWS LETTER
No. 24, March 1, 1944
Sgt. Charles N. Ables, Jr., USMC, wrote from Bougainville to the boys of Alpha Phi Omega:

"As you know, Jack Chandler and I have become the 'Rover Boys' of the fraternity. We've been to five countries already and we are still rolling along. When I say countries, I mean some lousy little tropical islands, because that's what the last four stops have been. I suppose you heard about our last little job. It was Bougainville, and believe me it wasn't exactly a picnic. It's a nice place to be from, but not such a nice place to be. When you are standing by the rail waiting to go over the side it's not at all like you'd think it would be. You have a strange feeling of calmness which lasts anywhere from the first few hours to the first few days. In my case it was days. Everything was running just like maneuvers 'til one night when a bomb hit just a few yards from me and several guys were killed and others wounded. I guess you know it was right then and there I decided this is really a pretty darn serious thing. No kidding, that is the most terrifying part of it all, to lay there hugging the deck and listen to the bombs swishing and then followed up by that all too familiar whoomp, whoomp, whoomp as they come smashing into the ground. You just can't help yourself and you lay there shaking all over. After they leave, you laugh at your buddy and he laughs at you for shaking so much. Chandler had his close call by snipers. You see, one day they were sent out to get a pesky one. Well, they sprayed the trees for awhile and decided they must have got the monkey and proceeded to go in swimming in the river. Chandler got out in the middle when all around him, ping, ping, ping, and the water splashed on all sides. Quite an embarrassing situation. He had to swim underwater to get to the little protecting bank by the river while someone took care of the pest.

"As you know, Chandler and I aren't even in the same outfits, but we've always been on the move together, and no matter where we go we keep running into each other. Up on Bougainville he was up to see me so much we had to dig my foxhole wider so he'd have room to jump in during air raids. Right now Jack is laid up with a pretty bad case of malaria; but so far I've been O.K. We are starting our second year overseas now. It was a year ago last week that we sailed away from good old 'Dago' and I'm afraid it'll be at least that much longer before we start heading back. Just before we left for Bougainville I had the chance to either make Sgt. or go back to the States for college training. You know good old V-12. Well, I figured that would be quitting at the wrong time so I guess I'm stuck at Sgt. for the duration.

"Pardon the typing, gents, but this is the first letter I've typed since about last May or June. I've got the Sgt. of the Guard tonight, and I have to sit in this office so I figured I'd give my fingers a little exercise. I've been typing a letter or a word then lashing out at a mosquito, but right now I can see where I've either got to donate all my time to the mosquitoes or get eaten alive, so I'll close now and drop me a line if you haven't anything else to do. Keep me posted on all the boys. I get the *News Letter* but not many of the old APO men seem to write in it."

On April 18, 1943, Alta S. Grant sent Dr. Post news of her three sons, Harold, Russell, and Floyd. She wrote, "I hear each week from Floyd and of course you know there is little they can say except they keep busy and are well—" A year later, Floyd was finally able to write a few details about some of the most harrowing island battles in the South Pacific.

April 4, 1944
Dear Doc:
Well Doc in these last 41 months that I have spent overseas I have really covered the ground. First it was Hawaii then Fiji, New Hebrides, Guadalcanal and now here. I haven't seen anything that I would really care to come back to, especially these South Seas gals. They are a big bring down.

Recently over here the Japs have been giving us a little bit of trouble. It seems as though they don't appreciate the fact that we had encroached up their rights of acquisition and so decided to run us off of the place. I don't see why they should be so indignant over the fact since we only took a small portion of what they had but never the less they do resent it. The way it all started was that they started to throw some artillery shells in our general direction and that did not suit us one bit. In retaliation we returned a little of the same plus a little more. The trouble with the whole deal was that it kept all awake no matter what time of the day that we chose to sleep. It is next to impossible to sleep when there is an artillery barrage in operation especially when the guns are so close by at hand. The last few days things have subsided which is highly appreciated by all of us.

Now the only thing that I am sweating out is this rotation of troops. I have spent more than my time in the tropics and am due for a return to the States any time now. It should come within a matter of a couple of months. I hope that I can get to San Diego before school closes for the semester.

Well Doc this is all for now. Keep the *News Letter* coming it is really appreciated by all of us.

Sincerely

Floyd

July 12, 1944

Hello Doc—

. . .

This war makes a fellow so weary and tired it's no wonder we're fighting like mad men to get it over with. I've only been over one year and it seems like five. I know how some who have been out longer must feel.

We've been from one end of the Solomons to the other [censored] and believe me it's been rough. I'll say one thing however and that is that there was never a dull moment—if you know what I mean. I believe the jungles on Bougainville are the most dense I've ever seen, full of "Wait a minute" vines and others of all descriptions. That's what made the progress of the war so slow in that sector. I couldn't understand what was meant when during the battle for Guadalcanal the headlines read "Terrific onslaught gains 75 yards for Yanks." No—I couldn't begin to understand until I saw for myself.

. . .

Well cheerio Doc. I'll see you in Tokyo—

Sincerely

Irving E. Lewis CM1/c
77C.B., Co A-6
c/o F.P.O.—San Francisco

Coral reefs hindered access to the Gilbert Islands. A coral atoll known as Tarawa proved to be one of the toughest landings. The Japanese were so well dug in to their defensive positions that they believed they could hold out against any attack. The Marines, together with Army infantry and supported by battleships and aircraft carriers, assembled a daunting invasion force. The beach landing depended on a vast number of men that could overwhelm the deep defenses.

Minesweepers went into the coral-ringed lagoon first and cleared a path for the personnel carriers. The flat-bottomed craft that ferried troops to shore were designated as Landing Craft, Vehicle, Personnel (LCVP), to distinguish them from other types of landing craft, such as those that carried tanks. Another type of vessel had treads that gave it traction in swamps. The military recognized the usefulness of this vessel in beach invasions and designated the new craft LVT, for Landing Vehicle Tracked, and modifications were made until this carrier essentially became a cross between a shallow-draft boat and a tank. LVTs were first used in combat at Tarawa, and during that invasion they were the only landing craft to make it all the way to the beach.[9]

The Battle of Tarawa was launched on November 20, 1943. Men and boats assembled off the coast, but the tide didn't peak as predicted, which meant many of the boats lacked the clearance to get over the sharp reefs. It was up to the LVTs to climb across the ragged coral. The Marines in the other landing craft were either stranded or forced to wade to shore. In a heroic attempt at rescue, the LVTs went back out and tried to ferry more men, but many of the craft were wrecked either by enemy fire or by the coral itself. The element of speed was lost, and almost 1,500 Marines were killed or wounded during the first day of the fighting.[10]

Those who made it ashore were immobilized and forced to fight unceasingly to hold their positions. Finally, another type of transport, known as the LCM—Landing Craft Mechanized—got to shore and unloaded tanks. The Marines moved slowly inland, divided the Japanese defenses, and directed another barrage by the Navy, knocking down more enemy guns. The assault's success was due to the relentlessness of the Marines, who kept moving more men and equipment ashore and pressing forward through days of constant battle.[11]

By the time Tarawa was in Allied hands, Marine casualties had risen to more than 3,000.[12] News of the battle's high cost stunned those at home, but the servicemen in the Pacific theater understood what they were up against, and they knew that more island invasions were still to come.

Planes were launched from the airfield at Tarawa to begin the assault on the Marshall Islands. After the Marshall Islands came still more cliff-barricaded, reef-ringed volcanic archipelagos. On and on the battles continued across the ocean, the U.S. military capturing one base after another but losing more men on the beaches and leaving more wreckage in the shallows.

THE AZTEC NEWS LETTER
No. 48, March 1, 1946

Sgt. Frank M. Watenpaugh, Jr., son of Mr. Watenpaugh of the faculty, is enrolled again after three years of service in the Army. . . . He was then stationed in Hawaii, Tarawa, and then at Hawaii again. On Tarawa, Frank was record clerk and helped in the making up of the weather maps. The forecasts from them were essential to the planes through their station.

Frank says that there are little cemeteries scattered over Tarawa. There are no weeds on the island, and the graves are in the white coral sand. "When the tide goes out, one can see thousands of shell casings on the beach. Those casings and the cemeteries are about all of the evidence of the fighting that took place over three years ago. It was nice to get away from the island."

Seven months after Tarawa, in June 1944, another landing took place at Saipan. Along with Guam, Saipan is part of the Mariana Islands, which are located east of the Philippines and south of the Japanese mainland. By the time of the landing at Saipan, invasion forces had learned how to overcome the coral, and more than 8,000 Marines made beach landings using LVTs.[13] Capt. Bill Stoll, whose letters follow, worked on these troop carriers during the invasion.

Capt. Perry DeLong survived a beach landing, and he expressed his gratitude to Dr. Walter Hepner, the college president, who joined in the Christmas letter writing campaign.

March 18, 1944

Dear Doctor Post

. . .

I am still at the boat basin near Oceanside, but have been transferred to the 5th Amphibian Tractor Bn. which is about ready to go across.

Amphibian Tractors have proved their worth as troop carriers over coral reefs and other inaccessible barriers to boats at Tarawa, and the Marshalls, and as a result are much in demand these days.

. . .

Sincerely,

Capt. W. C. (Bill) Stoll

5th Amphibian Tractor Bn.

July 15, 1944

Dear Dr. Post,

The division censor has just informed me that we may now disclose our location. I landed on Saipan, on June 15, along with the rest of the boys. Robert Sherrod, the *Time* correspondent, described the landing much better than I could ever hope to in the July 3 edition of *Time* magazine. However, I will say it was plenty rough and if our boys were not the fighting fools that they are, it may have been another story. My position was as Bn. executive officer of an Amphibian Tractor Bn. Saipan is surrounded by coral reefs which offered no resistance to the tractors and we were kept busy for many days at hard work with the helping to secure the island.

. . .

Sincerely,

Capt. W. C. (Bill) Stoll

5th Amphibian Trac. Bn.

c/o Fleet Post Office

San Francisco, California

February 24, 1944

Dear Doc—

I've just finished several samples of what the books rather prosaically term "Opposed Amphibious Operations" and [we] are still going around pinching our-selves in an attempt to dispel that "other world" sensation. Believe me, getting ashore when Mr. Jap is on hand and determined to prevent it is quite a feat in any man's war. I don't know how they did it but there was mail awaiting our return aboard ship and there big as life was my *News Letter*—in fact it was the only letter I did receive. I'll be more than glad to toot a horn at that reunion Doc, though for a while I thought it was going to be strictly duets between Gabriel and me.

. . . I especially want to thank Dr. Hepner for his Christmas card—it's a wonderful feeling to realize that while we may be gone, we're not forgotten. Realizing the reality of those old ties puts a lot more steam and determination behind one's efforts.

Some of the fellows seem to be getting quite a kick out of their war experiences. I wish I could feel the same but I've seen too many really fine boys drop to get any enjoyment out of this dirty business, and can only hope we may drive it through to a quick and complete finish. We certainly are going to do all we can toward that end and knowing you're all behind us is making a tremendous difference.

. . .

Sincerely
Capt. Chas. Perry DeLong
Hq. 1st Bn, 22 Mar.
c/o Fleet P.O.
San Francisco, California

October 10, 1944
Dear Lauren:—
You cannot appreciate in full my pleasure in receiving your letter. One paragraph touched me hard; it was the last one. "Some day we'll go out and see the afternoon scrimmages again."

Lauren it's things like that, that makes this all so worthwhile from my view point. When Washington called me two years and 5 days ago now and told me they had a part for me to play in this war we are in, I was proud about that call, the only request I made was that I be sent out to the forward areas where the real need for my type of work was, their only hesitation was over the fact that I was 40 years old and this island warfare was a young man's game, however I won my point . . .

When I waded ashore across the reef at Saipan, rifle high above my head looking at Mortar and Artillery shells falling on the beaches. My thoughts were of many things about like what a man must think as he walks up on the gallows to meet his creator. I realized then that life had been good to me, 3 fine children a wonderful wife and good friends. The faculty softball game at State went across my mind, I could see Walter Hepner very plainly trying to stop an infield hit, those stands where we have watched many boys at State do their stuff—all was there as clop clop ever nearer the shore came, suddenly Lauren it was the preservation of those things that caused me to be there, as I realized that peace came over me, the whistle had blown and the game was on, you would know that feeling that drops from you when in athletic combat.

The beach and tree area where we landed looked like all hell had broken loose, dead Marines, dead Japs, wounded and I swing into action to perform my task, had to use oxen the 1st days with poles Indian fashion to haul our dead to the cemetery, it is a long story too long for a letter. Some day when we sit in the old bleachers watching scrimmage I will tell you about it.

. . .

Always—
Orien (Junior) Todd

July 17, 1944
Dear Dr. Post—

. . .

After we left Hawaii we toured the Pacific for awhile & finally hit Saipan Island in the Marianas. My God, Doc, I once thought there could never be anything as bad as Tarawa was—that was before I'd seen Saipan. In many locations we had the Nips stacked up like cord wood. One of our guns accounted for 120 Japs during one of their mad Banzai night charges. One of the platoons in our company knocked out ten tanks during another, but previous, night counterattack.

Some of the Nip chow is quite tolerable—they had food dumps in numerous locations on the island. We had menus such as—curried rice & chicken, papaya & Saki; crabmeat cocktail, bamboo sprouts, tinned candied carrots & red salmon; canned pineapple, fresh bananas, fresh limes, mangroves, baked breadfruit & a variety of other foods—all very tasty & an immense relief from the "C" rations issued during the campaign.

Well, Doc, best I secure the butts & get off the firing line so until later.
Yours truly,
Guy Boothby

In the last weeks of July and the first part of August 1944, the Marines fought for Guam. Their job was to secure the beaches and push toward the high ground. Pfc. Jack Chandler, a veteran of Bougainville, landed on Guam and witnessed Japanese tactics that he described as fanatical. The defenders launched aggressive counterattacks against the Marines, including waves of banzai charges that brought them into range for hand-to-hand fighting. At a moment when the battle could have gone either way, tanks advanced to support the Marine position.[14] In the following letters, Chandler noted that the enemy sometimes prepared for suicidal attacks with a round of drinking. He described how the corpses stacked up and offered heartfelt gratitude for the tank support.

May 8, 1944

Dear Doc, and all,

I'm in a letter writing mood today, and better take quick advantage to drop you this long delayed line.

Number 25 arrived yesterday. The picture did more to revive old memories than anything has in a long time. It's funny how homesick a person gets when he sees something like that. Oh, well!

Things are going along pretty smoothly for me. No more malaria, no more jaundice. I still have the old jungle rot, though. I guess most of the boys down here know about that.

We've now been out of the States for about sixteen months, and here in the tropics for almost a year. I haven't seen a white woman since last June. I know what they mean by the "horrors of war."

Lately we've done nothing but train, getting ready for our next push. It looks as if it'll be a lot different from our push at Bougainville, and should be pretty interesting. I've finally gotten rid of my "walkie-talkie" (I ruined two of them in landings), and have landed a really interesting fast-moving job. We've been promised lots of enemy next time, so I have my entrenching shovel well sharpened. I'm a wave of destruction when it comes to digging a foxhole under pressure.

. . .

We have the ball rolling out here now, so maybe we'll be home before long.

. . .

Pfc. J. A. (Jack) Chandler

August 15, 1944

V-Mail

Hiya, Doc,

Well, here I am on Guam, still alive and unhurt, but don't ask me why. I've been a very lucky boy several times.

The shooting is about over, I guess, but it was plenty hot while it lasted. We saw lots of action, and we all got a chance or two to warm up our weapons. Believe me, the Nips know about it, too. My battalion certainly killed its share. If the Nips hadn't been such fanatics, I probably wouldn't be writing this letter. They pulled all of their Hollywood stuff, such as "banzai" attacks, etc., and that's where we really stacked them up.

We certainly had good support this time. The coordination between forces was very smooth. We're pretty sore at the Navy, though. You ought to see what they did to our liberty port! It doesn't even look like a city anymore.

The island of Guam is a very pretty one, or will be after it's cleaned up. The natives are very happy to see Americans again, and I don't blame them. That's all now, more later.

Best wishes to all,

Pfc. J. A. (Jack) Chandler

October 8, 1944

Hello, Doc, and all,

. . .

Our camp is well set-up, and the men are getting a well deserved rest. We certainly had a rough time for a while.

I caught my old job, walkie-talkie, on the campaign. I was attached to one of our rifle companies, and had a big time. There were a couple of times where I wouldn't have given a rusty carbine clip for my chances of coming out alive. I certainly take my hat off to the plain ordinary Marines who stick in that line with the rifles, Bars (Browning Automatics), and machine guns. It certainly takes guts to stay there, and in my opinion, they all rate medals. The Nips pulled three "Banzai" attacks on us, and I'm sure I would have cracked up if I'd been on the line, instead of twenty yards behind. I'm sure that at one time, we owed our lives to the fact that at one time the Nips were drunk, and failed to hit us with a concentrated counter-attack. Of course, that's just my personal opinion. There were lots of Nips around, and I could have used a barrel of grenades, if I had had them. There were lots of dead ones around the next morning too. (Thank God for the tanks!)

I made out pretty well for souvenirs. I picked up a lot of stuff, including two Nip flags, one battle flag, and one color, the kind with stripes. I had to miss a lot of stuff, a Samurai sword, for example, as I didn't have any desire to slow down 'till I got to a hole. Rifles, bayonets, and other Jap equipment was so abundant that we lost interest in it and threw it away.

. . .

I've been out here for twenty-one months now, and no relief in sight. I haven't seen a white woman or a liberty port in fifteen months. Something has to crack, but soon!

. . .

That's all now. I'm awaiting the *News Letter* as always,
Pfc. J. A. (Jack) Chandler

Hazardous beach landings were only the beginning. After the Marines secured an island, the Naval Construction Battalion (CB) cleared debris and built roads, airstrips, and even hospitals. Construction workers who joined the CB were called Seabees and often did double duty as fighting men, encountering pockets of resistance on Pacific islands even after an area had been declared secure. The Seabees went into action quickly, preparing the way for the next wave of attacks, often defending their positions as they worked. Their mascot was a fierce-looking bee wearing a sailor's cap and holding a machine gun, wrench, and hammer.[15]

February 11, 1944
Dear Mr. Post,—

. . .

I won't have to do any advertising for my outfit, Naval Construction Battalion or better known as Sea Bees, because the marines have already done it for us.

The miracles we have performed in the jungles of the south pacific can only be realized by those who have seen us work. I say miracles because we have surprised ourselves as often as we have surprised others.

. . .

Sincerely
Irving E. Lewis CM1/c
77 Const. Batt.
Co A-6, c/o Fleet P.O.
San Francisco, California

March 28, 1944
Southwest Pacific
Dear Doctor Post:—

. . .

When the Navy is covering a landing, they feel a personal responsibility for the Marines or Army or Seabees they are sending ashore. The Army and Marines are working more and more in conjunction and both the Navy and Marines are thankful that there are Seabees to help establish beach-heads and build advance bases. The Army Air Corps is a sweet sight to all of us at any time!

. . .

Cordially Yours,
Milton Effron, Pho M2/c
CBD 1008, HQS. CO.
c/o FLEET P.O.
San Francisco

September 12, 1944
Mariana Islands
Dear Doc:
You'd sure never know these islands around here anymore as the same ones we landed on such a short time back. Operations have sure been stepped-up plenty since the slow, grueling days back in the Solomons. We had complete support from the Navy and Air Corps and even some of the Army was around this time. The Seabees are really going to town getting the mess cleared up that the Navy barrage made, and it won't be much longer before we have a [censored] way out here.

. . . I wouldn't exactly say I was getting "Asiatic" but the fact that I've been out here 20 mos now and haven't see a white woman since a year ago July isn't exactly helping matters any. At least we have something to look forward to since we heard the First Division was finally sent home. So we figure on arriving back in San Diego by next summer.

. . .

Stf. Sgt. Charles Ables
3d Mar Div, Hq Co.

While the servicemen were trying to spot women, operators manning the relatively new Radio Detection and Ranging systems were searching for enemy planes and ships. The United States Signal Corps dubbed the technology RADAR, which measures the time it takes for a radio signal to bounce off an object such as a plane or ship and return to the point of transmission. Knowing the speed of the wave, the operator can determine the range, or distance, to the disrupting object. Great Britain was further along in developing this method of tracking objects and shared its findings with the United States in order to make use of their research labs' production power. Great

Britain used the technology to defend against bombing raids, and the U.S. Navy benefited by installing radar on its ships.[16]

Escort ships were tasked with defending convoys of slow-moving merchant ships. Armed with torpedoes and antiaircraft guns, the escorts were on the lookout for enemy planes and submarines. Radar made these smaller ships even more effective and design upgrades made them faster. They proved valuable for defending coasts and for covering the landing craft that brought troops to shore during beach invasions.

January 25, 1944
Dear Doc Post;

. . .

In less than two weeks I will go aboard a P.F. (Patrol Frigate) as a radarman and from there things should be different. The ship is near its commission time at Richmond and we expect to be on it within ten days of this date.

Incidentally, a Patrol Frigate is similar to a D.E. (Destroyer Escort) and are taking the Destroyer duties over in the various sections of the waters. It will be patrol duty and escort duty mainly, and should prove interesting work.

Our crew took over a P.F. last week to get acquainted with its gear and general set-up, so this type of ship will not be completely strange to us. Of course I was interested in the radar gear more than anything else and spent most of my time in the radar room. We were out six days so it gave us time to get acquainted with the two radar machines we have aboard and also gave us a chance to put them into operation. I might add that the gear is excellent and a pleasure to operate while at sea. Radar acts differently at sea than on land, therefore the practice we had last week was very helpful. It is a comparatively new weapon and consequently we have a lot to learn before we can be classified as good radarmen. So much for my activities!

. . .

Yours truly,
Jack Maupin Rdm3/c
Rec. Unit—Gov't Island
Barracks 6—Crew 16
Alameda, California

The capture of the Marianas put the Allies within striking distance of the Philippines and Japan. As quickly as they could, the Marines and Seabees leveled the ground and built airstrips, including runways long enough for the new B-29 bomber. One of the following letters estimated the cost of this long-range bomber, which was capable of reaching the Japanese mainland. Adjusted for inflation, $600,000 in 1944 is equal to approximately $8.5 million in 2018, and $3 million is equivalent to about $42.5 million.

✉ January 13, 1944

. . .

I suppose you would like to know what I am doing here on this field? Well I am going to a B-29 armament school. It is O.K. to tell you now, the plane I studied in Seattle, as it has been published in the papers. It was the Boeing B-29 or the super bomber, as the papers put it. I personally hope, that it can hang up as good a record as their B-17s have, but I am a little afraid that it can't, as there are a few more things on the plane that can go haywire (as the army puts it). They have had quite a little trouble with them so far, but that is expected of a new ship. I am sorry, that I can't elaborate on this plane, but as yet all of the details are a military secret.

> Thanking you kindly I am
> Yours
> Pfc Robert W. (Bob) Mossholder
> A.S.N. 39273359
> 33rd T.S.S.
> Lowry Field #1
> Denver, Colorado

✉ November 1944
Dear Doc Post,

. . .

I'm up here at the Second Air Force base of Alamogordo, New Mexico on detached service. I'm attending a thirty day course on the B-29 Super-Fortress. We are going to train combat crews on them at Biggs Field in El Paso. So the higher ups decided to send us to school to learn what we could about them. It took two years to put the first one together and they want us to know all about them in thirty days!!

To say the least Doc, I have never seen such a complicated mess in all my life. They are really immense. But for all their faults they are a darn fine bombing plane, and I'm elated to be one of those chosen to work on them.

Of course they are still hush-hush, but here are some figures & facts. 1st one cost 3 million, now they cost the citizenry $600,000 each. Carries 10 tons of jap poison. Speed—well over 350. Engine develops 2200 horse power each. Dual, tricycle landing gear (6 wheels in all). Pressurized cabins will allow plane to reach 40,000 feet and up. Quite a plane eh Doc? If you publish the letter please do not include the above figures. They are for your knowledge only.

. . .

Please give my regards to your charming wife.
Your friend and pupil
Bill Scarborough

December 23, 1944
Saipan
Dear Dr. Post

. . .

Living conditions are much better than we expected although I sometimes start to wonder why I didn't join the Navy.

Have recently found out that helmets have uses other than as shaving and laundry utensils. Occasionally we have to wear the damned things; since we brought in the B29s the Japs have been pulling a few raids and we've logged a few hours of fox hole time. Seen a few planes shot down; one landed a couple of hundred yards from my fox hole. However, about the only danger is from falling planes and shrapnel.

I was on the first B29 raid on Tokyo and have been on two since. Haven't been on a mission for three weeks; a crew from another squadron borrowed our plane for a raid and didn't bring it back so we've been getting our new plane ready to fly.

. . .

Best Regards,
Lt. F. C. (Frank) Heryet 0-7037116
879th Bomb Sqdn. 499th Grp.
APO 237c/o Postmaster
San Francisco

THE AZTEC NEWS LETTER
No. 35, February 1, 1945
Lt. Frank C. Heryet wrote (to someone else) from Saipan:
"Our crew was the first crew of the squadron to arrive here. While we were still putting up our mosquito netting, they threw a briefing at us for that first Tokyo mission. Well, I'm an old combat man now. I was on the first two missions over Tokyo,

skipped the third night mission and was on the next one. Didn't meet too many fighters or much flak on the first missions, I suppose because we had to bomb through the overcast. A few fighters pointed their nose at us and we threw a few tracers in their direction. They decided on discretion.

"I think the worst part of the mission is the half hour before the target. When you are finally on your run, things are so interesting and they happen so fast you don't have time to be scared. Of course, all the poor navigator has to do over the target is look, and think and sweat.

"I am a sight to scare babies about the time we go over the target. The navigator is the only man on the crew that can't sleep and you can imagine how tired you can get navigating 3000 miles together with the excitement."

The high altitudes (30,000 to 40,000 feet) at which the B-29 could fly took it beyond the reach of most antiaircraft fire, and it could cover vast distances, journeying more than 3,000 nautical miles on a bombing run.[17] By 1945, B-29s were coming in lower and dropping incendiary bombs that set Tokyo—urban, industrial, and heavily populated—ablaze. Damage estimates from the most devastating of those initial raids, conducted in March 1945, placed the death toll at more than 100,000 people during one night of bombing.[18]

The Allies gained territory with steady drives toward Japan in the north and toward the Philippines in the south. Peleliu (today part of the Republic of Palau) is in the Western Pacific and is strategically close to the Philippines. Over the course of two months in late 1944, the Marines struggled for control of Peleliu, and they succeeded at a terrible price. The Japanese, who had already lost their hold on a number of other islands, now stretched their fortified positions from the beaches to the interior, turning Peleliu's coral ridge into a nearly invincible citadel. Temperatures that soared to more than 100° Fahrenheit added to the overall misery.

Four Marine battalions took part in the assault that began on September 16, 1944. Peleliu's coveted airfield was captured and soon pressed into use to further the invasion. Gradually the Japanese lost ground, but they were loath to surrender. They pulled back into interlaced caves that allowed them to move supplies and reinforcements as the tide of battle shifted. Lethal crossfire held off the advancing Marines, savaging their every attempt to take the high ground. Allowing no quarter, the Japanese attacked during the night, trying to kill Marines while they slept, and snipers set up positions to continue the slaughter at daybreak.[19]

Two thousand Marines and infantry are estimated to have died in the bitter fighting. Losses among the 1st Marines mounted to one-third of the regiment's strength. Wresting the cliffs from the Japanese became a grim, hand-to-hand ordeal, and by the time it was over, the death toll for the enemy was approximately ten thousand. Soon the Marines were calling the vicious battle "Bloody Peleliu."[20]

Sgt. Allison Lutterman was with the 5th Marines, and he wrote his account of the fight on red-lined Japanese stationary. In describing the action, he used a football term that Dr. Post, a part-time coach, would have easily understood. He mentioned "D-Day," which has become synonymous with the Allied invasion of Normandy, but it means the day an operation is scheduled to begin. After all the fighting he had done, Lutterman questioned the notion of rest, even behind the lines.

A *News Letter* excerpt of Lutterman's other service referred to "Finchaven," and Dr. Post didn't correct the misspelling. During World War II, the name of Finschhafen, a town in Papua New Guinea, was often simplified.

✉ October 12, 1944

Dear Doc, et.al:

Received the September *News Letter* in my Peleliu Fox Hole a few days ago. We're back a few hundred yards now, resting ? for another go at the yellow so & so's. This has been by far the hardest fought & bloodiest fight so far. The news reports we've seen don't begin to give a picture of the Hell it's been for four long weeks.

A Lieutenant gave his life to save mine on D day. All I got was a tiny scratch on the leg. He started to enter a pill box which was supposed to be cleaned out. It wasn't & he jumped back with three .25 slugs in his stomach. I ran over to him and laid him down behind a pill box, dressed his worst wound and was about to start on the others when a Jap tossed a grenade at us which landed only a few feet away. I tried to pick the Lieut. up but couldn't as he was a pretty big lad, when I failed I turned to look for help. There was no one around. At that instant the Lieut. got to his feet, and with a neat football block, knocked me down & covered me with his own body, taking the full blast of the grenade. I got up & finally managed to half drag & carry (with his help) him out of danger, just as six Japs poured out of the pill box to be mowed down by the others who were near. A doctor & stretcher bearers came up then & he was evacuated. I heard later he had died.

There have been hundreds of heroic deeds Doc. Unbelievable feats of courage and endurance. The Japs were determined to hold this Gibraltar at all costs. We've killed them by hundreds and are now nearing the end Thank God. I've quite frankly seen all the war I care for & would be most happy to come home. I've never been so tired in all my life. Nor as scared.

. . . I'll be back to finish at State, as soon as Uncle is through with me. I for one will be most happy to kiss Uncle Monty's ugly pan.

That's about all for now. The artillery firing directly behind us has nearly shaken all intelligent thoughts from my head.

Cheerio to all Aztecs

Sgt. A. B. (Allison) Lutterman USMC

Hq. Co. 1st Bn. 5th Marines

F.P.O. San Francisco, California

THE AZTEC NEWS LETTER

No. 45, December 1, 1945

Pl. Sgt. Allison Lutterman, USMCR, breezed into the office after 29 months of rugged service with the Fifth Regiment of the First Marine Division. This was Allison's second hitch in the Corps as he had done four years earlier with four more years in the Reserve. Allison is one of the few Japanese-speaking Aztecs. That is one of his newer accomplishments, and it kept him in various kinds of interesting work such as interrogating prisoners and also trying to get them to come out of caves and surrender.

"New Guinea was not too tough. That was Finchaven. Gloucester was bad from the standpoint of terrain and weather. Peleliu awfully bloody and by far the toughest. It was on that island that a lieutenant was awarded the Congressional Medal of Honor for saving my life."

. . .

Allison looks mighty well for his four battle stars and his years—too many for the Corps to give him a commission on.

The successful capture of Japanese positions throughout the Pacific provided the Allies with bases for long-range bombers, assisted by fighter planes launched from aircraft carriers. All this firepower paved the way for MacArthur's famous return to the Philippines.[21] In 1942 he had been forced to leave the islands, and it wasn't until late in 1944 that he finally landed at Leyte Gulf. He soon repeated the dramatic performance of wading to shore at the island of Luzon.[22] The serviceman who witnessed it got the date wrong, as the battle for Luzon took place in 1945, not 1944, as he accidentally noted. His description of Gen. Douglas MacArthur, however, is undoubtedly accurate.

January 18, 1944 [*sic*; 1945]
Dear Dr. Post:

. . .

I am on an attack transport, the U.S.S. *Pierce*, which carries a herd of Higgins boats. We just got back to our base from the Luzon invasion. I saw Doug MacArthur come ashore at the beachhead, cameramen to the left of him, cameramen to the right of him, and cameramen in front of him.

Yours truly,
Tom Cullen

Pat Wyatt belonged to the Delta Pi Beta fraternity, and he did his best to keep Dr. Post informed about his situation, as well as the whereabouts of his fraternity brothers. He also had a penchant for illustrating his letters with cartoon likenesses of himself in his pilot's cap and parachute. Other images, sketched in colored pencil, reflected his views on wartime politics. On June 1, 1945, the war in Europe was over, but the fight in the Pacific raged on. Between bombing missions, Wyatt took time out to sketch a sad-faced Hitler next to a coffin decorated with a wreath and swastika. On one side of the letter is a list of countries initially conquered by Germany; the other side of the letter proclaims, "You Got Nothin'."

Beneath his colorful cartoons, Wyatt sprinkled into his prose his opinions of local flora, fauna, and the Hollywood actress Hedy Lamarr. When he ran out of paper, he flipped the stationery and kept up his commentary. He joked about everything except the utter destruction of Manila. On that point, he was somber. It's unlikely that the chaplain he mentions coined the phrase "Praise the Lord and pass the ammunition"—many military chaplains were credited with uttering that popular line. Wyatt was astute, ironic, and biased, and when it came to keeping track of his fraternity brothers, he was single-minded and intensely loyal.

THE AZTEC NEWS LETTER
No. 35, February 1, 1945
Lt. W.P. Wyatt, USMCR, wrote from the Southwest Pacific:
"I can't see how those jokers can send home letters saying where they are. I can't even tell you whether I lux my undies. All I can say is that I am on a rock in the Southwest Pacific. My plane, The Nervous Wreck, is holding out as well as any dive bomber can, and I am rapidly finding myself in the same category."

. . .

February 4, 1945
Philippines
Southwest Pacific
Dear Dr. P—
As I sit here carving my toenails with a bolo knife, I find my thoughts turning back to dear olde State and the wonderful *News Letters*—As the head belies I'm in the Philippines—Still flying the dive bomber and having a great time—Of course being roused out of a comfortable native-produced bamboo bed and into a foxhole at 1 A.M. due to some Nip "Washing Machine" is no great pleasure, but so fare the fortunes of war—

These people are extremely quaint in many respects—When we first landed here the people had been without clothing for 3 years, hence an undershirt or a towel will buy practically anything. The Japanese intervention hit these people quite hard and we have tried to help them by trading clothes for their articles— Consequently I'm now the manager of dogs, chickens, bolo knives, coconut candy, and various other pieces of merchandise. We have an outdoor shower and it [is] very embarrassing to have these Filipino girls strolling by selling their wares—

. . .

Lt. W. P. (Pat) Wyatt U.S.M.C.
Marine Scout Bombing Sqd. 241
E.P.O. San Francisco, California

May 9, 1945
Philippines
Dear L.C.P.—

. . .

As I related previously we moved to a new area sometime ago but still in the Philippines. Little bit stuffier than our other base and every day one can observe the battle of Wyatt vs. 10,000 flies—We have various forms of other insects in the form of centipedes, grasshoppers and of course good old 999% Malaria Mary— still no Delta Pi Betas. . . .

Not much doing down here Doc. Landed alphabet day and flew the first strike—My total now is 41, a mere drop in the bucket compared with some of the boys—if luck holds should get home around Sept.

I guess the surrender of Germany really has given the boost toward letter writing and consequently dwarfed our little intrigue—The boys did a beautiful job over there and I just hope we can perform a repetition here. . . .

Lt. W. P. (Pat) Wyatt U.S.M.C.
Marine Scout Bombing Sqd. 241
E.P.O. San Francisco, California

June 1, 1945
Philippines
Dear LCP—

. . .

As you probably guessed I was stationed on Luzon from the 1st of the year up until the present time or rather a month or so ago. Manila was really a wreck—My guess is approximately a 50 year reconstruction period will return it to a pre-war status. Certainly a shame, for one can easily see its former beauty.

. . .

Hope to see you soon LCP—
Yrs
Lt. W. P. (Pat) Wyatt U.S.M.C.
Marine Scout Bombing Sqd. 241
E.P.O. San Francisco, California

July 10, 1945
Philippines
Dear L.C.P.
Seems that all good things come at once and so it was as Ed, our smiling mail man, perched high atop his water buffalo dropped not one, nor two, but three *News Letters* into my throbbing flanges. I immediately dashed in and started penning furiously another thank you to you and your competent staff of morale boosters.

Only trouble I found with the latest issues of the *Letters* is the beautiful little chums adorning the cover—I can hardly keep track of where my *Letters* go. Ah me yes a pretty face (white) is really something around here. At the local picture

Letter from Pat Wyatt, June 1, 1945

the other night, upon the entrance of Hedy La M—one young man rushed down the aisle and started clawing the screen—We stoned him into submission and really enjoyed the picture—. . .

Also very grieved to hear of John R. (Jack) Nolan's death. Besides being a Delta Pi Beta, his father is a four striper in the Navy (Doctor) and his uncle is the famous Chaplain McGuire of "Praise the Lord and Pass the Ammunition" fame—I'm in great hopes Jack [will] achieve a niche in the State memorial honoring those who have fallen during the war—

Completed my 63rd strike today and those lil jerks are (out of paper) still shooting back—A strange tribe, these Japs.

Reckon I'm all out of thoughts for now—Your *News Letter* cover's extremely fetching and I might also add a great incentive to return to dear ole State—I'm having a heck of a time securing a skull for you Doctor—Settle for a water buffalo? That did it—

Yours

Lt. W. P. (Pat) Wyatt U.S.M.C.

Marine Scout Bombing Sqd. 241

E.P.O. San Francisco, California

THE AZTEC NEWS LETTER

No. 47, February 1, 1946

1st LT. W. PAT WYATT, USMCR

is on terminal leave. He has the Distinguished Flying Cross, the Air Medal with two Gold Stars, and the Navy and Marine Corps Medal. He was a dive bomber pilot in the First Marine Air Wing in the South Pacific.

The campaign to liberate the Philippines stretched from October 1944 through the following August. At Leyte, more than 3,500 Americans were killed, and 12,000 were wounded. Another 1,000 lost their lives fighting to liberate Manila. The Japanese fared much worse, with approximately 70,000 wounded and dead at Leyte and 16,000 casualties at Manila. For the local Filipino population, the final fight for the capital city cost more than 100,000 lives.[23]

THE AZTEC NEWS LETTER

May 1, 1944
No. 26

This Issue Sponsored
in part by
Phi Kappa Gamma

Edited by
DR. LAUREN C. POST
San Diego State College
San Diego 5, California

The Quad   (Photo by Cyrus J. Keller)

**To All Aztecs in Service
and Their Friends:**

We were held up for several weeks in the mailing of the last News Letter by the delay up in Los Angeles in getting the stencils made. When they finally came, we had a month's mail to go through for changes in addresses, and we had a lot of new stencils to cut all at once. The work was pyramided and with several changes in secretaries, we were practically swamped. At times it looked hopeless, but you can look for business as usual from here on.

If you missed out on any issues, let us know and we will try to get them to you. Dr. Harwood is helping in answering requests for addresses. See later note. The sororities are still helping with the folding and stuffing of the News Letters as well as carrying on the campus sales.

We still have about 400 names on the "addresses wanted" list. If you find that you are not getting the News Letter, just check up with yourself and see if you haven't moved or charged addresses. For the time being we are not changing your ranks on the mailing stencils, even if we note the promotions in the News Letter. Those changes cost money and work.

We have fared pretty well financially, but summer is coming on. We are going to need about $200.00 each month so there may be a little commercial on the third page.

I'm happy to report a relatively small number of casualties this month. I hope next month is better. By the way, we still like to hear of decorations. Let us know whenever you meet another Aztec, especially those from whom we have not heard. Sorry we had to cut your letters so much, but you will understand. Keep writing.

And again, best of luck,

Lauren C. Post
Editor of the News Letter

LT. MAURICE C. MORRELL

was killed in a plane crash in Italy on February 23, 1944. He previously had been awarded the Air Medal and the Oak Leaf Cluster for shooting down a Messerschmidt 109. He was a P-38 pilot.

LT. CLEA E. WILLIAMS

was killed in a plane crash in an emergency landing at Fort Worth, Texas.

SGT. KENNETH L. JOHNSON

who was with a bomber squadron APO, New York, is missing in action according to a verified note on his News Letter envelope which was returned. (This is all we know. LCP.)

CAPT. BOB BAUDER, USMCR

is back from the Solomons where he piloted a dive bomber on 39 missions over enemy targets in New Georgia, Bougainville and New Britain. He has been awarded the Air Medal and is now stationed at the Marine Air Depot at Miramar.

MAJOR EDWIN H. BREWER

who is stationed in Sardinia at a B-26 Marauder base as a squadron commander, played an important role in the Tunisian, Sicilian, and Italian campaigns. His unit was one of the first to bomb Florence and Cassino. As previously noted Major Brewer holds a

Silver Star, the Air Medal and Oak Leaf Clusters.

LT. THOMAS BRENT BURRELL

was awarded the Air Medal for completing five bombing missions from a base in England. Lt. Burrell is now in a hospital in England recuperating from wounds for which he received the Purple Heart. His Flying Fortress was called the "Squirmin' Squaw." See later note from Brent.

CAPT. RICHARD D. BUTLER

has just walked into the News Letter Office and our grilling has just brought out these facts. He piloted a B-24 on 28 combat missions, one of which had as its objective the bombing of the Ploesti oil fields. For this mission his group was awarded the Presidential Unit Citation. While in England Capt. Butler ran across **Capt. Robert L. Cardenas,** who recently joined his group.

Capt. Butler was in the raid on Kiel from which **Lt. Ross A. Tenney** is still missing. That raid took place on May 14, 1943.

Capt. **John F. Edwards** is another Aztec whom Capt. Butler saw. Their meeting was in Tunis.

LT. CHARLES CASTON

was awarded the Air Medal and the Distinguished Flying Cross. He has been in the Pacific area for over a year.

12

AZTECS OF FINE CALIBER

THE AZTEC NEWS LETTER
No. 21, December 1, 1943
Pvt. Shoji Nakadate wrote from Station Hospital Surgery, Camp Grant, Illinois:
"In the paper I read about Bert Tanaka, a former Aztec, who is now in Italy with the Fifth Army consisting of Japanese Americans and other Americans. There was an article of a former San Diegan so I thought I'd send it. Another Nisei (J.A.) and a former Aztec is T/3 Paul Kuyama, who is in Australia. Many more will be going shortly, I believe."

The Japanese attack on Pearl Harbor spurred the United States to step up the pace of industrial production, churning out planes and warships, and training the pilots, infantrymen, sailors, and marines who would take that machinery into war. The attack also fueled fears of espionage and sabotage, culminating in policies that led to the confinement of Japanese Americans in internment camps. Relocations began immediately after Pearl Harbor. Modern historians argue that the camps, which were operated and guarded under the Army's authority, were places of forced imprisonment, much like concentration camps.[1]

Japanese and Japanese Americans targeted for relocation were those living in the Pacific coastal states, which were deemed geographically essential to military interests. The military was given the authority to "enforce compliance" with the order, which was signed by President Roosevelt in 1942:

> Now, therefore, by virtue of the authority vested in me as President of the United States, and Commander in Chief of the Army and Navy, I hereby authorize and direct the Secretary of War, and the Military Commanders . . . to prescribe military areas in such places and of such extent as he or the appropriate Military Commander may determine, from which any or all persons may be excluded.
> Executive Order 9066[2]

Ten camps were set up around the country. The number of interned people has been estimated at more than 100,000, and perhaps as high as 120,000. More than half of those incarcerated were second or third generation, the sons, daughters, and grandchildren of immigrants. They were citizens, born in the United States.

The Manzanar War Relocation Center housed more than ten thousand Japanese and Japanese Americans during World War II. Ringed with barbed wire and guard towers, it was built in an arid region to the northeast of Los Angeles. This dusty camp deep in the Owens Valley, where rain from the Sierra Nevada Mountains scarcely reached the valley floor, was ideally suited for keeping people out of sight.[3]

Another 16,000 people were imprisoned in Arkansas, where two internment camps were built along the state's southeastern border. Unlike the desert of California's Owens Valley, the sites in Arkansas were marshy and overgrown, yet residents of the camps managed to clear and cultivate farmland. The locations were supposed to be self-sufficient. Those who lived there struggled to foster some kind of normalcy with recreation and schools, but families were forced to share cramped barracks with little privacy. Like Manzanar, the Arkansas camps at Jerome and Rohwer were surrounded by barbed wire and watchtowers.[4]

At the war's end, the camps were closed, and people who had been imprisoned were expected to leave with little assistance. Many had been forced to sell or abandon homes and businesses, had lost their possessions, and had nowhere to go. Those who had been brought to Arkansas were discouraged from settling there. Although the state had made land available to the federal government for internment, it also made sure that the families who had been behind the barbed wire did not feel welcome to stay once they were released. In 1943 the state legislature had passed a law that made it illegal for Japanese and Japanese Americans to become landowners in Arkansas. Eventually, this law was declared unconstitutional, but at the time it meant that a group of uprooted Americans found it even harder to resume their lives.[5]

During the war, second generation Japanese Americans were sometimes given permission to return to college, but most schools in Arkansas refused them admission. Two San Diego State College Japanese American students who had been released from the internment camps made their way to a military training center in Camp Chaffee, Arkansas. Going back to San Diego was out of the question. They had to stay out of the restricted zone on the West Coast.

The following letter, written by a serviceman stationed at Camp Chaffee, described a chance meeting with his former classmates.

May 20, 1943
Dear Dr. Post,

. . .

I have been at Camp Chaffee, Ark. since December fifteenth and although I was very disappointed in it, as a place to live then, I'll have to admit it is beautiful now. Everything is so green and the wildflowers are plentiful and so colorful. I'm in an Armored outfit but we do plenty of walking and my Phy. Ed. training comes in handy. I've still to get my first blister—it pays to know how to care for your feet. . . . While on the way back I was pleasantly surprised to hear someone call my name while we were rustling a snack to eat. It was Paul Yamamoto. He and his brother Johnny are being released from internment camp. They are both old Aztecs of fine caliber. They are moving inland to try to start over again. Paul said Johnny volunteered for the Army but got turned down on account of his knee—football.

. . .

Sincerely,
Pfc. Clifford E. (Cliff) Wells
Reg't Hq Co
62nd A.I.R.
446 Camp Chaffee, Arkansas
U.S. Army

Despite the prejudice leveled against them, Japanese Americans volunteered to serve in the military. Most were excluded from combat, and those who did fight were usually assigned to segregated infantry units comprised of Nisei—children born in the United States to Japanese parents. Others were trained as intelligence agents and as translators, and during the war their efforts uncovered enough information about Japanese strategy to help the Allies win key victories in the Pacific.[6]

Shoji Nakadate and his brother, Kakuya, were members of Nu Alpha Chi, an all-Japanese organization at San Diego State College. The club photo from 1940 shows only five members. When asked by the yearbook editors to state their purpose, they responded "incorporating all-Japanese students . . . in interest of fellowship." By 1942, membership in Nu Alpha Chi had grown to more than twenty, and the yearbook credited the club with promoting goodwill between "Japanese Staters" and the general student body. Just a year later, in the 1943 yearbook, the name of Nu Alpha Chi had disappeared. The editors paid tribute to the servicemen from State who were killed or listed as missing, but they made no mention of those who were forced to depart for internment camps.[7]

Shoji and Kakuya Nakadate were spared imprisonment because they were accepted for military service.

October 15, 1943
Dear Dr. Post:

. . .

I am doing work now in surgery and am enjoying it as I see various kinds of operations, as well as, assisting in them. I have been getting quite an experience as I would get in Medical School, as I have been in the Laboratory over a year and have had about a month of surgery to date. There are many things to be learned here.

. . .

Very Sincerely,
Pfc. Shoji Nakadate
A.S.N. 19068060
Station Hosp. Surgery
Camp Grant, Illinois
U.S. Army

Undated
Gen. Hosp.
Somewhere in France
Dear Dr. Post:—
This is just a short letter. More later when I feel better and able. I have been moved here after I was wounded more than two weeks ago. My left leg got in the way of a Jerry machine gun. I hope to get back at them soon.

. . .

Sincerely yours
Pfc. Shoji Nakadate
19068060
2628 Hosp. Section
A.P.O. 698 c/o P.M.
New York, New York

January 14, 1944
Dear Dr. Post,

. . .

Shoji Nakadate was a classmate of mine and believe me I was glad to see his letter about the Nisei troops—it is a documentation of the ideals we're fighting for.

. . .

Lt. Edward B. Davis, Jr. USMCR
B-1 19th Marines
3rd Mar. Div.
c/o. F.P.O. San Francisco

December 5, 1945
Birmingham General Hospital
Dear Dr. Post:—

. . .

In September I had a furlough home to S.D. but missed seeing you or my other friends at S.D. State as I went there before school session. Time flew so fast. In October I took the marital step and married Mary Su Gaye Hirata, formerly of Sweetwater Hi. Probably that was part of the reason I couldn't do as much as I wished in visiting all my school acquaintances.

Last Monday I was operated on again and had a bone graft from my ilium transposed to my tibia so I shall be in bed again for a while. I am hoping I'll be able to get out of bed by Christmas. In January I hope to get a convalescence furlough, then I shall be able to see all of whom I have missed in September and October. In the meantime, my regards and best wishes to all for the Christmas and the New Year.

Sincerely yours,

Pfc. Shoji Nakadate

Wd C-15S

Van Nuys, California

Shoji's brother, Kakuya, entered the Army Specialized Training Program (ASTP), which was developed at the end of 1942 to meet the increasing demand for engineers and language specialists. He was at Ohio University, and a similar program was also under way at Ohio State. The ASTP held classes at more than two hundred colleges and universities around the country. Four years' worth of academics, military education, and physical conditioning were crammed into a year and a half.[8]

February 3, 1944

Dear Dr. Post:

. . .

Our training schedule calls for pretty long hours, and we do quite a bit of studying among other things. It's very interesting work. The town here is very small, but our off duty hours during the week-ends are well taken care of because of the various campus activities which are open to us soldier trainees here at O.U.

. . .

Sincerely Yours,

Pvt. Kakuya Nakadate

A.S.N. 19088332

Co. A 1553rd S.U.

Men's Dormitory, 213

Army Specialized Training Program

Ohio University

Athens, Ohio

U.S. Army

July 6, 1944

Dear Dr. Post,

Recently, I received my *Del Sudoeste* from the Aztec shop; and like the *News Letter*, it sure did give me a lot of enjoyment. It certainly is "super." I especially like the pictures of our campus grounds and buildings, and it was swell seeing the photos of my Aztec friends. I passed my *Del Sud* around in my barrack to a number of my buddies (who attended other colleges), and they were amazed at the beauty of S.D. State and at the large number of Aztecs in the Service.

I've finished my course at the central signal corps school, and I've been transferred to my regular unit training outfit.

Sincerely,
Kakuya Nakadate
3168th Signal Serv. Co.
Barrack # 2696
Camp Crowder, Missouri

October 24, 1944

Dear Doc Post,

I have finally landed overseas after waiting for about 2 years for this chance to serve more actively. During most of the time in the States, I was doing limited service work; but recently I got back on general service work, and it certainly gives me a good feeling to be doing my part along with my friends and buddies.

As yet, I am not permitted to write and say where we are located. We are sleeping in our little pup-tents, and our food consists mostly of canned rations such as hash, beans, and veg. & meat stew.

Sincerely,
Pvt. Kakuya Nakadate
19088332
Cas. Det.—D APO #17374
c/o Postmaster
San Francisco, California

October 31, 1944

Dear Doc Post,

. . . As yet we aren't permitted to write and say where we are located.

I tried getting some coconuts, but I couldn't quite climb up to the top of the tree—so haven't tasted any coconut milk yet. I might ask one of the natives around here to get one down for me. My brother, Shoji, wrote me the other day from somewhere in France. He's getting along pretty nicely.

Sincerely,
Pvt. Kakuya Nakadate
19088332
3168th Sig. Sv. Bn. Det. "G"
A.P.O. 565 c/o Postmaster
San Francisco, California

December 12, 1944
"Somewhere in the Philippines"
Dear Dr. Post,

. . .

I'm now in the Philippines somewhere. I've met and made friends with a number of Filipino people, and they surely are nice people. They are a generous and very intelligent people.

My brother, Shoji, is in France, and he was wounded a little while ago. He's now in a hospital some place—perhaps in France.

In conclusion I might add that the coconuts here are very tasty, but the bananas don't go so good with me.

Sincerely,
Pvt. Kakuya Nakadate
19088332
3168th Sig. Sv. Bn. Det. "K"
ADSOS (SIG) APO 72
c/o P.M., San Francisco, California

April 14, 1945
Brisbane, Australia
Dear Dr. Post,
I'd like to thank you for *News Letter* No. 35 which I received while I was up in Manila, P.I.

By the way, Dr. Post, I was just transferred from the Philippines, and I was flown down here to another signal unit in Brisbane, Australia. I surely am glad to be down here where the weather is invigorating. The early mornings are very chilly and cold, but I like it a million times better than the humid heat of New Guinea and the Philippines.

While in New Guinea and in the Philippines (Leyte & the Manila area), I was constantly being mistaken for a Jap and I was having quite a few jittery experiences. My officers became alarmed and concerned about me and my predicament, and they took action and had me transferred down here. (*Please don't print this part of my letter.*)

Here is my new address:

Sincerely,

Cpl. Kakuya Nakadate

832nd Signal Sv. Bn., Det. 3

APO #923

c/o P.M.

San Francisco, California

THE AZTEC NEWS LETTER

No. 38, May 1, 1945

Pvt. K. Nakadate wrote from the Philippines:

"I recently took another boat ride, which was quite uneventful except for a couple of stormy days. At present, I'm living in a regular concrete building and it sure is nice to see streets, highways, buildings, etc. again.

"The treacherous Japs sure did a lot of terrible things here. They will have to be made to really suffer a great deal for all of their beastly inhuman doings, and let's hope that that day will come soon!

"My brother, Shoji, seems to be recovering very nicely from his wounds received in France."

THE AZTEC NEWS LETTER

No. 46, January 1, 1946

T/5 Kakuya Nakadate is home from the Philippines. He was in the service nearly four years and was overseas 14 months. He was [in] a signal unit that was moved around from one outfit to another, but he managed to get three battle stars. They are for the New Guinea, Leyte and Luzon campaigns. Nakadate had one great difficulty. Being of Japanese descent, he sometimes had trouble convincing Filipino soldiers (some of whom were guerillas) that he really was an American soldier. And the time in which he had to do the convincing was sometimes limited. It was all the more difficult when they understood practically no English at all.

On one occasion even Nakadate's Lt. had trouble convincing a Filipino Lt. of his nationality. Soon after they transferred him to a different outfit where he was safe.

Kakuya has been mustered out and plans on continuing his work in zoology.

Jim Hurley, whose letter follows, fought in Africa and Italy, and he wrote to Dr. Post with opinions on every subject—from striking miners to how long the war was likely to last. He also weighed in on the subject of Japanese Americans.

September 22, 1944
Dear Doc:

. . .

Again I want to say the [American] Legion is doing great things for the Vets. However, if the legion or analogous organizations continue to mess with the American Japanese they are in for trouble, as bad as if people do not change their ideas on the negro situation. The Japanese troops here in this theater have proven themselves to be some of the best troops to operate here. Their record has yet to be beaten by any of our other units. That goes for everything. The soldiers that are their division mates haven't enough praise for them, and when combat infantrymen praise anybody or thing it means plenty, for they are a skeptical lot, believe me. Anyone in this theater who has fought with them will be down on a unit in the States that says any derogatory thing about them or tries to discriminate against them. There are a lot of GIs over here too.

. . .

Pfc. Jim Hurley
Headquarters Fifth Army
A.P.O. #464 U.S. Army
G-3 Section

Internment camps for those of Japanese descent were in operation through 1944. Forty-four years later, in 1988, Congress passed legislation recognizing the need to make amends to those whose freedom had been annulled by forced incarceration. Families and their heirs received compensation and a letter of apology signed by the president. The Civil Liberties Act of 1988, signed by President Ronald Reagan, reads in part, "For these fundamental violations of the basic civil liberties and constitutional rights of these individuals of Japanese ancestry, the Congress apologizes on behalf of the nation."[9]

THE AZTEC NEWS LETTER

March 1, 1944
No. 24

This Issue Sponsored
in part by
Kappa Theta

Edited by
DR. LAUREN C. POST
San Diego State College
San Diego 5, California

To All of the Aztecs in the Service and Their Friends:

This little note marks the end of the second year of the News Letter as the copy for the 24th issue is all ready for the printer. In every way the News Letter has grown beyond all expectation, and it has met many unforeseen needs that arose during the past two years.

For next time you have the promise of the best issue ever in the Second Anniversary Edition. Be on the lookout for No. 25. Keep sending in the addresses, promotions and notes of news. We know that there are dozens of decorations that we never heard of. Send them in. It is a lot more fun to write about decorations and clusters than it is to report casualties.

Post-War Education (no pun intended as punning there means something else) has been in my mind lately, and some of us would like to hear from you on that subject. What are your plans, and what do you think will work out? We are all interested in you even if you may not have a chance to vote.

And again, best of luck.

Lauren C. Post
Editor of the News Letter

🕊

1ST LT. RUSSELL NEWBURY
was killed in action in Italy on November 7, 1943. Lt. Newbury was in the infantry and had been through all of the toughest campaigns with the Fifth Army in Tunis, Sicily, and Salerno, and he was still engaged in the northward march when he last wrote. (Russ was the first of the 1938 Frosh football team members to be killed in action. **Cpl. Bob Newsom, USMC,** is a prisoner of the Japanese, and **Paul Siraton** was killed in a plane crash in training. The rest of the old gang are still going strong and have more than ever to fight for now. LCP)

🕊

PVT. WILLIAM R. HEADINGTON
was drowned while on active duty in Saidor, New Guinea, on February 7th, according to a telegram just received by his mother, Mrs. W. R. Headington, of 2911 Gunn St., San Diego.

Pat Allard, left, and Leone Carlson check pictures for the service men's section (16 pages) of Del Sudoeste, this year's annual. See later note about sending in pictures and about ordering a copy. (Only three of the four sections of the AZTECS IN SERVICE picture panel appear here.)

THE THEATER GUILD
GIVES BENEFIT FASHION SHOW
FOR THE AZTEC NEWS LETTER
Tuesday, February 29—12:10
In the Little Theater
Tickets 25c

F/O JOSEPH K. ROBBINS
wrote to **Dean C. E. Peterson** from a German Prisoner of War Camp on Nov. 13, 1943:

"Dear Dean C. E.: Surprise! I am not certain, but I think I am one of the first Aztecs to land in a Prisoner of War Camp. Had a bit of tough luck over Germany. Mention my situation in the News Letter as I am not allotted sufficient writing paper here to contact my buddies. Please drop me a line, Dean, and I'll appreciate it."

Joe's address is

Prisoner of War Mail   Postage Free
F/O Joseph K. Robbins
American P.O.W.
Interned at M. Stammlager Luft 3,
Germany
P.O.W. #2161
Via New York
New York

🕊

W. C. BATCHELOR
who was reported missing in action after the U.S.S. Houston was sunk in the Battle of the Java Sea, has been reported a prisoner of the Japanese in Burma—two years later.

13

EXHAUSTION

THE AZTEC NEWS LETTER
No. 22, January 1, 1944
Capt. Delmar Dyreson who is a chaplain in the Army in Italy
holds church services right up at the battlefront according to a
nice long story in the *San Diego Tribune-Sun* of December 18.
(Drop us a line sometime, Capt. Dyreson. I am sure your many
Aztec friends would like to hear from you. LCP)
Dr. Lauren C. Post, Editor

The need for war materials drove industry booms in steel and coal at a time when organized labor was flexing its muscles in the United States. During the Great Depression, falling prices had forced the closure of many mines, sending shock waves of hunger and misery through communities that were already used to harsh and dangerous working conditions. When the National Labor Relations Act was passed by Congress in 1935, the United Mine Workers of America flourished, along with the Congress of Industrialized Organizations. The miners promised not to strike during the war, but in 1943 the leader of the United Mine Workers of America encouraged members to walk off the job. Half a million miners broke their word and went on strike. President Roosevelt placed the mines under government control, but he couldn't get workers back on the job until their wages were increased.[1]

The work stoppage meant supplies were slow to arrive as the Allies prepared to push from Africa toward Italy. Pvt. Jim Hurley was with the Third Infantry Division reinforcing General Clark's Fifth Army. Hurley penned his complaints to Dr. Post, along with observations of economic hardship and attempts at reconstruction in North Africa. His heart went out to those suffering deprivations in the aftermath of battle, but he had no pity for striking workers back home.

October 30, 1943

Dear Doc:

. . .

First, my first impression of North Africa is one of the prevailing odor of horse dung mixed in with unwashed bodies. . . . The Germans, with their usual thoroughness, picked the place clean leaving a poverty ridden land poverty stricken. . . .

To try to describe the city that we are near, without naming it is hard. . . . It is a mixture of ultra modern, that is curved fronts and corner windows, Mohammedan architecture, and old New Orleans. That makes it interesting. The streets are thronged with the Arabian lower and middle classes, the few white civilians of the mother nation, and soldiers and sailors of the united nations and their satellites. . . .

. . . There are signs of the invasion and naval engagements along the beaches. There are hulks of civilian ships, naval vessels of the opponents and ours, and barges in the areas close to shore. . . . The Stars and Stripes gives us a survey of home news. . . . Those damn miners should to the man be placed in the army and shipped over here and see how much the united nations and we fighting men . . . are dependent upon them. If they could but hear some of the stories that we hear from returning casualties, . . . of how it is to be continuously on the attack for 37 days without stopping for anything but exhausted unconsciousness or collecting an extraneous piece of scrap metal. . . . If the transportation system ties up as it threatens to with men and materials needed as they are at any front, and especially the Italian front, it might have the repercussions of losing a campaign or at least heedlessly and needlessly prolonging battle with the resultant loss in life and good American blood.

It makes your heart turn to ice when you stop to think that the American manhood that will be needed in the future, not only to straighten America out, but the world as well, is being wasted by those bastards at home, just so that they might have more time to get drunk and have intercourse with our bitches and fill their pocketbooks. If they could really see inflation as it is here. The franc which used to be darn near the equivalent of our dollar is now worth two cents. It takes 800 francs for clothing, if you have a clothing certificate which is based upon need, and woolen goods and cotton yardage are up in the thousands of francs. If the people have the cards they still can't get it. Food is scarce and high priced, but that situation is improving. . . .

I'll quit now as it is close to mid-nite and the censor'll shoot me anyhow as this is long and my writing you know would drive him to drink. . . .

Pvt. James R. (Jim) Hurley Jr.

A.S.N. 19111063

Co. "I" 15th INF APO 3

c/o Postmaster NY, NY

Jim Hurley's outrage stemmed in part from his own keen sense of duty. While at San Diego State College, he belonged to Alpha Phi Omega, an organization dedicated to national service. The group sold war savings stamps and bonds and sponsored the daily flag ceremony on campus. Hurley's awareness of wartime scarcity and inflation came with his education as an economics and finance major. In addition to his other campus activities, he belonged to Tau Sigma, the college's economics club, which featured speakers on business topics twice each month.

A 1942 yearbook photo captures a dapper young Hurley attired in a sweater and tie, posing with his chin in hand, his neatly trimmed sideburns framing his smiling face. He was never far from campus leadership, serving as president of his fraternity, Kappa Phi Sigma, and as treasurer for the Associated Student Body. His duties included balancing the council budget. A write-up in the 1943 yearbook stated that "students now associate money matters with him like jive with a jukebox."[2]

Jim's father, James R. Hurley Sr., wrote to Dr. Post, "Next to his home, S.D.S.C. was the dearest place on earth to him." At the end of August 1943, Dr. Hurley sent a picture of his son to Dr. Post for the Service Men's Panel. Less than three months later he wrote again, hoping that the geography professor could help him pinpoint his son's location. Dr. Post received enough clues and detailed descriptions to give him a pretty good idea of where many students were located, but he took care to keep hints out of the *News Letter*. If he was able to help Dr. Hurley, he did so privately.

November 13, 1943

Dear Doctor Post:

I am enclosing herewith a recent letter from my son James, the 2d—from North Africa. My principal reason for sending it is to see if you can figure out from its contents his present whereabouts in No. Africa, which sure is a big country. I am enclosing herewith a self-addressed, stamped envelope for your reply, if you will be good enough to make one briefly—and if you can decipher his chirography, which I admit is execrable. He comes by it honestly.

. . .

It would appear to me that James was endeavoring in every way admissible to give us an indication as to his whereabouts without transgressing censorship rules. I am of the opinion that he is not in Tunisia as he leaves the impression that French is the prevailing language in his vicinity.

Mrs. Hurley wants to preserve this letter, so I will ask that you return it to me at your convenience.

. . .

With continuing sentiments of highest esteem, I am

Sincerely,

J. R. Hurley, M.D.

9298 Lemon Avenue

La Mesa, Calif.

After North Africa was secure, Allied Forces moved on to Sicily, and then they attacked the coast of the Italian mainland, including Salerno. This strategy was favored by Winston Churchill, who famously remarked that it was a way to get at the "soft underbelly" of the Axis.[3] The Germans proved to have a tougher hide than the Allies had anticipated. Defensive lines blocked almost every advance, and the fighting on the Italian peninsula beginning in September 1943 inched along, brutal, bloody, and slow. Rome wasn't captured until nearly a year later, on June 4, 1944.[4]

Following combat in Italy, Private Hurley, usually a prolific writer, had little to say. Weary servicemen writing to Dr. Post often shied away from recounting the gory details of battle. Dr. Post, himself a war veteran, would have been able to read between the lines. The men blamed their reticence on the censor, and they admitted that they wanted to spare their families from war's atrocities. Their letters also hinted at their own psychological adjustments. Loss of innocence came with an initiation into a store of terrible knowledge. The men suddenly knew too much, and they weren't in a classroom where their kindly professor could guide them through an orderly analysis of events. Submerged in mayhem, many of them fell silent.

As an infantryman, Hurley absorbed the physical and mental blows of combat. He asked for forgiveness for his reluctance to share his own account. He would keep trying, he pledged. And if he didn't have words, he at least offered his love.

December 9, 1943
Somewhere in Italy
Dear Doc:
At last I reached my permanent outfit. As you can see it is part of the famous Third Division. I can tell you this because it has been released for public consumption.

Doc, I can see now why men on front line combat duty tend to drop from sight, at least postally speaking. The whole psychological situation precludes any form of constructive thought and tends toward atrophy thru inhibition. Furthermore, military censorship and the individuals' own desire to keep the hell of the front line existence from his loved ones keeps him from writing much. It is bad enough that he has to go through the horrors without creating further worry and heartbreak. It is time for the Air Corps with their glamorous life and way of living to sit and write exciting letters, but when it is over and if you can get an artilleryman or infantryman to talk about it, which will be hard, who has been thru a campaign, the story will be hard to believe. You have to be there to believe it. So much for the moans and groans.

. . . I know that this is a morbid letter, but will have to suffice I guess. The type of work that you are doing is even more appreciated where we are. More than we can say. Please keep it up and forgive us if we don't write. Keep the people writing for even if momentary relief to us. We will try to write them. Give my love to all.

Pvt. James R. (Jim) Hurley, Jr.
A.S.N. 19111063
Co. "I" 15th INF APO 3
c/o Postmaster NY, NY

One of Jim's friends, Lt. Russell Newbury, was also in Africa and then in Italy. The two men tried to find each other, but the war pushed them in different directions. Newbury's August 22, 1943, letter describes the fighting in Sicily. The Allies were able to reach the Italian mainland once it, and other islands, were captured. Jim Hurley fought on the Italian coast and eventually saw Rome, but his friend didn't get that far. The date of Newbury's death given in his father's letter differed from the official notice.

August 22, 1943
V-Mail
My Dear Dr. Post:
You don't know how much I appreciated your post card which was a little more personalized than the *News Letter*.

The *News Letter* still comes through even in the heat of battle. I received the last issue during the height of the campaign here in Sicily. . . .

My personal experiences over here are about a duplicate of the Tunisian affair. The landing operations were surprisingly easy compared to what I expected. It was mostly an artillery battle with lots of mountain climbing. However, the fighting close in was much more bitter than in Africa, much like a cornered rattlesnake would fight.

. . .

As ever,
Lt. Russell W. Newbury
Co. H. 7th INF APO 3
c/o Postmaster New York

January 25, 1944
Dear Dr. Post:
Thanks for your enclosure of the *News Letter*, and your kindly solicitude in regards to Russell—a thing thoroughly reciprocated on his part, I am sure, as he spoke many times of his warm appreciation of San Diego State, and its staff, and looked forward to again taking up his studies there.

I am sorry to report that your apprehension as to his present status is well founded. He was killed in action, in Italy November 7th.

Wishing for you and the institution to which you are attached, all success. I am

Fraternally,
W. R. Newbury
408 No Hill—12
Los Angeles, California

WAR DEPARTMENT
The Adjutant General's Office
Washington
In Reply Refer To AG 201 Newbury, Russell W.
(24 Jan 44) PC-G 0-1,284,192
9 May 1944

Mr. Lauren C. Post, Editor
Aztec News Letter
San Diego State College, California
Dear Mr. Post:
Your letter of 24 January 1944, addressed to Captain Dyreson, in which you request information concerning your friend, First Lieutenant Russell W. Newbury, has been referred to this office for reply.

I regret to inform you that the records of the War Department show that Lieutenant Newbury was killed in action on 11 November 1943, in Italy, the date he was previously reported missing in action. His wife, Mrs. Elsie C. Newbury, 1705 Leighton Avenue, Anniston, Alabama, was so informed in a telegram of 6 January 1944, and confirming letter dated 10 January 1944. An additional report received in the War Department discloses that Lieutenant Newbury was killed in action on 11 November 1943, near Caspoli, Italy. The report states further that the direct cause of your friend's death was shell fragment wounds.

Permit me to extend my heartfelt sympathy in your bereavement.

Very truly yours,
Robert H. Dunlop
Brigadier General
Acting The [*sic*] Adjutant General

Captain Dyreson was serving in Italy. He forwarded Dr. Post's inquiry about Russell Newbury to the adjutant general's office, and he made a personal visit, at Dr. Post's request, to see Jim Hurley. Even though chaplains were viewed as noncombatants, they were attached to military units and were often therefore in the midst of battle. They ministered to men of all faiths and to those whose faith was uncertain. When the fighting broke off and the doctors had given the best that medicine had to offer, it was often up to the chaplains to stitch together wounded souls.

March 2, 1944
V-Mail
Anzio Beachhead
Dear Dr. Post and Aztecs All:
Thank you for the interesting *News Letter* which arrives so regularly. I am sure the sun never sets on the Aztecs.

A man named Adolf Hitler has, by his military and political machinations, greatly interfered with my letter writing lately. . . .

As for war stories, the press supplies a goodly number. I am convinced, however, that the best stories can never be told, for their authors now sleep. It is always in a spirit of reverence for those who have given all that I relate any battle-field experiences. In that mood I tell you that the Boche airmen have interrupted two out of the last four religious services we've held. Both were later resumed and concluded in good order. What we begin, we finish. Could an Aztec do less?

So here we are, trading punches with the Nazis while we keep one eye cocked on Rome.

Keep the letters coming.

Greetings to all,

Chaplain D. L. (Delmar) Dyreson

Regimental Chaplain

7th Infantry Regt.

APO #3 c/o P.M.

New York, New York

Anzio lies just thirty-five miles south of Rome. The Allies made an amphibious assault there in January 1944. Unfortunately, Italy was only one battlefront, and resources were needed elsewhere. As forces were preparing to attack mainland Italy, the buildup for the invasion of Normandy was under way. For the amphibious assaults, troops needed flat-bottomed boats, designated Landing Ship, Tank (LST) and Landing Craft, Infantry (LCI), to bring equipment and men to shore. The landing craft for the operations had to be divided between Italy and France, and the Allies were slow to deliver sufficient troops to Anzio.[5]

In his early letters to Dr. Post, Pvt. Jim Hurley had anticipated a shortage of war materials. Thirty-six thousand men made it to shore on the first day of the Anzio offensive. By the end of the week, the Allies had nearly doubled that force, but over the next few months, the fighting bogged down. Men struggled to hold their positions on exposed, marshy beaches where they were surrounded by Germans and pinned under a barrage of shelling. By May, Allied troop strength swelled again, and the stalemate was broken. Still, casualties from shelling and combat fatigue were high on the embattled beachheads.[6]

"Shell shock," the term used in World War I for combat stress, was more broadly defined as "exhaustion" in World War II. Jim Hurley, the young finance student who loved his college almost as much as his family, served in student government, and excoriated striking miners, found himself trapped on a beach while artillery shells exploded all around him.

In February 1944, Hurley wrote to Dr. Post from the hospital. Just a few weeks later he wrote again, mentioning that he still hoped to find his friend Russell Newbury, but Russell had been killed in action three months earlier. As he continued to heal, Hurley stayed with his unit as a noncombatant. After reaching Rome, he took an account of the balance of war and cautioned those at home that more lives would have to be spent in battle.

February 28, 1944
Italy
Hi Doc:
Well, I'm in the hospital. Nothing serious and nothing to collect a medal for. I'm in on an exhaustion rap, which covers a multitude of sins, mostly of the neuropsychiatric type which again as you know is a wide field. I was sent in from the lines, which one I can't say, you guess.

. . .

I was first in the two metropolises in North West Africa. I see where a few of the boys that thirsted for action sure got it when they drew LST and LCI berths. I am well acquainted from first hand experience of their duties. . . .

Doc, the care of neural-psychiatric cases in this hospital is wonderful. They rehabilitate the individual with a planned program of sports and occupational therapy. When they think you are ready they try to find a job around the institution that is best suited to you.

. . .

I was glad to get your note concerning Lt. Newbury. However, at the time I got your letter we could not make contact due to our mutual business. I shall try again. . . .

Doc, the American Soldier has certainly proved himself in this theater in the recent period of time. I was there and saw him on one part of the front and acquaintances of mine in other units bear adequate testimony on the other front. Even though he is still somewhat confused as to what it is all about he is proving himself equal to and better than the best the enemy has to offer. We now are meeting some of the cream of the crops that Hitler had been saving. The German is a good fighter and has plenty of fight in him yet, plenty. We have no doubt who will win, it is a matter of when.

. . .

It rests in the hands of the psychiatrists whether they think I'll ever do combat again. I blew my stack & lost my marbles. No permanent after effects except a little deafness and visual trouble. If this letter seems incoherent please forgive me, I'm still a bit rusty in spots.

. . .

The ward boy is pissing up a storm so I'll have to roger and out. Keep the reunion going.

Pvt. James R. (Jim) Hurley, Jr.
A.S.N. 1911063
Co. "I" 15th Inf. A.P.O. 3
c/o Postmaster
New York, New York

Hurley's next letter, written less than two weeks later, explains again that he's in the hospital for "exhaustion." His prose reveals the landscape of combat stress. It was a specter that appeared in different forms to those in different war theaters. Infantrymen like Hurley, who made shore assaults, emerged from landing craft and waded toward the beach under hellish artillery fire and gunfire. The "screaming mimis" he mentions were German rockets nicknamed for the sound they made as they hurtled toward their targets. The intensity of battle combined with lengthy campaigns tore at the seams of sanity. Hurley clung to his correspondence with Dr. Post, grateful for every edition of the *News Letter*.

March 10, 1944
Still Italy
Dear Doc:

. . .

I'm in the hospital with what is known in the parlance as "exhaustion" which covers a multitude of sins. My sin was to get caught in the center of a concentration of "screaming mimi's" & get my marbles scattered all over the [censored]. . . . To top it off it took me 3 days to collect them. While my top was off I sure had me one hell of a time telling officers & noncoms off & even tried to pick a fight with a 6 foot Ranger. Wish I could have been there to enjoy it.

. . .

Couldn't contact Russ Newbury due to press of business. Hope to soon. Got 4 A.N.L.

Thanks.

Pvt. James R. (Jim) Hurley, Jr.
A.S.N. 1911063
Co. "I" 15th Inf. A.P.O. 3
c/o Postmaster
New York, New York

Doctors were well acquainted with battle fatigue. Treatment could be quick—just a few days away from the front lines—or, as in Hurley's case, the prescription was rest and light duties. The number of U.S. troops wounded in action during World War II is estimated at about 671,800,[7] and as many as half of all who were discharged from service throughout the war may have suffered from battle fatigue or exhaustion.[8]

April 15, 1944

Dear Dr. Post:

Thank you so much for your interest in James, Jr., and for asking the Chaplain of the 7th Infantry to look him up, and for letting us know about it. It was kind of you indeed, especially when you have so many Aztecs to remember, who are now serving their country. I do hope that the 7th is billeted near the 15th so that the Chaplain Dyreson can easily find James. The latter is having a rather difficult time of it, and to think that *somebody* was interested in him, and one who was capable of giving him spiritual consolation besides, will, I'm sure, give his morale a big uplift.

It was just too darn bad about Russell Newbury. James, I know, knew him well, and liked him, so we have not written James about Newbury's death. The former will find it out when he gets the latest *Aztec News Letter*, however, if he has not heard of it before. Being in a different regiment James had not run across him in Italy, or at least has not mentioned it in any of his letters though it's been several weeks, now, since we received a letter from James. In the last one he was about to be discharged from the base hospital, and sent back to his regiment via a replacement centre camp. James was in the Anzio beachhead landing operations, and his regiment, along with the balance of the 3rd Division, was still at Anzio the last we heard. We can only watch, hope and pray.

Thanking you again for your courtesy, I am

Sincerely yours,

J. R. Hurley, M.D.

9298 Lemon Avenue

La Mesa, California

Whether he was on the front lines, or with the "chair-borne infantry" (as he liked to call his position in the rear), Pvt. Jim Hurley was insightful, even prescient. He was always taking the pulse of the war, and he had an instinctive understanding of his enemy. He read the *Stars and Stripes*, the newspaper published for American servicemen that gave updates about the combat theaters, as well as news from home. As the fighting progressed in Italy and in France, many commanders became optimistic that the war might be over by the end of 1944. In one of his many long and thoughtful letters, Private Hurley cautioned Dr. Post against too much optimism. The Germans still had a lot of fight left in them, and the war was going to take a while longer.

Hurley also understood that after the Normandy invasion, all eyes were focused on northern Europe. His theater in Italy seemed forgotten, and his comments hint at a conflict that was playing out between the Allied leaders. The Americans wanted to concentrate their efforts in France. Hurley would have found a friend in Winston Churchill, who favored more support for the Italian campaign. In his letter, Hurley refers to the Normandy invasion as the "big show," and he uses an Italian word, "Tedeschi," for the Germans. The French often called Germans "the Boche," while Americans referred to them as "Jerry." More than anything, Jim Hurley wanted history to take note of what he and his friend, Russell Newbury, had accomplished.

✉ August 12, 1944
Dear Doc:

. . .

The type of entertainment over here is improving. The movies are more up to date. We are getting stage shows such as Lily Pons and Jack Haley and his luscious troop. . . . The best trooper of them all though, in my estimation, was Ella Logan which came to us in the Third up in the mountains. She sang under the most difficult conditions, to a bunch of tired and jaded doughfoots, in freezing weather out in the open, within cannon shot.

. . . As we progress up into the better part of Italy the change in the people is noticeable. Cleaner, better dressed, friendly and stuff has been leaking out on how these northerners have helped escaped prisoners. The partisans up here are of much value to our men. . . .

This is a rather poor letter, but I am not mad so I can't expound at length. Just don't let the people around there get too optimistic about the duration of the European war. It is rosy now, going great guns and all that, but there is a lot of ground to cover in more ways than one.

Good night

Jim Hurley

Headquarters Fifth Army

A.P.O. #464 U.S. Army

G-3 Section

September 22, 1944
Dear Doc:
. . .
I want to say that as far as the forgotten theater is concerned, we are experiencing some of the toughest fighting in Italy. Tedeschi is fighting like a cornered rat, and our fellows are fighting in as bad a piece of terrain as has been offered as a battle field. They are doing a wonderful job too. . . . The more I see of the American soldier the better man I think he is. . . . We have experimented with new equipment, tried new ordnance and supplies in the battle field, learned more about the German and how to handle him so that the big show could go off. I only hope that after the war we get the proper credit for what we have done. . . .

> Jim Hurley
> Headquarters Fifth Army
> A.P.O. #464 U.S. Army
> G-3 Section

THE AZTEC NEWS LETTER
No. 38, May 1, 1945
Jim, there are no forgotten fronts—not as long as there are Aztecs on them, and we have them on all of the fronts. I wish I knew the meanings of some of the big words you used, but you see, I was just a Navy man. . . . I hope your war is won before you get to read this. LCP.

> Dr. Lauren C. Post, Editor

Jim Hurley, Associated Student Body treasurer
Del Sudoeste, San Diego State College yearbook, 1942, Special Collections and University Archives, San Diego State University

THE AZTEC NEWS LETTER

The Victorious Aztecs and friends are invited to meet for their first Annual Reunion after the war at the above scene.

November 1, 1943
No. 20

This Issue Sponsored in Full by The Alumni

Edited by
DR. LAUREN C. POST
San Diego State College
San Diego 5, California

To all of the Aztecs in the Service and Their Friends:

There is never the least bit of trouble in making the deadline with the News Letter copy. In fact the struggle is the other way around—trying to keep from filling 12 pages of closely spaced copy too early in the month. What to cut and do every fellow justice and still make a publication that is readable for all is, of course, the problem.

If you don't get your copy each and every month, write and let us know. A

News Letter has been mailed to you every month since we first received your address. But if one was ever returned because of out-dated address, then the address was crossed off your card and your name was posted on our "Addresses wanted" list. We are helpless the moment your address changes, so let us know each and every time it changes, and then for good measure, drop us a line each time you get promoted. Or is it correct to continue to put 'A.S.' after the name of an ensign? Some of the real old timers are on the modest side when it comes to writing, but we still want to hear from you at least every 12 months.

We keep a complete file on those who are killed, missing, wounded, taken prisoner, or decorated. All such information is noted on the AZTECS IN SERVICE panel so you can scarcely imagine how much information the panel contains besides the actual pictures. Be sure to let us know if you were wounded or decorated.

We are having another "Open House" for the panel on Sunday, November 7,

from 3 to 5. Parents, friends, and the service men on leave or who are stationed in this vicinity are especially invited to pay it a visit.

And again, best of luck,
Lauren C. Post
Editor of the News Letter
PS. See letter to Wally McAnulty on last page.

A/C WARREN EDWARD HAND
was reported killed in a plane crash at Corpus Christi, Texas.

CAPT. JOHN W. BASSETT
who earlier had been reported killed in action in Attu has been awarded the Silver Star posthumously for gallantry in action. When the Japanese staged a fierce counter-attack, Capt. Bassett, who was in the Army Medical Corps at a forward echelon of his field hospital, organized a group of armed but leaderless soldiers and directed their fire to repulse three separate Japanese attacks. A stream on Attu has been named Bassett creek in memory of his intrepid stand.

14

THE HUMP AND
THE BLACK HOLE

In 1931 Japan invaded Manchuria, a region to the northeast of Beijing that borders the Sea of Japan. Fighting between Japan and China continued, and by 1937 numerous sparks had ignited into the Second Sino-Japanese War, which then merged into the conflagration of World War II. The United States tried to counter Japanese aggression against China by means of an embargo, but cutting off Japan's oil supply only made that nation more determined to find resources. Japan's next step was to take Burma (now Myanmar) in 1942, which was then under British rule. Situated between China and India, Burma offered a tenuous mountain passage between the vast, embattled regions of China and Southeast Asia. Next, Japan set its sights on India, which was also under British control.[1]

Following Pearl Harbor, the United States was quick to offer more assistance to China, and an all-volunteer squad of American pilots briefly captured the spotlight. The Flying Tigers, commanded by Gen. Claire Lee

Chennault, flew early missions with the Chinese Air Force until the Flying Tigers were replaced by regular U.S. Air Force units. Chennault believed that pilots should fly offensively as well as defensively, and he trained fighter pilots using the Curtiss P-40. In many ways, the small planes were outmatched by the enemy's technology, but the American Flying Tigers developed a ferocious reputation in the skies over Burma.[2]

September 27, 1943
Assam, India
Dear Doc. Post:
I just received *News Letter* No. 18, and it certainly brightened up a very rainy day.

It's hard to believe that Paul Fern and William Shropshire have gone West. So much good blood has been spilled during this war so far, hasn't it, Doc, and it's really a crime too. Boys like the two mentioned above, good American boys, killed because the damn Japs wanted a greater East Asia, well, they will sooner or later get that greater East Asia business crammed right down their throat. I'm hoping and praying when that final day comes, that I will have the profound pleasure of running hog-wild through the skies over Japan. From what I see over here that day is not far off.

. . .

Our operations around here require that we fly over the most rugged mountains and the most dense jungle to be found in the world. And when that fan and peanut grinder up front begin to run irregular, the gremlins really get in your cockpit and start to work, man, how they can work when something is wrong.

By the way Doc, I want to thank you very much for the Aztec Sticker, it's on the canopy of my plane right now. I'll enclose a couple of Indian Rupees, Doc, which are worth about .30, American money. Please send me a couple more stickers for my room and Out Shack.

. . .

I don't know whether I told you about meeting and talking with General Chennault, but it certainly gave me a thrill that I shall never forget. He is like a father to fighter pilots in this area, and if you have a problem on your mind you can go directly to him and he will help you solve it. Yes Sir! we look up to General Chennault as a sort of Fighter God. He seems to be another Sun-Yat-Sen to the Chinese population.

. . .

To close this letter I would like to express my deepest thanks as well as the rest of the gang's (all of them read the *News Letter*) for the appreciation and enjoyment we receive from your great *News Letter*. Viva La *News Letter*.

As Ever Your Reader and Admirer,
Lt. Dodd V. Shepard
A.P.O. 3969 NY, NY
89th Fgtr Sqdr. 80th group

November 8, 1943
Assam Air Base
Dear Doc;

I thought I had better drop you a line today acknowledging your letter which arrived yesterday morning. I just don't know how to express my thanks for the information and Aztec stickers conveyed in the letter, but thanks at any rate.

Today, which happens to be one of my days off, I was up in the foothills of the Tibetan Ranges of Mts. Doc, you have no idea of the beauty found there. The streams are blue with snow white foam and abound with trout, while the heavily forested hills, with their autumn colors, abound with deer of every description. We shot two and are having Venison tonight, which should sound very appetizing to you.

As for the war, well, we have been very busy with it, especially the past few weeks. Activity has stepped up a hundred percent during the past month, but of course the nature of the activity I can't divulge.

How are things going at State? From all indications I presume that State has dropped football for the duration, am I not correct.

. . .

Sincerely,
Lt. Dodd V. (Shep) Shepard
A.P.O. 3969 NY, NY
89th Fgtr Sqdr. 80th group

The China-Burma-India (CBI) theater was rich in resources but difficult to navigate, and keeping troops supplied was a constant struggle. Britain initially used the seven-hundred-mile-long Burma Road to deliver provisions to China, but after Japan captured key cities in Burma, the overland supply routes that sustained unoccupied Chinese territories were closed.

Gen. Joseph Stilwell, in command of the U.S. forces, hoped to build a new road through a high mountain pass in northern Burma, but until a land route could be constructed, Allied forces took to the air, flying cumbersome transport planes and ferrying hundreds of thousands of tons of war materials from India into China. The route took them over the Himalayas and 15,000 foot peaks beset with turbulent air currents, a dangerous passage that pilots dubbed "the Hump." Overloaded planes and exhausted crews resulted in accidents, and Japanese attacks often downed the unarmed transports.[3]

Military resources in the CBI theater were stretched thin, but help came from Pan American Airways. The company was founded before the war by a group of men with military pedigrees. As former Air Corps pilots, they saw the value of an international company that could land planes all over the world, and they quickly lined up investors. Originally, Pan Am delivered international mail, but when America began actively defending China, Pan Am used its considerable resources to do even more. The company took over the beleaguered China airways and became an owner of the China National Aviation Corporation (CNAC).[4]

Pan Am recruited expert pilots who could fly in any conditions, guiding their planes with instruments and by celestial navigation. Thanks to their company's deep pockets, skilled mechanics supported the flight crews, and they had access to the parts necessary to keep their planes in top working order. Pan Am's fleet included a modern new passenger airliner, the powerful DC-3, designed by Douglas Aircraft, which was modified for cargo transport. Pan Am moved its headquarters to India and recruited more pilots to fly the Hump.

June 25, 1945

Dear Doc—

. . .

I've flown The Hump about 200 times, Army count, single missions—and still going strong. . . . I've put in nearly 1000 hours on The Hump—and during that time, I've seen quite a bit of weather. The feat of navigating *around* mountains on instruments has to be learned carefully and reverently from older pilots who pioneered this route during the heyday of The Flying Tigers. . . .

Those lads hold records no one will ever be able to equal—most of them have crossed The Hump night and day, good weather and bad, for the past three and four years—until they are well over the 600 mark! The Army considers a man qualified to go home with only a few more hours than that. The real story of CNAC has never been told.

. . .

Capt. John P. (Pete) Billon, CNAC

One of Lieutenant Shepard's friends, Jim Dolby, flew transport planes over the Hump, but he longed for a P-38. The P-38 Lightning, made by Lockheed, was designed to fly at high altitudes, which made it ideal for crossing mountain ranges. Fast and quiet, the P-38 had a double tail section that engineers called a twin boom. The enemy viewed this effective fighter plane in a different light. The devilishly fast attacks made it seem "fork-tailed."[5]

Lieutenant Shepard flew a plane made by Vultee Aircraft called the Valiant. This tough little plane was fast and powerful but tricky to fly. It lacked hydraulics and earned the nickname "Vibrator" for the unnerving way different parts of the plane shook at varying speeds. After one harrowing encounter, Lieutenant Shepard sent Dr. Post a picture of his plane. Jim Dolby also described Shepard's battles. As combat progressed and stories were shared, the servicemen hinted that Dr. Post should expect a bit of exaggeration. They referred to these tales as "snow jobs" and competed to see who could give the best account.

When asked to explain the term, Dr. Post replied in the *News Letter*:

THE AZTEC NEWS LETTER
No. 34, January 1, 1945
The term Snow Job is perhaps best defined by a question that one sometimes hears even when the air temperature is rather high, "What kind of a Snow Job do you think you are handing me?" We call our unofficial lecture series by returning heroes our Snow Job series.

But sometimes I think the term is a misnomer for the series because the fellows are so modest—far more modest than I was after the other war. LCP.

Dr. Lauren C. Post, Editor

January 23, 1944
Dear Doc

Just a note to let you know how things are going out this way. The situation is changing over here and fast. The Japs seem to be bringing in a lot of fighter aircraft with which they intend to step up their attacks on us, our bases, and the transports flying the hump. At any rate I have had some hair raising scrapes with the Japs during the past two months.

Just five days ago I was leading a flight of four ships on a patrol over enemy territory when we encountered between twelve and sixteen zeros. Now, you can well understand that our position was rather precarious, but we managed to send them back minus three, and considering the number of planes we had, I don't think we did such a bad job.

By the way, I was promoted to a first Lieutenant about a month ago. Gosh, I really sweat that promotion out.

Enclosed is a picture of my Vibrator. Hope you like it.

Guess that's all for now Doc, but I'll keep in touch with you as time goes by.

Sincerely,

Lt. Dodd V. (Shep) Shepard

March 14, 1944

China

Dear Dr. Post:

. . .

I just got through, or rather, just got over spending a rip-roaring ten-day leave with Lt. Dodd Shepard. He is really doing a job to be proud of. One day during a raid on our field, Dodd and three others took on about twenty-five enemy aircraft. Dodd did an all-right job, I believe that he shot down a bomber and a Zero.

I had a little excitement myself the other day. I broke out of some clouds to find myself almost flying formation with three Zero's. Guess who ran back into the clouds darn fast? Oh, for a P-38 instead of that lumbering transport.

. . .

I'm sorry that this letter is such a poor one. The only excuse is that I must be "Hump Happy" (too many trips over the "Hump"). I should write it over but I have no more paper. The supper bell has just rung and there is a mad rush for the food, I guess that I had better go or I'll starve.

Sincerely yours,

Jim Dolby

A.P.O. 465 c/o PM.

New York, New York

The difficulties of traversing the land route that stretched from India through Burma to China were as numerous as the miles were long. Troops suffered the worst that the jungle had to offer, and supplies, including food, were slow to arrive.[6] The air route had its own dangers. An estimated

650,000 tons of war materials were flown across the Hump.[7] Some planes crashed, and others were reported missing, their cargo and crew vanishing over the Himalayas. Many in the region also felt frustrated that the struggle in India was overshadowed by other battle fronts.

One of the following letters refers to ringworm, a fungal infection caused by moist conditions. It could be treated topically, and the purple dye described was probably iodine. The professor mentioned in that letter, Dr. Robert D. Harwood, specialized in life sciences, and his expertise would have been handy for identifying the many types of snakes.

July 15, 1944
Somewhere in India
Dear Dr. Post,

. . .

Our main concern the past few weeks has been the weather. The rains of the monsoon have kept us pretty close to our tents. Due to the resulting humid atmosphere, things have taken to changing color. My cotton khakis are speckled with mildew, my wool uniform's pale green and fuzzy with mould, my pistol and knives are brown with rust, my silver musical instrument a strange lavender color from God knows what, and my complexion is assuming a weird yellow cast. Of course, those of the fellows who have picked up ringworm (and there are quite a few) do me one better with their brilliant splotches of purple dye, which cure is supposedly preferable to the disease.

I slaughtered with a huge tent-stake mallet a small snake that crept in out of the rain the other evening. The natives identified the mangled remains as being those of a cobra. Their identification was accompanied by much gesturing with the hands, simulating the characteristic hood and striking movement of the cobra. The fact that these Indians tend to refer to every reptile that crawls about their country as a "cobra" leaves me with doubts, however. Perhaps Dr. Harwood can render an opinion on the subject: the critter was a poisonous snake about 18″ long with markings similar to those of a diamond back rattlesnake.

. . .

Yours sincerely,
Lt. Donald B. (Don) Smith 0-581228
317th Fighter Cont. Sqd.
APO—9687 c/o Pm
New York, New York

✉ October 9, 1944
China
Dear Dr. Post,

. . .

Out here we often feel we're living in another world, fighting another war. The emphasis on plans for celebrating "V-Day" back in the States following the collapse of Germany has earned for our particular sector of World War II the title of "The Forgotten Front." Even the Hollywood stars who start-out this way to give their "all" for the boys consistently run-out on their commitments because they find CBI-land both unpleasant & unglamorous, despite the fact they are given the finest in accommodations that each locality has to offer and are handsomely reimbursed by the government to make up for lost paychecks at home. This isolation from the American soil and the American mind, coupled with a confusion of ideologies, sometimes finds us questioning our most fundamental convictions.

. . .

Sincerely,
Lt. Donald B. (Don) Smith
317th Fighter Cont. Sqd.
APO 210, A-H, c/o PM
New York, New York

✉ November 10, 1944

. . .

Probably it won't be against regulations to tell you China National Aviation Corporation's job—flying the "Hump." That is a well known fact. The company has been in existence a very long time and originally established the route a long time ago.

. . .

Saw a very incredible sight not long ago. The population of this city in India is so large that every night a few thousand of the Indians die on the streets, and are collected the next day—piled in ply-wood fashion with tiers of wood and a layer of bodies and burned. It's really something to see.

. . .

My best regards to you and all of the Aztecs on campus.
Capt. John P. (Pete) Billon, CNAC
APO 465
c/o Postmaster
New York City, New York

In India, too much rain damaged crops and led to famine, and the usually fertile area of the Bengal delta wasn't able to support its dense population. While the land route was closed, Calcutta (now Kolkata) couldn't import food from Burma. Calcutta was no stranger to misery. In 1756 British troops stationed at a fort for the protection of the East India Company were captured in a local rebellion. More than a hundred men perished from suffocation and other injuries after being crammed into a tiny prison. The incident helped give rise to the city's unfortunate nickname, the Black Hole.[8] For the servicemen, conditions were harrowing in city and jungle alike.

Lt. John Muelchi was fighting battles as vicious as the viper-infested terrain. His letters hint at the many ways he adapted to a combat theater comprised of troops from different nationalities, along with a changeable command structure. He improvised when necessary, especially when it came to supplementing his diet of rice and military rations with wild game. He made the most of fishing and hunting opportunities, but his love of the outdoors stopped short of snakes. The Thompson he refers to in one of his letters was the Thompson submachine gun, also called the Tommy gun. Muelchi was clever and innovative, but he was powerless to alleviate the suffering of the local population.

August 2, 1944

Greetings Busy One:

Just a line to let you know that all is well in the Black Hole of Calcutta & that the *News Letter* has arrived for June & July. Someone on the other side of this damp territory must have wanted to peruse a good paper as they arrived one day apart.

. . . It has been ten months since my last flight & crackup! Time really fleets away. It has been a nice rest though.

Attended a none too appetizing sight last week. Our abode is only a couple of blocks from the "Burning Ghats," so last Friday we journeyed up to the daily 5 P.M. cremations. There are plenty of them. (952 people died over the weekend in this city.) They stack up a bunch of logs & place the body on top. The fire is started first & a solemn ceremony is held during the roast. It's not too thorough, the ceremony or the cremation. Some stomachs in our little group were not in tip top shape that day, so I'll have to leave the description out as we suddenly had other places to go but fast. We did get pictures of it but they aren't exactly pleasant to look at even if you have an able stomach.

They used to make the wife or wives dive on top of the deceased, but that's out now. They got timid & refused. As late as 1900 the priests had huge logs suspended over the fire & if they could get the mate over the pile, the log was cut loose & pinned her on the pile. It fell with enough force to break the back or spine so that a change of heart was useless. It's illegal now.

That's all for now, Doc, except that usual thing, a new address! . . .

'Bye for now & keep 'em coming.

Salaam,

As Ever,

Lt. J. A. (John) Muelchi

APO 465—4th P.R.S.

August 17, 1944

Hi Doc:

Ah! ah! ah! don't tear that hair. There isn't much left & I'm fairly certain this will be my last new address for a while. Be calm.

. . .

Right now we are putting the finishing touches on the Chinese division I'm with & they should be ready to move out soon. This is a pack outfit & I'm only here in the way of an assistant liaison officer & also to refresh my paltry knowledge of Field Artillery.

I happen to be the first F.A. pilot to hit these parts & they don't quite know what to do with me. It has all been hashed out now & action is in the offing.

We have a nice spot here. We're in the jungle & supplement our Chinese ration of rice daily with what we can get with a carbine, rifle, or pistol. Have had dove for the last two days. Have to be careful where you hit them, or they fly to pieces. Today we exterminated a wild boar & good old pork chops are on the menu.

Had a nice experience just before I sat down to record this note. Was laying on the floor, in a rather indisposed manner, reading. Suddenly, I had a feeling I wasn't alone. I looked around the room, or better yet, the bamboo floor of my tent & gazed right in the eyes of a young viper coming through the floor. I bet I jumped ten feet straight up. I threw every book, shoe, or loose object I had at him & never hit the snake once. He was as scared as I. He finally found the exit. I almost shot him, but thought better of it. We have a bunch of trigger happy guards around here & that is the best way in the world to set off every Thompson in camp. It's okay during daylight hours.

If we stay here until mating season is over (September 1st) the local keeper of the forest is going to take us cat hunting on elephants. Hope we remain.

. . .

No Aztecs, no nothing up here, just heat & mosquitos. Ah, for a tall, *cool* one.

Sincerely

Lt. J. A. (John) Muelchi
A.P.O. 689
Northern Combat Area Command

December 18, 1944

Hi Doc:

Rec'd the December issue of the *News Letter* several days ago, but have just got around to acknowledging it. We have been indulging in a little battle over here for about ten days. You probably heard of our hollow victory. The downfall of the surrounded territory came about on December 15. There has been a bit of indecision [on] the part of our commander on the advisability of our moving on into more opposition.

Our Artillery was given credit for the breaking of the siege. I went into the conquered area for the last three days and we really gave them a good pounding. We all started out with the intentions of obtaining all of the weapons of war of the enemy that we could carry. As usual, we wound up grabbing Burmese items. I got a Buddha, some vases of small size out of the same temple, a few bells, and a pair of spurs that belonged to some unfortunate Nip. I wound up trading my Buddha for a rifle, why I don't know. We had an entire day of stiff bartering here after everyone had obtained a bit of loot. As usual, we found that The Sons of Heaven were very well supplied and were well cared for.

Guess we have the best outfit in this area. It is strictly American and we even have command function. That is something new for this place. Everyone seems to be well satisfied with our work so far, so we shouldn't encounter any difficulties. You have probably heard a million times before about what excellent jungle fighters they are and how well they dig in, so there is no use of lingering on that subject. You come to realize very quickly in this theatre that there is no such thing as a pushover victory. We really earn and pay a good price for everything we get.

Got myself a swell fishing kit and am going to embark on an expedition this afternoon. Have a nice river that came with the taking of this place. 'Tis rumored that it is well stocked with some large game fish. I have heard tell they are Pike. No one seems to know for sure, and so I aim to find out.

Guess you are still tops, Doc. . . . I never fail to show your production all over the place and watch the envious eyes.

. . . The Colonel has just returned and I am sure to get a chewing if I don't submit to his wishes pretty soon. So-o-o, before trouble descends in torrents on my shoulders, I will have to say Adios for now. Best wishes to you and Mrs. Post.

As Ever,

Lt. J. A. (John) Muelchi

The Aztec News Letter
Special Edition—Christmas—1943

AS OUR CAMPUS LOOKED IN THE GOOD OLD DAYS WHEN WE HAD GASOLINE AND TIRES

To All Aztecs in Service:

Eight years ago when I was a "freshman" here at San Diego State College I dreamed of an institution whose influence some day would extend far beyond the region located south of Los Angeles. Little did my most fanciful flights of imagination indicate to me that Aztec spirit, contributions, and leadership would reach into all the far corners of the world. The messages in your letters and the reports of your activities and achievements from other sources all indicate that Montezuma's sons, and daughters, too, are true warriors of determination, courage, efficiency and humility. I like your letters. You see, Dr. Post lets me read a few of them! And I, too, look forward each month to the receipt of my copy of the News Letter.

I only wish that I might have known each one of you personally as I have known some and with whom I am privileged to correspond regularly—but that is wishful thinking. However, I do wish for you every success and all the joy and satisfaction that is at all possible under the unique circumstances in which each one of you may find himself in this holiday season. When you return to the campus won't you put a call to my office on your list of "musts"? The opportunity to greet each of you is a privilege which I covet.

Sincerely,

Walter R. Hepner

At this Christmas time we are thinking of our State College representatives all over the world. We have the faith that you are spreading our spirit of friendship wherever you are. We proudly follow you in your various ways and eagerly wait to welcome you home.

Very sincerely yours,

Mary Mendenhall

Season's greeting and salutations! For awhile we felt at a dead end in this war effort, but your interesting letters and the now more frequent visits of former Aztecs who have seen service all over the world keep our fingers on the pulse of every activity. You have shown that you have what it takes and we are proud of you. At this time particularly we want you to be sure of our love and best wishes.

C. E. Peterson

15

BY GUESS AND BY GOD

THE AZTEC NEWS LETTER
Special Edition, Christmas, 1943
To All Aztecs in Service:
Eight years ago when I was a "freshman" here at San Diego State College I dreamed of an institution whose influence some day would extend far beyond the region located south of Los Angeles. Little did my most fanciful flights of imagination indicate to me that Aztec spirit, contributions, and leadership would reach into all the far corners of the world. The messages in your letters and the reports of your activities and achievements from other sources all indicate that Montezuma's sons, and daughters, too, are true warriors of determination, courage, efficiency and humility. I like your letters. You see, Dr. Post lets me read a few of them! And I, too, look forward each month to the receipt of my copy of the *News Letter*.

. . .

Sincerely,
Walter R. Hepner
[President, SDSC]

Consolidated Aircraft Corporation, founded in New York by Rueben H. Fleet, expanded its operations in 1935 and moved to a new factory in San Diego. The facility merged the powerhouse of mass production with continuous operations to produce a greater number of planes in a shorter amount of time. By the beginning of World War II, Consolidated was already the largest employer in San Diego. It was building planes so fast that in 1938, more production space was added, and two years later, the factory grew even more. By 1940 the combined indoor and outdoor areas for production totaled nearly 3 million square feet. During the war years, San Diego's population grew by about 75 percent, with as many as 1,500 workers arriving each week. Consolidated is estimated to have employed up to 36 percent of the wartime workers in San Diego.[1]

In 1943 Consolidated merged with another aircraft company, Vultee, which was operating near Los Angeles. The Consolidated Vultee Aircraft Corporation soon became known by its compact name, Convair. The company made the B-24 Liberator, a bomber that saw action all over the world, including the Pacific battles in the Solomon Islands and New Guinea and over the Himalayas in the China-Burma-India theater.[2]

One of the B-24 Liberator's most tragic missions was a raid against the Ploesti oil fields in Romania. On August 1, 1943, 178 B-24s carrying heavy loads of bombs and extra fuel took off from Libya and headed for Ploesti. In an effort to surprise the enemy, the planes kept radio silence and then descended to a low altitude to make their attack. The Germans were waiting with devastating antiaircraft fire, and by the time the raid was over, 80 percent of the Liberators had been damaged or lost.[3] Those who made it back received the Air Medal for meritorious achievement, and one of the pilots writing to Dr. Post was recommended for the Distinguished Flying Cross, awarded for heroism or extraordinary achievement.

February 8, 1944

V-Mail

Dear Doc. Post

I have finally found an opportunity to write and let you know that I am no longer a test pilot at Wright Field. I was sent over to England and am now engaged in flying one of San Diego's own products—mainly the B-24 "Liberator." I have earned the "Air Medal" for raids over enemy territory and our entire group was given a citation for the raid on Ploesti so each one of us gets to wear the citation decoration. It's a Presidential Citation.

. . .

I will send a picture for the board as soon as I get them from London and in the meantime give my regards to Doc. Livingston and Dean of Men Peterson. I will write again—send me the *News Letter* at my new address. Thanks a million, and best to you and all—!

Still an Aztec,

Capt. Robert L. (Bob) Cardenas

44th Bomb Group

506th Bomb Squadron

A.P.O. 634 c/o Postm.

New York, New York

May 9, 1944

Somewhere in Italy

. . .

Yes, I am here to tell you that I have been on some interesting and disastrous raids. One of which was on a certain well known oil field. I have been recommended for the D.F.C. and I already have the air medal with one cluster and the "Purple Heart." I received the Purple Heart as a result of coming back from a raid and I lost one of my two remaining engines. I had to land in a certain sea and our plane broke in two. Lost 4 members of my crew and we were picked up by the British shortly before the Germans arrived on the scene. I never want to experience it again. I am and have been a Flight Leader in a Heavy Bombardment Group.

. . . If you divide the distance to L.A. by 4 you will know the number of missions I have been on. Ha! Ha! That *News Letter* really hits the spot. Keep it coming.

Sincerely,

1st Lt. Frederick B. (Fred) Smith

0-663193

460th BGP (H) 761st Sqdn. (H)

A.P.O. 520 c/o P.M.

New York, New York

News was often frustratingly incomplete, and Dr. Post did his best to keep up with the notifications. Sometimes he had to wait until the men returned to learn all that had happened. Captain Cardenas, who wrote about the raid on Ploesti, survived a number of mishaps before making it home.

THE AZTEC NEWS LETTER
No. 33, December 1, 1944
Capt. Robert L. Cardenas walked into the office. He is a great walker. He walked into Switzerland after having been shot down by flak on his 22nd bombing mission. That was just the beginning of his walking which seems to be still quite a mystery.

The 22 bombing missions were made out of England and apparently some of them were plenty rough. He was on the first Berlin daylight raid. He completed four other missions that week to Berlin, and the Germans were waiting for them with both fighters and flak. Bob gave our fighter boys a real plug for the wonderful job they are doing in escorting our bombers, both in and out as well as over the target. On one mission Bob returned with two engines out, one of the twin tails partly blown off, the wing badly shot up and several hundred holes in the ship. That mission brought a recommendation for the Distinguished Flying Cross.

On the last mission the ship was not shot up quite so badly, but she was on fire with gasoline spilling all over the place. He got out just as the ship exploded. He didn't tell it all but it was about the most unusual type of experience any of the Aztecs have had. Bob is expecting to be sent to Wright Field for test pilot work.

(Bob was about the most chased man at Sadie Hawkins Day. The gals took one look at him and decided that there was a man really worth going after. He got caught. LCP)

Dr. Lauren C. Post, Editor

When raids were conducted at night, the planes were less likely to be hit by antiaircraft fire, but bombardiers had more trouble finding their targets. When fighter planes launched from carriers at night, pilots had one of the most difficult tasks: they had to find their way back to the deck of the ship with little to light the way.

✉ November 3, 1944
Dear Doctor Post:

. . .

I'm still one of the many fighting the so called battle of the Atlantic, flying over-loaded torpedo bombers from an undersized flat-top. The only thing of interest that happened to me in this battle is that I helped set a world's record of a number of hours flown in a set number of days from a carrier. I don't hold much personal interest in this record because they had me doing the night flying—over a hundred hours of it in a month—along with 25 to 30 landings aboard the carrier in the black of night. And, Doc, believe me, it was black—blacker than the coal bins of hell. Yeah—they light the carrier's deck—but you couldn't read the top line of an optometrist's card at 3 inches by the light they use. It was truly a "by guess and by God" operation and I think god had it more than once.

. . .

Until later—Sincerely—
Lt. J. R. Gabrielson
VC19 c/o FPO
New York, New York

Roy Grimse earned the number one spot on the college tennis team in 1940, playing alongside Burdette Binkley, the young man who, before his plane was shot down, assured his parents that he had found peace. Grimse worked in Hollywood as a cameraman and he brought his photographic skills to the battlefront. A *News Letter* account of his service described his close brushes with sniper fire and a land mine. The half-track referred to had front wheels like a Jeep and tank-like treads at the rear.

THE AZTEC NEWS LETTER
No. 34, January 1, 1945
Lt. Roy J. Grimse filmed a complete record of the capture of one of the Palau islands and the speedy construction of an airbase on that jungle island. Riding in with the assault forces, Grimse and his men photographed all phases of the battle. They then

mounted their cameras on jeeps and bulldozers to film the
work of the AAF aviation engineers in hacking out the airstrip.
He had several narrow escapes from sniper's bullets and he
was thrown from a half track when it hit a land mine.

Photographers documented the images of war, and reconnaissance
units tried to determine the location of targets so that bombers could strike
with maximum effect. Reconnaissance missions required the speed of fighter
planes, the altitude capabilities of transports, and the range of bombers.
The planes were usually unarmed, flying stealth missions without the protection of an escort group, and pilots took even more risks to get good
photos. Grimse loved flying, but he also had to endure a long voyage on the
open ocean.

February 18, 1944
V-Mail
Dear Doctor,
Just a few lines from a very mediocre sailor. It's a usual clammy cold rough day,
on one hell of a big ocean, and though most of my outfit has overcome its varying
stages of seasickness, I still have spasmodic reoccurrences, much to my discom-
fort. My outfit is functioning exceedingly well in all photographic procedures,
and we all look forward to obtaining some of the best action shots in our theatre.
Maybe some time you will see some of our aerial shots in the local reels, I hope.
We certainly have the experienced men and the best of materials, and if we can
get the chance of being there at the right time, I know we will produce the results.
Our motto being "Kill 'em with Film" we're hoping the best, and I will let you
know soon as possible if we are living up to it.
     To date I haven't hit upon any fellow Aztecs on this vessel.
Very Sincerely,
Lt. Roy J. Grimse 0-866907
7th AAF, CCU, APO #953
Postmaster, San Francisco
California

August 27, 1944
Dear Dr. Post,
     . . .
Now I am in a Photo Reconnaissance squadron in the South West Pacific. . . .

We fly the PB4X which is the Navy designation for the good ole B-24. Instead of bombs we carry cameras and extra fuel tanks in the bomb bay. . . . On our last mission we got our tail shot up quite a bit. First, 20 MM shot out the elevator tab and then a burst of AA knocked out the rudder tab. It was nothing serious but plenty of excitement. There were about 25 Jap fighters after us and they were the best I have seen yet.

. . .

Your Friend,
Lieut. Edwin H. (Ed) Voorhees USNR
Photo Sqd One (VD-1)
FPO San Francisco

Different planes were designed to do different jobs, including transport, escort, and bombing over short and long range. Some aircraft functioned in versatile roles. The P-47 Thunderbolt and P-51 Mustang flew as fighter planes and as escorts for long-range bombers. As fighter-bombers, these planes were also effective in ground attacks. Lt. Robert Macdonald wrote poetically about the P-51. Lt. Le Roy Morgan bemoaned the lack of liquor and the fact that the *News Letter* couldn't find him in the European Theater of Operations. (In chapter 5, Lieutenant Morgan also offered good-natured complaints about Lieutenant Chase.)

The gratitude expressed in the letters below covers all things important to an airman—a fast plane, a good drinking buddy, and the protection afforded to the crews of heavy bombers by pilots in fighter planes.

April 28, 1944
Dear Dr. Post—

. . .

We started out here flying the P40 but have now switched to the P-51c "Mustang." She's as fast as any made, handles like a cradle, and climbs to over 40,000 ft. like a homesick angel.

Upon completion of training here we'll ship over, altho to which theater is still a question.

Best of Luck, Doc
Sincerely
Lt. R. M. (Robert) Macdonald 0-820631
440th Fighter Sqdn.
PAAF, St. Pete., Florida

March 27, 1944

England

Dear Doc

. . .

Liquor over here is damn near as hard to get as a bath. I had a drink 5 days ago. As to baths. Let's just say I stink and leave it at that.

I was wondering if any of the old crowd out of '42 are over here in P47s. Every time I come back I swear the first one of those jokers I run into I'm going to kiss him. The "Heavy" crews really like those P47 boys.

I haven't rcvd a *News Letter* since I hit the ETO. How come? Can't they be sent here? If not send mine to my wife at 1947 Linwood, S.D. and she will put it in a pkg.

Thanks

Lt. L. A. Morgan 0-695688

389 Bomb Gp (Heavy)

565 Sqdrn

APO 634

New York, New York

April 8, 1944

England—Damit!

Dear Doc

I recvd the March 1 issue of the *Aztec News Letter* a day or so ago. It was sure welcome. I've been stuck in the hospital having my bean sewn up where Jerry bounced a piece of flak off it. It sure seemed good to hear of old friends again.

News from over here is limited not only by so little taking place but the blasted censors won't let you comment on anything but the fact that you eat & sleep.

I have managed to contact only one Aztec over here, my step-bro, Chapman Bone. We plan to "pin one on" as soon as we can get together but there lies the hitch. If I get a pass they fly him & vice versa. It looks as if we will have to go over the hill.

So Long,

Lt. L. A. Morgan

P.S. Don't Rick about rationing. Everything over here is rationed except frostbite, flak, and venereal disease.

May 10, 1944

Dear Doc

I just returned from what someone laughingly christened a 7 day rest leave. I have yet to see a man do more resting than he can manage on a quart of Scotch.

With much moaning at the Limey rail system I got out & saw my step bro', Chap. Bone. He got a two day pass. We went to London. We got stinkin.

He is in a Photo Recon outfit. I'm in Heavy Bombardment. The wind blew and the "stuff" flew. I envy him. A photo recon pilot can live to a ripe old age. I maintain he gyps the army every day he lives. He claims I rob my wife of her insurance every day I live. Mebe we are both right.

I'm being heckled to go to chow so I'll pipe down.

So Long

Lt. L. A. Morgan

THE AZTEC NEWS LETTER

June 1, 1944
No. 27

This Issue Sponsored
in part by
Delta Chi Phi

Edited by
DR. LAUREN C. POST
San Diego State College
San Diego 5, California

**To All of the Aztecs in Service
and Their Friends:**

If the envelope of your copy is marked up with a single forwarding address, it is time for you to write in. **Keep sending** in those changes in address as fast as you move.

We are still adding names to our mailing list, and there are still available back numbers of the **News Letter.** But on the other hand, if you feel that you no longer enjoy reading the **News Letter**, and would rather have your copy go to someone else, **kindly drop us a card to let us know.**

Some of you may wonder about announcements of weddings, engagements, and also about furloughs of the men stationed in the States. Well, we just haven't been putting any of them in. I am looking forward to the time when someone can do all of that for our readers just as a real society editor would. Of course, that will be after you "secure this war" as the Marines say.

Graduation is to be on June 16 this year, and at that time we are to have a real Open House for the picture panel showing the AZTECS IN SERVICE. Put it on your must list for that time as it will be dressed up better and more complete than ever.

And again, best of luck,

Lauren C. Post,
Editor of the News Letter

🎏

**To the High School Seniors
Visiting State College Campus:**

At the end of each letter or news item there appears the name of a high school. It is the school from which the writer or the person named in the news item graduated. We who are at State College are proud of those Fighting Aztecs, and we thought that you would be interested in knowing that these service men and women who are making good

THE ARCHWAY AND OUR SERVICE FLAG
Aztecs killed in action and in training, 45; Aztecs missing in action, 20; Azte taken prisoner, 12; Aztecs decorated or wounded, 120. (Photo by Cyrus J. Kelle

in the armed forces graduated from your own high school alma maters. The printing of the high school names was our simple way of pointing out the connecting link between the high schools, State College and the armed forces.

Take a few copies of the News Letter to your teachers, parents and friends. They will be interested in the activities of the former students of your various high schools.

Lauren C. Post,
Editor of the News Letter

CAPT. ROBERT L. CARDENAS

was reported missing in action in th European area. Capt. Cardenas was heavy bombers, and his group had bee cited previously for bombing the Ploes oil fields. (San Diego High.)

🎏

CAPT. ARCHIE WARREN CHATTERLEY

who has been credited with shootir down 7 enemy planes, is missing in th European area. A fellow pilot reporte seeing him parachute from his plan

16

ANY GUM, CHUM?

THE AZTEC NEWS LETTER

No. 27, June 1, 1944

Aztecs killed in action and in training, 45; Aztecs missing in action, 20; Aztecs taken prisoner, 12; Aztecs decorated or wounded, 120.

Graduation is to be on June 16 this year, and at that time we are to have a real Open House for the picture panel showing the AZTECS IN SERVICE. Put it on your must list for that time as it will be dressed up better and more complete than ever.

And again, best of luck,

Dr. Lauren C. Post, Editor of the *News Letter*

I n Great Britain, the bombing was interminable. The Germans hit London early in the war in a sustained attack known as the Blitz. In fall 1940 bombs fell on London every night, and the following spring, incendiary bombs set the city ablaze. During one horrid night in May, an estimated two thousand fires swept through the city. Other industrial centers were also targeted, including Bristol, Newcastle, Plymouth, and Portsmouth.[1]

The British prime minister, Winston Churchill, insisted that Great Britain staunchly resist any compromise with the enemy. In his speeches, he encouraged the British people to remain firm, but their faith was sorely tested. During the bombing, Londoners took shelter underground in the subway tunnels, and the images of their stoic and orderly endurance became legendary.[2]

July 21, 1943

Dear Dr. Post.

Yesterday I received the *Aztec News Letter* #16, and believe me when I say I was never more happy than when I read thru the magazine and saw of the daring and highly meritorious work of my fellow-classmates, in all branches of the Armed Forces, and in all theatres of War.

. . .

We have made several trips to the great capital of London, and thoroughly enjoyed ourselves upon sight-seeing all the famous and interesting places one hears about in history-making news back home. As you know by what you read in the papers, London has been and continues to be bombed almost every day, and you can never imagine the untold misery and loss of lives, besides indescribable damage bombs can cause. Sections of the great metropolis have literally been wiped out and all one sees are debris and wreckages all around. In spite of all this, British people surprisingly still maintain a very high and undaunted Morale, and very valiantly do their best to see the War through at the quickest time possible.

. . .

Awaiting eagerly *News Letter* #17. I remain,

Sincerely Yours,

Enrique A. Rivera

Hq. Co. 850 Engr Avn Bn

A.P.O. 644 [censored]

New York City

Early in 1944, London was bombed again in what was called the Baby Blitz. The writer who described it, Moira Bainbridge, was the daughter of a British Army officer, and she had met the Posts on a visit to San Diego. In the *Aztec News Letter* dated March 1, 1944, Dr. Post wrote, "Some time ago she asked Mrs. Post to direct any of our friends to her address, and she offered to help them. Perhaps she did not know how many friends we had, but you may call on her or drop her a card."

✉️ July 21, 1944

London

Dear Dr. Post

Thank you very much for 3 *Aztec News Letters* which have just come. It is so interesting to read of many men, with such widespread & different experiences.

. . .

My flat has been blitzed again & this time lost all its windows & become uninhabitable, though fortunately we & the furniture are unhurt. So for the present we are in the country & though I can't welcome people to my home, I will always be glad to hear from them & maybe we can arrange to meet.

. . .

Here is a story which I think shows the spirit of people here even after five years of bombs or the threat of them. The head of the Women's Voluntary Services went to the scene of an "incident" early one morning. As she was going into the room of a nearby house, being used for enquiries, she noticed a woman smile & said "How nice to see you smile. It does help to cheer one up. I do hope you'll have good news." "There can be no good news for me," replied the woman. "My son has been killed & my 2 children are buried in the debris of our house, but if you think that by smiling I can help someone, I will go on smiling."

Yes the news is good & we have just had word of the attempt on Hitler's life. It looks as if we might just begin to allow ourselves to hope we shall be out of the front line soon & the fighting, or most of it over in Europe soon.

. . .

Everyone is stowing evacuees from London into odd corners of their homes, all over the country. It's rather more difficult than in the Battle of Britain, after the strain & stress of five years of the front line, & all the restrictions on daily life which this involves, but people are very kind & helpful & it's all working very well.

. . .

Well I must stop. We both send you & Mrs. Post all kinds of good wishes & hope that day won't be far distant when we can welcome you to this country & show you something of it.

Yours sincerely,

Moira V. Bainbridge

11 Braemar Mansions

Cornwall Gardens

London S.W. 7

England

Bombing raids against Germany became more effective as the Allies coordinated their efforts with long- and medium-range bombers. Industrial centers, factories, and railroads were targeted day and night. Several big thrusts began late in 1943 and continued through spring 1944. Berlin was attacked repeatedly by the British and the U.S. Army Air Forces. By the war's end, the Allies were also dropping incendiary bombs, which set fire to whatever was left of the infrastructure.[3]

✉ March 11, 1944

V-Mail

Dear Dr. Post;

. . .

You are certainly correct about the intensity of our Air Attack over here, and though I was only able to complete six missions before I "hit the jackpot," I managed to see plenty of action. I can truthfully say that "Jerry" is a tough and courageous foe, and that I've been scared stiff on several occasions. There is no doubt as to the final outcome of this terrible mess; I only hope and pray that it may be soon.

I'm coming along in great shape and should be out of the hospital before many months have passed. My Navigator, Lt. M.O. McGurer of Kalamazoo, and I were awarded the Military Order of the Purple Heart and the Air Medal since we've been in the hospital.

I'll be looking forward to the next *News Letter*.

Your friend,

Lt. Thomas B. (Brent) Burrell
0-735261
1st Genl. Hospital—Ward 12
Detachment of Patients
A.P.O. 517 c/o PM
New York City, New York

Undated
Dear Dr. Post.
. . .

For the last 6 mo I have been caring for German prisoners and if they are a good sampling, we will have to do plenty of fighting before the Germans will ever quit. The ones I had were an arrogant, belligerent, stubborn bunch of Neurotics who were sure they couldn't lose.

It's a real pleasure to hear about the school & what the Aztecs are doing. Thanks & good luck.

Capt. James R. Phalen
0-428304
APO 7753 c/o P.M.
San Francisco, California

In Britain, not enough food could be locally produced, and Germany made it hard for imported supplies to reach British ports. The specter of wartime hunger wasn't new. Starving a population into terms of surrender was a common tactic, and the British had faced similar shortages during World War I. Milk, sugar, and other staples were scarce, and even tea was hard to get. Ration coupons were a fact of life. Gardens supplemented the produce that had disappeared from store shelves, but it was harder to replace grains and meat. Years after the war, the London Housewives' Association celebrated when the limitations on the sale of meat were finally removed.[4] Fuel and wood were also scarce, and at Christmas, parents did their best to make toys from what little they could find. Years of war had restricted their diet, but the children showed their own ingenuity.

November 12, 1944
Hello Dr. Post,

. . .

From the port we landed at I had a train ride and saw quite a bit of the English countryside and it is truly beautiful, all so green and fresh but this is easily understood as it rains quite a bit. What surprised me most was at the quite frequent stops, at these stops the English kids would run up to our train and beg for gum, candy, cookies, and other sweets while the older people would ask for American Cigarettes. The favorite phrase over here seems to be "any gum chum."

I have seen quite a few towns that have been bombed, among them are Liverpool, Bristol, & London. The people just laugh it off and think nothing of it. I don't seem to understand this view but I suppose it is the best way to look at it. London is a big historical city and I enjoyed seeing all the sights. Westminster Abbey is a magnificent sight to see, it is truly a beautiful bit of construction. . . .

An Aztec,
Pfc Chris M. Franovich 39279587
Btry—A—492nd Armd. F.A. Bn.
c/o Postmaster—A.P.O. 261
New York, New York

December 27, 1944
England
V-Mail
Dear Dr. Post,

. . .

Gave an Xmas party for the English children yesterday and really had a time of it. We decorated the mess hall & had a Christmas tree that was very nice. We had lots of food for the kids. Consisted of bread, butter, jam, cheese, baloney, salami, pickles, weak tea, hot chocolate, fruit juice & lemonade. They really dove into it. The school teacher said that many of the children had not slept the nite before because of the nervous disorder & probably would not sleep that nite because of stomach disorder. Real truthful these English. When our Santa Claus, called Father Xmas here, entered, the children almost tore him apart. Each kiddie received five candy bars, a couple of packs of gum & some cookies in addition to the Red Cross boxes packed in the states. They really had a fine time

& I am sure if the people at home could have seen the joy the Red Cross boxes brought to these children, the contributions to the Red Cross would be much greater. Too much credit cannot be given to the Red Cross for their efforts here.

Visited London & failed to be impressed. I'm already wanting to see San Diego again. Will close now hoping you all had a Merry Xmas & a Happy New Year.

Sincerely,

Capt. James E. (Jim) Stacey 0-454491

Co. M 271st Inf. APO 917

c/o PM

New York, New York

THE AZTEC NEWS LETTER

August 1, 1944
No. 29

**This Issue Sponsored
in part by
The Faculty**

Edited by
DR. LAUREN C. POST
San Diego State College
San Diego 5, California

**To All of the Aztecs in Service
and Their Friends:**

Your friends at home and elsewhere
in the service are interested in you and
dozens of them have been very happy
to hear, as the reports came in, that you
came through D-Day all right. If you
only knew that, more of you would have
dropped a card to us even though you
are very busy.

As of this date (July 13), I have
checked various sources, and really, it
seems that State College did not lose
a man in Normandy or the English
Channel. Paratroopers, glider pilots,
LST men and a good many others have
written in, we have heard through various sources, and we have watched the
newspapers, and yet, only **Lt. James
White** was wounded. There is not another single casualty that we know of.
It is almost unbelievable that we could
have made the invasion without an Aztec being lost. Perhaps that comes
from expecting you to come through all
right rather than expecting to necessarily lose heavily in men.

And for those of you who are fighting elsewhere. We are aware of the
Saipan, Italian and other campaigns,
and we know that Saipan was really
rugged. We know that some of you
are engaged in every action. We want
you to know that we follow you in
thought, and nothing pleases us more
than to get word from you that you
pulled through another one all right.

Will each of you just let us know that
all is well after each campaign so that
we can pass the word to your friends.

Let us hear from you, and again, best
of luck!

Lauren C. Post
Editor of the News Letter

The Quad (Photo by Fay Landweer)

LT. WENDELL E. LANGFORD

was killed in a plane crash at Hammer
Field near Fresno.

LT. MAURICE G. WILSON

was killed in a plane crash on the east
coast.

IST LT. FREDERICK B. SMITH

who was recently reported missing in
the Mediterranean area has since been
reported killed in action. Lt. Smith
piloted a B-24 on many missions in that
theater and had been awarded the Air
Medal with several Oak Leaf Clusters,
the Distinguished Flying Cross and the
Purple Heart. (This Lt. Smith is the one
who played Frosh football in the fall of
1938 and was from Shelbyville, Indiana.
He should not be confused with the
Fred Smith who played guard in 1942
nor the Fred Smith who is doing graduate work in Geography at the University of California. LCP.)

CAPT. CLAIR V. BERDEL, USMCR

was reported missing in action. He had
been on duty in the Solomons earlier as
a torpedo bomber pilot.

CAPT. RICHARD BURCH

was reported missing in action over
Germany on June 20. Previously he
had been on duty in the Aleutians.

LT. EDWARD L. IMBLUM

was erroneously reported a prisoner of
the Germans by the last **News Letter.**
He is still missing. I can't account for
the error other than to say we made a
mistake, probably by confusing two
names. Let's all hope that we can have
a more favorable report to make on
Lt. Imblum. LCP.

LT. AUGUST FLEISHBEIN

who was a bombardier in England, has
been reported missing in action from a
mission over Europe.

CAPT. ARCHIE WARREN
CHATTERLEY

who was reported missing from a flight
over Europe in the last **News Letter** is a
prisoner in Germany. Capt. Chatterley
did a tour of duty with the RAF before
going into the AAF and was reported
by **Capt. Richard Butler** to be one of
the hottest pilots he had ever seen. He
had shot down seven German planes.

IST LT. WILLIAM LANSILL

who was previously reported missing
from a flight over Holland has since
been reported a prisoner of war in Germany.

17

THE PRICE OF THIS
VICTORY

Before daybreak on June 6, 1944, the day known as D-Day, U.S. and British paratroopers began dropping through the dark skies into Normandy, France. Their mission was to hinder the German advance toward the coast where more Allied troops were about to reach land. The paratroopers descended through antiaircraft fire. Many of the troops missed their landing zones because of poor visibility in the cloudy, predawn operation. Those who came down in flooded canals and could not get free of their chutes were drowned.[1]

Paratroopers were infantrymen, and once on the ground they battled like regular infantry units. Their supplies were limited to what they brought in by air and what arrived on glider planes. They fought to capture bridges and crossroads, then they maneuvered to connect with reinforcements. Up and down the coast of Normandy, more troops were fighting their way onto the beaches. If their coordinated assaults failed to push inland, the paratroopers would be trapped in enemy territory. An estimated 11,000 Allies were wounded or killed during the first twenty-four hours of the invasion.[2]

✉ Undated

. . .

I am in a fine outfit and we are really ready to go. We are the 1st Regt to go over-seas as an Expert Infantry Regt. As my company leads the Regt in the number of men qualified I usually throw my chest out another inch when passing the other 1st Sgt's.

I have trained the boys since they just came into the Army and although their average age is 20 they are plenty rugged. The average weight is about 165 lbs. We can't have them too heavy as it causes too many broken legs.

We are somewhere in England and are a part of the 1st Allied A/B Army which looks like a wonderful outfit. I have met a lot of the Parachute troopers who went through the school while I was an Instructor there. The tables are reversed now as I first taught them how to jump and they are now teaching me practical things about combat. I even saw some of the Canadians who went through Parachute school while I was there. They have really had some experiences since they left Benning. Some of the old men are gone but the losses aren't too heavy considering the missions they were on.

Well Doc I have to get back to work. I will write and tell you of any unusual experience we may have.

As ever
1st Sgt. R. J. (Joe) Carter 19088518
Hq. Co. 1st Bn. 513 Pacht. Inf.
APO 452
c/o P.M.
New York, New York

Pvt. Herman Addleson's family owned a watch and jewelry store in San Diego. They contributed money for the *News Letter* and asked that Herman's mother be included on the mailing list. Addleson was recogniz-able on campus as a small man whose smile bore the mark of the cleft lip he had surgically corrected so he could enlist.[3] He embraced his nicknames and often mentioned his friends, including Clarence and Andy Randeques, proprietors of the campus café. More than anything, Addleson loved being a paratrooper.

✉ November 17, 1943

Fort Benning, GA

I am now a qualified Paratrooper, and am really proud to be one. Made five jumps, three from 1200 ft. and two from 800 ft.

My first jump was Monday, Oct. 18. 1943, a day I'll never forget as long as I live. We were all up at 5:45 AM that morning, many of us had had a very restless night. Our thoughts ran in common I guess, for our past seemed to flash through all of our minds. It was cold & foggy that day & as we marched over to the field, we were all trying to sing. Yes, sing, even if our voices did crack a little. Everyone was excited, nervous & mostly scared. As we took our parachutes out of the bins, I looked at mine & I guess I said a prayer. "Please dear chute open for me." As we lined up, 24 men in front of the plane, my knees felt like water. Before we got into the plane we were checked five times to make sure we had everything O.K.

As we stepped in the plane & sat down, buckled ourself to the seats, everyone was joking & trying to sing. Before we knew it the plane went down the runway & we were looking at the ground disappear beneath our feet.

There's a fellow called the "jump master" who gives the orders. When we were at 1200 ft., everyone trying to cheer-up everyone else, the jump-master's voice sounded like some immortal soul. "Get Ready," he hollered. At this point every man turned white, or all colors. Yes, the big ones, tough ones, officers & soldiers, were scared. A pin could be heard, that's how still it became. Only the roar of the motors. The next commands came very fast. "Stand up," every one of us managed to stand and grab the cable above our head. "Hook up, Check Equipment," & "Sound Off," were all done automatic. Then "Stand in the Door," everyone fixes his eyes on the door. The jump-master taps the first man & "go." Out we go, & when you leave the door the prop-blast takes you away. You drop 75 ft. to 100 ft. before your chute opens. In that time, you don't know you're falling. When you hear a crack of a whip sound, & you look up & there is the most beautiful sight in the world. The Canopy is open & all is fine. You descend about 19-20 ft. per second so you are down before you know it. After you're on the ground, the tension over, you holler with joy & slap each other on the back. Each jump after that is the same only with more tensifying [*sic*] fear as you know what's coming. Yet it is safe as driving a car or anything else that has the word safe with it. Don't forget, it's right here, where the boys are separated from the men.

Pvt. Herman Addleson

Paratroops

Co. N. 1st P.T.R. 3rd Bn.

February 10, 1944

Hi Doc:

Yes, Sir!, we are now on the boat, destination unknown.

You've heard how tough the paratroops are. How rugged in physical endeavor, but what you don't know is how these same men felt as we boarded the ship & left the soil of U.S.A.

From the "Staten Island Ferry" to the boat, was something to witness. First we joked and kidded as we passed familiar signs along the harbor like "Maxwell House Coffee," "Bethlehem Steel," Colgate Soap & Perfume" & then that thing that stopped the crowd, the "Statue of Liberty."

Tough guys had tears in their eyes, many stood gazing open-mouth, many a heart was in one's mouth, with a feeling of emptiness in one's pit of the stomach.

The Statue of Liberty was beautiful & as she disappeared, Long Island came into view, then Brooklyn, & what memories & laughs we all had.

Then as some giant hand pushing us way out, land seemed far off, New York skyline seemed to diminish. When that disappeared & possibilities of seeing land of U.S. was gone, we just leaned back & silence was a bliss as we all thought of what we left behind & what we are fighting for.

That's about it Doc. Just thought I'd drop my thoughts. This boat is so compacted a sardine has more room than we do. Please excuse the writing as I'm doing it under very hazardous conditions.

Give my regards to Andy, Clarence, & all there.

Keep sending the *News Letter* to me.

Also hello to Lionel Chase, Bill Koller & Tom Rice. Hope to meet you guys again.

Always

"Little Geronimo"

Pvt. Herman Addleson 39259380

Co. 13 Inf. A.P.O. 15152

c/o P.M. New York, New York

May 1, 1944

England

Hello Doc. Post & all at School,

Here I am in England. Nice country for those who like it.

. . .

Sure glad to get my morale builder today. I got *News Letter* of March. Seems like a lot of Aztecs are over here, yet I haven't been able to get around to locate any, except Tom Rice & Guy Sessions, buddy paratroopers. We are all going to give those Nazis hell on "D" day, so you can see old Aztec is well represented in the Airborne outfit.

. . .

If I get back alive, tell "Cotton" to move over with the snow jobs, I'll really have the latest stuff.

Good luck to you Doc.

As Ever

Herman "jockey" Addleson

Co. I 3rd Bn.

502nd Prcht. Inf.

APO 472 c/o PM

New York, New York

P.S. Give my regard to Andy, Clarence, C.E. Peterson & everyone there at State.

September 28, 1944

Dear Dr. Post—

I received the issue of the *Aztec News Letter* with a mixture of feelings—some reminiscent, some a longing for the good old days at State. Unfortunately, during my college life, I had to work 8 hours a day as well as attend school and I didn't have a chance to enter into the campus life and campus friendships as much as I really desired.

However, there was one little fellow we all knew, Herman Addleson who was killed on D-day, and this fellow was my friend. I can remember lying on the grass discussing our ideals and hopes, and so I believe I can qualify to say to all our fellow Staters that the price of this victory is written in memories of men like that—not just flesh and blood, but the dreams and aspirations of men who will live forever in our memories. May their memories and ideals reflect in the way we live and in our accomplishments.

. . .

Hope to see you again before too long.

William C. Boyd

October 6, 1944

France

Dear Doc Post,

. . .

Doc, when I first glanced at the latest *News Letter* I received quite a shock; there on the front page was the news of the death of a very old friend of mine, Paratrooper Herman Addleson. It's still a very hard thing for me to believe.

I ran into Herman in Columbus, Georgia, last Nov. I had just begun Basic at Fort Benning, and he had just finished his qualifying parachute jumps. He told me how thrilled and pleased he was to be in a swell outfit like the Paratroops.

. . .

Pfc. Ben Siegel
Co. E., 376th Inf. A.P.O. [page torn]
c/o PM., New York, New York

August 29, 1944
Dear Dr. Post:
Back again. Had an easy ride this time and was able to see more of France. Southern France is really gorgeous, but later for that. On returning I received a lot of back mail. In one of the letters was a clipping announcing the death of Herman Addleson. That was quite a blow to me for I'd heard before that he was o'keh. I didn't know Herman personally but felt awfully close to him as I'd fought with his forces for quite a while. He was a member of the greatest group of men in the World! They saw more Hell in one day than any of us see in a lifetime. Only two out of every ten returned. I wish you'd tell the people back home that, though Herman was a small man, he and his buddies packed a wallop so powerful that they held out for over thirty days against forces none of us were prepared to meet, holding the most important beach heads in this war. I wish Herman could see what he and his made possible. I'm sure he'd get just as big a thrill in seeing the Eiffel Tower as he did the Statue of Liberty. His group, incidentally, received the Presidential Citation, the highest award for gallantry for an organization.

. . .

As ever—
James W. (Willard) Wallace
87th TCS 438th TCG
APO #133 c/o PM
New York

Pvt. Herman Addleson made his first training jump as a paratrooper on October 18, 1943, and lost his life in the D-Day landings on June 6, 1944. The Star of David marks his grave at the Normandy American Cemetery and Memorial in France.

Sgt. Tom Rice and Myron (Guy) Sessions were "buddy paratroopers" of Addleson. They were in the 501st Parachute Infantry Regiment, and

PVT. HERMAN S. ADDLESON

This year's annual, **Del Sudoeste**, was dedicated to the Gold Star men. In it are pictures of those who are listed below. You may procure a copy of the annual for $3.08 by ordering through:

**The Aztec Shops
San Diego State College
San Diego 5, Calif.**

You may also order last year's annual at the same address. **El Palenque**, which is the college literary magazine, can be purchased for 25 cents. **Jayne Dempsey** and **Jeanne Oncley** edited the annual, and **Phyllis Kefalas** edited **El Palenque.**

(The above are not connected with the **News Letter** and should not be ordered through this office.)

Pvt. Herman Addleson, whose picture appears above and also in the annual, was chosen by your editor to introduce the topic of annuals as he was, according to the many notes that have come in, one of our most beloved and missed Gold Star men. We all loved Herman for his willingness and cheerfulness, and we miss him at every basketball game and every other college function. Too bad we can't run all of the pictures of our 95 men killed but you may see the pictures of the following in the **Del Sudoeste** for 1945:

John E. Abbott, R. L. Adair, Herman Addleson, Martin F. Anderson, Roger Armbrister, Allen Bailey, John W. Bassett, Jack N. Berg, John Burdette Binkley, John William Borum, Warren Brown, Wesley E. Carter, Thomas H. Cozens, T. J. Davies, Sherman Denny, Charles Dowell, W. P. Eby, Howard J. Engle, George J. R. Ewing.

Paul A. Fern, Howard Flisrand, Lyman J. Gage, Joseph Norman Gates, Frank J. Guasti, Warren Edward Hand, W. Headington, Arthur N. Kelly, James D. Koester, Robert J. Landis, Wendell E. Langford, Maurice C. Morrell, Kenneth B. Moyer, Raymond W. Mueller, Frank Oliver, Robert C. Peterson, Craig Potter, George D. Rosado, Frank Ryan.

Richard J. Sawaya, Edward L. Searl, M. B. Sherwood, William B. Shropshire,

Robert H. Smith, J. Stevenson, Clarence F. Terry, Walter L. Tichenor, Leo P. Volz, Donald Webber, Clea E. Williams, Maurice Wilson and Louis Massey Winn.

THE DEVELOPING STATE COLLEGE PROGRAM
By President Walter R. Hepner

Your **Alma Mater's** future is bright! The enrollment dropped from 2300 in 1940-1941 to 900 in 1943-1944 and then it came up to 1200 this last year. Our plans are set for 1500 students for 1945-1946.

Our budget will provide for fifteen additional faculty members. The enlarged instructional staff will make possible the offering of eighty-five additional courses spread over twenty-six different subject fields. Former faculty members who will return next year are **Professors Baker, Haskell, Lesley, Mead, Nichols** and **Ross.** Those who have resigned are **Professors Allen, Calland, Eubank, Gross, Hunt** and **Messner.**

Post-war building plans include provisions for an Art Building, an Industrial Arts Building, and additional housing for Science, Speech Arts and Radio, and Commerce.

The Legislature has passed a bill which authorizes the College to give graduate courses which lead to the General Secondary Supervisory and Administrative Credentials. When **Governor Warren** signs this bill, which we are fully expecting, the State Colleges will become full-fledged teacher training institutions.

We sincerely hope that many of you former **Aztecs** and your friends will be able soon to take advantage of the expanded opportunities here at **State.** Our interest in your activities and our hope for your early return to civilian status are matched only by our appreciation of the contributions you are making in your various and far-flung assignments.

OUR ATHLETIC PROGRAM
By Dean C. E. Peterson

San Diego State College will field a football team next fall, and if man power and transportation do not take a decided turn for the worse, a fairly complete schedule of competitive sports will be included in the plans for the 1945-46 college year.

There are a number of problems facing the administration in making the decision. Many colleges have sidestepped it and plan to re-enter the field a year later. Whether or not there will be sufficient manpower to field a team, whether transportation problems will be worse than they were during the past year, and whether a schedule could be secured, are among the problems faced by the Student-Faculty Athletic Committee. Another important item to be

considered was that if the war was to take a decided optimistic turn, some of the men who are on military leave would return to the college where they are naturally entitled to their position and plans had to be made for coaching on a part time basis. **Bill Cortz,** in another article gives you an excellent idea of the assistance which will be given the sports program for the coming year.

In order to determine the available man power the county and city high schools were canvassed and a poll taken of the available football material in college. It was thought after a rather thorough check up that sufficient men would be here to field a team. Letters were then sent out to every college in Southern California and the University of Arizona to determine whether or not a schedule was possible. Santa Barbara, University of Arizona, and California Polytechnic Institute have decided not to field teams for the coming year. The College of the Pacific had a schedule with the larger colleges and said that for financial and prestige reasons it was to their advantage to schedule the service teams and the members of the Pacific Coast Conference. However, a very acceptable schedule was finally arranged after making a tour of the Southern California college group. The schedule at present, which lacks verification in one or two items, is:

University of Redlands, here, September 29.

California Institute of Technology, here, October 6.

U.S.C. Junior Varsity, October 13.

Bye, October 20.

Fresno State College, at Fresno, October 27.

Pomona College, here, November 3.

San Jose State College, here, November 16.

It was necessary to schedule some of the colleges earlier than was desirable because they were dependent on military units for men to play football, and many of them feel that they will lose these military units the latter part of October.

Many problems are still ahead before **State** is back in the sports program in full stride. The field has to be reconditioned; the staff has to be augmented; and most of all, some of the fine athletes who represented **State** in the past and who are called into service, will probably have to clean up this war situation and then return to **State** and carry on in the **Aztec** uniform. Many have already written in telling of their plans, and we are expecting a return of a large number of our students who still have a number of years to finish at **State** and elsewhere before their education is completed. We all hope and pray that that day of return will be soon at hand.

16

Addleson was with the 502nd, both part of the 101st Airborne Division. Rice was ill during his trip to Europe, and he compared the voyage to a quiet meeting of the Woman's Christian Temperance Union. Once in battle, his experience was anything but serene. He described his harrowing jump and witnessed the gliders as they brought in more equipment. The officer he refers to was Brig. Gen. Don Forrester Pratt of the 101st Airborne Division. One of Rice's letters noted the exact time of his jump, down to the minute. H-Hour was the time when a combat operation was scheduled to commence. "H minus five" meant five hours before combat.[4]

February 3, 1944

Dear 'Doc' Post,

Received no. 22 just before leaving the States. Enjoyed reading & rereading it on board ship for I was confined to an isolation ward and saw little of the broad Atlantic. Mumps only last a short time. The trip was uneventful as a WCTU reunion. . . . Herman Addleson should be on his way over soon. I hope I bump into some Aztecs in the near future, plenty of them over here I imagine. . . .

Cordially,

Sgt. T. M. (Tom) Rice 19164859

501 Parachute Inf. Co. C

APO 472 c/o PM

New York, New York

June 28, 1944

France

1900 [hours] Wednesday

Dear Doc. Post,

Myron G. Sessions, Herman Addleson and I have been on the continent since D day at H minus five hours and we weren't early either. Jumped in Normandy at 1:31 AM June 6, D day. The reception which was given us was really torrid. They threw everything at us including the kitchen sink. The sky was lit up as bright as day, ack-ack bursts, streams of red, green and white tracers converged on us and showery bursts of flares outlined us in the sky as we neared our drop zone. I was no. 1 man waiting to push the equipment bundles out on the "go" signal. As soon as we sighted the French coast we stood up and hooked up. The flak was coming in the door and I could hear it clattering against the fuselage beneath me. The "go" signal came and the bundles were cumbersome to get out because we [were] trying to avoid ack-ack by fishtailing and diving. After the bundles cleared the plane the men began to get out at double time. As I left the plane my arm got hooked in the door and I was hung up with my arm inside and body outside, finally slipped free when I straightened my arm. We were at about 500 feet then and going about 135 mph, couldn't slow down cause we would be an easier target. We were getting enough flak at the time anyway. Luckily I wasn't hit at all. My wristwatch came off and is probably in the possession of the crew chief now. I came in on a field which was patterned by canals. I didn't get wet even though my 'chute reinflated and I was being pulled toward a canal. I cut the suspension line in time. I couldn't get out of my harness because I had so much equipment on, couldn't even get my weapon out. Finally had to cut my way out. We organized and raised hell behind enemy lines 'til the Seaborne troops reached us. Gliders came in after we started on Hitler's SS men and General Pratt was killed in one as it struck an anti-airborne obstacle not far from where we were. The gliders were duck soup for those Nazi machine gunners as they came in at about 100 feet. You can't conceive of the magnitude of this airborne invasion, it was really gigantic.

Since our arrival on French soil I have had some close brushes with Hitler's Satellites and came out the lucky one thus far. One can't be too cautious at any moment or during any movement.

It seems that every French farm house has a wine cellar with four or five casks of about 75 gal. capacity full of cider, even some hard stuff has been uncovered. The fruit in the orchards is getting ripe and the summer storms are frequent. A lot of this fighting has been from hedge row to hedge row, no picnic.

Received the June edition of the *News Letter* which was a dilly, really enjoyed it and passed it on. Gotta go now.

Sincerely,
Sgt. T. M. (Tom) Rice 19164859
501 Parachute Inf. Co. C
APO 472 c/o PM
New York, New York

Tom's friend Guy Sessions jumped into France and then into Holland. On the back of his V-Mail dated October 18, 1944, Dr. Post wrote, "He was wounded previously during the big invasion & had been awarded The Purple Heart."

June 18, 1944
V-Mail
France
Dear Dr. Post

It's quite a long time since I've had a chance to write and let the old alma mater know how things were going where I'm located. But now it can be told and I can say that I along with another Aztec, Sgt. Tom Rice, were among the first Paratroopers to jump in France. We both had a lot of interesting experiences and plenty of narrow escapes since we've been over here but we've both weathered the first two weeks of the storm. It's needless to say how important that Tom and I get our *News Letters* each month. We look forward to each new issue with all the more enthusiasm. Hoping to receive many more copies of your fine publication.

> I remain
> Sgt. Guy Sessions
> Co. C. 501st Para. Inf.
> A.P.O. 472 c/o PM
> New York, New York

October 18, 1944
V-Mail
Somewhere in England
Dear Doc Post,

. . . I jumped in Holland, September 17, with the 1st Allied Airborne Army and was doing okay too. That is until Oct. 5, when I was wounded by machine gun fire which broke my right leg. I'm resting quite comfortably in a fine hospital in England and am being excellently taken care of. It's going to be a long grind before this thing is healed. But one day when it is I'll probably be dropping into the college to see you and the rest of the folks. Oh yes, Tom Rice is still in good health and going strong with the old outfit.

> As ever
> Sgt. Guy Sessions 39271070
> Det. of Patients
> U.S. Hosp Plant
> A.P.O. 350 c/o PM
> New York, New York

THE AZTEC NEWS LETTER

No. 36, March 1, 1945

Sgt. Guy Sessions, who jumped with the paratroopers on D-day in France and who did a great deal of fighting after that, is in Torney Hospital at Palm Springs. He was brought back on a ship and then across the country on a hospital train. He is in a cast with traction and weights.

Glider planes, towed by transports and then released, could bring additional troops and larger guns into enemy territory. Paratroopers were sometimes scattered following their jumps, but the gliders were able to more accurately deliver men and equipment to the target destination. In later wars, gliders were replaced by helicopters, but during World War II these silent planes provided important backup.[5]

The letter below was damaged, but not censored.

August 18, 1944

England

Dear Doc,

Received *News Letter* #29 and I certainly was glad to hear that so many of the boys came through the D-Day landings safely.

. . .

There's not much I can add to the accounts [page torn] given of our particular part in the initial landings [page torn] that I know of not a single glider pilot who does [page torn] put the paratroopers in a degree heretofore unknown. Those boys were at a tremendous disadvantage when they were dropped in there, and no one needs to tell of the splendid job they did while they were over there.

Those boys in the medical outfits cannot be praised too highly, either. I know of many an airborne man who would not be alive today had it not been for the tireless efforts of those medics—many of whom made excellent targets for German snipers, and many times the snipers did not fail to take advantage of it, either.

Hope we all are back home before much longer!

Yours for a quick victory

Gordon C. Chamberlain

THE AZTEC NEWS LETTER
No. 31, October 1, 1944
Lt. Gordon C. Chamberlain was awarded the Air Medal for "superb performance in initial troop carrier phases of the invasion" of Europe. He piloted one of the first gliders to land in France.

One of the first airborne attacks across the Rhine River took place in September 1944 and included an attempt to bring paratroopers into the Netherlands. The plan called for capturing key bridges to clear the way for an advance into Germany. The initial wave of Operation Market-Garden made it across the Rhine, but additional forces missed their landings. By the time the paratroopers had struggled back to where they were supposed to be, the Germans were waiting to deliver a death blow.[6]

On March 23, 1945, the Allies tried again to cross the Rhine. The following day, 2nd Lt. Gordon C. Chamberlain, the glider pilot who hoped for a quick victory, lost his life in a crash. He had been awarded the Air Medal with two oak leaf clusters and the Purple Heart. In May 1945, just months after his death, the Netherlands was liberated from German occupation. Lieutenant Chamberlain is buried in the Netherlands American Cemetery and Memorial.

✉ Undated
Dear Dr. Post:
Just a line to let you know I am still alive and griping. As you probably know we made the Jump across the Rhine landing between Wesel and Hammerkorn. I was sorry to hear about Chamberlain, a lot of the Glider pilots were killed during this operation. The air corps dropped us about 3 miles from our D.L. and it took some time to fight back to it. In the mean time the Gliders came in and hit their LZ and we hadn't cleared it yet. The Gliders really caught Hell as the Krauts were waiting for us. Most of the tree landings were casualties. All the Krauts needed was a target and a Trooper hanging in a tree is like shooting a duck on water. I have to run now. By the way my new address is

Lt. Richard J. Carter 0-2016409
Hq. Co. 1st Bn 513 Prcht Inf.
17 A/B Div APO 452
c/o P.M. New York, NY
As ever
R. J. (Joe) Carter

Another letter from Joe Carter is at the beginning of this chapter.

Willard Wallace was a glider pilot, affectionately called a "Glider Rider" by fellow Aztec Pat Wyatt. Wallace flew with the 74th Troop Carrier Squadron, part of a Carrier Group that towed gliders into the Netherlands, delivered fuel and supplies, and brought paratroopers across the Rhine. He was friends with Lieutenant Chamberlain, and in a short note on June 19, 1944, he wrote, "We were both in on the initial invasion. I guess the papers have told all about it so I won't enlarge. It was exciting and a truly wonderful show. I was awfully glad I got a ring side ticket."

Wallace had written to Dr. Post in August 1944 to share his grief over the death of paratrooper Herman Addleson. Eight months later, he wrote again, this time to grieve the loss of Gordon Chamberlain and other dear friends.

April 9, 1945

Dear Dr. Post:

I just got number 36 and decided I was long over due on a letter. A few changes have been made since I last wrote. We did a little more work and have since been trying to keep up with Patton with gas. I believe that you heard that Gordon Chamberlain was killed on this last mission. I saw him in the field but there wasn't much anyone could do. He landed his load in good condition though and took good care of his troops. We had heavy casualties all around this time. They used a new weapon on us and really tore us apart. As a result of the casualties we received several replacements, two of whom were from San Diego State, Lts Totten and Russell. . . .

I was awfully sorry to hear about Don Webber and Charles Dowell. Seems like last week I was out on a picnic with Don, his wife and child. At that time he'd just returned from his tour of duty in the Pacific. I hope people won't forget about Don, Chuck, and all the others when the last card is played.

. . .

Well, so long for now. Thanks again for all the news.

James W. (Willard) Wallace

74th TCS 434th TCG

Wallace wrote more to his sister, Janice, about his experiences before and after the Normandy invasion. She excerpted one of his letters for Dr. Post.

✉ Undated

Dear Doc Post,

. . . In case you haven't heard from Willard, I'd like to quote a letter I received from him. Part of it was written before the invasion—part after he got back to England:

"I'm sitting in my tent just wondering what's going to happen next. We were supposed to have gone in last night but the weather played a dirty trick on us. We were all ready to go, packed, loaded and eager. Now we have to wait for a day or two. Maybe we'll move tonight. Our job is to go in the night before the invasion (D minus one day) and hold all roads leading inward. I'm carrying a heavy machine gun squad (in a glider). We'll land about 5 miles inland on the Cherbourg peninsula. The main attack is on the north shore. We land south-east of it to hold a Panzer division that is farther south-east which may move up (probably will). We land about two o'clock in the morning. The invasion starts at five o'clock. By nine o'clock we should have re-inforcements and be able to rest awhile. They say those left will be evacuated for another trip over. It's going to be a big show. I sure hope I get to see the whole thing. Some dumb English girl sent over a false report that it had already started. That means they'll be waiting for us." (He tells me a little of what he thinks of the English people—censored!)

He wrote this after he came back:

"Yes, I'm all intact. Saw a great show from the ring side and didn't have to pay a penny. It was horrible but a great show. I didn't get a scratch. On top of that they gave me seven days off. I spent a grand time all through the Isle but mainly in Edinburgh."

That's just about all in that letter—he's been writing almost every other day since—and in every letter he asks for food! He said he paid $1.75 for a small orange and was lucky to get it.

. . .

Sincerely,

Janice Wallace

57 W. 58th

New York City

THE AZTEC NEWS LETTER

No. 32, November 1, 1944

F/O James Willard Wallace was struck in the face and temporarily blinded while making a landing with his glider in Belgium

and crashed it. He ended up in the hospital with a broken back and three broken ribs. Until that landing Willard had been lucky both in Northern and Southern France and had been awarded the Air Medal and the Oak Leaf Cluster.

THE AZTEC NEWS LETTER
No. 43, October 1, 1945
F/O James Willard Wallace is a student on campus after an interruption of four years, 19 months of which he spent in overseas service as a glider pilot. Willard took part in the D-Day invasion of France. They were quite early as they landed four hours ahead of H-Hour. He and his fellow crew members held their objective until the beachhead was extended to them.

Willard's second landing was in Southern France. That one was much easier. It was a vacation compared with the first landing.

His third landing was in Holland. Then he landed in Malmedy and his last was across the Rhine. Willard has the Air Medal, with four Oak Leaf clusters and the Purple Heart. Altogether he had 121 discharge points.

Allied troops were sweeping across Europe with the force of a thunderstorm. The tone of the letters, so grim during 1943, resounded with an optimism that reached as far as Africa.

June 7, 1944
"Still Somewhere in No. Africa."
Dear Doc—
News of the French invasion hit us early yesterday morning, first reported by German sources & then confirmed by the Allies. As most of us expected, Americans accepted the announcement calmly and with a sense of relief now that long-awaited D-day had arrived.

Local French sailors & soldiers presented a striking contrast as they shouted deliriously & paraded up the streets, waving flags & singing their anthem.

As for the Arabs—they took advantage of the careless friendliness that pervaded and made it a field day for pick-pockets.

. . .

Not much excitement around here. We had a wild time a few nights ago, however, when a terrific windstorm tipped our tent, blew away our mess hall and sent our latrine crashing down a mountainside. Luckily, no one was in it at the time!

. . .

So long for now. And please give my regards to Mrs. Post.
Laurence (Larry) Madalena
90th AA Gun Bn, Btry D
APO 512; c/o PM
New York, New York

In France, Capt. Richard Bate described his first view of German prisoners, whom he sarcastically called "Supermen." He helped bring down a German Focke-Wulf fighter plane and described how the American foot soldiers, called doughboys, were slowly gaining ground.

July 13, 1944
France
Dear Dr. Post,

. . .

After training in the U.K. for the better part of a year, the AAA outfit I'm with finally made the big jump. We didn't make the 1st boat over, but the tub we rode in didn't scrape her bottom on the sands of France but twice before we made up the pay load. We came over in a British boat whose captain was 20 and whose 1st mate had reached the ripe old age of 19. They were grand chaps though and in spite of their age they certainly knew their business.

As we came ashore we were greeted by piles of American wreckage of all sizes from jeeps to tanks. As we progressed further inland there were still piles of wrecked guns & equipment, but much to our delight it was mostly Jerry stuff. It was just off the beach that we saw our first "Supermen," hundreds of them, in a big barbed wire cage.

The first night ashore I slept in an open fox hole about 2 feet deep. The next, and each succeeding night I slept in a fox hole 3 feet deep with a 2 foot dirt roof. I found out that a lot of our boys caught cold in open fox holes—stone cold.

There was certainly no flag waving as we rolled inland, just a lot of solemn dazed looking people standing around their wrecked homes. Most of them practically in rags. The little children all waved and scrambled gleefully for the bits of candy and gum the men threw to them, but it was days before I saw a French adult with a smile on his face.

All the towns I have visited so far with the exception of one over in the British Sector have been hit very hard by the battles that have torn through them. Some are absolutely leveled to the ground and others only partly destroyed but regardless of the extent of the destruction the French people move back in and start patching up as soon as the military authorities will permit.

. . . I went into a farm yard the other day to find a place to locate my Command Post and the old farmer came solemnly out and started "parle vousing" at me. I motioned for him to wait a minute while I hailed a corporal who speaks French. Through the corporal, he asked me if I would want to use his whole house or could he move his family into the attic instead of out to the barn. He also wanted to know how much milk and butter I would be wanting for my men. When I had the corporal tell him I didn't want his house or his milk and butter that I just wanted to set up in his orchard he was absolutely amazed and bubbled over with thanks.

. . .

We saw our first action the second day we were on French soil; two of my guns shared in the destruction of a FW 190. Since then we have managed to keep in fairly close touch with "Herman's Boys." The going is pretty slow since most of it has to be hedge row to hedge row stuff pushed through by the Doughboys. Day and night the country resounds with the boom of big guns the great majority of which are ours. And hardly a day has passed without our seeing or hearing formations of our planes passing over on their way to plaster Jerrie's front lines or rear areas.

. . .

Sincerely,
Capt. R. L. (Richard) Bate
Btry "D" 461 AAA Bn
APO 230
New York, New York

In September 1944 Sgt. Robert Kelly chronicled the details of his cross-country trek. He poured out his thoughts, including his admiration for the resilience of the human spirit, into a single sentence.

September 7, 1944
France
Dear Doc
In the fields of France, as in the fields of home, there are rain and wind and the fickle sun, all of which I've come to know quite well, living on the ground at the

edges of restricted towns, sleeping in pup tents by hedgerows, in forests, by paths of mud; living with a fire, water and some rations; smiling to the people who smile at our passing, who cheer and hold up the two-fingered "V" and kiss their hands—who wander about their broken churches and crumbled homes; mouthing stiff French phrases, bargaining for eggs or milk or cider, inquiring vainly for wine; asking myself how a whole nation of people can return with life for these windowless towns of shutters and bars, and how they can supply food where there is none, make clothes and machines and tools in these shells of buildings, recreating a supply, and exchange and a power to purchase; shaking my head at the gutted cities, exclaiming at the beautiful land, cursing my lost mail, shaving my shivering face, singing slightly off key, fingering the currency of three nations, writing letters to those whose answers are lost on my twisted way from home—and noticing now that my socks are wet and cold and need changing.

Yours,

Sgt. Robert G. (Bob) Kelly

19155223

INF. Co. F. APO. 15374

c/o P.M. New York, New York

Mary Lacour, a WAC, faced off with a different kind of foe as she kicked up her heels at a Sadie Hawkins dance. Weariness was pushed aside in favor of celebration, and in Paris, the lights blazed again.

November 17, 1944

France

Dear Dr. Post—

As usual, my *Aztec News Letter* inspires me to write the latest news from this part of the feminine fighting world. . . .

Thought you might be interested in what happens when a group of GI joes and janes get together far away from home. The fellows and gals in our headquarters decided that just because we were in France was no sign we should abandon the good old customs we had in the states. So we threw a Sadie Hawkins Day dance on November 11. The WACs were allowed to wear any variation on the GI theme of clothing they wanted—and believe me, they did! There were about fifty French girls invited as well, and you should have seen the looks they gave the WACs when they went into action. Don't believe all you hear about the infallible charm of these mademoiselles—haven't met a GI yet who wouldn't trade a bushel of them for an American girl. The main complaint seems to be that they can't learn to dance our way. . . .

Sincerely

Mary Lacour

THE AZTEC NEWS LETTER

No. 32, November 1, 1944

Pfc. Mary H. Lacour, WAC, is serving in France with the Twelfth Army under General Bradley. She is doing secretarial work.

December 10, 1944

Somewhere in France

Dear Doc:

. . .

France is very beautiful. I am set up fairly well with three rooms of my own—a tent, a front yard and a slightly used fox-hole. I did get into Paris not long ago and found that it is still living up to its reputation of being a very beautiful city. The language handicap is fairly rugged but by using a combination of French, German, English and Indian sign language accompanied by a pencil sketch one seems to manage quite O.K.

The French people are very warm and friendly and will render any assistance possible. . . .

It certainly was good to get into Paris, where black-out is practically nil, after twenty-seven months of black-out in England and Ireland.

. . .

All my best wishes to you and yours for a very Merry Christmas and a Happy New Year.

Ever your friend

Maj. George E. Piburn, 0-431587

20th Air Disarmament Sqdn (prov)

APO 639, c/o P.M.

New York City

THE AZTEC NEWS LETTER

September 1, 1944
No. 30

This Issue Sponsored
in part by
Phi Sigma Nu

Edited by
DR. LAUREN C. POST
San Diego State College
San Diego 5, California

**To All of the Aztecs in Service
and Their Friends:**

This summer has been an exceedingly busy one for the **News Letter.** Address changes have come in at the rate of about 250 per month. But even so we know that you are not sending in the changes as you should. Since we do the addressing with a machine, we probably still have some dead ones among the addresses. In case you get two copies or in case you no longer care to receive the **News Letter,** just let us know. And on the other hand, we are always adding new names, so don't be afraid to send in the addresses of your wives or families or friends whom you think should like to get our publication. Also, we have a good many back numbers which you may get by asking for them.

The **News Letter** office is now A. 109. That is the room next to the **Placement Office.** It is easier for us to handle news and new addresses which come to us in writing than over the phone. **Dr. Harwood** still answers most of my mail that requires answering. **Dr. Watson** handles that which has to do with the registrar's work. When we edit we have to cut more than ever as the volume of mail is enormous, but keep writing. We would like to hear from some of you who ran out of ink over 12 months ago. And again, best of luck!

Lauren C. Post,
Editor of the News Letter.

PVT. HERMAN ADDLESON

was killed in Normandy on D-day when he landed with the first paratroops. The official notification came to his parents following the official message saying that he was missing. Unfortunately, a fellow Aztec had reported Pvt. Addleson as being in France with him, but he seems to have been in error. One of Herman's last letters to the **News Letter** was written as his ship left an American port:

"We are now on the boat, destination

The Quad (Photo by Fay Landweer)

unknown. You have heard how tough the paratroops are. What you don't know is how these same men felt as we boarded the ship and left the soil of the U.S.A.

"From the Staten Island Ferry to the boat was something to witness. First we joked and kidded as we passed the familiar signs, Maxwell House Coffee, etc. and then that thing stopped the crowd. It was the Statue of Liberty. Tough guys had tears in their eyes, many stood gazing with open mouths, and many a heart was in one's mouth. The Statue of Liberty was beautiful, and then came Brooklyn, and what laughs we had. Then as though some giant was pushing us away, the New York skyline disappeared. Then we all leaned back and thought of what we left behind and what we are fighting for."

LT. MAX BINSWANGER

is missing in action again. This is the second time Lt. Binswanger has been of-

ficially reported missing in action. See his letter in the last issue of the **News Letter** which tells of his having been an internee in a neutral country and his later resumption of flying duty.

SGT. REGINALD C. FERGUSON

is missing in action from a bombing mission over France on June 8. Sgt. Ferguson was a gunner on a B-17.

S/SGT. HOWARD FLISRAND

was reported wounded and also missing in action in the European theater of operations.

LT. JAMES C. HARDIN

who has been piloting P-38s in Italy has been reported missing in action. Lt. Hardin had been awarded the Air Medal and the Presidential Unit Citation and had also been given credit for shooting down an ME-109.

18

WHAT IT FEELS LIKE
TO BE FREE

THE AZTEC NEWS LETTER

No. 22, January 1, 1944

Ens. William R. Kruse wrote from North Africa:

"I've been assigned to an L.S.T. She's not beautiful but she's a good ship. Most of the others on board have seen action in Sicily and Italy and I expect to see some more before we get back to the States. I'm looking forward to it—that's why I joined the service.

"Haven't seen any Aztecs yet but I know there are several in the vicinity because they are registered in the States log back at the Red Cross Club."

(Now, Bill, if you had given me their names, I could give you their addresses so you could find them. LCP)

Dr. Lauren C. Post, Editor

Bill Kruse graduated in 1942 with a bachelor of arts in physical educa-tion. He played center in varsity football, earned a place in the letter-man's club, and was a member of the Sigma Lambda fraternity. His athletic training made him a good judge of field strategy and overall coordination between forces during an invasion. As he delivered supplies and troops to

France, he watched as enemy planes were shot down, and he was close enough to mine-damaged Allied transports that he assisted with rescuing casualties. He viewed the efforts of others as inspiring and called his own job "routine."

The "buzz bombs" he describes in a letter were V-1 flying bombs, sometimes rather glibly called doodlebugs because of the insect-like sound made by their pulsing jet engine. This early type of guided missile had a range of more than a hundred miles and was used against London late in the war.[1]

In one of his letters, Kruse described the way his ears had become attuned to the sound of these bombs, though he questioned their nickname. Kruse also had a chance to see part of the Westwall (Allies sometimes called it the Siegfried Line), a series of defenses comprised of nearly four hundred miles of bunkers and barricades, including concrete blocks called dragon's teeth that could stop tanks.[2] Some of the structures had been in place since World War I, and Hitler used every resource, including civilians and forced labor, to shore up what was left of his defenses.[3]

The one thing that Lieutenant Kruse had not yet seen was his baby daughter.

July 15, 1944
England
Dear Doc—

. . .

Well, Doc, I've seen my first real action in this war, and although there were many things not pleasant, it was quite an experience. There were so many incidents, that I won't attempt to go into a description of them at this time. Suffice to say, it was an example of perfect teamwork and coordination between Navy, Army, and Air Corps—both British and American forces. They all did a wonderful job getting the invasion off to a good start. Since D-Day we have been quite busy ferrying men and materials from England to France. Some wit pointed out that England had risen 18 inches out of water since D-Day—presumably due to transfer of men, vehicles & supplies.

. . .

As ever
Lt. (jg) Bill Kruse

August 12, 1944
England
Dear Doc Post

. . .

My activities on D-Day and thereafter were so routine and uninteresting that they are hardly worth mentioning. Our ship was part of the Western Task Force which landed on the right flank of the French coast. Our ship was scheduled to arrive in the afternoon of D-Day, so we only saw the pre-landing show from a distance. We had a good view of the bombing and naval gunfire support prior to the initial landings, and I want to go on record that I've never seen, or hope to see in the future, anything that can compare with it. They did a superb job in our sector, because by the time we arrived in the area, everything was quiet and serene. We watched a follow-up force of gliders come in about dusk, and that too was an awe-inspiring sight.

The next morning we moved in to the beach to start our unloading in a supposedly swept channel. However, a small control ship came along side and told us to move over to starboard, and just about the time our bow started to swing, a minesweep formation just ahead of us blew three mines faster than I can write this. Life-preservers were quite popular from then on, and I think some of our men slept in them. Just shortly after we anchored, we saw our first enemy planes—four FW 190s came in out of the sun and strafed the beach. I'm happy to report that all four were shot down.

We unloaded during the night, and returned to the outbound convoy area. On our way out, we stood alongside an LST which had been mined, and removed quite a few casualties. This also was right in the middle of another minefield, but we were lucky again and got away without any complications. Just shortly after we anchored again, a small tender blew up and sank just a few hundred yards off our port bow, so we put our small boat in the water, and gathered a few more survivors. The trip back to England was very uneventful and has been very routine ever since then.

We have been making the long run to the London area our last few trips and I'm getting to be quite an authority on the rocket-bombs, or "buzz-bombs" as they are affectionately (?) called. We have had several opportunities to observe them at close range, one time almost too close, and they are really a vicious little item. The sound they make is quite individual, doesn't sound like any plane, and once your ears become tuned to it, you unconsciously find yourself listening for it every time the air raid sirens blow. We are back on the south coast now and breathing much easier.

. . .

Adios for now, give my regards to everyone at school.

As Ever

Lt. (jg) Bill Kruse

✉ August 15, 1944

[Dr. Post penciled "$5" on this letter, indicating the amount sent by Eileen Kruse.]

Dear Dr. Post,

I received your card asking for a picture of Bill in his uniform. I just received one from him taken over in England and that is the only one I think you could use. I wouldn't give it up for anything but I wonder if you might be able to take a copy off of it. . . .

I am enclosing another small check which I hope will help out some. Our daughter is fine & is 8½ mos. old now. I would give anything if Bill could see her. Let me know about the photograph.

Sincerely

Mrs. Eileen Kruse

Box 521

Vista, California

✉ October 8, 1944

England

Dear Doc—

. . .

We have been working pretty steadily shuttling between England and France. I had a chance to go ashore in Cherbourg a while back and see for myself what a war-torn city is supposed to look like. Surprisingly, there wasn't nearly the damage that I'd expected. In fact, except for a few isolated spots, it hadn't been damaged at all. I went through one of the large forts, part of Hitler's vaunted "west wall," and it was really a fortress. Our bombers did quite a job on some of them, but others were almost intact. All in all, it was quite an interesting trip—and well worth while.

. . .

We are sweating out a voyage "state-side" right now. I am sure hoping that we will make it. I've been overseas 13 months now, and away from Calif for 19, so I'm really ready for a little sunshine & pleasant weather. Also I have a daughter who will soon be a year old, that I've never seen. I've got lots to look forward to, if we are chosen to go back to the States.

Give my regards to everyone at school. Adios.

As Ever

Lt. (jg) Bill Kruse

The U.S. Army Civil Affairs Division, established in 1943, grew out of the military's need to stabilize cities and to rebuild the infrastructure and governments that had collapsed under the weight of warfare. In Civilian Affairs Training Programs at campuses in the United States, students learned military governance, economics, and languages. When they transferred overseas, they were tasked with setting up military governments in defeated territories. Civil affairs officers also oversaw the transition of occupied cities, such as Paris, after enemy forces were expelled.[4]

Private Henri Jacot grew up in Neuchâtel, Switzerland, attended State, and went through the Army Specialized Training Program to learn German. In one of his letters to Dr. Post, he added a plea: "Please don't misspell my name." Jacot was posted with the European Civil Affairs Regiment. Each regiment trained companies for different countries, and Jacot was in Paris after that city was liberated on August 25, 1944.

Resistance fighters in France had organized under the direction of the exiled general Charles de Gaulle, and they undermined the Germans at every opportunity.[5] Jacot's letters reference the FFI, the French Forces of the Interior, the formal name of the French resistance. Not everyone in France actively opposed the occupation, and after the liberation, those who had collaborated were dealt with harshly, including women who had catered to German officers in the Paris brothels. Jacot was amazed at how quickly the French reestablished order. He reveled in their gratitude, understood their rage, and admired the renaissance of Paris and its residents.

August 12, 1944

Somewhere in France

Dear Dr. L.C. Post,

. . . Six weeks of basic with combat engineers in MS. made a soldier out of me (my record says so). After this rough life I was sent to A.S.T.P. at Ohio State

University. There I learned German language and area. . . . Now I'm overseas. My tough luck sent me to England, where I spent a lovely spring; Normandy where I'm spending the summer and I hope by winter I'll be getting my mail at the Riviera. . . . "D" Day came along and for the first time I was doing a constructive job. I'm proud of my Civil Affairs Detachment because we won our first round & for the first time I'm able to report something worthwhile besides traveling. . . . Since I've been in France I've seen most of our occupied territory. It's the tough luck that the army made me a Pfc with a General's job. So long and hello to everyone in State.

> Your friend
> Pfc. Henri Jacot 39041973
> D3C1-CoC-1st ECAR-ECAD
> APO 658 c/o PM
> NYC, New York

THE AZTEC NEWS LETTER
No. 33, December 1, 1944
Pfc. Henri Jacot is serving as an interpreter, and he is also interrogating German prisoners in either France or Germany. He wrote his family that they live in officers' quarters captured from the Germans. He speaks French, Spanish and German besides English.

✉ January 6 [1945]
France
Dear Dr. Post,
Since the Normandy days we have been received as the victorious liberators. Never in our lives will we experience such mass appreciation. The feeling was mutual as we admired their fortitude during the occupation.

On our way to Paris they gave us everything including the kitchen sink. Cider, cognac, flowers, tomatoes, apples, bread, & everything they hold dear. Paris was liberated Friday night & we entered at sunrise next day. Paris was glowing with fight & fury. Barricades & snipers. Lots of street fighting but in a couple of days everything became a thing of the past. Every day something new started. Peace & order re-established. The renaissance of Paris is the most amazing thing I've ever witnessed. The speed of it was startling. The food supply came in and Parisians fed the population, the "metro" began service, movies started, then the theatres, the opera & Paris with its sidewalk cafes was again on its own. Now Paris has become a G.I. city. All G.I.'s are amazed at this jewel. Paris is going in smooth wheels but relatively few saw the mobs fighting, the FFI's catching snipers, Frenchmen killing collaborators (after being judged); the hair cutting of "chaise longue" blondes, and the general cleansing of their institutions.

During this crucial point, I lived very closely to the people in their homes, work & entertainment because of my Civil Affairs work. For several weeks I saw them acquire their liberty. They had almost forgotten what it feels like to be free.

. . .

Thank you

Pfc. Henri Jacot

Capt. Chas. W. Nolen wrote from the South Pacific:

"Have been moving a bit since I last wrote. Have been placed in command of this unit and we moved into the Solomon Islands. Here we are in contact with the Japs and have been in several air raids. You should see a night raid. It's really a beautiful sight. **Maj. Rodney** and **Wally** left us for a joy ride, but we are having all of the fun. You might tell Maj. Rodney that he owes me that T. S. slip which he promised me in a conference we had one day. Congrats to **Tom Chavis.** Wish I could be stationed some place where the love bug would bite me too.

"Oh yes, **Bob Harer,** my 1st Sgt., got himself skinned up a little diving for a foxhole the other night. He said that was the fastest he ever moved since he played football at State. Was surprised at **Muelchi** kicking about a soft job. Seems to me he was always looking for one. Tell **Ralph McQuaid** to drop by to see me. He knows the outfit.

"By the way, Doc, I'm keeping that wing I promised you in mind. Certainly enjoy the News Letter. Heap good work!"

The **Robert W. Richardsons** have announced that Margaret Ann, aged 2 years and 4 months, has a little playmate, Robert Talbot Richardson, born December 16, 1943. The Richardsons have been in Washington for nearly two years and are still to be convinced that icy storms of winter and the muggy heat of summer there are as pleasant as San Diego weather.

Roy M. Cleator, CSK, wrote from his new station in the South Pacific:

"Several days ago **Lt. Clair Berdel** flew down to see me. He is a Marine flier with months of combat. Today I found **Lt. Clelland Wharton** (HOD) along the road. Together we went to the hospital and saw **Chet De Vore.** He had a little wound in his leg but looks fine. (Chet is back on duty now. LCP.) As you might guess, the Aztec scandal flew thick and fast. Also met **John Sellwood.**

"I see **Norm Strohte, John Porter,** and **Bill Lyle** quite often. I believe that a fellow would see more Aztecs around here than in San Diego. We all get the News Letter and are never without one —if the mail slips in.

"You might be interested to know that we run our own little pet shop here. At the last census we had two dozen cats and kittens, the same number of dogs and puppies, one billy goat, one tailless monkey, tropical birds, and last but not least, me. They call me **snafu.** I believe that is some kind of animal."

A/C A. D. Henehan wrote from Marana Air Field, Tucson, Arizona:

"**Bob Milton** is an upperclassman here. We enlisted together but they had me in C.T.D. for so long that I missed his class. He leaves tomorrow for Advanced. Henehan remains a solitary being on this desert waste for four more weeks—life is a trap!

"Please send me any News Letters that I've missed, and I have missed 'em! (Which ones? LCP.)

Some notes contributed by Miss Christine Springston from her Christmas mail: From **Lt. (jg) Robert S. Hamilton** who is at Harvard:

"Rounded out my 16th month as instructor at Harvard today and am celebrating with the San Carlo Opera Company.

"We applauded 'Winged Victory' in which we saw our own **John Tyers.** He has three dramatic minutes to himself— more than any other in the play except, of course, the six principals."
From **A/C C. O. Ayers** at Iowa City, Iowa:

We have a real good chorus here— 110 voices and it's really swell.

WHO—WHAT—WHERE

A/C Remo Sabatini is in WTS-CAA, Pella, Iowa. ☆ **Lt. Comdr. Clifford E. Smith** is still in the Aleutians. ☆ **Lt. C. A. Boyer,** USNR, is on an LST, FPO, SF. ☆ **Ens. Geraldine M. Francisco** is at the Chaplain's Office, Mare Island Navy Yard. ☆ **Lt. Robert Durbin** is in the Camp Pickett area in Virginia. ☆ **Alex Calhoun, PhM1c,** is at Dispensary Unit I, USNTS, Newport, R. I. ☆ **Donald L. Harvey** has been promoted to Chief Torpedoman. He is still on a sub tender in the Pacific. ☆ **Bob Cozens** now goes by the rank and title of **Maj. R. C. Cozens.** He has completed 25 missions but merely gets a change in duty. (Not bad for 25 months of service from the day he entered the service. LCP.) ☆ **Lt. Dodd V. Shepard** changed the name of his plane (a fighter in Assam) from **"Monty"** to **"Joe Aztec."** (Had he not shot down the Zero, we would never forgive him for that. LCP) ☆ **Ens. George L. Stillings** has a new ship address, FPO, N. Y. ☆ **Sgt. John R. Rowe** is at Camp Stewart, Ga.

Pvt. George M. Ellis wrote from Morrisville Maneuver Area, Fort McClellan, Alabama:

"I'm not doing anything special except beat my brains out in the goldarned infantry. I've been privateering for about a year now—with four months out due to a slight disrespect I had for my best friend—my rifle. Maybe that's why they gave me a machine gun and mortar outfit. I can't very well injure

myself with them except to break my back. It's the same old stuff week in and week out—instructing the same old weapons — walking on the same old stumps—pulling the same old pack— looking out for the same old tin hat.

"Just finished two weeks at instructor's school and my head is buzzing about cam levers, rear shoulders, and breech lock pins, etc. Worse than finals.

"By the way, Doc, where do you get this sunny south stuff? 12-15 degrees at night and 32 degrees in the daytime with a lot of snow! Probably we'll have a tidal wave next week."

Lt. Charles R. Smith wrote from Army Air Base, Santa Ana:

"Just came back from a few days after visiting my family in Tucson, and noticed enclosed picture in Santa Ana Cadet. I had a chance to visit **Hal** and **Morry** just once while they were in Santa Ana.

"Certainly do appreciate your News Letter every month, particularly as it gives me a chance to stay up with all the youngsters who are lucky enough to . get across. No, I haven't given up hope —I'm still sweating out an assignment.

"Good luck to all the gang and here's hoping we can have that final Reunion soon." (The picture showed a squadron basketball team and a big shiny trophy that the boys had won. In the picture were **A/C Hal Summers** and **A/C Morrie Shepherd.** LCP.)

Capt. Douglas L. Inman, USMCR, wrote from Camp Lejeune, N. C.:

"Whoever said that this is the 'Sunny South' was a little off the beam. Not long ago we had six to eight inches of snow followed by zero to ten above weather. That in a country fresh out of fuel and anti-freeze, is something —the only difference between this and Boston is that here there is no Cocoanut Grove to burn down and never was.

"Had a pleasant surprise this morning when the corpsman told me the Lt. across the hall was from San Diego too— everyone knows that's where I am from! Found out it is **Lt. D. Asquith,** an old Stater from the class of '32.

"Who can tell me where 'Gunner' Chase is? Last I heard he was basking in San Diego. I'd appreciate a letter from said Gunner giving me the word on what goes on there."

(It's **Lt. Lionel Chase,** Student Pilot Group, Lockbourne AAB, Columbus 17, Ohio. LCP.)

Notes from Miss Deborah Smith from her Christmas mail:
A. A. Ault, CBM, wrote from the Pacific:

"It seems like such a long time since I marred the attendance record of A Capella. I guess it has been about five years. You don't know how much I

4

19

THE FRONT LINE DOUGH

THE AZTEC NEWS LETTER

No. 23, February 1, 1944

Pvt. George M. Ellis wrote from Morrisville Maneuver Area, Fort McClellan, Alabama:

"I'm not doing anything special except beat my brains out in the goldarned infantry. I've been privateering for about a year now—with four months out due to a slight disrespect I had for my best friend—my rifle. Maybe that's why they gave me a machine gun and mortar outfit. I can't very well injure myself with them except to break my back. It's the same old stuff week in and week out—instructing the same old weapons—walking on the same old stumps—pulling the same old pack—looking out for the same old tin hat.

"Just finished two weeks at instructor's school and my head is buzzing about cam levers, rear shoulders, and breech lock pins, etc. Worse than finals.

"By the way, Doc, where do you get this sunny south stuff? 12–15 degrees at night and 32 degrees in the daytime with a lot of snow! Probably we'll have a tidal wave next week."

W artime experiences varied for men and women in different branches of the service. For the most part, those writing to Dr. Post praised the efforts of everyone else, but bitterness occasionally crept into the letters. When it did, it was often a complaint from someone on the ground who had suffered through combat and had little patience for any attempt to make warfare seem glamorous. The task of first assault often fell to the Marines, who were trained to make amphibious landings; to paratroopers, who dropped in behind enemy lines and then fought on the ground; and to Army infantry, whose mission was to hold on to the new territory and keep advancing.

Foot soldiers in World War I and World War II were called doughboys. The nickname is sometimes attributed to the field rations the men ate or to the dust that coated them after a cross-country trek. Other possible origin stories point to the way they cleaned their uniforms or to the sound their marching feet made on muddy ground.[1] Whatever the source of their name, their job was to dig in, advance, and dig in again, the dirtiest work of war. An aura of toughness surrounded them, and hardship dogged their footsteps. In general they were perceived to have less education and to have come from a lower social standing than their counterparts in the Air Force and Navy.

Two champions of the lowly doughboy who gave them a voice and brought their spirit to life were Ernie Pyle and William (Bill) Mauldin. Mauldin's cartoons featured the characters Willie and Joe, who stoically endured infantry life. Pyle's journalism gave his readers a realistic glimpse of war from the perspective of the foot soldier.[2] The odds were stacked against the doughboy as he trudged toward combat and fought to stay alive.

THE AZTEC NEWS LETTER
No. 27, June 1, 1944
Pfc. M.P. Vander Horck wrote from Italy:
"Judging from what I have read this war is being admirably and truthfully reported in story and picture and it's a pleasant feeling to know that the folks back home are getting an unbiased account of our lives over here. My favorite reporter in this respect, and I think this applies to most of the soldiers, is the inimitable Ernie Pyle, who has an uncanny talent for putting the real thoughts of the boys into print. I have often wondered how the things he writes get past the censors, but that's the beauty of our American newspapers."

THE AZTEC NEWS LETTER
No. 28, July 1, 1944
Sgt. John R. Rowe wrote from New Guinea:

. . .

"By the way, you were the person who started me reading Ernie Pyle's column in the Tribune. He came to S.D. not many years ago, and I remember how interested you were in his visit. Didn't he visit the campus? My wife clips his columns out of the paper every day and sends them to me. Boy, what a writer he is. I found out a long while ago it is the little things in life that make it what it is. His writing is perfect, and he never misses the human angle."

The following writer was determined to air his grievances, and he tried to cram his complaints onto a V-Mail form, which was much too small. This did not dissuade him. He simply ended each note with "to be continued" in parentheses and carried his train of thought onto the next form. He addressed three separate V-Mail letters, all written on the same day. His tirade mentioned the infantry, tank, and cavalry units and tank destroyers (TDs) that battled enemy tanks. "Burp gun" was an Allied nickname for a German submachine gun.

✉ May 10, 1945
V-Mail
Austria
Dear Dr. Post,
I lost contact with you and the *News Letter* back several months ago when my outfit went into combat. Recently my brother Bob, who is in a glider outfit back in France, sent me the March and April issues.

I guess I should have known better than to read them though, as they always have a depressing effect. It seems as though everybody is either a lieutenant in the Navy or in the Air Force. Or at least that they are the people who count.

I venture to say that the vast majority of these big shots have never seen a war being fought and probably never will. Yet we get replacements from the Air Force—men who have never heard a shot fired in anger—yet wearing bronze stars, unit citations, and battle stars. The 11th Armored Division—anybody back there ever heard of it?—probably saw more action in a hour back in the bloody snow of Belgium than all the experiences of these big shots put together. (to be continued)

Sure, the Air Force and Navy have lost a lot of men. But—how nice it must be to die on a nice clean deck in nice clean clothes with a stomach full of good, warm food. How nice it must be to die in a nice clean plane doing something you like and knowing that a bed, hot chow, women and everything warm await you at your base.

I wonder if these big shots have ever seen a mangled buddy lying in a stinking gutter in a lousy, stinking Krout town (?) I wonder if these heroes have ever lain on a snowy hill, half frozen, always hungry and scared, and listened to the strangled wail of "Medic" on a dark night; knowing that the medics are too busy to help most of the wounded, knowing that to attempt to evacuate the wounded is almost impossible. Have they ever heard artillery crashing down on their stranded unit for 12 hours straight, slowly dying minute after minute? Have they ever sat all night in a frozen foxhole and listened to panzers moving just over the hill, knowing that if they attacked there would be no stopping them? (to be cont.)

I doubt if any of these beribboned glamour boys have ever seen or done any of these things.

Do the people at home realize who has actually fought this war? Don't they know that the only men in this huge Army and Navy who have ever faced the enemy are in line infantry, tank, TD, and cavalry outfits?

It is very amusing, in a Mauldin sort of way, when somebody in my squad gets a hometown paper and reads about how T/Sgt. Johnny Jones is now battling bravely on the Paris front with an Ordnance outfit, or about Lieut. Sam Squirt who is in a finance disbursing outfit stationed near London, or about how Lt. Col. Joey Smith, age 20, who is in a bomber group in England, has just received his third oak leaf cluster or his Presidential unit citation.

I guess the people back in the States really eat that stuff up. Of course it's not nice to talk about the infantry medic who walked out in the street of a dirty German town under a hail of burp gun fire to treat a wounded man and got himself shot in the back. There's going to be a lot of bitter, club-footed men when the doughs come home.

Sincerely,
S/Sgt. Wm. B. (Bill) Boone, 39292936
Co. A, 63rd Arm'd Inf. Bn.
APO-261, c/o PM
New York, NY

The argument didn't end there. Even Dr. Post's secretary came into Staff Sergeant Boone's crosshairs. The following letter was written from a spa town named for its hot springs. The war in Europe may have been over, but the well of bitterness was overflowing.

July 15, 1945
Bad Hall, Austria
Dear Dr. Post,
I received your letter of June 17th and also the June and July *News Letters* and wish to thank you for them.

I appreciate your desire to keep feuds out of the *News Letter* and I certainly didn't intend to start one. Few people are in a better position to appreciate the work of other branches of the service than the front line dough, and, believe me, we don't make a habit of belittling the efforts of others. We have seen at first hand what the bombers have done to German morale and industry. Many of us feel personally indebted to Thunderbolt pilots whose skill and courage saved our skin.

But any dough will get very angry when somebody belittles the infantry and heaps its praise on other branches.

If your secretary thinks I am good at slinging the bull and would make a good fiction writer perhaps she would like to take a trip overseas and see for herself. I hear that there are plenty of good openings for Wacs and Nurses. As for her remark about "deserving a better fate than the infantry," perhaps it would astound her to hear that we are not ashamed of being infantrymen. Astonishing as it may seem to her civilian mind, the most respected man in the ETO is the Joe who wears the combat infantry badge. When I was on furlough in England, many G.I.s were so ashamed of their Air Force patch that they came up to me and explained that they had fought with such and such an outfit until badly wounded and returned to a soft job back in rear echelon. She must be one of those people we have read about who can't seem to make any sense out of what made Ernie Pyle and Bill Mauldin so famous. A Joe from a Graves Registration outfit once told me that if only every civilian could be forced to work on his detail for a month there would never be any more wars—in spite of the schemes of Hearst and the rest of the Russia-baiting U.S. press. The G.R. boys are the guys who follow the front line troops to pick up their bodies and bury them.

You mentioned something about the Air Force losing more men than the infantry, but I think you are mistaken there. According to the casualty list published in the *Stars and Stripes* there were about 180,000 men killed in the ETO, 110,000 of which were infantrymen. It is true that for a while the Air Force fought the war alone, but when the infantry entered the picture its 24 hour day quickly caught up with the Air Force's 8 hour type of fighting in the matter of time in combat—it seems to me.

Remember that in the infantry you fought until you were killed, wounded, captured or the war ended. In the Air Force you flew 30 to 50 missions and, if you survived, went home with the D.F.C. and an Air Medal for each five missions.

The Third Inf. Division alone had about 45,000 casualties, including 6,000 dead—(almost half a division in dead alone). That means that at the end of the war, if you were an original member of the Third you were either dead and buried, severely wounded and back in the U.S., or had been wounded three times. The only original members in that division and in many other veteran outfits at the end of the war were cooks and clerks. The rest were either dead, badly wounded or recently liberated from prisoner of war camps.

I realize that this sort of talk is senseless and gets you nowhere. But I wanted to explain a little of the bitterness that a lot of us feel.

There are a lot of other reasons for our bitter feelings, too. Things like having our cigarette rations stopped once the war ended and our morale was no longer important; the way the USO and movie stars have capitalized on the war to make a name for themselves by putting on a few shows in London and Paris (now they sometimes even venture as far as Munich) and then returning home to tell the world how they entertained the front line troops; the way the G.I. on pass is treated in cities he "liberated" such as Paris, Luxembourg, Liège, etc.; the way the Military Government forgot their "campaign promises" on what was to happen to our German friends once the war ended; the way our beloved "free" press is so energetically and systematically strumming up bad feeling against Russia; the way the G.I. Bill of Rights looks so good but means so little; the army's point system of discharge which was supposed to have been a result of soldiers' opinions. All these things and a few more have left their effect on a lot of G.I.s.

I know you are a busy man, Doctor, so I won't take up any more of your time. Thank you very much for the *News Letters*.

Sincerely Yours,

S/Sgt. Wm. B. (Bill) Boone, 39292936

Co. A, 63rd Arm'd Inf. Bn.

APO-261, c/o PM

New York, NY

Staff Sergeant William Boone wrote that "the most respected man in the ETO is the Joe who wears the combat infantry badge." This award was given to those who had faced fire and the risk of injury during active ground combat.[3] Planes, artillery, and weapons of modern warfare increased the distance between combatants, but the infantryman brought the battle to his foe. He gained an intimate knowledge of war's most brutal deeds by closing with an enemy to kill or be killed. Added to the injury was the insult that some of the battles fell beneath the notice of journalists and those at home.

Pfc. Edward W. Creekmur earned the Combat Infantryman Badge and a Purple Heart. He was wounded in the Hürtgen Forest near the border between Belgium and Germany. The fighting in Hürtgen began in September 1944 and continued sporadically with terrible losses that weakened Allied forces. The cost to the Americans in a few months' time was more than 30,000 casualties.[4] The Germans quickly counterattacked in another region of dense forest through Belgium and Luxembourg. That assault, known as the Ardennes Offensive, nearly broke the Allied line.[5]

The Allies held. Barely.

In the United States, the enormous campaign in the Ardennes came to be known as the Battle of the Bulge, and it consumed the press. After the Ardennes, the focus was on victory, and scant words were spared for the horror that had to be endured beforehand. The families of those who had fought at Hürtgen had a hard time piecing together a picture of what had happened in that small patch of forest. The troops that ventured into the Hürtgen Forest waded into the worst kind of trap. The German artillery was dug in and waiting to ensnare the Allies in dense underbrush and tangles of barbed wire while firing from bunkers hidden in the cover of trees.[6]

After an initial round of battles in Hürtgen Forest, there was a brief break in combat, followed by more battles in mid-November. During the short cease-fire, Edward Creekmur managed to get off a letter to his mother. Before she heard from her son again, she received news from the War Department.

THE AZTEC NEWS LETTER
No. 34, January 1, 1945
Pfc. Edward W. Creekmur has been reported missing in action in Europe. He was with the infantry and has been missing since November.

January 29, 1945
Dr. Lauren C. Post;
On Dec. 4-1944, we received a telegram from the War Dept. saying "our son, Pfc. Edward W. Creekmur, was reported missing in action since Nov. 15 in Germany." We had a letter from him written Nov. 12; something happened between Nov. 12

and 15, 1944; we had no more word concerning him, until Jan. 24, we received a letter written by him, on Jan 7. from a hospital somewhere in France. He wrote, "I feel better and better; all I now need is time, and I'll be as good as new. Due to circumstances beyond my control, I have not received any mail for quite some time. However, the future holds better prospects. We had a nice Christmas here. The Red Cross supplied the Christmas packages, and the chaplain supplied the spirit. I heard Major Glenn Miller's band from my bed in the ward. They were practically outside my door. Sure sounded good."

Needless to say we were overjoyed to receive this letter. The War Dept. in a telegram yesterday, said they will "forward by letter the name of the hospital (where Ed is) and details."

I received the two *Aztec News Letters* and immediately sent them on to Ed, by first class mail. I believe Ed would enjoy the *News Letter*—and will keep you posted as to his address.

Am enclosing a one dollar bill, to help on the postage or whatever you wish.

Very truly

Mrs. A. S. (Anna) Creekmur

4030 Chamoune Ave.

San Diego 5, California

May 5, 1945

Dr. Lauren C. Post—dear Sir:

Pfc. Edward W. Creekmur is now convalescing at DeWitt General Hospital at Auburn, California, from wounds received during the Hürtgen Forest fighting in Germany. . . . [He] had been wounded by an 88 mm shell fragment, that tore through his body. One result was partial paralysis of his left leg, which is now under treatment. While hospitalized in England, he received the Purple Heart Medal. Since his arrival at DeWitt Gen. Hosp. he has been awarded the Combat Infantryman's Badge.

He thoroughly enjoys the *Aztec News Letters*. In them he sees the names of many fellows he knew at State. Please continue sending the *News Letter* to my address, and I will re-mail it to Edward. This one dollar bill will help defray expenses—postage, etc.

Very truly

Mrs. A. S. (Anna) Creekmur

4030 Chamoune Ave.

San Diego 5, California

P.S. Edward says "he owes a lot to a lot of people." He had 16 pts. plasma and 3 quarts of blood poured into him. He highly praises the doctors, nurses and Red Cross.

Edward Creekmur recovered, and after the war he taught math at a community college in San Diego. He couldn't run due to his leg injury, but he liked to walk, and he exercised regularly on campus. Professor Carl Lutz, a colleague of Dr. Post and Creekmur, recalled seeing Creekmur in the locker room and described his stomach as a "mass of scar tissue."[7]

Another infantryman, Pfc. Chester Hagman, survived the German counteroffensive, and he offered his perspective of battle as only one who had been on the ground can understand it.

September 23, 1945

Dear Dr. Post;

Here I am in the States safe and sound after knowing six months of combat as a machine gunner in the Infantry.

Sometimes, as I think about it, I don't feel that I should still be alive. I had so many friends killed around me that it seems odd that I should be spared. One of the facts about warfare that most people do not realize is that a small group of men do the actual fighting. The front lines are usually small foxholes widely spaced. It is a rare thing to see any officer above a captain even near the front. The only support the rifleman usually has is his brain and his rifle.

Death becomes so commonplace that we used to eat our K-ration lunch right by the side of bloody corpses.

The number of men in the rear of the front lines is amazing. The further back one goes the more crowded it becomes. On the front line there is plenty of elbow room.

I was in combat with the 103rd Division, but when the war was over I was transferred to the 5th Division. Right now I am at Camp Campbell, Kentucky taking a silly training program that makes us all think the army doesn't know the war is over.

All the fellows want to get home, but discharges are coming slow. I hope to be out sometime this winter.

Yours truly

Pfc Chester A. Hagman

The Aztec News Letter is published monthly as a service to the **Fighting Aztecs** who have attended **San Diego State College** and their friends. It is mailed to all **Aztecs in Service** for whom we have addresses whether they actually graduated from **State College** or not.

It is also mailed to civilians, parents and wives of our service men and friends of the college.

Every former **State College** student in service should keep the editor informed of his address changes, his promotions and items of interest.

STATISTICS:

Aztecs in service (grand total)	2,800
Women in service	135
Discharged, mostly on medicals	75
Prisoners of war	30
Missing in action	25
Wounded in action	72
Killed in action and training	81
Decorated	216
Commissioned officers	1,200
Aztecs overseas	1,000
Domestic mailing list	1,800
Campus distribution, about	500
Printing of average issue	3,700
Printing of this issue	6,000

The **News Letter** is supported by contributions of civilians and service men and to some extent by on-campus sales. It is sold only on the campus.

A PICTURE PANEL

showing **Aztecs in Service** is maintained in the Administration Building of the college. Pictures should not be over 2½ inches high for the head and shoulders. We still need about 1,000 pictures.

CENSORSHIP

may be lifted somewhat if and when the war in Europe folds. Your editor has tried faithfully to hold down in the publishing of addresses and APO numbers. The object was to make sure that the **News Letter** would be an aid rather than a hindrance to the winning of the war. After V-E Day we may be able to give better service. LCP.

WANTED—BACK NUMBERS

of the **News Letter**: Number 14 (April 29, 1943) and 19 (October 1, 1943). We are making up some sets to bind and the number of sets that we can make up will depend upon how many of the above numbers we can pick up. You may get back numbers for almost any other month. Thanks. LCP.

The 24 veterans who attended **State College** last semester carried an average study load of 13.7 units. They made a grade point average of 1.46 which is well above the general average. There were no disqualifications.

CAMPUS NEWS
By Connie Frith

(This is Connie's last column of **Campus News**, at least for a while. She is getting married. The date is set as April 28th, and the lucky man is **Cpl. James Lloyd Haight, AAC,** Fairmont AAF, Fairmont, Neb. Connie leaves the **Aztec** and **Aztec News Letter** staffs with the good wishes of many, many friends. She has been a hard worker, and we hope we can find a worthy successor for her. Thanks, Connie, and best wishes. LCP.)

March was a month in which several **Aztec** servicemen recited wedding vows with **Aztec** co-eds. On March 1, S/Sgt. **Robert A. Wade, U. S. Army,** (Sigma Lambda) and **Gloria Winke** (Phi Kappa Gamma) were married. Serving as best man and maid of honor, were former Staters S/Sgt. **H. Billy Miller** and ex-Wasp **Frances Coughlin,** while **Lt. (jg) Nord Whited** was one of the ushers.

Lt. Col. **John E. Fitzgerald, jr., U. S. Army Air Corps (Hod)** and **Carol Remington** (Theta Chi) were married on March 17.

The marriage of **Lt. (jg) Nordstrom Whited, USN Air Corps** and **Barbara Wiese,** (Phi Sigma Nu) took place on March 25th.

Inter-fraternity sports, under the direction of **Bill Cordtz,** began this month with Basketball. Four fraternities, **Eta Omega Delta, Phi Lambda Xi, Epsilon Eta,** and **Sigma Lambda,** are participating. The three other frats, **Delta Pi Beta, Kappa Phi Sigma,** and **Sigma Delta Epsilon** do not have enough members to play, as yet. Other sports to be scheduled are miniature golf, badminton, track and volleyball.

Steve Porter was appointed by the A. S. Council as Senior Manager of Baseball, soon to be scheduled.

Joe Rodney (formerly Major, USA) and **Mrs. Rodney** are the proud parents of a daughter, **Patsy,** born March 1, weight 7 lb. 6 oz.

Mary Peck, Aztec songbird, has made a Decca recording with **"Hail Montezuma"** and **"The Fight Song"** on one side, and a smooth rendition of **"Always"** on the other side. Record can be purchased through bookstore.

Fred "Buzz" Holding, basketball player, was elected by students to reign as **"St. Patrick"** at the Shamrock Shuffle, W.R.A. sponsored event.

March 19, **Cetza** held its annual celebration of **"Hello Walk Day,"** and all **Aztecs** received name tags bearing the words, **"Hello"** and **"Smile."**

Treble Clef gave their annual concert on Sunday, March 25, to a large audience in Russ Auditorium. Proceeds all go to the pipe organ fund.

OPEN HOUSE WILL BE HELD
for the
PICTURE PANEL

on Sunday, April 8, from 2 to 5. Visitors are invited to come and make the occasion a **Little Reunion.**

EL PALENQUE

which is the college literary magazine will be out the first week in May. To date the Navy has contributed most to the service men's section. The price is 25 cents and it may be purchased through

The Aztec Bookstore,
State College,
San Diego 5, Calif.

DEL SUDOESTE

which is the college annual, will be off the press in a few months. This year it is being edited by **Jayne Dempsey** and **Jeanne Oncley.** It is to have a special feature on **Aztecs in Service,** and a later notice will tell you that it can be ordered through the **Aztec Bookstore, State College, San Diego, Calif.** It is still possible for you to get a copy of last year's annual also.

COMMERCIAL

This issue of the **News Letter** is a sort of "supreme effort." We hope you will like it. But don't expect this much every month. You may have a colored picture just once or possibly twice a year; you may have 16 pages only when correspondence and news force us up to 16.

This issue took a lot of mid-night oil. The stencil cutting for the addressing machine required extra work. There are 400 changes per month which have to be searched, carded and stenciled.

We are still out of the red, but that is about all. We are looking for better times ahead. So, send in your changes of address, promotions and items of news, and from time to time help us out with our bills. Thanks to all of you who have contributed so generously to date. LCP.

T/5 WHITWORTH W. HOSKINS

was wounded in action in Luxembourg on January 29th according to a last minute bit of news. Whit was in an Air Borne Infantry outfit along with **1st Sgt. Joe Carter** who had previously reported jumping in a blizzard about Christmas time. They have had their share of combat duty. Whit is now in a hospital in England and was slated to come back to the States, but in his last letter to his mother, **Mrs. Alice B. Hoskins,** of 2322 Whitman St., he is to go back to his old outfit.

2

20

IN ACTION WITH PATTON

THE AZTEC NEWS LETTER
No. 32, November 1, 1944

. . .

Over 800 Aztecs are overseas. We have lost more than 60 in action and in training. The overseas mail has slacked off a little in the last week or so—possibly due to so many men being tied up in combat. We want to hear from you after each campaign, at least. It is always comforting to your friends to know that you are still kicking and able to write. I repeat, we do like to hear from you after we know that you have gone into combat. Figure it out.

. . .

Dr. Lauren C. Post, Editor

THE AZTEC NEWS LETTER
Third Anniversary Edition
No. 37, April 1, 1945
STATISTICS

Aztecs in service (grand total)	2,800
Women in service	135
Discharged, mostly on medicals	75
Prisoners of war	30

Missing in action	25
Wounded in action	72
Killed in action and training	81
Decorated	216
Commissioned officers	1,200
Aztecs overseas	1,000
Domestic mailing list	1,800
Campus distribution, about	500
Printing of average issue	3,700
Printing of this issue	6,000

✉ January 23, 1945

Dear Dr. Post,

Sorry not to have written before but news from Joe has been quite scarce the last two months. Joe is now in action with Patton. I don't know too much because only two of his letters in 60 days have come thru—one took 46 days, the other less. He has been in the front lines since Christmas nite but actually jumped into action New Years' Day during a blizzard. According to the papers here—neither weather or Germans stopped them. They were the "elements" of Patton's Army to first meet patrols with the 1st Army. Joe says he's crazy about the French people—they seem so sincere and genuinely like the Americans.

Joe's last letter—Jan 6—came this a.m. and was written in Belgium. He has had no home letters in almost two months but they have been moving so fast (the letter says) that it is impossible for mail to catch up to them. Joe says he is quite proud of his outfit—each man has proved his worth. All his men are 18 and 19 so that's a lot to say.

. . .

I have kept all the copies of the *Aztec* for Joe—I look forward to it each month to see if Joe or John has written. Once for a solid 30 days, a letter in it was the only news I had of Joe. Right after it, they held up the mail over there for 26 days.

. . .

Sincerely

Mrs. R. Joseph Carter

Letters from R. J. (Joe) Carter appear in chapter 17 and later in this chapter. Gen. George Patton Jr. would have understood Mrs. Carter's frustration with a slow-moving supply chain. In some ways, Patton was so far ahead in his thinking that it seemed nothing could keep up with him. He outpaced and outmaneuvered the enemy, frustrated his superiors, and at times was so prescient in his battle strategy that he was poised and ready for action when his army was needed the most. He was accused of risking lives, credited with stunning victories, criticized by the press, and known for motivating his men to move rapidly under adverse conditions.[1]

The following writer referred to Patton's rapid advances, but in editing for the *News Letter*, Dr. Post crossed out that line. He didn't want to alert the enemy to the movement of Patton's troops.

April 12, 1945
Germany
Dear Dr. Post—

. . .

Things are going great at this end of the line. Our boss Gen. Patton really keeps us moving as you can plainly understand. Don't imagine it will last very much longer. They're getting pretty well cornered.

. . .

Sincerely,
Jack Hudson

Patton was from a family of pioneers, and he grew up hearing about the heroic deeds of relatives who had fought for the Confederacy. His own wartime training came in an era that saw dramatic shifts in military equipment and technology. He was quick to adapt and trusted his instincts, sometimes over the orders of his superiors. His unyielding personality was shaped by his religious faith, and his ferocious determination caused him to push those under his command to extremes.[2] Patton's Third Army moved rapidly across France toward Germany, only to run out of gas— literally—outside the German city of Metz.[3]

The following *News Letter* excerpt describes the conditions under which James W. (Willard) Wallace delivered fuel to the front lines. Wallace took part in the Normandy invasions. More of his letters are in chapter 17.

THE AZTEC NEWS LETTER

No. 39, June 1, 1945

F/O James W. Wallace wrote this note from Germany: (He asked us not to print it, but since the newspapers have already told of gas being flown in to Patton's men, the fact is known to all. LCP.)

"We were flying gas in to Patton's men lately. On one trip we flew in and noticed two fighters take off just before us. When we landed we were told to take cover in nearby trenches by the ground troops. We couldn't figure it out 'til these two fighters circled and made a screaming pass at the field. They were two Me-109's flown by Germans who had just evacuated the field. That gives you an idea how fast the move is. At many fields, there are German ships in perfect condition left by the Germans in their haste to get away from the tank men. It's really a miracle how these boys have pushed.

"We took some Frenchmen, who had been held prisoners by the Germans for six years."

Allied supply lines were strained as they rushed to get enough materials to those at the front, and Patton seethed at the delay. The setback gave the Germans time to fortify their positions. Metz lay between France and Germany, and Hitler had given orders to Metz and other strongholds along his defensive line that troops should not surrender. In November 1944 Patton's army finally moved to take the city, battling for days through bad weather. With Allied air support, the Germans were finally forced out, and the heavily defended city fell.[4]

December 5, 1944

Dear Doc.

Just a few lines to let you know that I am still part of the race. I am in combat with a unit of the Third Army; just now we are in Germany. We helped to change History a little with the fall of the impenetrable fortress city of Metz.

. . .

As Ever,

Alfred (Al) Rhodes

Hitler then ordered the Ardennes Offensive, and in December 1944 that fierce German counterattack nearly broke the Allied line. Patton's instinct, even before receiving orders, was to redirect his troops toward the "bulge" where the Germans were about to push through. Recognizing that whoever controlled Bastogne, a crossroads in the Ardennes, would have an advantage, the Allies sent the U.S. 101st Airborne Division and part of the 10th Armored Division to hold the town, but they were surrounded by German forces. To help lift the siege, Patton's army covered almost a hundred miles in a matter of days. The weather cleared long enough for C-47 transport planes to drop supplies to those trapped.[5]

Capt. Mason Harris survived the siege and continued with Patton's forces into Germany. The photo of Harris with his teammates from the championship basketball team is in chapter 6.

✉ January 30, 1945
Dear Doc:

. . .

I am at present in Belgium in this nice snowy & cold climate. My unit was in on the battle of Bastogne, which was quite an event and a job well done. There are so many things which I could tell of that particular fight but can tell you in part of my own reactions, especially after we were getting low on supplies and we got our first supply by air. I have never seen anything so beautiful as those C47 & fighter protection as they came in low, circled, & got their signal from the pathfinders who were dropped the day before, and then came back & started their drop of supplies. Those colored chutes as they floated down were beautiful & words can't describe the feeling of not only my self but all of the others. Of course we had a couple of more supply days & then they sent in some gliders in about 3 days afterwards & then more gliders. Doc it's not possible to put on paper what one feels in those instances. There were many grim sights such as you've probably heard but it all came out in the end. . . .

Mason W. Harris
Captain 705 TD Bn.
A.P.O. 403 c/o P.M.
N.Y. N.Y

THE AZTEC NEWS LETTER
No. 37, April 1, 1945
Capt. Mason Harris was killed in action in Germany. He had been with an armored division under Gen. Patton and had been among those to hold out in the city of Bastogne when that city was surrounded during the German break-through. He had written since that time, and his letters appear elsewhere in this issue. Capt. Harris is the third member of the championship team to go, the other two being Ens. Milton (Milky) Phelps and Lt. (jg) Paul Fern. Mrs. Harris was an Oregon girl, and their little daughter whom Mason had not seen is three months old.

. . .

February 24, 1945
Germany
Hello Dr. Post,

. . .

Yes, I am in Hitler's vaunted fortress Germany. The only catch is that it is not so vaunted as they want you to think. The other night I slept in one of his Pillboxes and they are good. They are built in the ground with four to six feet of concrete supported by iron rods for protection. They have from three to six rooms in them with bunk beds for the men. The only trouble with them is that they are damp & stuffy but that is completely overshadowed by the safeness!! The only way to knock them out is to blast them by T.N.T. but that is not usually needed as the Krauts usually give up before that is necessary. It makes it easier for all parties concerned that way but in a way they are damn lucky to get off that easy.

. . .

I remain, as ever,
Pfc Chris M. Franovich, 39279587

Another letter from Chris Franovich is in chapter 16.

THE AZTEC NEWS LETTER
No. 41, August 1, 1945
Chris sent two Nazi flags that are very gaudy. We haven't decided whether to put them on the wall or the floor, but thanks a million for them. LCP.
Dr. Lauren C. Post, Editor

Sgt. Thomas M. Rice parachuted into Normandy on D-Day, June 6, 1944. (His letters about D-Day are in chapter 17.) He was part of the 501st Parachute Infantry Regiment with the 101st Airborne Division, and after the invasion of France, he fought in the siege at Bastogne. In one of his letters to Dr. Post, Rice quotes from a citation for a soldier who came to his rescue. Rice, the platoon leader, had been badly wounded and lying in an open field under enemy fire. In the *News Letter*, Dr. Post reported Rice's actions in many battles, along with a list of his awards. Privately, he called the young man's mother.

Rice recovered and was among the first to reach Berchtesgaden in the Bavarian Alps. With his exceptional eye for detail, he took stock of the equipment left in disarray by retreating troops. The planes he mentioned are the Messerschmitt Bf 109 fighter, the Junkers Ju 52 transport, and the Junkers Ju 88 bomber. The Luger and the Walther P38 are German pistols. Rice also described his view of Hitler's Eagle's Nest, a remote mountaintop retreat. He couldn't resist a touch of irony as he noted that the "hideout" was in plain view. As the German command collapsed, the remnants of resistance camped in the surrounding mountains. A fragment of the German forces harried the victors with sporadic machine-gun fire, while the Allies took inventory of Nazi wealth.

May 1, 1945
Tuesday
France
Dear Doc Post,

. . . The past four months I have been convalescing in England from wounds received at Bastogne where our division held out. My life was saved by a member of my squad while on patrol behind the enemy lines. He received the bronze star for his actions. Enclosed is an excerpt from the citation; as a member of a combat patrol of six men whose mission was to outflank enemy positions in the town and seize the village crossing an open field the patrol encountered an enemy tank and several enemy infantrymen. While engaging the enemy, his platoon leader was seriously wounded (I got hit twice once in the right forearm and left thigh by breaking bones machine gun fire) and lying in an exposed position. Aware that the approach to the platoon leader was covered by intense enemy machine gun fire, my rescuer crawled forward under direct fire from the tank and returned over the same hazardous terrain. With complete disregard for his own personal safety he saved my life and was awarded the bronze star. I am truly indebted to this fellow who really came through when the chips were down and things seemed really rough. Things happen like this quite often and usually the award doesn't fit the deed.

. . .

Sincerely,

Sgt. T. M. (Tom) Rice 19164859

May 30, 1945

Berchtesgaden, Germany

Dear Doc. Post,

Enclosed are a few news items I thought might interest you. We are stationed here at Berchtesgaden, the home of Hitler's elite corps of SS troops, being quartered in very modern two story battalion capacity buildings. The camouflage of the installations as well as "der fuhrer's" hideout is perfect. His Eagle's Nest is plainly visible and only 6000 feet above sea level. It sticks out like a sore thumb on this precipitous mountain. Snow is still very deep at higher levels and the weather is very pleasant. The RAF really cratered his hideout but the Eagle's Nest is intact. The SS men really had a layout up here with every conceivable convenience available.

Many of the fellows are finding caves laden with rich treasures of art, currency and even great caches of arms have been dug up. Small groups have been going out on five day trips hunting and fishing around the numerous lakes. It takes an .03 with a scope to get these mountain goat, but the deer are readily rendered lifeless by our M1s with the nose cut off the bullets and holes drilled in them. There are large Jerry vehicle depots all over this area and almost everyone had a car or cycle at one time or another whether it be diesel or gasoline. ME 109s and Junker 52 & 88 are still standing on airdromes near Munich. They used the autobahns as landing strips and interception bases.

There are still thousands of die hard SS men hiding out in these mountains of the Bavarian National Redoubt Area. Even children are carrying concealed lugers and P38s. One of these kids drew a luger on [one] of the boys and offered to trade it for two bars of chocolate. The gun was fully loaded and off safety. This is hard to believe but true. Propaganda of all nature is being unearthed and the children flock to our chow lines. Every once in a while machine gun fire is heard echoing through the area as one of our boys is being fired upon. These SS men who are still hiding build fires out in the open every night and fire flares. Sometimes a mountainside is completely illuminated by their activities.

. . .

Thanks for calling my mother on the telephone; it was very thoughtful of you.
Sincerely,
Sgt. T. M. (Tom) Rice 19164859

THE AZTEC NEWS LETTER
No. 46, January 1, 1946
S/SGT. THOMAS RICE
of the 101st Airborne Division is home after two years of service in Europe. Tom's experiences run all of the way through
from D-Day in Normandy where he earned the Bronze Arrowhead through France, Bastogne and the Bulge, Rhineland
and Central Germany. For action in the Bulge his outfit was
awarded a Presidential Unit Citation, for action in Holland he
was awarded a Bronze Star, for some other action his outfit was
awarded a Belgian Unit Citation, and somewhere along the
line Tom picked up a Purple Heart with an Oak Leaf Cluster for
wounds received in the left thigh and the right arm.

He is still undergoing treatment for one of the wounds but
expects to be back at State College in February.

The Rhine River descends from the Swiss Alps and courses through
half a dozen countries, demarcating the borders between Germany and
Switzerland and Germany and France. The waters of this massive river
drive trade and industry, and the castles along its banks, considered to be
among the most beautiful in the world, are proof that this passageway has
been heavily defended for hundreds of years.

The Germans were determined to halt the Allied advance and prevent the Allies from crossing the Rhine. The town of Remagen, Germany,
bore the brunt of the fighting in March 1945, at one of the few crossings
that had not yet been destroyed. The Germans did their best to blow up
the bridge there, but the Allies captured it and made enough repairs for
troops and tanks to flow into Germany.[6] The strain proved too much for
the bridge. A few weeks after it was captured, it collapsed, but the damage
to Germany was done—the Allies were across the Rhine. Engineers wasted
no time in constructing more bridges to get more troops and equipment
into Germany.[7]

Town by town, Germany fell under Allied control. The two cities mentioned in Capt. Jim Stacey's letter, Düren and Kassel, are about 135 miles apart by air, and both suffered from heavy bombing. Stacey also wrote to Dr. Post about the 88-millimeter anti-tank, antiaircraft artillery used by the Germans in an effort to bring down the Allied planes.

Stacey had written previously to Dr. Post from England. In that letter (chapter 16), he described a Christmas party for children that featured Father Christmas handing out Red Cross boxes. After seeing combat, Stacey's appreciation for aid and the generosity of those who delivered it extended to medics on the battlefield. He offered his impressions of the Russians, including an officer who, at first glance, reminded him of the timid cartoon character Caspar Milquetoast. (In *News Letter* No. 40, Dr. Post changed the name to Caspar Milktoast.) When it came to the locals, however, Captain Stacey couldn't laugh. He detested what he considered to be hypocrisy on the part of the German populace.

April 21, 1945
1st Army
Germany
[V-Mail]
Dear Dr. Post:

. . .

We are here in Germany as per usual and the reception, while it has slackened some in the last day or so, can still definitely be termed as hostile. These people are really using everything including the kitchen sink to try and stop us but I am afraid that it is no use. Have really learned to appreciate the air corps, for Doc, they really have done a job over here. I have seen the results of their work on Duren and Kassel and the only complaint I have is that they rarely leave enough buildings standing to provide billets for my men. Duren was the most bombed out place I have ever seen and there wasn't one building in the entire city, which must be as big if not bigger than San Diego, which hadn't been hit. They really worked it over. . . . At Remagen, we crossed the Rhine on the largest pontoon bridge ever built. Over 1000 feet of it and it was a dandy. The medics were the most abused group of individuals in the states and over here they are doing a wonderful job. I am speaking only for the front line aid men for they are just about all we see. I have never seen one refuse to go out to aid a wounded soldier regardless of the fire on that area. They do this despite the fact that they are marked as targets with the four white circles on their helmets with the red cross in it and experience has proved that the Jerry is not prone to cease firing on the aid man. We have lost too many [medics for their deaths] to have been accidents. Guess I shall close now with regards to all my friends in the service and home.

Sincerely,

Capt. J. E. (Jim) Stacey 0454491

Co M 271st Inf APO 417

c/o PM, New York, NY

THE AZTEC NEWS LETTER

No. 38, May 1, 1945

Capt. James E. Stacey wrote from Germany:

"The one thing that we never heard about the Germans was their artillery. From all the papers that we read they have none and what they have, they can't use. That was just the writer's idea. They have plenty of it, plenty of ammo, and they know how to use it. Their 88 is a favorite weapon; however, the thing we hate most is mortars, because you can't hear them coming. These American lads sure confuse me—they are the most curious people in the world. They will pick up anything, a habit liable to be fatal, but I have noticed the change in this company. Now they look and leave things alone. They seem to have an endless supply of energy and although they complain, they are usually in fine spirits. I believe it is their sense of humor which makes them impossible to beat.

"Recently we took a town and immediately pushed on to secure it against counter attack, which never came. We set up just before dark and dug in. We had only our ponchos and as it rained and snowed and got cold, we spent a miserable night and part of the day out there before we received orders to pull back to town and get the men under cover. This we tried to do, but I say *tried*, because while we were freezing, the rest of the division moved into town and fixed themselves up swell. We got what places we could, and because of my exalted position in the company, was given special consideration. I got to sleep on a meat block."

May 12, 1945
Dear Dr. Post:

. . .

As you probably know, our division, the "Fighting 69th," was the 1st to contact the Russians. It was a Los Angeles officer that made the contact. California scores again. However it wasn't our regiment altho we met them soon after. They are truly a bunch of characters. Real screwballs but they get the job done. I met one major that was a real Caspar Milquetoast in the flesh but later I found out that he had been a sniper and accounted for a whole bunch of the enemy as his chest was covered with ribbons. I did notice a strange thing; the Russians do not wear ribbons but rather the entire decorations and these they continue to wear even when fighting. One really put a slam on the American scotch when he drank a water tumbler full down without pausing or even blinking and then said "Pretty good wine but rather sweet." I guess they must practice drinking gasoline or a reasonable substitute. I volunteered, as did practically everyone else in the division, to go along when the division commander and the Russian commander met. I was elated when I got an ok but all I got for my troubles was a long ride and was so far from the meeting place that I couldn't even see the town when they were meeting. We provided flank protection or something but it really taught me to observe the one fundamental of the army, "Never volunteer for anything."

. . . Shall close for now and hope VJ Day is soon coming.

Sincerely,
Capt. J. E. (Jim) Stacey 0454491
Co M 271st Inf APO 417
c/o PM, New York, NY

July 25, 1945
Dear Dr. Post:

. . .

We have just finished our part in a search for black market operators, contraband, deserters and PWs from the German army. From all reports it was quite a success. In searching the houses you run into many hard luck stories and each has a reason why they should be excluded from the search and ready to tell on their neighbors. I can't imagine the American people, if we were occupied by a victorious enemy, trying to curry favor like these former members of the "Superrace."

They have no feeling of guilt and everything is blamed on the Nazis and so far none admit to being a member of the party. You are sometimes tempted to feel sorry for some of the older people but when you find pictures of them with their hands upraised in the Nazi salute, smiling and cheering, you feel nothing but contempt for them. Their attitude seems to be that the Nazis are no good because they lost but had they won, they still would have supported them 100 percent. I still cannot understand why the German peoples themselves wanted war because Germany is by far the prettiest country that I have seen since arriving in Europe.

. . .

> Sincerely,
> Capt. J. E. (Jim) Stacey 0454491
> Co D 175th Inf APO 29
> c/o PM, New York, NY

The campaign to cut across Germany was a race to ford its many rivers. The town of Wesel, in western Germany, lies at the junction where the Rhine meets the Lippe River. When Wesel came under heavy Allied bombing in February 1945, the Germans resorted to their usual defensive tactics, trying with all their might to blow up the bridges that spanned both rivers.

If the Allies couldn't cross on foot, they were determined to proceed by air or boat. On March 24, Operation Varsity was launched, bringing together the combined strength of two elite paratroop units, the American 17th Airborne Division and the British 6th Airborne Division. First, an amphibious assault ferried ground troops across the water, and then the airborne divisions dropped in behind enemy lines. The speedy massive attack drove the enemy back from the riverbank. The Allies erected more bridges and pushed deeper into German territory.[8]

April 15, 1945

Dear Dr. Post,

Since last writing to the *News Letter*, I've changed outfits. It's the 224 Medics with the 17th Airborne Division.

We crossed the Rhine in gliders and dropped by parachute to help the British Second and the American Ninth across.

My glider landed with only a couple of bullet holes, but several caught fire and others were badly machine gunned.

The medics set up amid artillery fire and as the days went on, followed to Munster where we left the British. The British commando is, incidentally, a wonderful fighter. All Germans say "Deutschland ist Kaput."

We are now in [censored] in a tavern to catch our breath, wash up and write letters. We found an old phonograph and with the help of a screwdriver, it plays wonderfully—after you drop 10 Pfennig in the slot.

Pvt. Harold Stark
224 Med Co 17AB Div
APO 452 c/o PM
New York, New York

Two armies, the First and the Ninth, set out to flank and surround the Germans, but a combination of resistance, not enough bridges, and poor roads threatened to bring troops to a standstill. Whit Hoskins, a member of the Delta Pi Beta fraternity, and fellow Aztec Joe Carter were with the 17th Airborne. Once they were successfully across the Rhine, they moved rapidly to secure more bridges and opened up routes for the infantry to pour through. Their fast advance made it possible for the two prongs of the Allied attack to surround and ensnare 325,000 German soldiers in what became known as the Ruhr Pocket.[9] Hoskins was awarded the Silver Star, the third-highest military award for valor, for gallantry in action against an enemy. The medal added to his points for discharge, but he was short of the number needed to get home. (For more on the point system, see chapter 22.)

THE AZTEC NEWS LETTER
No. 38, May 1, 1945
Cpl. Whitworth W. Hoskins who is with the 17th Airborne Division has been awarded the Purple Heart and the Distinguished Service Cross.

June 1, 1945
Sterkrade, Germany
Dear Doc Post,
It's been many months since I've written word one. But it's always many months before I write. My last was shortly after our mission in the Belgian Bulge. Of course, we had other names for it, unprintable names, naturally.

Since then the 17th Airborne has made military history with its airborne mission across the Rhine and its aid in the enveloping of the Ruhrland, forming the Ruhr pocket, and later aiding to close that pocket. Since, we have occupied a portion of the Ruhrland.

I'll always feel, and I believe it was proven so, that the defeat of the German army in the west took place in Belgium. After the Bulge, the main enemy was old man weather. Why do I say after the Bulge. Certainly during it, also. But weather rather than opposition was the main factor in the comparatively slow advance during the early spring. [page torn] was real war, at its worse. After the Roer crossing and especially after the Rhine, going was much easier, though much more rapid. When the war ended, we were already doing occupational duty.

Joe Carter received a battlefield commission for his work in Belgium. He is now in charge of one of our Displaced Persons camps. I see him very frequently because I have to service his medical section and keep medical records on his camp.

Our only contact with other Aztecs is through the *News Letter* because we have no other Aztecs among us, that we know of. That being our only contact with the Aztecs, the *News Letter* has become a monument to us. A monument of things gone by and of things to come. We're all eagerly looking forward to those things to come, those things the Allied Nations have given so much in human life and injury to build and maintain.

. . .

Since I last wrote, I find I have the Silver Star to add to the rest of my points, which still fails to make me enough. Seems unless a man has a child or two he stays. I think the system is entirely fair, but it certainly leaves me with the feeling that I'd left something important undone. Now I know how important. But if we all go on doing our own small share, it makes our one big share as the U.S. Army.

Next time I write, I'll visit the latrine before hand and get all the latest lies, rumors and orders. Then I'll have a real story. Only trouble is, I always get the rumors from there that I started two weeks before. Strictly as a morale booster, of course.

Sincerely yours,
Whit Hoskins
Delta Pi Beta

THE AZTEC NEWS LETTER
No. 38, May 1, 1945
1st Sgt. Richard Joseph Carter wrote from the 17th Airborne Division:

"I wrote once that my boys were ready and eager for combat. Things have changed; we were thrown in as shock troops west of Bastogne. After numerous attacks, we chased the Nazis back to Germany. We drove 45 miles in less than a month. Pretty good, considering that we had no heavy equipment, no snow equipment, etc. Hoskins is okay in more ways than one—he is up for the Silver Star and deserves more."

Annihilation from German war tactics came in many guises. Those captured were often forced to work in factories. In addition to the Jews who were used for labor, the Nazis added millions of Polish and Soviet prisoners to their workforce.[10]

April 6, 1945
Somewhere in Germany
Hello "Doc"—

. . .

I've been in France, Belgium, Holland and now Germany. Every time I get to where I can ask for wine, women, or song in one language we move to another country and I have to start all over again.

We were talking with some Russian slave laborers with the help of one of the men in the company who speaks Russian and they said they had been waiting for us for four years. The Germans branded them with tattoo marks and every time they would run away they would tattoo them again. One guy looked like a bill board.

. . .

I remain—
"The Swede"
Pfc. Charles M. Snell

May 7, 1945
Somewhere in Austria
Dear "Doc"—

. . .

Guess it won't be long now till you will be hearing from some of the boys who were prisoners of the Germans. Our division alone has set free some 15,000 of them, at the same time capturing some 14,000 Nazis. Haven't seen any Staters over here but have glimpsed some of the prison camps and talked to the inmates. The stories of Nazi atrocities are rather subdued than exaggerated and I know that you can hardly believe what has been told. Personally I don't believe there is any such thing as a good German unless it's a dead one and these riflemen believe in lots of good Germans.

The Germans are supposed to be civilized and to have had the benefits and culture derived therefrom but it seems only to have developed the evil in their brains. We expect something of this nature from the Japs but it stops all description to see this.

Am sweating out a furlough to the States before going to the So. Pacific but may go directly there from here.

Have survived three major battles and been awarded the combat infantryman's badge. Am feeling fine tho' somewhat thinner than when I was at State by some 25 lbs. No purple heart thank you, just a few grey hairs (ha). Thanks for the *News Letter* Doc, and keep up the good work—

"Swede"

Pfc. Charles M. Snell

As the Allies began liberating concentration camps, the Nazis attempted to move their victims by train or forced march. Thousands died during those futile evacuations. Allied commanders were inclined to view the local population as complicit and sometimes drafted civilians to bury the bodies.[11]

June 8, 1945
France

. . .

My division, the 97th, will return to the States in July for 30 day furloughs, then we are scheduled to go to Fort Bragg, North Carolina for Pacific training. Our battle history mainly concerns the Ruhr and Czechoslovakia. Just before the end of the war we cleared the town of Schwarzenfeld where a notorious German atrocity camp was. Instead of flying white flags of surrender—the inhabitants hung from every window white flags with black marks on them. Even some of the German citizens were sickened by the sight of some 300 Polish victims which had been thrown on the bank of the town's main river. The people claimed it was all the fault of SS troopers but all through our journey in Germany each civilian blames the other or the soldiers blame the SS. We made the people of the town bury the bodies, but the darkness of their activities & cruelties will remain and stand out on them for a long time to come as did the black on their surrender flags. It will be a long time before Germany can rise again, to commit such deeds, and we are doing our utmost to see that they never do.

Thank you again for the swell *News Letters.*

Sincerely,

Gordon Luce

June 15

Bad Klosterlausnitz, Germany

Dear Dr. Post:

. . . Our unit is slated as occupational troops. Although, some may be sent home and others to the Pacific area.

It was a hard blow, learning that we would remain, but we are all hoping we won't have to stay here too long. . . .

No doubt you read in *Life* magazine, the atrocities of the concentration camp, Buchenwald, in Weimar, Germany. I "visited" the camp, and although it was pretty well cleaned up, I could almost "feel" the presence of the people who were imprisoned there.

The town we are in was formerly a health resort. It is very beautiful country, but even at this late date, rainy and cold. There is a large maternity hospital here, and every once in a while we are called on an emergency. We have quite a few civilians who come here for treatment, mainly because we have more of a complete dispensary.

Well, I hope that in a few days, we learn our orders have been changed and on our way home.

Thanks again,

Manuel Doria

June 30, 1945

Germany

. . .

We were recently billeted in Trier, the oldest town in Germany. In the days of Constantine it was the seat of the Holy Roman Empire. There are still some of the old Roman ruins standing. The city is such a mess that it is difficult to tell which are the old and which are the new ruins. Everywhere is rubble & debris. Each town we go through seems to be worse than the previous one. Such destruction— block after block, it was apparently so systematic.

We flew along the Moselle River where General Patton crossed & over the Siegfried Line. We saw the dragon teeth. All the pill boxes have been blown up. Flame throwers must have been used because some of the remains looked burnt.

Surely with all that has happened to Germany in this war, some of it will be brought home to the people. We've seen so many German prisoner camps. Along the highways & byways is wreckage—maybe a tank, maybe a truck or car, or a crumbled house. Yet with all of that, Germany is beautiful. Outside of the States and next to Hawaii, the Rhine Valley is the most beautiful spot I've seen. I have a full appreciation of the beauty of "Castles on the Rhine."

With best regards

Ferne Downes

The battle for Nuremberg in April 1945 struck at the heart of the Nazi regime. It had been the site of Nazi rallies and the place where Hitler announced that Jews were no longer citizens of Germany.[12] The Germans surrendered the city after days of bombardment. Harold Dill captured a stamp from the Bavarian State Police in the Fürth district, so the symbol of the Nazi party appears on his letter. The old part of the city, where the Holy Roman Empire had once held court, was destroyed in the fighting. After World War II, the city again became a center for the courts, where military tribunals brought to justice those who had perpetrated war crimes.[13]

August 21, 1945

Nuremberg

Hello Doc—

Just a line to let you know where I am. Arrived here right after the squadron did in April and was really glad to join an outfit permanently after three years of nothing but the training command.

Nuremberg, I believe, was about the worst hit of the larger cities of Germany. The old walled city section was leveled to the ground.

The situation is pretty well in hand here now as we have so far "liberated" a Coca-Cola plant and an Ice Cream factory and so have plenty of both which makes it much easier to live. We occupy a former "Kraut" training field that was left pretty well intact. Hangars, barracks, mess halls, etc. are all in very fine shape.

When the war ended all Luftwaffe planes were ordered to come in here and land. We had to go out and "escort" some of them in though. When they did come in, they would land "wheels up", wreck their planes so that we couldn't use them.

Harold W. Dill

21st August 1945
Nurnberg, Germany

Hello Doc —

Just a line to let you know where I am. Arrived here right after the squadron did in April and was really glad to join an outfit permanently after three years of nothing but the training command.

Nurnberg, I believe, was about the worst hit of the larger cities of Germany. The old walled city section was leveled to the ground.

The situation is pretty well in hand here now as we have, so far, "liberated" a Coca-Cola plant and an Ice Cream factory and so have plenty of both which makes it much easier to live. We occupy

Letter from Harold Dill, August 21, 1945

You will note the stamp at the top of the page. Got that at Gestapo Hdqrs in town along with various other souvenirs.

Don't expect to see San Diego for another year or so as we are occupational. Have flown around the continent quite a bit. Been to London, Paris, Rome, Graz, Linz, Vienna, Munich, Hamburg, Cologne, Liège, Brussels, Rotterdam, The Riviera, and many other places. Got some good pictures of Berchtesgaden & Salzburg. It really breaks the monotony to be able to go up in the blue and fly around a little.

Will close for now. Say hello to everybody for me.

Regards,

Harold W. Dill

THE AZTEC NEWS LETTER

Five of the 75 married women students on the State College campus. They, along with many other married women students, have gone into extracurricula activities with the spirit and enthusiasm of the students that you used to know. See last page for names and some of their activities.

January 1, 1945

No. 34

This Issue Sponsored in part by Phi Sigma Nu

Edited by
DR. LAUREN C. POST
San Diego State College
San Diego 5, California

To All of the Aztecs in Service and Their Friends:

At the moment of this writing, the news is not the kind that makes a New Year's greeting an easy, casual thing. It is reminiscent of the news that came in from Salerno when a comparable greeting had to be written. State College Aztecs lost their lives at Salerno, but the war went on. Today we have many more Aztecs in the First Army; more lives have been lost, but still progress is evident. The war is closer to its end. In view of what happened during 1944, we can expect that a tremendous lot will be accomplished during 1945. May this year see each of you succeed in your various duties and get home for leaves if not for permanent residence.

May the New Year bring Victory and those opportunities that should come with the Peace with a minimum loss of life.

And again, best of luck,
Lauren C. Post,
Editor of the News Letter.

P.S.: Keep writing and should you come to San Diego don't forget to pay the campus a visit. LCP.

CAPT. ROBERT J. LANDIS
was reported killed in action in France.

LT. WALTER L. TICHENOR
died of battle wounds on August 30. He had been overseas for 27 months and had served in Iceland, England and France. He had been awarded the Purple Heart.

21

V-E DAY

THE AZTEC NEWS LETTER

No. 34, January 1, 1945

To All of the Aztecs in Service and Their Friends:

At the moment of this writing, the news is not the kind that makes a New Year's greeting an easy, casual thing. It is reminiscent of the news that came in from Salerno when a comparable greeting had to be written. *State College Aztecs* lost their lives at Salerno, but the war went on. Today we have many more *Aztecs* in the *First Army*; more lives have been lost, but still progress is evident. The war is closer to its end. In view of what happened during 1944, we can expect that a tremendous lot will be accomplished during 1945. May this year see each of you succeed in your various duties and get home for leaves if not for permanent residence.

May the *New Year* bring *Victory* and those opportunities that should come with the *Peace* with a minimum of loss of life. And again, best of luck,

Lauren C. Post,

Editor of the *News Letter*

World War II did not end easily. The Axis powers in Europe capitulated to the Allies even as the war in the Pacific continued. Late in April 1945 the European surrender began with German forces yielding in Italy. That small stream of submission turned into a cascade of surrenders at the beginning of May. Berlin was captured, and then the Germans gave up control of Denmark and the Netherlands. Bavaria fell, and the might of Germany drained away across the continent. On May 7, 1945, Germany signed the Act of Military Surrender, and the following day was designated as Victory in Europe Day, or V-E Day.[1] People the world over turned out to celebrate in public, though many reserved at least a few private moments for prayerful reflection.

Sgt. Robert Kelly understood that he was witnessing the raw emotions of a rare moment in history. Another of his poetic letters is in chapter 17.

April 12, 1945
Germany

. . .

I searched until I found an old French grammar. I used to read it at night in my pup-tent, studying by the light of burning grease. . . .

As we moved across the country and into Belgium, I went into every door that opened. I sat in the kitchens and talked. I slept behind countless windows, in beds of all descriptions. . . . I heard them say, "We watched and watched for your coming . . ." or "It was three in the afternoon. I was by the church. I heard a shout and someone called that the Americans had come. And—heavens above!—you *had*!" or "Mary was anxious for your coming. She waited and asked. She couldn't leave her bed to watch. She was always hungry. She died the day before—oh tell me why *the very day before*?" or "We don't know where to begin . . . who to trust . . . what to try to do . . ."

Never again would it be there to be seen; a whole society, a whole race with all the thousand tiny complexities and normalcies of living laid open, laid bare, twisted and turned about and spilled in the streets, receiving us to sudden intimacy, smiling on us and crying and praying for us.

. . .

Sincerely,
Robert Kelly

Albert Lepore gave a whirlwind account of his unit's race through Germany, crossing rivers, uncovering enemy machine guns, and opening warehouses stocked with liquor. His brother, Lt. Louis R. "Louie" Lepore Jr., was half a world away, fighting with the 27th Marines, 5th Marine Division on Iwo Jima. Al got word of him through the *News Letter* and commented on the family luck that saw both brothers through combat. On April 17, 1945, Louis wrote, "I was very fortunate and didn't even get a scratch. . . . I still don't see how I came out so, because enough fellows got hit around me and I had a couple of pieces of shrapnel glance off my carbine."

May 11, 1945
Austria
Hello Doc!
. . .
Our outfit has really been roaring along until we screeched to a halt here in Austria. We wound up at the time as the farthest East of any American troops. I don't know if since then the other prong of the 3rd Army arrived at Prague proceeded farther East. No map!

But, Doc, you should see these Jerries—If the "SSers"—Hitler's alleged Supermen are really sad looking sacks—Plenty meek for the most part, and humbly grateful that they are in our hands instead of the "Russkis." Oh but these Jerrys fear the Russians!
. . .
Our outfit crossed all of Germany entering in the vicinity of Pirmasens and leaving between Braunau & Passau. This caused us to cross the Rhine (our Division made one crossing, bridgehead), the Danube, the Regen, the Inn, the Isar, all of them sizeable streams. The Danube proved to be the roughest. My own assault boat was dipped twice.
. . .
We walked into Coburg—fought only in its South & Southeastern outskirts near the railyards. But Bayreuth was different—all the bridges were blown—so Nicht Tanks! Snipers were really thick in the environs & fringes—especially along a ridge which overlooked our avenue of approach—we hauled 5 MGs out in only a few hundred yards.

Bayreuth was pretty well taken over before very long. It didn't take too long to find Wehrmacht warehouses—we really liberated 3 star Hennessy, Sparkling Burgundy & Champagne—Found it in quantities in different Nazis hangouts— the boys keep themselves under control—oh sure you'll get one or two that will imbibe too heavily—but it's uncommon—at least in this outfit.

Do you know that some of the first details that I found out about my brother and Iwo Jima were in the *News Letters?* Looks like Louis was the only Stater of that group of 4 that came out unscathed. Just old Lepore luck I guess. Sure hope it holds out for him.

. . .

I've done very little souvenir hunting—a foot soldier just carriers too much to begin with—Finally wound up with only my cartridge belt, ammo, chow, shovel, compass, canteen & carbine—period.

Say hello to all on campus—

Sincerely

Albert R. (Al) Lepore, 01312953

Co. A. 5th Inf. A.P.O. 360

c/o P.M. New York, N.Y.

THE AZTEC NEWS LETTER

No. 45, December 1, 1945

CAPT. ALBERT R. LEPORE

was awarded the Silver Star Medal for gallantry in action in the taking of Bayreuth, Germany. Al has been in the ETO for 10 months and has been in France and Germany most of the time.

May 28, 1945

Caserta, Italy

Dear Doc

. . .

As the return address indicates, yours truly has been promoted. It was really quite an occasion, as it came at 4:30 PM on 7 May 1945, and at 5:20 PM on that day we received word that Germany had surrendered unconditionally. I guess that my being promoted was too much for the Krauts.

. . .

My fondest regards

Bernie Carroll

June 11, 1945

Dear Sir:—

I received a letter from our son Tom, the end of last week, and thought you might like to know his reaction to VE Day.

The letter is dated May 8, 1945, and he was down in a place called Manby in England. Had been in London for several days on business for the R.A.F. and was on his way back to Castle Kennedy in Stranraer, Scotland, where he has been stationed as a Senior Instructor for four or five months. He received the rank of Flying Officer last December.

This is part of his letter home[.]

"Dear Mother and Dad: VE Day, the day we fought and worked for so long and hard is here at last. I wondered what it would be like this "V Day," and here when it has come the people at this place do not feel much like celebrating or having a joyful time. Feel more like going to church and thanking God that the fighting is over. As for myself; I could not go out for a lot of laughing to day for I am thinking back over the past few years, of what I have seen and been through, of all the boys I have known that will never come back, of the sad hearts of their mothers and dads. Here I sit in my room at Manby thinking over it all and wondering what is ahead of us.

I know the way you must be feeling about the news today—very thankful but sad, and much to be thankful for."

Tom expects to be home this summer and we shall be so happy to have him here. It is three years past since he joined the R.C.A.F. and two years since he landed in the British Isles. He was in the thickest of the fight so we feel very thank[ful] he has come out of it all, as he has.

. . .

I remain,

Sincerely,

Mrs. Hugh (Agnes) W. Milligan

4743 Marlborough Drive

San Diego 4, California

THE AZTEC NEWS LETTER

No. 40, July 1, 1945

Pfc. Theodore W. Livingston wrote his parents from Czechoslovakia:

"In V.E. Day our squad and a few other fellows boarded a truck to move to this location—Instead of white flags all the houses flew the Czech flag. The streets were jammed with people dressed in their best, who showered us with flowers and wreaths. They had bunting stretched across the streets and quite a few tall fir trees had been cut. These were stripped of bark and branches up to within 8 feet of the top and the bare poles 'barber poled' with red, white and blue bunting. About every other person had a plate of cookies or cakes. The alternates had a pitcher of milk or a bottle. We couldn't stop in all the towns, so we had to disappoint many of the people and let them feed those who came later.

"When we arrived in this town our jeep and truck were swamped with people.... When they heard we would stay they all wanted an American in their homes.... I am in a very modest but scrupulously clean house with an American-worshipping 12 year old son and a vivacious 16 year old daughter. As soon as we entered, the latter wanted to know if there would be dancing at night. Soon everyone was asking the same question.... Therefore it was arranged for 7:30.... Then some one got the bright idea of autograph hunting. We started signing name and the date on money, photographs, in books, Nazi orders, etc. I think I signed my name 500 times.... The band must have done some secret practicing for it was surprisingly good. Of course we had a pretty hard time getting the idea of the whirling polkas, and whatever else they do, to the great enjoyment of the old folks sitting around the walls. The more tangled up we got, the harder they laughed. . . . Then there were speeches and cheering which, of course, we couldn't understand except for an occasional mention of American.... We try to keep them from going 'hog-wild' with enthusiasm and hospitality, but after six years of oppression that is hard to do."

It took time for information about all those who had been held prisoner to reach Dr. Post's office, and he refrained from celebrating while he waited for the news. Each month he tallied up the number of men and women in service and made note of those who had been reported as missing, killed, or captured. "Kriegies" was a slang term for Allied prisoners, from the German *Kriegsgefangener*, a prisoner of war.

THE AZTEC NEWS LETTER

No. 39, June 1, 1945

To All of the Aztecs in Service and Their Friends:

There has been a change in the war since last we went to press. V-E Day has come and gone, but without celebration on the campus or in San Diego. It was rather an occasion for rededication of ourselves and our efforts toward the completion of the task that lies ahead. No local Aztec would have felt right celebrating when each and every one of us has close relatives and acquaintances in actual combat against the Japanese.

Your editor has made a sincere effort to keep track of our men in both theaters of operation, and a close checkup is being made of our men who are missing or who have been prisoners in Europe. . . .

Should you get information about any of the 22 prisoners or the nine missing Aztecs in the ETO, please let us have it so that we can publish it. And let us hope that all of the news is good news.

And again, best of luck!

Dr. Lauren C. Post, Editor

THE AZTEC NEWS LETTER

No. 39, June 1, 1945

Lt. Kenneth E. Barnhart, Jr. cabled from Europe to his parents that he was liberated, well, and would be seeing them. The cablegram which came on May 15 was the first to report liberation of any of the 22 Aztec prisoners held in Europe.

The statistics changed month to month, and by the time the next issue was published, Dr. Post confirmed "that every one of the 25 State College Aztecs who had been held prisoner in Europe has been liberated."

THE AZTEC NEWS LETTER

No. 40, July 1, 1945

Lt. Richard F. Kenney who was a low-number prisoner (POW No. 1747) came home after 22 months in prisoner camps. He had a couple of low visits on the campus and appeared to be perfectly well. He will be ready to go again, if necessary, after his 60 day leave.

Richard told many stories of happenings in prison camps, some with humor, and others in a different mood. His experience, although not as bad as some, is not the kind one would ever want to repeat. He told of solitary confinement and interrogating when his arms were badly burned from his crash landing. Altogether it was pretty rough.

Richard had flown P-38s when the going was rough back in North Africa. He was shot down on his 27th mission.

THE AZTEC NEWS LETTER
No. 40, July 1, 1945
Lt. George Scott is home following his liberation. He had quite a time of it in the prison camp according to Richard Kenney. It seems that Scott had drawn a picture of Hitler (with a noose around his neck) and one of the ferrets found it on his bunk.

THE AZTEC NEWS LETTER
No. 40, July 1, 1945
Capt. Griffith P. Williams has been liberated and was first reported to this office as being well by Lt. Larry Devlin who saw Griff in Paris. Griff was the first Aztec to give us a Snow Job at State College. That was back in the summer of 1942 when we were working on *News Letter* No. 4.

He was shot down on July 4, 1943 over Sicily and his pals reported that he didn't have a chance as they had seen his plane go down in flames. We are looking forward to a further report on Griff as on the other Kriegies as they check in on their 60 day leaves.

The Allies took control of Germany and established zones of occupation. By August 1945, plans for a postwar German government had been drawn up under the shared authority of the United States, Great Britain, France, and the Soviet Union. Military commanders assisted in establishing a transitional government, and occupational troops continued in Germany into the 1950s.[2]

A new government wasn't the only thing that had to be established. For many citizens, every aspect of life had been demolished. Cities and their supporting infrastructure had been bombed and burned, sometimes to the ground. Homes, businesses, and the agriculture to support a population had disappeared. Those now freed from labor and prison camps swelled the ranks of the homeless and displaced. An estimated eight million people had been displaced, and many found themselves in new camps managed by the United Nations through its Relief and Rehabilitation Administration. Some people who had been uprooted began returning home as soon as they could. Others made plans to start over in a new country. Many Jews relocated to the partitioned land, Palestine, which became the state of Israel, and thousands more emigrated to the United States.[3] The efforts of repatriation continued for years, and camps for displaced persons remained in Europe for more than a decade.

Capt. Ralph Bailey, an army chaplain, wrote a detailed letter each Christmas season to friends, including Dr. Post. After the war, Bailey ministered to occupation troops across Germany. He sprinkled his prose with humorous and heroic stories, and he gave testimony to the human suffering caused by war. Mingled with his gratitude for victory was his keen awareness that rebuilding nations and cultures ripped apart by combat would take time.

Christmas, 1945
Bavaria, Germany
Greetings to You!
Last week several of us were climbing a snowy slope to the ski jump, each man silently thinking his own long thoughts as we plodded through a Christmas-card world, when a young soldier stopped in his tracks. "Chaplain," he brought up without preliminaries, from that deep well of loneliness that every old-timer over here understands, "if I'm not home by *next* Christmas, my wife not only will have to be reintroduced—she'll have to be reconvinced!"

. . .

Speaking more seriously now, despite the fact that we are not beyond longing for our homes and families, and despite those Occupation problems and personnel headaches that press dispatches have so colorfully pointed up for you, what impresses me is the number of men I talk with every day who have what it takes to go on with a hard job when the bands have stopped playing, and the folks at home have stopped cheering. Under fire, I witnessed self-sacrifice that will live in my memory forever; but just as lasting will be memories of unsung heroes I see putting herculean effort into their Occupation jobs, often in the face of discouragements, confusions and conflicts that soon would break the spirit of lesser men. And they stick to their high vision of an effective peace in the full knowledge that each day over here, for them personally, is just plain self-sacrifice, untinged by any of the glamor that may have been a spur when flags were waving.

As for me, I'm busier, if possible, than when we were in combat. Troops are spread out over many miles, and I must keep on the leap from dawn until midnight, the last hour of each day being reserved for the daily communique to my wife. Nevertheless, what a difference between this December and the last one, when I remember writing my Christmas letter to you under the sketchy shelter of a pup-tent, my combat boots almost top-deep in mud, our guns roaring in my ears. Tonight I am writing this in a heated office, my typewriter on a desk instead of on my knees. Last winter we slept in our bedrolls on frozen ground, or under any shelter we could find. This Christmas no one is shooting at us, we sleep in dry bunks, and have always before us the jolly possibility of a short rest in Switzerland, on the Riviera, in Paris, or perhaps Prague. In other words, those of us who went through last winter at the front find the Occupation soft going, no matter what its rigors for the newcomer, and we are deeply grateful.

My observation of the civilian situation here is much as it has been described for you in the press. Thousands of displaced persons (men, women and children) constitute one of the most heartbreaking problems. With German civilians, because of enormous destruction of buildings, a chief concern of many is shelter. It probably is difficult for you (living in what one of our sergeants always refers to as the one spot on earth that makes sense) to imagine what it is like where several families, clinging to one small house, must cook, eat and sleep in relays. As winter closes in, there is some disturbing evidence of cold, hunger and unrest, and Occupation forces, plus other agencies, are certainly not unmindful of urgent need for alert, intelligent action in the crucial months ahead.

And you? Please find time for a note. I appreciate so much all the letters I have received this year, as our friends are our strongest links with the sane and happy homeland we remember. Each friendly letter somehow makes it easier for us to remain away from those we love so long as our country needs us here—doing what we can to help secure peace in a world that as yet seems none too secure. Meantime, a happy Christmas to you, and don't forget us in your prayers.

Sincerely

Ralph R. Bailey

Chaplain (Capt), AUS

THE AZTEC NEWS LETTER

The Belles of the Blue Book Ball. Top row: Adrienne Wueste, Pat Allard (Queen), Barbara Mackay. Lower: Barbara Wiese, Dorothy Jorgenson, Mary Helen Ramsey.

March 1, 1945

No. 36

This Issue Sponsored in part by Shen Yo

Edited by
DR. LAUREN C. POST
San Diego State College
San Diego 5, California

To All of the Aztecs in Service and Their Friends:

This time it is Iwo Jima. Cotton Gilliland, Ted Thomey, Ross Workman, Chuck Ables, Jack Chandler, Bill Stoll, and Jack Edwards are there on the beaches, and dozens of other Aztecs are either on the beaches or in some capacity nearby. We cannot take our minds off of Iwo even though we know that the hazards of any of nearly a thousand other individual Aztecs may be as great. Aztecs in Germany, France, Italy, the Philippines and a hundred other spots should feel that they also are close to our hearts. We know that future months also will be rough, but in the meantime, let us hear from you after each of the current campaigns.

Many a fine letter had to be reduced to a single statement, hence the great extent of the WHO-WHAT-WHERE department. We try to include all of the names mentioned each month for it takes only a line to inform your friends that you are well. When we consider that the killed, missing, prisoners and the mustered out Aztecs (not including those incapacitated by severe wounds, combat fatigue and sickness) number over 200, our readers will appreciate the importance of a statement saying that YOU are well and carrying on.

For the 36th time we go to press, and believe it or not, it was the 36th time that was hardest. During the month many hundreds of yellow data cards came in bringing new names and addresses along with more information. (Keep sending them in, please.) There

22

TOKYO'S FRONT PORCH

THE AZTEC NEWS LETTER

No. 36, March 1, 1945

To All of the Aztecs in Service and Their Friends:

This time it is Iwo Jima. Cotton Gilliland, Ted Thomey, Ross Workman, Chuck Ables, Jack Chandler, Bill Stoll, and Jack Edwards are there on the beaches, and dozens of other Aztecs are either on the beaches or in some capacity nearby. We cannot take our minds off of Iwo even though we know that the hazards of any of nearly a thousand other individual Aztecs may be as great. Aztecs in Germany, France, Italy, the Philippines and a hundred other spots should feel that they also are close to our hearts. We know that future months also will be rough, but in the meantime, let us hear from you after each of the current campaigns.

. . .

The next issue begins the fourth year with a special edition and a colored picture. And so for the 36th time,

Best of luck!

Lauren C. Post

Editor of the *News Letter*

The Allied campaign across the Pacific had, as its ultimate goal, the defeat of the Empire of Japan. Slowly but surely, Japan's control of territory and resources collapsed. Capturing Iwo Jima, which lies south of Tokyo and has several airfields, took just over a month, from February through March 1945. The initial assault delivered 9,000 Marines to the shores of the volcanic island. By the end of the first day, 30,000 men had made their way onto the beaches. Always tenacious, the Marines pushed forward to take the high ground. They mustered more firepower and forces and hammered away at the entrenched enemy.

By this point in the war, each side understood the other's strategy. Expecting a devastating artillery barrage designed to shake them out of their bunkers, the Japanese dug in even deeper. They had mastered the art of connecting their caves with a network of tunnels, and their forces moved like a tide. When one group of defenders was flushed out and killed, additional troops flowed in and surprised the advancing Marines. In return, the Marines became more aggressive, clearing the Japanese positions with grenades and flamethrowers.

Nearly all 20,000 Japanese defenders on Iwo Jima were eventually killed. Only a few hundred Japanese troops were captured, although several thousand remained in hiding in the reinforced caves even after Allied victory. By the time the island was secured, an estimated 6,000 Marines had lost their lives. The number of American wounded had risen to a staggering 25,000.[1]

The historic flag-raising on Iwo Jima is the indelible image of victory in the Pacific. The flag atop Mount Suribachi meant that an American claim had been staked on Japanese soil. The scene became fixed in the minds of Americans and in the lore of the Marine Corps. Capturing Japanese territory was so important that one of the servicemen included some of the sand from Iwo Jima in his letter to Dr. Post.

March 8, 1945
V-Mail
Iwo Jima
Dear Doc,
They really picked a rugged spot for us this time. Ordinarily this island wouldn't be worth two cents but as it is we're paying a terrible price for it. This place could very easily be described as "Hell's Last Acre."

. . . Then of course Jack Chandler is here too. We've been on every campaign together now. He came padding back from the front lines a couple days ago hiding behind a beard and lugging a Nip rifle with him. He and all the others on the lines are taking a beating but once we secure this "hole" we'll really have one foot on Tokyo's front porch.

S/Sgt. C. N. "Chuck" Ables

USMCR

3rd Mar Div, HqCo. (G2)

c/o F.P.O.

S.F. California

More letters from Chuck Ables and Jack Chandler are in chapter 11.

THE AZTEC NEWS LETTER

No. 37, April 1, 1945

S/Sgt. Charles Ables came through all right at Iwo Jima. He is [with] the Headquarters of the Third Division, and his job is to keep a progress map of activities. He wrote his mother that the early hours of battle were, "the worst I have ever seen."

THE AZTEC NEWS LETTER

No. 37, April 1, 1945

Pfc. John A. [Jack] Chandler, also of the Third Division, came through so far without a scratch. He has been out up on the line most of the time and he wrote his mother: "Am here on Iwo Jima. Have been on the line. It's the toughest yet but I'll be all right. I saw Charles today and he is safe. Please tell his folks.

"This is a funny fight. I have been under a lot of fire but have seen only one live Nip. They are all around though, and are throwing lots of stuff back at us. Please don't worry too much about me as I am going to be OK."

THE AZTEC NEWS LETTER

No. 38, May 1, 1945

Pfc. Jack A. Chandler wrote from Iwo Jima:

"Iwo Jima is just about ours. It seems almost a nightmare, these last two weeks. This is the closest I have ever been to hell, and I have seen all the war I want to see. It doesn't sound very heroic, does it? I have been attached to an infantry company and have seen more grief than I ever dreamed could exist. I thought I had seen some bad times on Bougainville and Guam, but nothing like this. The Third Division really did a job. This is not a very cheerful letter, but it is the way I feel at present. Sorry. Chuck Ables is OK."

May 10, 1945

Dear Doc:—

I suppose you are getting your classes ready for finals again. Well out here we are sort of getting ready for our finals with the Honorable Nipponese. Looks as though the Nips would flunk, doesn't it?

I am enclosing a small dash of dirt. It is genuine Iwo Jima sand, picked up on the original invasion beach (but not during the invasion) quite close to Mount Suribachi. It is slightly on the volcanic side, as you will notice. You might like to add it to your collection, if any, of terra-not-so-firma from out of the way places. If you don't have this sort of a collection and wish to start one, I was just kicking the idea over in my mind that with all your service contacts, you could gather an astounding collection of valuable (well interesting anyway) sand, dirt, gravel, etc. from everywhere. A word about it in the *News Letter* would surely do the trick and you would no doubt be deluged with dirt.

Having a wonderful time but don't necessarily wish any of you were here.

Regards,

George Bergman, CY, USNR

c/o ComTransDiv 69

Flt. P.O., San Francisco

THE AZTEC NEWS LETTER

No. 40, July 1, 1945

I took the Iwo Jima sand over to Mr. Brooks for the geology collection. He was very glad to get it, and I think that we may start something along the line you suggested. Dr. Harwood gets bugs from his former students, Mrs. Harvey receives plants. Some day I'm going to put in a want ad for photographs of house types, racial types, physiographic types, and also aerial views that show village and field patterns. More about this later. LCP.

Dr. Lauren C. Post, Editor

After Iwo Jima was relatively secure, the Seabees set to work immediately to get the airfields in good repair. They made it possible for the P-51 Mustang to fly as an escort for the B-29 Superfortress. The powerful and accurate Mustangs fended off enemy fighters as the B-29 bombers made raids on Japan. Lt. Frank Heryet, a B-29 pilot, described the coordination between the bombers and their fighter support in the *Aztec News Letter*. More of Heryet's letters are in chapter 11.

THE AZTEC NEWS LETTER
No. 38, May 1, 1945
Lt. F.C. Heryet writes from somewhere in the Marianas:
. . .
"Yesterday was a red letter day for the B-29s in this area. It was the first time we had fighter protection to Japan. Our ship was up for 100 hour inspection, so we did not go on that mission, but I've heard all about it from members of the squadron who did go, and I thought you might be interested in some of the events.

"The B-29s rendezvoused with the P-51s off the Empire and things started happening soon after. Groups of P-51s would zoom 5,000 or 6,000 feet above us and a few minutes later a Japanese fighter would spin down in flames. Over land they shepherded those Jap fighters away from us and chased them all over the sky. The only time they'd come near us was when they'd go through the formation in a futile effort to get away from a P-51. One Jap pilot bailed out when his ship caught fire and he didn't wait to slow down before he pulled his rip cord. The chute opened and yanked the harness and every stitch of clothing off the poor chap and he went tumbling through one of our formations, naked as the day he was born.

"From the way it was described to me, it seems that the sky was filled with falling Nip fighters, Japanese parachutes and even pieces of the target. Unfortunately, there also was a B-29 burning from a phosphorous bomb hit.

"As you can judge, every B-29 crewman worshiped those P-51s. Those Jap fighters have given us plenty of rough times, especially over Tokyo, but yesterday most of the worries were from flak. I think one B-29 pilot expressed the sentiments of

every crewman when he drooled over the interplane communication, 'Oh you P-51s, I loves you, little sweethearts, I
loves you.'

. . .

Dr. Post, we feel we owe those fighter pilots a great deal;
that's an awful long way for a man to fly, fight, and return alone.
But we don't forget the debt we owe to the men who took Iwo
Jima and made fighter protection possible for us, and gave us
an emergency landing field half way home from Tokyo."

Landing parties needed to get even closer to the Japanese mainland. For
that purpose, Okinawa was the next objective. The struggle for Okinawa
began late in March 1945 with an American naval and air attack against
Japanese bases and battleships. On the first day of April, Easter Sunday,
the combined efforts of the Marines and army divisions brought 60,000
men to the beaches. They pushed toward the cave-pocked hills where a
defensive force of 100,000 Japanese was dug in and waiting.[2] American
troops inched forward, and as the fighting took its toll, reinforcements
moved up. The Japanese had established a nearly unbreakable line, but
at one point they emerged from the shelter of their caves. As soon as the
Japanese came out of hiding to counterattack, they lost their advantage
and were overwhelmed.[3]

The fight for Okinawa was particularly personal for Dr. Post, as his
nephew was there. Cpl. Bill Post wrote to his family, and Dr. Post occasionally gave an account of him in the *News Letter*. Another *News Letter*
mention of Corporal Post is in chapter 9.

THE AZTEC NEWS LETTER
No. 40, July 1, 1945
Cpl. William L. Post, USMCR was wounded in the leg by shrapnel on Okinawa on May 14. He was hospitalized for a while but
rejoined his outfit and was with the boys when they finished
the fighting to secure the island. He is in an engineering Bn. of
the Sixth Marine Division. This is his second tour of overseas
duty with the Marines. (Bill is your editor's nephew. LCP.)
Dr. Lauren C. Post, Editor

The Japanese did not give up easily. On just two days in April, they
flew 355 kamikaze missions against American naval ships in Japanese

waters. The suicide planes carried payloads of fuel and explosives intended to do as much damage as possible. Aircraft carriers were favorite targets, but smaller ships were more vulnerable and more likely to sink when hit. In response, the Allies sent up more fighter patrols and gave them a broader range in hopes of detecting and destroying the incoming Japanese planes. Kamikaze attacks continued throughout the Okinawa campaign, killing more than 1,400 Japanese pilots, and sinking 29 U.S. Navy ships. Another 120 vessels were damaged, bringing the death toll of America sailors to more than 3,000.[4]

January 16, 1945

Dear Doc:

Since Nov 5th I've been slightly "incapacitated," so I haven't been able to write, altho I wanted to. I had a little run-in with a "suicide" that day, and he had a plane (with "meat balls" on it)—I didn't have even a water pistol! Ha!

Kidding aside, Doc—I'm finally walking a little all by my lonesome, and as soon as I can get around well enough by myself it looks like I'll head for the states (S. Diego, I hope) to have the reconditioning job finished up. Doc just told me they've done all the skin-grafting they are going to do out here.

. . .

Tell all the gang "Hello"—and also that you can't keep an Aztec down!

As ever—

Barney Carman

October 19, 1945

Dear Dr. Post,

. . .

On the 21st of June, while we were operating at Kerama Retto just west of Oki-nawa, a kamikaze smashed into our photographic lab, producing a concussion which wiped out all of the interior of the ship from frame 20 to 37 and from the keel to the superdeck. A bomb stowage magazine was broken open in the blast, but though tails were torn from the bombs and their paint singed off by fire, they miraculously escaped detonation. Fifteen hours after the crash all of the fires were extinguished. A few days later the rent in the hull was repaired, and we led a convoy of damaged ships back to Saipan. Fifty-six casualties resulted from the fracas, but I got off unscathed. I was one deck above the last injured deck at the moment of impact.

. . .

Best luck.
Lt. D. V. Miller
USS *Curtiss*, AV-4
FPO San Francisco, California

Japanese naval commanders were also expected to fight to the death against what had become a superior Allied force in the Pacific. In a bizarre twist on an amphibious assault, the Japanese navy sent its largest battleship, the *Yamato*, along with a small convoy toward Okinawa. One version of the plan called for the ships to run aground and disgorge their crews, who would fight on foot, but none of them ever touched land. U.S. aircraft carriers launched two waves of dive-bombers and torpedo-bombers, and they succeeded in making multiple direct hits on the mighty *Yamato*, which capsized and exploded.[5]

Allied fighter pilot strategy called for hitting the enemy vessels primarily on one side, if possible, which made it more likely that a crippled ship would sink. After the huge *Yamato* was attacked and began to list, its commanders took extreme measures to keep the prized battleship afloat. Members of the ship's crew were drowned in a futile attempt to counter-flood and stabilize the ship.[6]

In the following letter, the pilot's shorthand refers to battles in which his Grumman Hellcat Fighter was hit by antiaircraft fire, including fire from a Japanese destroyer armed with five-inch guns. The writer claimed his wounds were minor; he only mentioned in passing that he received a P.H., or Purple Heart. "Zeke" and "Tojo" were nicknames for Japanese fighter planes.

June 14, 1945
Dear Doc:

. . .

I've flown some very interesting missions this time out—over Tokyo three times, Iwo, Okinawa strikes & support, & over Kyushu, Inland Sea, & Shikoku. (I've got a good notion to come back to State & *breeze* thru that "Geog. of Asia"!) Also had a hand in the sinking of the *Yamato*.

Have been pretty lucky—have had my Hellcat hit three times by A.A. [antiaircraft] (once by a Jap DD five-inch in Tokyo Bay) and twice by aerial gunfire—but only received a few minor cuts myself. I went back later to the place where I got the P.H. & we set fire to the town, put the AA outa business & shot down a

Zeke & a Tojo over the joint. Vindictive, wot! Still haven't been able to get that big, flat flying boat—have a total of seven "kills" for this cruise, but all Jap fighters.

Remind me to tell you about the "typhoon" when I next see—quite an experience.

I'm now C.O. of the Fighter Bomber squadron, & really have a great bunch of boys. I'm very proud of them.

We've been out of the States but eight months, however, our losses have been pretty high, so I expect to be visiting the old school again shortly. . . .

Well, Doc, keep up your good work (I think *you* know there is still a war going on!) & give my regards to all

Luck

Lt. E. S. (Ed) Conant

On Okinawa, the rains poured down, and the misery continued. Combat fatigue took on new dimensions. Men had no place to sleep in the water-logged ground and no place to dig a latrine. Marines struggled to keep a grip on their weapons and their sanity. On both sides, the remains of those killed decomposed under the eyes and noses of the living.[7]

By June 1945 Okinawa had amassed more casualties than in any of the fighting elsewhere in the Pacific. The death toll for the Japanese was more than 100,000. More than 7,000 Americans were killed in the fighting on land and nearly 5,000 more were killed in the naval battles. The number of Americans wounded in the island invasion climbed to more than 31,000.[8]

In the following letter, Chester DeVore was hopeful that the fighting would ease after the capture of Naha, the capital of Okinawa. He also asked Dr. Post to check the rainfall facts in his textbooks. When Dr. Post excerpted this letter for publication, he omitted the details about specific injuries. He may have thought it was too much information for wives and mothers.

May 31, 1945

Okinawa

Dear Doc Post;

I just received the 1 Apr *News Letter* and it made me decide to write this letter.

Our Battalion is in reserve so we all are trying to catch up on living—such things as sleep, chow, etc. have been a little hard to obtain lately.—I don't know if this Okinawa deal is very impressive in the news, but it is rough in comparison to the other fights I've been in.—Casualties have been high—Nip artillery & mortar fire the main cause.—Our division has been on the right flank attacking toward Naha for some time and finally we walked in the other day. Maybe from now on it won't be as tough as it was—the Nips are falling back and once they are out of their holes they're easy.

The day before Perry DeLong was hit I saw him and we had quite a conversation about old times at State & how we met on Guam under similar circumstances—he told me then he didn't see how his luck could hold out—his gear was filled with holes, a bullet had taken the zipper off his jacket—Guess we all wonder at times.—The best information I have is that he was hit in the leg and also the penis—sure hope nothing too serious.

. . .

Does it say in the book that it's supposed to rain every day on Okinawa—if it doesn't re-write that chapter—Mud & rain have really hindered this fight and there seems to be no end to either. The weather has really changed in the 60 days we have been on here.—

Guess I'll sign off for now Doc.—I hope the next time I report in—it's in person.—

Sincerely

Chester (Chet) DeVore

Sgt. Allison Lutterman was with the Fifth Marines on Okinawa. He worked in the command post and promised to try to find Dr. Post's nephew, Bill, with the Sixth Marine Division. Previously, in the fall of 1944, Lutterman had been on Peleliu, where he wrote, "A Lieutenant gave his life to save mine" (chapter 11). On Peleliu and Okinawa, the terrain and the Japanese defenses were similar. As with his earlier letter, Lutterman wrote on red-lined Japanese writing paper.

May 14, 1945
Okinawa
Dear Doc:

. . .

Our Picnic is over for certain. These ridges & caves are as bad as Peleliu. The Japs are dug in beyond description or belief. I've been in some of the caves which run completely through the ridges with dozens of corridors & side rooms. How they can live in them like rats is beyond me.

The fighting has been tough but my job has kept me pretty much in the C.P. where we had shells & mortars coming at us as well as sniper fire, but none of the Banzai! stuff that our line companies have. For most of the time I've slept in a tomb with four others. The Japs had removed the porcelain urns with their grisly contents so they made safe, warm & dry bomb proofs. The Hon ancestors failed to disturb my sleep.

This will undoubtedly be the bloodiest yet when it's over. They're throwing everything they have into it. I've seen several suicide planes do their stuff. It's sickening.

I enjoyed the copy of *The Aztec* & like the idea of a memorial for the fellows who went out. I'll contribute as soon as I see the paymaster. All I have at the moment is invasion money & that's not much good. I'm enclosing a 10 yen Jap note as a souvenir for you.

Keep pitching Doc, & here's hoping I see you very shortly.
Sincerely
Pl. Sgt. A. B. (Allison) Lutterman
Hq. Co. 1st Bn. 5th Marines
F.P.O. San Francisco

THE AZTEC NEWS LETTER
No. 40, July 1, 1945
Graduation ceremonies were held in the Open Air Theater Friday afternoon, June 15. The graduating class hit a record low of 65 members, since this, as you remember, is the group that was the freshman class when we began to fight.

Japan had lost its dominance in the Pacific, it was critically short on resources, and it was fighting a desperate, suicidal war. Even after many of its cities, including Tokyo, had gone up in flames following devastating incendiary bombing raids, the nation did not intend to surrender. Those who had been part of the island assaults in the Pacific and had experienced the intractable strength of Japanese resistance understood the need to bring a strategy of total destruction to the Japanese mainland. The Allies insisted on unconditional surrender, and the Japanese had a penchant for fighting to the death. Faced with a choice between a land invasion and the use of a new weapon of unimaginable magnitude, the Allies opted for the atomic bomb.[9]

Also at issue was the projected number of Allied casualties if Marines and infantry came ashore in a land invasion. Pacific commanders estimated that an initial landing would cost 100,000 wounded and killed and that a subsequent thrust at the main island would come with a price of another 250,000 casualties. Military leaders also knew that as the fighting continued, more American prisoners were dying.[10]

Hiroshima lies nestled on the coast of Japan's largest island, with a busy port and active railway lines servicing industry and the military. It had escaped the incendiary bombs suffered by other cities, but that was soon to change. Nagasaki's picturesque waterfront had hosted European traders in past centuries. Now its waterways were used by the Imperial Japanese Navy, and it was a manufacturing center for steel and other war materials.

The Allies had already secured air bases close enough to Japan to launch the long-range B-29 bomber. The first atomic bomb, a uranium bomb weighing more than 9,000 pounds, was dropped on Hiroshima on August 6, 1945. The second, a plutonium bomb weighing more than 10,000 pounds, was dropped on Nagasaki on August 9, 1945. Though some damage estimates vary, in each city approximately 70,000 people were killed instantly. In Nagasaki, another 75,000 were injured. Within a year of the Hiroshima bombing, more than 118,000 people were thought to have died from the effects of burns, radiation, and other bomb-related injuries.[11]

Several servicemen who saw the effects described them to Dr. Post. Cpl. James West served with the headquarters in charge of the Western Pacific, and he got an aerial view of the bombed cities. Guy Boothby noted the physical destruction and commented on the psychological toll that the war had taken on civilians. He did his best to win over the local children.

✉ October 5, 1945

Dear Dr. Post,

Well, "Doc," it's been quite some time since I last reported in—must be at least a couple of monsoons ago. Time seems to glide by out here like the current of a stream gliding through a slough—you hardly notice it until you look backward and see the distance covered.

The "Second" has been around a little since I last wrote—a short run up to Okinawa and at present am doing occupational duty in Nagasaki—Kyushu Is[land]. Nagasaki city is in bad shape—the damage done by the bomb was tremendous. The loss of life was heavy—the people were & in some of the outlying districts still are very much afraid of us. You know, Doc, the propaganda the Japanese government put out about us was the best "secret weapon" the Marine Corps had—the Jap troops were so well indoctrinated as to our so called ferocity that in many instances they were practically beaten before we made a beachhead on their Pacific islands.

The rural sections inland from Nagasaki are very beautiful. Nearly all the land in the valleys and up on the hills is terraced—there is not a foot of arable land that is not under cultivation. The rock wall terraced orchards—oranges, peaches, persimmons—are things of near perfection. They would put our southern California orchards to shame—all of them have the appearance as though they had been laid out & maintained for demonstration purposes. The people on the farms are much healthier, cleaner, & happier than their compatriots in the city—after seeing the town that is easily understandable. There is a Japanese—teaches English in a school near here—went to Northwestern for three years—her description of the atomic bomb is quite graphic—can't give it to you through the mail but will when I see you. Incidentally, she's a very nice & interesting girl.

The reaction of the farmers in areas where no Americans have been before is very enlightening. I & my interpreter have been on quite a few two-man reconnaissance patrols up into the hills. On several instances we came unexpectedly upon workers in their fields. In all cases they showed great fright & on two or three occasions the women dropped their hoes & ran screaming into the brush with the men a close second behind them. One time our jeep rounded a bend in the narrow road and almost ran into a group of children returning home from school. Their abject terror was pitiful—all of them literally dived off the road into a rice paddy & lay in the mud with their hands over their heads & moaned. It took us half an hour & a sack of candy to convince them that we were not going to shoot them or stick them to a tree with a bayonet—we finally left them with doubtful smiles on their faces.

. . . I've got plenty of points & 28 months over but at present no prospect of getting home—anyway that's another story and as they say here it's "Sayonara" for now.

As ever,

Guy Boothby

November 22, 1945
1130
Iloilo City, Panay, P.I.
Dear Dr. Post;—

. . .

My team stayed up in Aomori Prefecture for two weeks picking up records the Japs forgot to burn, and doing some other investigating. We rode down to Tokyo in a second-class evack (which wasn't so bad), and then flew back to Manila. We flew over both Hiroshima and Nagasaki, and I can truthfully say our air force really did a completed job there as well as all of the other large cities. . . .

By the way Doc, when we were driving around up in Aomori Prefecture, we discovered a group of well camouflaged 16″ guns which were trained right on Misawa Airfield. I believe part of the 11th Airborne was scheduled to jump over that field if the invasion plans had been carried out. From all of Japan that I saw by jeep, train, plane, and boat, I'm sure it would have been a *rough* battle if we had made the invasion.

I'm glad to hear the Aztecs have started winning some football games. Let's keep up the good work.

Will close now and get down and have some of that good ol' Thanksgiving Turkey!

Sincerely yours,
Cpl. James (Jim) H. West 39735246
Recovered Personnel Detachment
Hq AFWESPAC
APO 707; c/o PM
San Francisco, California

December 17, 1945
Hiro Wan, Japan
Hello Doc,

. . .

We got stuck with ferry duty from Kure to Matsuyama so I imagine we will be out here for quite awhile. The duty is actually very soft consisting of a three hour run every other day and always in calm water *but* it's just too far from the States.

I have seen the results of the atomic bomb at Hiroshima, the wreckage of all type [of] Jap warships in this area, the customs and habits of the Japanese. It's amazing how these little people could ever start a war.

. . .

Doc, I've wondered what a collection of paper money you have made from what the boys send in. I imagine you have already received some yen but here is one more for the collection, also a few dollars for the *News Letter.*

I'll drop you another line soon Doc. Until then,

Sincerely
James E. Bunker
Merry Christmas

Emperor Hirohito had announced Japan's surrender on August 15, 1945. The surrender documents were signed on September 2, on board the USS *Missouri*. Gen. Douglas MacArthur took part in the ceremony to end the war, and then, as the Pacific commander, he began the work of the occupation of Japan.[12]

La Verne Brown Jr., a naval ensign, described subdued emotions when word came about the war's end. Many sailors went about their duties while their minds teemed with thoughts of home. For others, occupational duties were just beginning. Albert Cech was on a transport that arrived in Tokyo Bay on the same morning the surrender was signed. His convoy delivered the first occupation troops to a newly established American base in Japan.

August 19, 1945
USS *Biloxi* (CL80)
Dear "Doc" Post

. . .

There was little rejoicing on the "Bee" when the official word was received, though everyone was greatly relieved at the news. There had been so much scuttlebutt and so many rumors, intercepted Jap broadcasts and news items of premature celebrations back in the States; we had just given up holding our breaths. We were eating breakfast in the wardroom when an announcement was made over the 1MC—general announcing system—that the President had declared the Japanese acceptance of our peace terms. There was a weak cheer, a flurry of half-excited whispering—then the bugler blew "Officers' Call" and we hurried to quarters, as per the plan of the day.

That night we had a bit of a peace celebration back on the main deck aft. . . . Now we're slowly getting back into the peace time groove, and everyone is busy counting points and worrying about how to get some more points. They certainly learn about mathematics in a hurry when the discharge system is announced.

. . .

Sincerely,
La Verne W. Brown, Jr.
Ensign, U.S.N.

September 2, 1945
Dear L.P.
Greetings from Tokyo! In company with a vast task force composed of transports, cargo ships, and escorts we have just steamed in to participate in the first landing of sea-borne U.S. Army forces on the soil of Japan—under the protecting guns of

the greatest combat fleet ever assembled. Aboard the U.S.S. *Missouri,* anchored nearby, the surrender is being signed that brings to an end this greatest of all world wars.

At the time of this ship's commissioning, March 11th at San Pedro, California, most of us didn't expect to be debarking troops on Nipponese shores within six months—and even the most optimistic among us didn't dream that those landings would be unopposed. It's a real thrill to be here on the scene and see world history being written under our very eyes.

. . .

Yours very truly,
Lewis Estep
USS *Gasconade*
APA 85, Fleet Post Office
San Francisco, California

September 6, 1945
Dear Mr. Post,

I wish at this time to send "Greetings from Japan" to you and to all of my Aztec friends. The large convoy, of which my A.P.A. was a part, paraded into Tokyo Bay on Sunday morning 2 September Japanese time. Our arrival was timed so as to take place while the surrender ceremony was in progress. It was a grand sight to see the U.S.S. *Missouri* (lined with officials) and surrounding combatant ships as we steamed slowly past in a long single column. The sky added to the scene, being full of carrier-based planes and B-29s.

Our convoy was the first to land sea-borne occupational forces on Japan. Thirty minutes after the surrender was signed the transports were anchored off the new American Naval Base at Yokohama and troops were going ashore. The invasion (our Division's part in it) went off well enough to receive a "Well Done" from Vice-Admiral Wilkinson.

It was a wonderful adventure to be here for the opening phase of the occupation of the enemy's homeland.

Fellow Aztec,
Albert J. Cech

VICTORY EDITION
No. 42, September 1, 1945
To All of the Aztecs in Service and Their Friends:
V-J means much to your editor. I can no more describe the meaning than you can, but I'll say this. I know that you will be

coming home. I used to bid goodbye to fellows who were about to ship out. I seldom knew just where they were going, but by their training I could tell what kind of duty they would have. We could wish them the best of luck and then hope for the best when we heard and read the reports telling of casualties. And the printing of the casualties up front in the *News Letter* was especially hard for one who knew so many of them.

Thirty-one issues of the *News Letter* (numbers 11–41) were edited in keeping with the censorship rules to which all publications were voluntarily subjected. The censor was on our mailing list, and he complimented the *News Letter* in its adherence to the rules of security.

Now censorship is off. Addresses can be printed, and for the first time in 31 months, the *News Letter* can serve one of the original functions that the editor had in mind when it began— that of helping our Aztecs find each other the world over. This time you can find the overseas men who are near you.

In this Victory Edition we can at least in a small way honor the men who are on the ships and in the combat units that helped win this war. It is too bad that we can't run them all, but we will run them as you send them in, and we will also adjust your ranks as we know many should be.

. . .

The editing has not always been easy. In imagination sit yourselves down with several hundred letters and decide which 10 per cent you will include. It's extremely difficult at times. I can only hope that all in all, the *News Letter* shows the true Aztec spirit and carries a maximum of news. We'll be seeing you!

Sincerely,
Lauren C. Post,
Editor of the *News Letter*

Robley Baskerville	Nancy Williams	Jeanne Oncley
writer of the **Collegiate Corner**	writer of **Aztec-nicalities**	writer of **Covering the Campus**
in the **Tribune-Sun** on Tuesdays	in the **Union-Tribune** on Sundays	in the **Daily Journal** on Thursdays

Photographs through courtesy of Maybelle Smith, Valley Studio, El Cajon

(Ask your families to clip these columns and mail them to you.
Also ask for the **Service Edition** of the **Union-Tribune** edited by **Henry Love.**)

Edited by
DR. LAUREN C. POST
San Diego State College
San Diego 5, California

**September 1, 1945
No. 42**

This issue sponsored in part by
Delta Chi Phi

**To All of the Aztecs in Service
and Their Friends:**

V-J means much to your editor. I can no more describe the meaning than you can, but I'll say this. I know that **you** will be coming home. I used to bid goodbye to fellows who were about to ship out. I seldom knew just where they were going, but by their training I could tell what kind of duty they would have. We could wish them the best of luck and then hope for the best when we heard and read the reports telling of casualties. And the printing of the casualties up front in the **News Letter** was especially hard for one who knew so

many of them.

Thirty-one issues of the **News Letter** (numbers 11-41) were edited in keeping with the censorship rules to which all publications were voluntarily subjected. The censor was on our mailing list, and he complimented the **News Letter** in its adherence to the rules of security.

Now censorship is off. Addresses can be printed, and for the first time in 31 months, the **News Letter** can serve one of the original functions that the editor had in mind when it began—that of helping our **Aztecs** find each other the world over. This time you can find the overseas men who are near you.

In this **Victory Edition** we can at least in a small way honor the men who are on the ships and in the combat units that helped win this war. It is too bad that we can't run them all, but we will run them as you send them in, and we will also adjust your ranks as we know many should be.

These addresses were copied from cards run off from our address stencils. On them not all ranks have been brought up-to-date. When you write we

will make the corrections.

This time we sacrificed long letters so as to get in the addresses from which you can get a lot of news. The news is really in the addresses—if you can dig it out. For example, **Edward L. Thomas,** U.P. correspondent, described for his readers the most powerful armada ever assembled for a single naval operation for which he listed 133 naval vessels. Among the ships named were the **South Dakota, Missouri, Massachusetts, Essex, Ticonderoga, Yorktown, Wasp, Independence, Flint, Cogswell, Norman Scott, Borie** and the **Wadleigh.** We had men, besides naval air men, aboard them all. And if the surrender of Japan is signed aboard the Missouri, we may have a man there to witness it along with **Ed Thomas** to report it. How many of you remember **Ed Thomas** as our **Aztec** publicity man and **Lt. Robert Hamilton** as a history student at **State College** and a teacher in one of the city schools?

And now let me take this opportunity to compliment our **Aztec** fighting personnel for keeping mum when the chips

23

WHO'S GOT THE POINTS?

THE AZTEC NEWS LETTER
No. 23, February 1, 1944
There will be perhaps several millions of war veterans to return for more education. The government undoubtedly will send many of them to college. Their education programs may be vastly different from anything we have known to date. Certainly there is an uncharted course for many an individual college.

. . .

But a man in a foxhole today is probably more interested in the big Reunion. We'll try to do something to make them feel glad they came home. I'd even like to see Perry DeLong and Johnny Fox and others join in with the Aztec band to do some real tooting at the Reunion. And the Men's Glee Club would welcome John Tyers, Benny Lamb, Bob Austin, and a lot of others back into ranks for a few of the old songs on the same occasion. I'm looking forward to that myself with a great deal of pleasure. Drop around one of these days and we'll talk it over. LCP.

Dr. Lauren C. Post, Editor

As the war ended, all thoughts turned to home. The military had a plan for the fair and orderly discharge of personnel that could be summed up in a word: *Points.* The number of points accumulated depended on a person's age, the type and length of military service, and the number of dependents in a family. Men and women began frenzied calculations, tallying up their years of service, adding points for the medals they had received, and happily counting their children.

Even as servicemen and servicewomen longed to be reunited with loved ones, they understood that some would have to remain for the work of occupation and transition. Those who had endured the most combat could expect to go home first, but many complicating factors had to be considered. Officers might be redeployed if they were needed elsewhere, and highly trained medical personnel were kept longer. Nurses were always in demand, and they watched others leave with fewer points, while they kept adding to their totals. Anyone deemed vital to military effectiveness might remain behind. One serviceman wrote that he needed more than one hundred points, due to his location. As the military adjusted its estimates for the number of necessary troops, it gradually lowered the number of points required for discharge.[1]

THE AZTEC NEWS LETTER
No. 39, June 1, 1945
The Point System has turned all of the Army men into mathematicians. What Aztec has the most points? And will you let us know how the points came? Also who is the first Aztec to be released under the new system?

June 11, 1945
Augsburg, Germany
Dear Dr. Post—
. . .
The Company has been overseas for 32 months, made D day landings at N. Africa, Sicily, Salerno, Anzio and So. France—been in French Morocco, Algeria, Tunisia, Sicily, Italy, Corsica, France, Germany & Austria. Hope the next stop will be the U.S.—

I have 87 points but it may not mean much especially since I am an officer and the work we are doing is pretty much of a necessity—(Message Center, Radio & Wire for 7th Army).

My points figure out 43 for months in the Army, 12 for overseas, 20 for awards, and 12 for the boy I haven't seen as yet. They're all figured as of 12 May & then we add 2 more each month we are here as Army of Occupation.

The picture is of Dachau Concentration Camp—represents one day of Jerry's dirty methods—

S'long & thanks again—
John Fitch

✉ August 10, 1945
Chateau Thierry
Camp San Francisco
France
Dear Doc,

. . .

I'm a "Free reinforcement" here, and they don't know what to do with me. I had hopes that being surplus I would be able to get a discharge, but it seems to be the opposite. You have to have over 100 pts to get out of the theater and my 89 look mighty small.

. . .

I'm glad to see that so many of the POW were home and in good health.

About all for now Doc, maybe I'll be back home going to school again one of these days.

George T. Forbes, Jr.

John Orcutt was a member of the prestigious Oceotl Society, a men's service group tasked with three important jobs—protecting campus traditions, boosting morale, and initiating incoming freshmen to college culture. Membership was reserved for sophomores and juniors with a record of superior involvement in school activities.[2] As his military service came to a close, Orcutt promised he would find his way back to State, even if it meant crossing the ocean by canoe, porpoise, or in a swimsuit. The Jantzen bathing suit he mentions was initially designed for members of a rowing club who wanted to stay warm on the water.[3] The line about "refugees from MGM" refers to photos in the *News Letter* of college women. They weren't really Hollywood actresses, though they must have looked that way to a homesick serviceman. Orcutt was fed up with Red Cross doughnuts, and he finally sailed for home in spring 1946.

✉ September 13, 1945
Kassel, Germany
Dear Dr. Post,

. . .

I have just come back from a mud flat near Reims, France called Camp Detroit where they specialize in pneumonia, malnutrition and sending people home. They sent my outfit home, gave me my chance at pneumonia (I failed—only got a head cold), gave me a bag of Red Cross doughnuts and said go east young man. The young man boarded a train, aided and abetted by a platoon of narrow minded MPs, and here he is—bloodied and bowed.

It's one of these deals—don't look now, but I think you're going to be army of occupation. Points, points, who's got the points? Not Orcutt—Maybe I should take out citizenship papers.

My present home is a very comfortable one—they've stuffed me into a garret room of a modern apartment building. All of the modern conveniences—hot and cold running mice. Only one narrow stair leading up to my sanctum—I can easily defend it from as many as three duty sergeants at once!

I came here, I thought, as a photographer, but upon arriving, the 1st sergeant said if he ever needed me he would look me up. That's the last I've heard from him. My present plans are to hibernate this winter and try to sneak down to a boat next summer in time to get home for the fall semester at dear old State. Happy day!

Please save a seat for me in the café, sign me up for the ping pong team, and persuade those beautiful refugees from MGM that have appeared on the *News Letters* not to graduate until we "foreigners" get back to America, and more especially to State.

Keep a candle burning in the café window and if they don't give me a boat ride, I'll ride home piggy back on a porpoise.

Hopefully yours,
Cpl. J. A. Orcutt
19162945
Hq & Hq. Sqdn
10th Air Depot Group
APO 149
c/o PM New York, NY

March 5, 1946
Kassel Air Depot
Dear Editor,
This is to inform you that I wish my name to be taken off the mailing list of the *News Letter*—not because of any dissatisfaction over the number one morale builder on my part, but rather, because the army has become so desperate to appease congress on the redeployment question that they are shipping my body home. I am going home on three counts—points, months of service, and my subversive attitude.

I traversed the ocean blue to Italy in a convoy consisting of four ships—THE NINA, THE PINTA, THE SANTA MARIA, and a canoe commandeered from a Miami Beach amusement concession. From Italy to France I travelled on the SS Brighton—a Limey beer keg—but now, I'm informed that I will travel in style— an excess of boats, yet. My intentions are modest, however, and I will merely requisition promenade deck aft for my quarters.

Knowing the army, upon reaching the port, I expect to be handed my travel orders, two red cross doughnuts, a Jantzen bathing suit and a map of the Atlantic. They've been floating our mail over in bottles for months now, so with a favorable current, I still expect to make San Diego in time to start the April semester which I understand will be offered to veterans and other displaced persons.

I had intended to major in music appreciation, but understand that the juke box has been removed from the café, so perhaps I will have to choose a less cultural subject.

In the event, barring accident or sudden death, any friends I might possess may locate me for the next year or so in the deck chair that will be placed in a sunny spot in the quad upon my return. I intend to write a book there exposing the army. I'll be wearing knickers, high button shoes, a serape, and smoking a Turkish water pipe.

Thanking you for many enjoyable issues of a truly fine project, I remain—
in a state of animated suspension,
J. A. Orcutt

Servicemen and servicewomen weren't the only ones figuring a way to get home. Men who had been held prisoner were eager for freedom, and joyful reunions were soon under way. Details on the conditions of imprisonment slowly emerged, though many who had endured despicable treatment were not inclined to share their experiences.

✉ Undated
Dear Dr. Post,

. . .

We got back Stateside on the ship that brought the first internees from the Philippines. There were 375 of them aboard. They represented about 10% of all the internees left in the Philippines and were the only ones physically fit to make the trip.

You probably saw their pictures in the paper. They didn't look so worse for the wear. But I saw the men without their clothes, (the bare facts so to speak) and they reminded me of the pictures of starving Europeans after the last war.

. . .

Yours,
Bob Lando

✉ May 25, 1945
Dear Dr. Post:—
Just a line to let you know I have just received a Cablegram from over-seas from Warren. He said, "All is well, see you soon all my love, Warren—"

I enjoyed reading the June issue of the *Aztec News Letter*. . . . One of the mothers of a P.O.W. received a letter from one of the pilots written on the 12th of May saying he was one of the fellows who were ferrying the boys out of Luft I—said there were 10,000 Prisoners there. They were taking out the British first and on the 13th were starting to take the Americans—I received a note from one of the boys who knew Warren at the camp last Monday—saying, "I have made my way through the lines from the Camp which Capt. Chatterley has been held. As I had his address and knew your concern, I am writing to inform you he is safe and will be home soon." There have been many conflicting rumors about Luft I, so will have to wait until some of the boys arrive home to tell us about it.

Most sincerely
Mrs. Laura E. Chatterley
1036 Bush St.
San Diego, California

July 10, 1945
Dear Dr. Post:—
Thanks for the *News Letter* again. Warren has arrived home safely at last. It doesn't seem possible to see him looking as well after all he has been through. The boys' Morale has certainly been high. We should be very proud of them—He is just like Dr. Barnhart's son, doesn't want to talk. So I guess we will have to be satisfied and thankful they are home with us again. I think he plans to go out again if they will let him.

Thanking you very much for your interest in him.
Sincerely
Mrs. L. E. (Laura) Chatterley
1036 Bush St.
San Diego, California

Finally, the end of the war brought a different kind of confirmation for families who had been holding to the slim hope that perhaps a missing loved one had been captured, even if the prisoner status had never been reported. Now, at long last, those families were forced to accept the finality of death.

May 15, 1945
Dear Mr. Post,
. . . I shall tell you what little we know about Jack. Most of it we heard from a young Captain who had been with him in North Africa and who was there at the time he was reported missing. They had been in North Africa nearly a year, having gone in with the invasion force on Nov. 8, 1942. Jack was First Pilot of a B17 and most all of his work had been in that plane.

He left La Marsa Aerodrome in N. Africa on the morning of Aug. 26 in a P38 Lightning, his first mission over enemy territory in that type of plane. He reported by radio over Salerno in Italy and nothing more was ever heard from him. The captain told us that within twenty minutes from the time they lost contact with him they had planes out searching for him and that everything humanly possible was done to locate him but that no trace was found of him or his air craft. They thought, from the fact that they lost contact so suddenly, that it must have been enemy action, as he was over enemy territory. We have held on to the faint hope that perhaps when Italy and Germany surrendered there might be a chance he had been a prisoner some where but we have never heard any thing at all. The captain told us that when they went into Italy six weeks later that they had hope of finding some trace of him but never did. Jack always enjoyed being at San Diego and I know from the number who visited him when he was in the hospital down there that he had many friends, and he always made many friends wherever he went. We were and are very proud of him but our hearts will ache for him the rest of our lives.

Very Sincerely Yours

Mrs. John Frost

Etiwanda, California

THE AZTEC NEWS LETTER

Victory Edition

No. 42, September 1, 1945

THE LITTLE REUNION

We are going to have a lot of Little Reunions in getting ready for the Big Reunion, and each is to bring a great many old-timers together.

The first Little Reunion will take place at the opening football game where we will have an Aztec Reunion Section at Balboa Stadium—West Side and from the 50-yard line north. Be There. Aztec service men, alumni, and faculty members are especially invited to sit there, and any alumni stationed in this vicinity are asked to help welcome Aztec service men on leave or who are just returning.

. . .

San Diego State College

Offers Educational Opportunities
For Returning Service Men and Women

News Letter No. 25, April 1, 1944

24

EDUCATIONALLY
SPEAKING

THE AZTEC NEWS LETTER

No. 22, January 1, 1944

There is no doubt that you will get college credit for your military service—six units for completing basic and nine additional units for getting the commission. But you needn't make the request now. My own case may be used as an example.

I had not gone to college when I was in World War I. Two years after the war was over I entered college, presented my honorable discharge to the registrar, had my training evaluated and was granted the credit. Unless you have a special reason for getting the credit now you may safely wait until you return to college to request the credit.

Dr. Lauren C. Post, Editor

The United States mobilized more than sixteen million troops for World War II, and when the fighting was over, the number of veterans streaming back to cities and towns exceeded anything the country had ever seen.[1] In 1944 Congress passed the Servicemen's Readjustment Act to help ease the transition back into civilian life. Lacking formal support following World War I, many returning veterans became mired in the hardship of the Great Depression. This time, the goals were clear. Those who had served would receive assistance in gaining a college education and in purchasing a home. The law, known as the G.I. Bill, also included provisions for health care and set aside unemployment funds for those who could not readily find work.[2]

THE AZTEC NEWS LETTER
No. 29, August 1, 1944
THE G.I. BILL OF RIGHTS:
EDUCATIONALLY SPEAKING
(This seems to be the most concise and complete statement available on what the government will do for you if you want more education or training.)

"When a veteran qualifies for a college, school or training course, the Government will pay up to $500.00 per year to cover tuition, laboratory fees, cost of books, etc. The student will also get $50.00 per month living allowance, plus $25.00 per month if he has a wife or other dependents. He may choose his school, but he must keep up with his work or he will be dropped.

"If a veteran was under 25 when he entered the service, he may return to school even though his education was not interrupted. That is, he may have left school and been working when he entered the service. But anyone who was 25 or over when he went into the service must show, in order to qualify, that his education was 'impeded, delayed, interrupted, or interfered with.' However, any veteran who desires a refresher or retraining course may take such a course for one year.

"A veteran who qualifies for college or other schooling will be able to remain at Government expense for one year. Then, if he qualifies for further education, he can remain for the length of time, up to a total of four years, that he served between Sept. 15, 1940, and the end of the war. He has until two years after his discharge or after the war ends to return to school. The Government-paid education program stops seven years after the war ends."

(Are you going to avail yourselves of this opportunity? If so, do you think you will come back to San Diego State College, and what do you want to study? By the way, when you write in for information along this line, please direct your questions to Dr. Donald R. Watson, who is our Registrar. LCP)

Dr. Lauren C. Post, Editor

To hasten the journey home, the Navy pressed combat ships and non-combat transports into service. Beginning in September 1945 and continuing for a year, Operation Magic Carpet facilitated the movement of troops bound for the United States. The first priority was getting prisoners safely out of the camps. After that, another rush was on to bring troops back in time for Christmas. In December 1945 more than three hundred vessels, including carriers, hospital ships, and cruisers, made it their mission to get men home. From the latter half of 1945 through the beginning of 1946, naval ships transported an estimated two million people.[3]

Sgt. Allison Lutterman, whose life had been saved on Peleliu and who had sheltered from bombs in a tomb on Okinawa, now turned his attention to peaceful endeavors. He wanted to teach, and he sought the advice of his mentor, Dr. Post. Lutterman's other letters are in chapters 11 and 22.

November 22, 1944
Dear Doc:

. . .

Doc, what kind of course are we going to be able to take to fit on for teaching in High School. Would it be possible to get a B.A. there at State in say two years, summer included, that would give a High School credential in Science, History & Languages? Will any allowances be made for our service, eliminating physical culture & some of the orientation courses? In other words, will the course be streamlined to such an extent that we will not have lost too much time over here?

. . .

Sgt. A. B. (Allison) Lutterman, USMC
Hq. Co. 1st Bn. 5th Marines
F.P.O. San Francisco, California

Men and women wanted to pick up where they had left off, but a note of anxiety, often camouflaged in a humorous aside, was evident in their correspondence. Readjustment would take time, and the habits of combat might not be cast off so easily. Separation counselors received more training to assist those whose mental health had been affected by war.[4]

December 28, 1944
Alsace-Lorraine
Dear Doctor Post

. . .

Doc I'm still a little bit undecided as to what I will do if & when I get home. In case I decide to return to State, will you set out a plot 16 feet by 16 feet for

a pyramidal tent. I think I will have to live on the campus in it until I get used
to civilized homes and ways of living. I've only been living in them 2 years now
(pyramidal tents I mean).

. . .

Best Regards

George T. Forbes, Jr.

January 23, 1945

War Department Personnel Center

Fort Sam Houston, Texas

Dear Doc Post,

. . .

I have been assigned to Personnel Counselling in a Separation Center interviewing men being separated from the service. The government is going to great effort
to help returning veterans back into their proper place in the civilian world. Our
service offers the men information on jobs, education, veterans' rights, etc. Also
if a man has any personal problems he wishes to discuss the counsellor will offer
the appropriate help in this field. All our counsellors have considerable training
and/or experience in personnel Psychology to fit them for this work.

It can easily be seen how varied this would be when the incoming men are
returning from every battle front in the world and are all kinds of men.—My only
desire above this would be to work at it in California so I could direct potential
students to the beautiful campus of SDSC.

. . .

So Long for this time,

Sgt. Charles V. Harrington

526 Castano Ave.

San Antonio, Texas

Everyone coming home either asked for help, offered help, or understood the need for support, even if it was just to return to a familiar routine. For each serviceman or servicewoman, the time and requirements for
healing differed, but all those from State had one thing in common: they
could seek out Dr. Post. He may have been a geographer by training, but
he knew the landscape of recovery as well as anyone. For Aztecs, the path
home led to his campus office whenever possible.

News Letter No. 44, November 1, 1945

September 16, 1945
Dear Dr. Post,
At long last I can write this letter. I have the necessary points and within the next few weeks should be homeward bound to see the family that I have acquired since I left. I still find it very hard to believe that I have a daughter old enough to be toddling around.

. . .

I believe I am going to attempt my first few months of civilian life by returning to school. It seems to me there would be no better way to reactivate a long dormant brain than by studying and no better way to cure a sleeplessness and nervousness than by falling back into the old, and believe me Doctor, easy routine of school. I could work 14 hours a day and it would be far easier than this 24 hour stuff I have been on for the past five years.

. . .

I hope I can see you soon Doctor.
Lt. Robert (Bob) Wilber

Dr. Post had his own ways of enticing servicemen back to San Diego. The *News Letter* featured photos of college women, including song and cheer leaders. This strategic effort to make men yearn for their campus worked like a siren's song.

THE AZTEC NEWS LETTER

November 1, 1944

No. 32

**This Issue Sponsored
in part by
Phi Kappa Gamma**

Edited by
DR. LAUREN C. POST
San Diego State College
San Diego 5, California

To All of the Aztecs in Service
and Their Friends:

The semester is a third gone. D notices have gone in, and we are already thinking of the Christmas letters. Other college activities are swinging along somewhat as they used to before the war. There is a difference in the feeling on the campus this fall and last, but it is difficult to give the reason for it. The Frosh class is larger, probably because the city is larger. The 25 veterans pepped it up some, but they didn't change the entire campus. Just think what it will be like when all of you come back.

We have changed about 300 address stencils since the last **News Letter** was mailed. You are really moving about, but keep sending the changes. Here is something that many of you have never realized. It is not enough to just tell the Post Office that you are moving. Send a card to the **News Letter** giving the new address. Your carelessness in that little detail has caused 400 **Aztecs** to miss out on the **News Letter**.

Over 800 **Aztecs** are overseas. We have lost more than 60 in action and in training. The overseas mail has slacked off a little in the last week or so — possibly due to so many men being tied up in combat. We want to hear from you after each campaign, at least. It is always comforting to your friends to know that you are still kicking and able to write. I repeat, we do like to hear from you after we know that you have gone into combat. Figure it out.

And while you are tied up in the winning of the war, we are trying to keep you in touch with each other and with the campus. We are getting organized for bigger and better things after the war, and we hope that you are not disappointed.

And again, best of luck!

LAUREN C. POST,
Editor of the News Letter.

Montezuma overhears 1st Lt. Wallace McAnulty hand Dr. Post a real Snow Job after his 45 months of overseas service. Wally had lost none of the sparkle that appeared in letter No. 1, News Letter No. 1. He is on a new assignment at Fort Bliss, Texas.

LT. RAYMOND W. MUELLER, USMC
was killed in action in the South Pacific.

KENNETH B. MOYER
passed away in a San Diego hospital recently following a long illness. Previously he had been in Army hospitals and had been given a medical discharge last May.

LT. AMOS NORWOOD
was killed in action in France in July, 1944.

LT. GEORGE ROSADO
was killed when the B-25 of which he was pilot crashed near Victorville, Calif.

LT. ROBERT HARLAN SMITH
was killed in action over Germany on July 7. He was co-pilot of the **Blue Blazing Blizzard** and was a veteran of 43 bombing missions. Last month the **News Letter** had reported that he was a pris-

oner, but that report was an error, one made in some unexplainable way, but nevertheless an error. We are sorry to have to state that the latest report is that Lt. Smith was killed. L. C. P.

LT. KENNETH E. BARNHART, JR.
who was a navigator on a B-24 flying missions out of Italy, was reported missing in action over Hungary about two months ago. He has since been officially reported a prisoner in Germany. He has been awarded the Air Medal for the missions he has flown.

LT. MAX BINSWANGER
paid the campus a visit after having been an internee in a neutral country and a prisoner of war of the Romanians. He had flown 27 missions as a pilot of a B-24. On one mission, while flying near the Swiss border, he saw **Capt. Robert Cardenas** in trouble with an engine on fire, and his tail gunner saw the

25

THE LAST BLUE CHIP

In 1942 when the Philippines fell to the Japanese attack, Cpl. Bob Newsom was initially reported missing. Eventually, his mother learned that he had been taken prisoner and transferred to an internment camp in Japan. In her correspondence with Dr. Post, Bertine Newsom remained hopeful, even though she received scant news. Her son was limited to writing just twenty-five words on a post card. The letters from Bertine Newsom are in chapter 8.

In 1945 word finally came that Bob Newsom had been liberated, and his friends from State were among those who celebrated. In the *News Letter* account of Newsom, Dr. Post noted that he had been on Corregidor Island, a military fortification known as the Rock, and at Cabanatuan, the location of a prison camp in the Philippines.

Howard Kucera, one of Newsom's friends, also remembered Lt. Russell Newbury, who had been killed in action in Italy in 1943. Howard helped make the arrangements to have Russell's belongings shipped home. More letters about Newbury are in chapter 13.

September 28, 1945

Dear Doc Post,

Have been neglecting to write as you know. But just rec. the Oct 1 issue of the *News Letter* and saw right away the piece on Bob Newsom. Our Marine. Was rather relieved to know that the old timber topper was still kickin' and coming home. I am going to try and see If If, I can get hold of him if he comes thru Frisco. I know a Lt in the Navy here that has something to do with meeting repatriated prisoners of war so maybe he can do something for me in that category. Let's hope so, and I think it would be a pretty good surprise for Bob if old "Kucy" showed up to meet him, if I am not too late already. I'll do my best there. Only wish dear old Russ could be with me. But that is something else. Losing Russ to me Doc, was the thing that really hurt. I was scheduled to marry some gal up here and she two timed me as most of these damn war time women seem to do, and so I am still lucky and single. I've still two years to do as I am Regular Navy and the point system doesn't mean a thing to the reg. Nav.

. . .

Best to all,

Sincerely,

H. S. (Howard) Kucera

THE AZTEC NEWS LETTER
No. 44, November 1, 1945
SGT. ROBERT NEWSOM, USMC
was the most welcome visitor to come to the State College campus in many a month. He had spent three and a half years in Japanese prison camps after having been taken prisoner on Corregidor early in 1942. Bob had enlisted in the Marine Corps in 1939 and was in the old Fourth Marines. He fought on Bataan and crossed over to the Rock and was there when it folded.

Bob was kept at Cabanatuan for a few months and then was taken to a rice field near Davao where he worked in all phases of rice production and did every type of menial work under most difficult conditions. In June 1944, he was taken to Japan and from then until his liberation in August of this year he worked in a copper mill with 600 other prisoners. Bob refused to go into gory details, but he did say that the Japs didn't like big men and that he had it rougher than average in his group on account of his great size. His weight fluctuated from 245 before the war to 159 when he had pneumonia. He had malaria in Davao 18 times, and they had practically no quinine. He had several different diseases, but he survived apparently with no permanent bad effects.

He is looking fine and has 90 days in which to get rested up. He is not sure about his future plans but he still likes the Marine Corps.

Bob was a member of the 1938 Frosh football team and, of course, was looking for Russell Newbury who was killed in Italy two years ago. Incidentally, your editor had written Bob a letter in 1944 telling about several of the old gang. All that could be said about Russell was that Bob wouldn't be seeing him.

Bob pondered over it, but never quite figured it out. Any way, we were mighty glad to see Bob.

Pvt. Jim Hurley, the young man who looked after the campus finances as treasurer of the Associated Student Body and who was trapped on the beach at Anzio while artillery shells exploded around him, had written to

Dr. Post that "[I] blew my stack & lost my marbles." Although his concussion rendered him unconscious and affected his vision and hearing, he described his injuries as "Nothing serious and nothing to collect a medal for." He didn't want to be awarded a Purple Heart. His only hope was that "after the war we get the proper credit for what we have done."

Jim Hurley's father, also a faithful writer, tallied up his son's medal count. In addition to the Combat Infantryman Badge, he earned the Arrowhead device for participation in an amphibious landing. Before his honorable discharge, Jim helped others get home, a task that would have appealed to his sense of fairness.

August 31, 1945

Dear Doctor Post:

. . .

It might interest you to know that James R. Hurley, Jr., has been promoted to Corporal (T/5) and has been presented with the Good Conduct Medal, and the Combat Infantryman's Badge, and wears three bronze stars on his Mediterranean theatre of Operations Ribbon. He has latterly been stationed with what is left of the 5th Army Hq. at a beautiful resort in the lower Alps on a lake not far from Verona. . . . In his last letter he said that the Hq. Company had been alerted for transfer to the States as a unit about Sept. 1st, subject to change, of course. So while there is slight possibility that he will be discharged very soon—he says clerks are badly needed in the mustering-out paper work,—and that he will likely be held in until almost the last. . . .

With continuing sentiments of highest esteem, I am, with best wishes,

Sincerely yours,

J. R. Hurley

9298 Lemon Ave.

La Mesa, California

THE AZTEC NEWS LETTER

No. 44, November 1, 1945

T/5 James R. Hurley is back in San Diego with his honorable discharge after three years of service. He was overseas 24 months all of which time he was in the MTO. First he was in North Africa and next he went into Naples. That was in October,

1943, and he joined the Third Infantry Division in November. There he soon learned that Lt. Russell Newbury had been killed in the Third on November 7.

Jim's first fighting was in the Casino front when they were screening for the 36th Division. That was in the dead of winter with a lot of rain and sleet and a lot of cold weather. On January 1, they pulled back from the front and went down to Naples to train for Amphib warfare in preparation for what turned out to be the Anzio show. He landed with the first wave at Anzio at 2 A.M., and they set up a perimeter defense. Jim was on the extreme southern end of the front. In February he was pulled out and sent to a hospital down at Naples for treatment for concussion. After that he was reclassified and put in Hq. of the Fifth Army working in G-3 Operations section. There he worked for a time in Gen. Mark Clark's private war room. He also worked under Gen. Truscott.

Jim has the MTO ribbon with four battle stars and one bronze arrowhead beside the Combat Infantry Badge.

Hurley had been assisted by a regimental chaplain with the 7th Infantry, Capt. Delmar Dyreson, who wrote to Dr. Post, "At my earliest opportunity I shall look up Pvt. James R. Hurley, Co. I., 15th Infantry, APO #3. Thanks for letting me know about him."

THE AZTEC NEWS LETTER
No. 38, May 1, 1945

Capt. Delmar L. Dyreson has returned to San Diego and will rest for a time at Carmel-by-the-Sea. His record as released by PRO is a most enviable one. He was awarded the "Bronze Star for meritorious service in direct support of combat operations during the Sicilian campaign while a member of the Third Infantry Division."

Chaplain Dyreson went ashore on D-Day of the North African invasion with a battalion aid station, landing on the Fedala-Casablanca beachhead. He was cited for saving the lives of 37 soldiers, members of his boat. During landing operations, the boat, under fire of enemy machine guns and mortars, rammed another landing craft and was sinking. The chaplain swam to shore under hostile gunfire, carrying a rope as a guide line.

In addition to the Bronze Star, Chaplain Dyreson wears five stars on his North African-Italian campaign ribbon for participating in five campaigns, as well as the coveted combat infantry badge and the America Defense Medal. He was in four amphibious landings and saw action on the Italian "winter line" and at the Anzio beachhead.

The servicemen who had been stationed in remote combat theaters understood that their efforts might be overlooked. In places like India, where planes plummeted from the high altitudes into forbidding mountains, and in the Hürtgen Forest, where dense foliage hid booby traps, the suffering didn't always filter into the news. Chester Hagman, an infantryman, knew that some heroic stories would never be told. (Hagman's letter describing fighting on the front lines is in chapter 19.) When the fighting was over, Hagman spoke for those who could no longer speak for themselves. Following his letter is a page from the campus yearbook. Hagman's photo is in the second row from the bottom.

February 17, 1946
Dear Dr. Post;

. . .

I had a great deal of excitement while I was overseas in combat. I went on line during the winter, just in time for the big German counter-attacks. I joined my squad as last ammo bearer, but within a month I was first gunner. Advancement was rapid because gunners did not live long.

During one fight, several of us were getting ready to make a dash down a street under sniper fire. Suddenly a mortar shell burst a few feet away. Our first gunner, who was standing by my side was killed. The remainder of us were not hurt. So I took his pistol and the machinegun tripod, and off we went down the street, leaving him there in the snow.

Quite often our squads would only contain 3 or 4 men. Our officers had to help carry ammo. Often too, they would stand guard with us. Rank meant nothing on the Front Line. It was what a man had inside of him that counted.

Right now we get a great deal of amusement from the numerous awards that the Army and Navy are passing out to the Armchair Commandos. It has become now so that one can figure that the more ribbons a man wears, the less combat he saw. In fact many of the awards are given to non-combat men.

All this is amusing, because anyone who was really in the fight, knows that the real heroes are dead. They fell, over there, in the mud, or snow, or rain, and the ground was stained with their life blood.

Some were blown into so many pieces that parts of them were never found. Some were cut in half and lived for a few awful moments. Other men were shot in the guts and died a slow, painful death.

These men were the heroes, but they are dead. Already many people have forgotten them.

Sincerely,

Chester A. Hagman

Throughout the war, the *News Letter* had grown in size as well as reach, expanding into a publication with eight, twelve, even sixteen pages. Dr. Post sometimes printed little "commercials" to solicit funds. As men and women were discharged, they happily wrote to tell him to save the postage. He delighted in welcoming them home and kept his office lights burning until all the Fighting Aztecs were accounted for.

Toward the end of the war, Dr. Post cast his mind back to his own war experiences, reflecting on the loneliness that gave him the inspiration for the *News Letter*.

THE AZTEC NEWS LETTER

No. 35, February 1, 1945

. . . My recollection of standing watch on a destroyer in 1918 made me visualize the need of getting news to our men who are in this war—something to think about as they gaze into the blackness hour after hour. I often wonder how many thoughts go through a man's mind during a four-hour watch on a dull, dark night. Oft-times, it's the dull watches that are hardest. LCP.

Dr. Lauren C. Post, Editor

Lt. Lionel Chase spent his combat tour flying planes, amassing medals, searching for his friends, and enthusiastically describing all of it, including his attempts to get his hands on Coca-Cola. When he had completed

(This cut is from a page in the service men's section of the new annual, Del Sudoeste, edited by Pat Allard and Leone Carlson. There are 16 such pages in the book. Ed Herzig can supply a certain number of annuals for $3.00 each at the Aztec Bookshop or $3.25 each mailed to domestic addresses. LCP.)

Lt. (jg) Walter Harlin
1st Lt. Z. Allen Barker
Harold H. Niewoehner, Sp(M)2c
Lt. Joseph F. Cobb
H. W. Martin

Capt. Bernard T. Harmer
Ens. Giles T. Brown
Lt. J. C. Hellyer
Ens. W. H. Looney
Sgt. Warren C. Golson

Lt. (jg) Jack M. Vogel
Ens. Murl J. Gibson
Ens. June Herzig
Pfc. Morrie A. Naiman
Pvt. Bill Simonsen

1st Lt. Gustav Swab
Lt. Roger W. Armbrister
(Killed in plane crash)
Loren Scholz, A.S.
Pvt. Margaret Wiltse

Capt. Esther E. Pease
Lt. (jg) E. Lynn Kemp
Lt. Charles J. Keeney
Ens. Richard Coburn
Lt. Lee B. Williams

Lt. Comdr. Clifford E. Smith
Lt. Charles M. Witt
Cpl. Vernon J. Smith
Lt. H. Ted Reynolds
Lt. John Doyle

Lt. (jg) Viola Leigh Tatum
Ens. Richard Davis
Ens. David Steinman
Pvt. Chester A. Hagman
Thomas Roche, QM3c

Ens. Donald E. Newman
Ens. H. B. Walton
A/S Charles Norman Janke
Ens. Ed Moore
Ens. Jack R. Walden

Yearbook photos from *Del Sudoeste*, San Diego State College
Yearbook, 1944, reprinted in *News Letter* No. 28, July 1, 1944

enough missions, he returned to the States, and tried without much luck to master a few of Dr. Post's rope tricks. When it was his turn to be mustered out, he planned to pay a visit to his mentor and friend.

October 1, 1945
Dear Doc:

I've been five kinds of a goon about writing. Since I last wrote, I've been stationed at Second Air Force headquarters here in Colorado Springs, flying a desk again.

After V-J Day, I initiated proceedings for a release, and on the 3rd of this month, I proceed to separation center at Lowry Field.

The *News Letter* came this morning, and in it I see names that stir old memories. . . . I can hardly wait to come home and visit the old campus, and sit in your office in one of those good old bull sessions.

. . . No one can possibly tell you what a magnificent job you have done in making life a little more livable for the guys overseas, and in making this inactivity on this side a little easier to take.

In my own experience, your *News Letter* has been something that really helped when I was down to the last blue chip.

I will be home to thank you personally about the middle of this month.

. . .

Sincerely,
Lionel E. Chase
1st Lt., Air Corps
Headquarters Second Air Force
Office of the Air Inspector
Colorado Springs, Colorado

THE AZTEC NEWS LETTER
No. 44, November 1, 1945

Civilian Lionel Chase walked into the *News Letter* office in a brand new plaid suit (swindled or con-man type) wearing a discharge pin. You will remember Lionel as one of our most productive correspondents from the MTO back in the days of the Tunisian, Sicilian and Italian campaigns. He flew 50 missions as a B-17 pilot and came home in October, 1943 wearing the Air Medal with nine Oak Leaf Clusters. He also has the campaign bar with four battle stars and a Presidential Unit Citation.

. . .

Lionel expects to be a salesman soon, "Either selling lawn-mowers to the Eskimos or skis to the Arabs." Thus the AAF loses one of its more colorful pilots.

Long after the war was over, until Dr. Post retired in 1969, visitors continued to drop in at his campus office to express their appreciation for the *Aztec News Letter*. Lauren Chester Post died in 1976. His funeral at Greenwood Memorial Park in San Diego was standing room only. An estimated three to four hundred people turned out to pay their respects to the man who held a community together during World War II.

CONCLUSION

D
r. Lauren Chester Post and his Fighting Aztecs didn't set out to write a history of World War II, and yet page by page they did just that. Their correspondence describes an American path through World War II that started in the Pacific, crossed North Africa, swept through Europe, and came full circle back to Japan. In this account of war, students of history will recognize the struggle to advance over rough terrain toward peace, and students of literature will appreciate how the storytellers are flawed, heroic, and entirely human.

Reading so many letters is like gathering bits of a mosaic, and each intricate piece has its own beauty. Each letter is whole by itself, yet is also a fragment of a bigger story. The tales they share are dramatic and intimate, like parachuting through antiaircraft fire or sheltering with a friend in a foxhole. It's surprising on the surface how much humor is woven through the words. Then again, humor has always been a way to deal with hardship. Handwritten pages give testimony to the fact that war can produce heartache and gratitude in equal measure. The letters describe such strange ironies as the feeling of calm during the chaos of battle. They provide eyewitness accounts of individual moments that add up to something greater than the sum of the parts. Alongside the mundane tasks of drills, transport, and chow lines, the letters shine with a belief in country and a genuine desire to work for the common good.

When Dr. Post's students ventured from the ivory towers of academia to blood-red battlefields, the *Aztec News Letter* did more to keep them connected than any military communiqué or radio broadcast. The *News Letter* was powerful enough to reach from the frosty peaks of the Himalayas to the smallest, most insect-infested island in the Pacific. It was flexible enough to accommodate the rules of censorship and strong enough to last four full years. The forty-eight issues were produced with the diligence and regularity of a military drill. No matter where the war took them, when servicemen and servicewomen opened the *Aztec News Letter*, they were home again.

As a war veteran and professor, Dr. Post seemed to have an unerring instinct for meeting the needs of his students. From classrooms to combat theaters, his words stayed with them. He honored their service and never lost track of their whereabouts, even on the "forgotten fronts." He reminded them that they had a home on campus and in the hearts and minds of everyone who read their letters. The many different war experiences depicted by the servicemen and servicewomen from San Diego make up a universal story of struggle and sacrifice. Our understanding of the human dimension of war is greater, thanks to the work of Dr. Post and the letters from his Fighting Aztecs and their families.

Author's Note

D r. Post compiled the *Aztec News Letter* using excerpts from thousands of letters. The original letters are archived at San Diego State University. Many times over the course of two and a half years, I visited the university library's Special Collections reading room. Each week I looked forward to sitting down with the letters, as one might meet an old friend to catch up on events. I read every letter, absorbing the stories and experiences of the Fighting Aztecs. Gradually, a war that had been fought before I was born became personal in a way that I never expected. After a while, I came to understand that reading the letters was changing me.

We cannot separate ourselves from the consequences of war. When we rush to put its unpleasantness behind us or when we reduce the complexities to sound bites, focusing merely on victory or defeat, we lose sight of what happens to those who are thrust into combat. Fighting changes not only the world, but the minds, hearts, and even the souls of those required to carry out battlefield orders. I have read dozens of books and articles on political decisions, battle strategies, weapons, and even weather conditions that affected the outcomes in World War II. Those articles enhanced my understanding, but nothing impacted me as completely as the voices of Dr. Post's students.

I was moved by the exuberance and exploits of the pilot Lionel Chase, and by the stamina of Wally McAnulty, who played football and then settled into the defensive line in the Pacific theater. My heart ached when I read paratrooper Herman Addleson's description of the Statue of Liberty as his ship sailed out of New York, and I wept when I learned that he died on D-Day in Normandy. And I shared in a sense of wonder as Burdette

World War II San Diego State College Servicemen's
Correspondence Collection, 1941–1946, displayed in
the reading room at Special Collections and University
Archives, San Diego State University. The collection
can also be viewed online at sdsu.edu.

Binkley wrote about his belief in something greater than himself, shortly
before his plane was shot down over North Africa. The simple, beautiful,
and profound prose of the Fighting Aztecs brought home for me the meaning of war.

These letters are a gift from a group of students who shared what
was in their hearts and minds as history unfolded around them. The war
changed them, and their efforts changed the world.

Acknowledgments

As a writer, I believe in the power of words, yet they seem inadequate to express my gratitude to the many people who have offered so much help, encouragement, and wisdom. To those listed here, please know that my appreciation is heartfelt and everlasting.

I am profoundly grateful to Seymour Dussman, whose generosity of spirit and deed helped bring this work to a much broader audience.

Before this book was conceived, the project was an unwieldy thesis. I am indebted to my gracious and rigorous adviser, Judith McDaniel, who saw me through every stage of research and writing. I was also fortunate in that Union Institute and University specializes in interdisciplinary research. Two outstanding historians helped me in my literary approach to the letters. For their expertise and unflagging support, I am grateful to Woden Teachout and Loree Miltich.

Special thanks to Jonathan McLeod, professor of history at San Diego Mesa College, and to Professor Emeritus John Steiger, and Professor Emeritus Carl Lutz, who assisted me in getting the inside track on Dr. Post's life.

The research for this book would not have been possible without the help of Robert Ray, Director of Special Collections and University Archives at San Diego State University. He has been a wonderful guide to the letter collection and generous in his assistance over the years. I am also grateful to archivist Amanda Lanthorne and all the staff who keep the documents and artifacts in good order. Thanks to their tireless efforts, the words and works of others remain alive for us all.

Thanks also to Laura Davulis, who first championed this book, and to Emily Bakely, David Bowman, and the wonderful team of the Naval Institute Press, as well as Sarah C. Smith, who helped bring the work to its final, polished form.

Writing is a solitary practice, but good writing requires friends. My comrades in arms for this project are Deborah K. Reed, Leo Dufresne, Graeme Ing, and Daniel Jeffries. They are tough, honest, and dedicated to the craft of writing.

I have worked closely with Deborah K. Reed, fellow author and co-writer on many projects, including our book, *The Chamber and the Cross*. She has provided wise critique and keen advice through countless drafts and revisions. She scouted the terrain and took the initiative to forge a path through the thickets of marketing and publishing. I have learned more from her than anyone else, and she has my highest regards and gratitude.

Abbreviations

AAA	antiaircraft artillery
A.A.B.	Army Air Base
AAF	Army Air Forces
AAFFTD	Army Air Forces Field Training Detachment
A.A.F.L.T.D.	Army Air Forces Liaison Training Detachment
ADSOS	Active Duty Service Obligations
A.F.S.C.	Air Force Service Command
AIR	Airborne Infantry Regiment
AMMI	aviation machinist's mate I (instrument mechanic)
ANC	Army Nurse Corps
APA	attack transport
APO	Army post office used for Army and Air Force mail
A.S.N.	Army Service Number
ASTP	Army Specialized Training Program
AT	advanced trainer
BCD	Battlefield Coordination Detachment
BGP (H)	Bombardment Group (Heavy)
Bm. Gp. or Grp.	bombardment group—a group of bomber aircraft
Bn.	battalion
BOQ	bachelor officer quarters
Btry.	battery (unit of artillery)
CA (AA)	Coast Artillery (Antiaircraft) Regiment
CAS	Close Air Support
CB	Naval Construction Battalion (Seabees)

CBD	Construction Battalion Detachment
CBI	China-Burma-India Theater
CNAC	China National Aviation Corporation
Co.	company
Cpl.	corporal, United States Marines
C.Sp. (A)	Chief Specialist (Athletic Instructor)
CY	chief yeoman
DD	destroyer
DE	destroyer escort
Det.	detachment
DE-V(G)	designation for deck and engineer officers, general detail, USNR, used through 1944
ECAD	European Civil Affairs Division
ECAR	European Civil Affairs Regiment
ETO	European Theater of Operations
FFI	French Forces of the Interior, the French resistance
F/O	flight officer
FPO	Fleet post office used for naval mail
Hq., Hqtrs., Hd., or Hdq.	headquarters
INF	infantry
LCI	Landing Craft, Infantry
LCVP	Landing Craft, Vehicle, Personnel
LST	Landing Ship, Tank
Lt. (jg)	lieutenant junior grade
LVT	Landing Vehicle Tracked
LZ	Landing Zone
MCWR	Marine Corps Women's Reserve
ME	Messerschmitt
Med. Adm. C.	Medical Administrative Corps
MOMM 2/c	motor machinist's mate second class
MTO	Mediterranean Theater of Operations
NAS	Naval Air Station
O.C.S.	Officer Candidate School
Pfc.	private first class, United States Marines
PhM 3/c	pharmacist's mate, third class

PM	postmaster
POW or PW	prisoner of war
PRO	public relations officer
P.Sgt.	platoon sergeant
Pvt.	private—entry level rank in the Army
RAF	Royal Air Force
R.C.A.F.	Royal Canadian Air Force
R.T.U.	Replacement Training Unit
SC-V(G)	designation for a supply officer, general detail, USNR, used through 1944
Sgt.	sergeant
SOS	services of supply
SP(T) 3/c	specialist, teacher, third class
Sq., Sqdn., or Sqdrn.	squadron—a unit of aircraft
S.R.A.A.F.	Santa Rosa Army Air Field
SS	Schutzstaffel—Protection Echelon of the Nazi Party
S.Sgt.	staff sergeant
Sv.	service
SW	South West (South West Pacific theater)
T/3	technician third grade
TC	Transportation Corps
TCG	troop carrier group
TCS	Troop Carrier Squadron
TD	tank destroyer
USCGR	United States Coast Guard Reserve
USMC	United States Marine Corps
USMCR	United States Marine Corps Reserve
U.S.M.S.	United States Maritime Service
USNR	United States Naval Reserve (now the United States Navy Reserve). During World War II, nearly all of the members of the Naval Reserve went on active duty.
USO	United Service Organizations
V-E Day	Victory in Europe Day
V-J Day	Victory in Japan Day
VP	Navy Patrol Squadron

WAAC	Women's Army Auxiliary Corps
WAC	Women's Army Corps
WASP	Women Airforce Service Pilots
WAVE	Women Accepted for Voluntary Emergency Service
Y2c	yeoman second class
YF	Navy lighter
YP	yard (harbor) patrol boat

Notes

Chapter 2. Waiting for Something to Pop

1. "U.S. Seacoast Defense, 1781–1950: A Brief History," Coast Defense Study Group, accessed December 20, 2016, cdsg.org/the-world-war-ii-era-1940 -1950.
2. John Costello, *The Pacific War, 1941–1945* (New York: Harper Perennial, 2009), 225–26.
3. "Last Outposts of Empire," in *The California Missions*, ed. Dorothy Krell (Menlo Park, Calif.: Lane Publishing Company, 1979), 33–43.
4. Lynne E. Christenson, Alexander D. Bevil, and Sue Wade, "San Diego State College Historic District: The Mediterranean Monastery as a College Campus," *San Diego State University Occasional Archaeological Papers*, accessed December 20, 2016, soap.sdsu.edu/Volume1/SDSCollege/college .htm.
5. International Committee of the Red Cross, "The Geneva Conventions of 1949 and Their Additional Protocols," accessed December 20, 2016, icrc .org/eng/war-and-law/treaties-customary-law/geneva-conventions/over view-geneva-conventions.htm.
6. American Red Cross, "World War II Specialized War-time Services," accessed December 20, 2016, www.redcross.org/about-us/history/red -cross-american-history/WWII/specialized-services.

Chapter 3. Dead Ahead

1. Natalie Nakamura, "San Diego and the Pacific Theater: Consolidated Aircraft Corporation Holds the Home Front," *Journal of San Diego History* 58, no. 4 (2012): 221–46, accessed December 21, 2016, www.sandiego history.org/journal/v58-4/v58-4Nakamura.pdf.

2. Boeing, "B-25 Mitchell Bomber: Historical Snapshot," accessed December 21, 2016, www.boeing.com/history/products/b-25-mitchell.page.

3. Alan Axelrod, *The Real History of World War II: A New Look at the Past* (New York: Sterling, 2008), 162–65.

4. Griffith P. Williams, "WW II Revisited: The First Air Attack against Japan, The Recollections of One Participant" (unpublished memoir, 1993), Special Collections and University Archives, San Diego State University, 1-1. Note that pagination in this manuscript starts over in each chapter, so page references in these notes are to chapter and page number.

5. Williams, "WW II Revisited," 1-2.

6. Annalisa Underwood, "Evolution of the Aircraft Carrier," *Navy Live*, accessed December 21, 2016, navylive.dodlive.mil/2015/04/12/evolution -of-the-aircraft-carrier.

7. Williams, "WW II Revisited," 2-1.

8. Ibid., 2-2.

9. Ibid., 2-4.

10. Ibid.

11. Ibid., 3-2.

12. Ibid., 3-3.

Chapter 4. The Missing American Airmen

1. Williams, "WW II Revisited," 2-3.

2. Alan Axelrod, *The Real History of World War II: A New Look at the Past* (New York: Sterling, 2008), 164.

3. Williams, "WW II Revisited," 3-4.

4. Ibid., 3-6.

5. Antony Beevor, *The Second World War* (New York: Back Bay Books/Little, Brown and Company, 2012), 56–65.

6. Williams, "WW II Revisited," 3-6.

7. Ibid., 3-6 and 3-7.

8. Ibid., 3-7.

9. Ibid., 3-7 and 3-8.

10. Ibid., 4-4, 4-7, and epilogue.

11. Axelrod, *Real History of World War II*, 165.

Chapter 5. Happy Landings

1. Beevor, *The Second World War*, 59–60.

2. Ibid., 60.

3. Axelrod, *Real History of World War II*, 137.

4. Ibid., 221.
5. Costello, *The Pacific War*, 253–63.
6. Axelrod, *Real History of World War II*, 216–18.
7. Beevor, *The Second World War*, 308–11.

Chapter 6. Such Swell Kids

1. David Vergun, "Casualty Notification Process Emphasizes Dignity, Respect," ARNEWS, U.S. Army News Service, March 11, 2014, accessed December 28, 2016, www.army.mil/article/121623/Casualty_notification _process_emphasizes_.
2. Axelrod, *Real History of World War II*, 47–49.
3. U.S. Army, "Army Air Forces," accessed December 28, 2016, www.army .mil/aviation/airforces.
4. Smithsonian National Air and Space Museum, "World War II Aviation," accessed December 28, 2016, www.airandspace.si.edu/exhibitions/world -war-ii-aviation-dc.
5. Air Force Historical Support Division, "Medals for Valor and Meritorious Service," accessed December 28, 2016, www.afhistory.af.mil/FAQs/Fact Sheets/tabid/3323/Article/753768/medals-for-valor-and-meritorious -service.aspx.

Chapter 7. African Branch of San Diego State College

1. Rick Atkinson, *An Army at Dawn: The War in North Africa, 1942–1943* (New York: Picador, 2002), 6–7.
2. Ibid., 148–50.
3. Ibid., 293.
4. Ibid., 499–515.
5. Frank Thompson, "The Lost Remake of Beau Geste" (Los Angeles: Men With Wings Productions, 2013), available at San Diego State University Library Media Center.
6. Marek Lazarz, "Re: San Diego State's Doolittle Raider, Griff Williams," message to Robert Ray, director, Special Collections and University Archives, San Diego State University, June 5, 2015.

Chapter 8. In Our Great Sorrow

1. Costello, *The Pacific War*, 171–72.
2. International Committee of the Red Cross, "The ICRC in WWII: Overview of Activities," accessed December 29, 2016, www.icrc.org/eng/resources /documents/misc/history-world-war-2-overview-020205.htm.

3. Axelrod, *Real History of World War II*, 160.
4. Atkinson, *An Army at Dawn*, 453–59.
5. Ibid., 536–37.

Chapter 9. An American Kid

1. Robert Fikes Jr., "Supreme Sacrifice, Extraordinary Service: Profiles of SDSU Military Alumni" (San Diego, Calif.: San Diego State University Library and Information Access, 2016).
2. *Del Sudoeste*, 1943, SDSU Yearbooks, SDSU Library and Information Access, accessed January 3, 2017, library.sdsu.edu/scua/digital/resources/sdsu-yearbooks#1940-1949.
3. *Del Sudoeste*, 1944, SDSU Yearbooks, SDSU Library and Information Access, accessed January 3, 2017, library.sdsu.edu/scua/digital/resources/sdsu-yearbooks#1940-1949.
4. "Department of Defense Directive: Special Separation Policies for Survivorship," Department of Defense Issuances Program, accessed January 3, 2017, www.dtic.mil/dtic/tr/fulltext/u2/a269410.pdf.
5. "V-Mail," Smithsonian National Postal Museum, accessed September 2, 2017, Postalmuseum.si.edu.
6. Fikes, "Supreme Sacrifice, Extraordinary Service."
7. Theresa L. Kraus, "The CAA Helps Americans Prepare for World War II," accessed January 3, 2017, www.faa.gov/about/history/milestones/media/The_CAA_Helps_America_Prepare_for_World_WarII.pdf.

Chapter 10. Roger and Out!

1. San Diego State University Division of Student Affairs, "SDSU Traditions: History," accessed January 4, 2017, go.sdsu.edu/student_affairs/traditions.aspx.
2. National Museum of the U.S. Air Force, "AAF Training during WWII: Link Trainer," accessed January 4, 2017, www.nationalmuseum.af.mil/Visit/MuseumExhibits/FactSheets/Display/tabid/509/Article/196852/link-trainer.aspx.
3. Judith A. Bellafaire, "The Women's Army Corps: A Commemoration of World War II Service," U.S. Army Center of Military History, accessed January 4, 2017, www.history.army.mil/brochures/WAC/WAC.HTM.
4. Becky Schergens and Elizabeth L. Maurer, "Honoring Rosie the Riveter and the Women Who Won the War." National Women's History Museum, March 20, 2017, accessed December 14, 2017, https://www.nwhm.org/articles/honoring-rosie-riveter-and-women-who-won-war.

5. George Washington University Department of History, *The Eleanor Roosevelt Papers Project*, accessed January 4, 2017, www2.gwu.edu/~erpapers/teachinger/glossary/int-congress-work-women.cfm.
6. Jennifer Casavant Telford, "The American Nursing Shortage during World War I: The Debate over the Use of Nurses' Aids," *Canadian Bulletin of Medical History* 27, no. 1 (2010): 85–99.
7. Ibid., 85–99.
8. Heather Willever and John Parascandola, "The Cadet Nurse Corps, 1943–1948," Public Health Reports *PHS Chronicles* 109, no. 3 (1994): 455–57.
9. Kraus, "The CAA Helps Americans Prepare for World War II."
10. Texas Woman's University Libraries, "History of the WASP," accessed January 4, 2017, http://www.twu.edu/library/wasp-history.asp.
11. Ibid.
12. Beevor, *The Second World War*, 501–5.

Chapter 11. No Relief in Sight
1. Costello, *The Pacific War*, 112–16.
2. Ibid., 142–48.
3. Beevor, *The Second World War*, 344–52.
4. Ibid., 353–55.
5. Axelrod, *Real History of World War II*, 233.
6. Ibid., 232–48.
7. Ibid., 224–27.
8. Costello, *The Pacific War*, 422–24.
9. Axelrod, *Real History of World War II*, 236–38.
10. Costello, *The Pacific War*, 436.
11. Ibid., 432–39.
12. Axelrod, *Real History of World War II*, 238.
13. Costello, *The Pacific War*, 476–79.
14. Mark A. Kiehle, "The Battle of Fonte Hill, Guam, 25–26 July 1944," *Marine Corps Gazette*, July 2003, accessed January 5, 2017, www.mca-marines.org/gazette/battle-fonte-hill-guam-25-26-july-1944.
15. Navy Seabee Veterans of America, accessed January 5, 2017, nsva.org.
16. Axelrod, *Real History of World War II*, 73–74.
17. Costello, *The Pacific War*, 547–48.
18. Axelrod, *Real History of World War II*, 335–36.
19. Beevor, *The Second World War*, 626–27.

20. Costello, *The Pacific War*, 496–98.

21. Ibid., 525–30.

22. Ibid., 503.

23. Axelrod, *Real History of World War II*, 267–73.

Chapter 12. Aztecs of Fine Caliber

1. National Archives, "Japanese Relocation during World War II," accessed October 21, 2016, www.archives.gov/education/lessons/japanese-relocation.

2. National Archives, "Document for February 19th: Executive Order 9066, Resulting in the Relocation of Japanese," *Today's Document from the National Archives*, accessed October 21, 2016, www.archives.gov/historical -docs/todays-doc/?dod-date=219.

3. National Park Service, "Manzanar National Historic Site, California," accessed October 21, 2016, www.nps.gov/manz/index.htm.

4. Rohwer Japanese American Relocation Center, accessed October 21, 2016, rohwer.astate.edu/.

5. Russell E. Bearden, "Japanese-American Relocation Camps," *Encyclopedia of Arkansas History and Culture*, accessed October 21, 2016, www.ency clopediaofarkansas.net/encyclopedia/entry-detail.aspx?entryID=2273.

6. Stephen C. Mercado, review of "Nisei Linguists: Japanese Americans in the Military Intelligence Service during World War II," by James C. McNaughton, *Studies in Intelligence* 52, no. 4 (2008).

7. *Del Sudoeste*, 1942, SDSU Yearbooks, SDSU Library and Information Access, San Diego State University, accessed October 21, 2016, library. sdsu.edu/scua/digital/resources/sdsu-yearbooks.

8. Ohio State University, "Evaluation of Courses of the Army Specialized Training Program," accessed October 21, 2016, library.osu.edu/documents /university-archives/subject_files/Army%20Specialized%20Training %20Program%20(ASTP).pdf.

9. Public Law 100-383, 100th Congress, August 20, 1988, accessed October 21, 2016, https://www.gpo.gov/fdsys/pkg/STATUTE-102/pdf/STATUTE -102-Pg903.pdf.

Chapter 13. Exhaustion

1. "Organized Labor and the Depression, The New Deal, and World War II," Southern Labor Archives: Work n' Progress—Lessons and Stories, part 4, accessed October 22, 2016, research.library.gsu.edu/c.php?g=115684&p =752252.

2. *Del Sudoeste*, 1943, SDSU Yearbooks, SDSU Library and Information Access, San Diego State University, accessed October 22, 2016, library.sdsu .edu/scua/digital/resources/sdsu-yearbooks.

3. Axelrod, *Real History of World War II*, 197.

4. Beevor, *The Second World War*, 568–73.

5. Ibid., 571–73.

6. Ibid., 540–43.

7. Axelrod, *Real History of World War II*, 354.

8. Mathew J. Friedman, "History of PTSD in Veterans: Civil War to DSM -5," PTSD: National Center for PTSD, accessed October 22, 2016, www .ptsd.va.gov/public/PTSD-overview/basics/history-of-ptsd-vets.asp.

Chapter 14. The Hump and the Black Hole

1. Beevor, *The Second World War*, 552–57.

2. Ibid., 270.

3. Axelrod, *Real History of World War II*, 256–57.

4. Steve Weintz, "How America's Airline Went To War," Pan Am Historical Foundation, accessed October 24, 2016, www.panam.org/war-years/400- how-america-s-airline-went-to-war-2.

5. P-38 National Association & Museum, "Lockheed P-38 Lightning: The Plane That Changed the Course of History!," accessed October 24, 2016, www.p38assn.org.

6. Beevor, *The Second World War*, 555–57.

7. Axelrod, *Real History of World War II*, 257.

8. Ben Johnson, "The Black Hole of Calcutta," Historic UK, accessed October 24, 2016, www.historic-uk.com/HistoryUK/HistoryofBritain /The-Black-Hole-of-Calcutta.

Chapter 15. By Guess and by God

1. Nakamura, "San Diego and the Pacific Theater," 221–46.

2. Nakamura, "San Diego and the Pacific Theater."

3. Beevor, *The Second World War*, 453–54.

Chapter 16. Any Gum, Chum?

1. Axelrod, *Real History of World War II*, 77–80.

2. Beevor, *The Second World War*, 137–39.

3. Axelrod, *Real History of World War II*, 299–303.

4. "1954 Housewives Celebrate End of Rationing," BBC News, accessed November 4, 2016, news.bbc.co.uk/onthisday/hi/dates/stories/july/4/news id_3818000/3818563.stm.

Chapter 17. The Price of This Victory

1. Beevor, *The Second World War*, 575–58.
2. Axelrod, *Real History of World War II*, 311.
3. Donald H. Harrison, "The Wax and Addleson Families: Military Service Abroad and on the Homefront," San Diego History Center, accessed January 12, 2017, www.sandiegohistory.org/journal/wax-addleson-families -military-service-abroad-homefront/.
4. Axelrod, *Real History of World War II*, 301.
5. Beevor, *The Second World War*, 575–78.
6. Axelrod, *Real History of World War II*, 320–22.

Chapter 18. What It Feels Like to Be Free

1. Nigel Blundell, "Terror of the Doodlebugs: Sinister V-1 Flying Bomb That Menaced Britain 70 Years Ago," *Daily Express*, May 31, 2014, accessed January 14, 2017, www.express.co.uk/news/uk/479386/Terror-of-the-Doodle bugs-Sinister-V-1-flying-bomb-that-menaced-Britain-70-years-ago.
2. Axelrod, *Real History of World War II*, 322.
3. Beevor, *The Second World War*, 640–43.
4. Cristen Oehrig, "Civil Affairs in World War II," International Security Program, Center for Strategic and International Studies, accessed January 14, 2017, csis-prod.s3.amazonaws.com/s3fs-public/legacy_files/files/media /csis/pubs/090130_world_war_ii_study.pdf.
5. Axelrod, *Real History of World War II*, 66–67.

Chapter 19. The Front Line Dough

1. "Why the Term Doughboy?," *Marin Journal* (San Rafael, Calif.), October 19, 1922, accessed January 7, 2017, cdnc.ucr.edu/cgi-bin/cdnc?a=d&d =MJ19221019.2.43.
2. "Ernie Pyle," Indiana University Media School, accessed January 17, 2017, mediaschool.indiana.edu/erniepyle.
3. "Combat Infantryman Badge," U.S. Army, accessed September 3, 2017, https://www.army.mil/symbols/CombatBadges/infantry.html.
4. Beevor, *The Second World War*, 650–51.

5. Axelrod, *Real History of World War II*, 323–25.

6. Beevor, *The Second World War*, 650–51.

7. Carl L. Lutz, interview by the author, June 24 and 25, 2015.

Chapter 20. In Action with Patton

1. Axelrod, *Real History of World War II*, 313–14.

2. George Forty, *Patton's Third Army at War* (Philadelphia: Casemate, 2015), 52–66.

3. Beevor, *The Second World War*, 633–34.

4. Ibid., 649–50.

5. Axelrod, *Real History of World War II*, 323–25.

6. Beevor, *The Second World War*, 724–25.

7. Axelrod, *Real History of World War II*, 325.

8. Matthew J. Seelinger, "Operation Varsity: The Last Airborne Deployment of World War II," National Museum of the U.S. Army, January 20, 2015, accessed January 19, 2017, armyhistory.org/operation-varsity-the-last-air borne-deployment-of-world-war-ii/.

9. Beevor, *The Second World War*, 746.

10. "Forced Labor: An Overview." *Holocaust Encyclopedia*, accessed January 19, 2017, www.ushmm.org/wlc/en/article.php?ModuleId=10005180.

11. Beevor, *The Second World War*, 729–30.

12. "The Nuremberg Race Laws," *Holocaust Encyclopedia*, accessed January 19, 2017, www.ushmm.org/outreach/en/article.php?ModuleId=10007695.

13. Axelrod, *Real History of World War II*, 360–62.

Chapter 21. V-E Day

1. Beevor, *The Second World War*, 757–60.

2. "Allied Occupation of Germany, 1945–1952," U.S. Department of State Archive, accessed January 20, 2017, https://2001-2009.state.gov/r/pa/ho /time/cwr/107189.htm.

3. "World War II: Displaced Persons," Jewish Virtual Library, accessed January 20, 2017, www.jewishvirtuallibrary.org/displaced-persons.

Chapter 22. Tokyo's Front Porch

1. Costello, *The Pacific War*, 542–47.

2. Beevor, *The Second World War*, 702–4.

3. Axelrod, *Real History of World War II*, 279–80.

4. Beevor, *The Second World War*, 704–5.

5. Ibid., 704–5.
6. Yoshida Mitsuru, *Requiem for Battleship Yamato*, trans. Richard H. Minear (Annapolis: Naval Institute Press, 1999), 73–83.
7. Beevor, *The Second World War*, 706–7.
8. Costello, *The Pacific War*, 578.
9. Axelrod, *Real History of World War II*, 334–36.
10. Beevor, *The Second World War*, 772–73.
11. Axelrod, *Real History of World War II*, 347–49.
12. Ibid., 349–51.

Chapter 23. Who's Got the Points?

1. John C. Sparrow, "History of Personnel Demobilization in the United States Army," Department of the Army Pamphlet no. 20-210, July 1952, 39–44, accessed January 26, 2017, www.history.army.mil/html/books/104/104-8/CMH_Pub_104-8.pdf.
2. *Del Sudoeste*, 1943, SDSU Yearbooks, SDSU Library and Information Access, accessed January 26, 2017, library.sdsu.edu/scua/digital/resources/sdsu-yearbooks#1940-1949.
3. Adrienne Denaro, "Jantzen," *Oregon Encyclopedia*, accessed January 26, 2017, www.oregonencyclopedia.org/articles/jantzen/#.WNXUOTvyvIU.

Chapter 24. Educationally Speaking

1. Axelrod, *Real History of World War II*, 354.
2. "Education and Training: History and Timeline," U.S. Department of Veteran's Affairs Veterans Benefits Administration, accessed January 27, 2017, www.benefits.va.gov/gibill/history.asp.
3. Stewart B. Milstein, "Operation Magic Carpet," Data Sheet 31, Universal Ship Cancellation Society, April 2008, accessed January 27, 2017, www.uscs.org/wp-content/uploads/2012/04/DS31_Operation-MagicCarpet.pdf.
4. "History of the Field," Boston University School of Medicine Mental Health Counseling and Behavioral Medicine Program, accessed January 27, 2017, www.bumc.bu.edu/mhbm/about-us/history-of-the-field/.

Bibliography

Atkinson, Rick. *An Army at Dawn: The War in North Africa, 1942–1943*. New York: Picador, 2002.

Axelrod, Alan. *The Real History of World War II: A New Look at the Past*. New York: Sterling, 2008.

Beevor, Antony. *The Second World War*. New York: Back Bay Books/Little, Brown and Company, 2012.

Berg, Temma. "Truly Yours: Arranging a Letter Collection." *Eighteenth-Century Life* 35, no. 1 (Winter 2011): 29–50.

Carpenter, Clarence R., and Clarence E. Glick. "Educational Plans of Soldiers: A Study of Soldier-Students at Biarritz American University." *The Journal of Higher Education* 17, no. 9 (1946): 469–73, 498.

Costello, John. *The Pacific War, 1941–1945*. New York: Harper Perennial, 2009.

Del Sudoeste. SDSU Yearbooks, 1940–1949. San Diego State University Library and Information Access. Available at http://library.sdsu.edu/scua/digital/resources/sdsu-yearbooks#1940-1949.

Edelman, Bernard, ed. *Dear America: Letters Home from Vietnam*. New York: W. W. Norton, 2002.

Fikes, Robert, Jr. "Supreme Sacrifice, Extraordinary Service: Profiles of SDSU Military Alumni." San Diego, Calif.: San Diego State University Library and Information Access, 2016. Available at http://www.sdsualumni.org/s/997/images/editor_documents/Chapters/veterans2016.pdf.

Forty, George. *Patton's Third Army at War*. Philadelphia: Casemate, 2015.

Hallet, Christine E. "The Personal Writings of First World War Nurses: A Study of the Interplay of Authorial Intention and Scholarly Interpretation." *Nursing Inquiry* 14, no. 4 (2007): 320–29.

Harari, Yuval Noah. "Military Memoirs: A Historical Overview of the Genre from the Middle Ages to the Late Modern Era." *War in History* 14, no. 3 (2007): 289–309.

Huntsville, Sandra, Tamara Rowatt, Lisa Brooks, Victoria Magid, Robert Stage, Paulette Wydro, Steve Cramer, et al. "Measuring School Spirit: A National Teaching Exercise." *Teaching of Psychology* 31, no. 1 (2004): 18–21.

Hynes, Samuel. *The Soldiers' Tale: Bearing Witness to Modern War.* New York: Penguin, 1997.

Johnson, Teresa. "Ensuring the Success of Deploying Students: A Campus View." *New Directions for Student Services* 126 (2009): 55–60.

Krebs, Ronald R. "The Citizen-Soldier Tradition in the United States: Has Its Demise Been Greatly Exaggerated?" *Armed Forces & Society* 36, no.1 (2009): 153–74.

Lutz, Carl L. Interview by the author. June 24 and 25, 2015.

Manchester, William. "Okinawa: The Bloodiest Battle of All." In *The Best American Essays of the Century*, edited by Joyce Carol Oates and Robert Atwan. New York: Houghton Mifflin, 2000.

Meyer, G. J. *A World Undone: The Story of the Great War, 1914–1918.* New York: Delta, 2007.

Miller, Delbert C. "Effect of the War Declaration on the National Morale of American College Students." *American Sociological Review* 7, no. 5 (1942): 631–44.

Mitsuru, Yoshida. *Requiem for Battleship* Yamato. Translated by Richard H. Minear. Annapolis: Naval Institute Press, 1999.

Moad, James A., II. "Re-imagining the Past through Letters." *War, Literature and the Arts: An International Journal of the Humanities* 19, nos. 1–2 (2007): 323–36.

Mosse, George L. "Two World Wars and the Myth of the War Experience." *Journal of Contemporary History* 21, no. 4 (1986): 491–513.

Nelson, Robert L. "Soldier Newspapers: A Useful Source in the Social and Cultural History of the First World War and Beyond." *War in History* 17, no. 2 (2010): 167–91.

Oxford, J. S., A. Sefton, R. Jackson, W. Innes, R. S. Daniels, and N. P. Johnson. "World War I May Have Allowed the Emergence of 'Spanish' Influenza." *The Lancet: Infectious Diseases* 2 (2002): 111–14.

Poore, Paul. "School Culture: The Space between the Bars; the Silence between the Notes." *Journal of Research in International Education* 4 (2005): 351–61.

Ramsey, Edwin Price, and Stephen J. Rivele. *Lieutenant Ramsey's War: From Horse Soldier to Guerrilla Commander.* Washington, D.C.: Potomac, 2005.

Robinson, William J. *Forging the Sword: The Story of Camp Devens.* Concord: Rumford, 1920.

Samet, Elizabeth D. "Leaving No Warriors Behind: The Ancient Roots of a Modern Sensibility." *Armed Forces and Society* 31, no. 4 (2005): 623–49.

Shapiro, Seth, and Lee Humphreys. "Exploring Old and New Media: Comparing Military Blogs to Civil War Letters." *New Media & Society* (2012): 1–17.

Shay, Jonathan. *Odysseus in America: Combat Trauma and the Trials of Homecoming.* New York: Scribner, 2002.

Stanley, Liz. "The Epistolarium: On Theorizing Letters and Correspondences." *Auto/Biography* 12 (2004): 201–35.

Telford, Jennifer Casavant. "The American Nursing Shortage during World War I: The Debate over the Use of Nurses' Aids." *Canadian Bulletin of Medical History* 27, no. 1 (2010): 85–99.

Tregaskis, Richard. *Guadalcanal Diary.* New York: Modern Library, 2000.

Werrell, Kenneth P. "The Strategic Bombing of Germany in World War II: Costs and Accomplishments." *Journal of American History* 73, no. 3 (1986): 702–13.

Wilson, C. B. "School Spirit in a Democracy." *National Association of Secondary School Principals Bulletin* 25 (1941): 37–40.

Williams, Griffith P. "WW II Revisited: The First Air Attack against Japan. The Recollections of One Participant." Unpublished manuscript, 1993. Held at Special Collections and University Archives, San Diego State University.

Wimmer, Andreas, and Brian Min. "From Empire to Nation State: Explaining Wars in the Modern World, 1816–2001." *American Sociological Review* 71 (2006): 867–97.

Woodruff, Todd, Ryan Kelty, and David R. Segal. "Propensity to Serve and Motivation to Enlist among American Combat Soldiers." *Armed Forces and Society* 32, no. 3 (2006): 353–66.

World War II San Diego State College Servicemen's Correspondence Collection, 1941–1946. Created by Lauren Chester Post. Special Collections and University Archives, San Diego State University.

Index

Note: italicized *page numbers* indicate photographs.

About the Author

LISA K. SHAPIRO began teaching in 2003, and her community college classrooms have always been filled with veterans. As a creative writing instructor, she encourages the soldiers, sailors, and Marines who are transitioning back to student life to put their stories on paper. She is the author, with Deborah K. Reed, of the novel *The Chamber and the Cross*. Shapiro holds degrees in management and literature and is an assistant professor in business administration at San Diego Mesa College, where she developed the entrepreneurship degree. She has taught creative writing courses throughout San Diego.

The Naval Institute Press is the book-publishing arm of the U.S. Naval Institute, a private, nonprofit, membership society for sea service professionals and others who share an interest in naval and maritime affairs. Established in 1873 at the U.S. Naval Academy in Annapolis, Maryland, where its offices remain today, the Naval Institute has members worldwide.

Members of the Naval Institute support the education programs of the society and receive the influential monthly magazine *Proceedings* or the colorful bimonthly magazine *Naval History* and discounts on fine nautical prints and on ship and aircraft photos. They also have access to the transcripts of the Institute's Oral History Program and get discounted admission to any of the Institute-sponsored seminars offered around the country.

The Naval Institute's book-publishing program, begun in 1898 with basic guides to naval practices, has broadened its scope to include books of more general interest. Now the Naval Institute Press publishes about seventy titles each year, ranging from how-to books on boating and navigation to battle histories, biographies, ship and aircraft guides, and novels. Institute members receive significant discounts on the Press's more than eight hundred books in print.

Full-time students are eligible for special half-price membership rates. Life memberships are also available.

For a free catalog describing Naval Institute Press books currently available, and for further information about joining the U.S. Naval Institute, please write to:

Member Services
U.S. NAVAL INSTITUTE
291 Wood Road
Annapolis, MD 21402-5034
Telephone: (800) 233-8764
Fax: (410) 571-1703
Web address: www.usni.org